D0153514

IMPERIALISM AND THEATRE

"Imperialism" is a transnational and transhistorical phenomenon; it occurs neither in limited areas nor at one specific moment. In cultures from across the world theatrical performance has long been utilized as the disseminator of a dominant ideology or the place for colonized revolt.

Imperialism and Theatre is a uniquely comprehensive and timely collection of fifteen essays from noted scholars and theatre practitioners, exploring the impact of imperialism and colonialism on the theatre, performance and dramatic texts. Writing on the theatre of both colonizers and colonized, the authors examine the function of theatre and performance both in support of and in resistance to imperial ideology.

Spanning global and historical boundaries, the essays engage in current theoretical issues while shifting the focus from the printed text to theatre as a cultural formation and locus of political force.

J. Ellen Gainor is an Associate Professor of Theatre Studies at Cornell University. She is the author of *Shaw's Daughters: Dramatic and Narrative Constructions of Gender* (1991) and has also written on imperialism and colonialism in the drama of George Bernard Shaw and Athol Fugard.

IMPERIALISM AND THEATRE

Essays on World Theatre, Drama and Performance

Edited by J. Ellen Gainor

London and New York

First published 1995
by Routledge
11 New Fetter Lane, London EC4P 4EE

Simultaneously published in the USA and Canada
by Routledge
29 West 35th Street, New York, NY 10001
© 1995 J. Ellen Gainor;
individual chapters © 1995 individual contributors;
this collection © Routledge

Typeset in Garamond by
J&L Composition Ltd, Filey, North Yorkshire.

Printed and bound in Great Britain by
Biddles Ltd, Guildford and King's Lynn.

British Library Cataloguing in Publication Data
A catalogue record for this book is available from the British Library

Library of Congress Cataloguing in Publication Data
Imperialism and Theatre: Essays on World Theatre, Drama and Performance /
edited by J. Ellen Gainor.
p.   cm.
Includes bibliographical references and index.
1. Theater – Political aspects.   2. Theater and society.
3. Theater – Political aspects – Developing countries.   4. Theater and
society – Developing countries.   5. Intercultural communication.
I. Gainor, J. Ellen.
PN2049.I47 1995   94–35439
792—dc20

ISBN 0–415–10640–0 (hbk)
ISBN 0–415–10641–9 (pbk)

In memory of Michael Quinn,
who shall be greatly missed

CONTENTS

CONTENTS

ILLUSTRATIONS

CONTRIBUTORS

Nora M. Alter is Assistant Professor of German in the Department of Germanic and Slavic Languages and Literatures, the University of Florida, where she teaches film, media studies and theory. Her degree is in Comparative Literature and Literary Theory from the University of Pennsylvania. She is author of the forthcoming book *Vietnam Protest Theatre: Staging the Television War in the US and Abroad (1965–1979)* (Indiana University Press), and has written on German cinema, including Harun Farocki and Wim Wenders, on Chester Himes, and on Peter Brook.

Sudipto Chatterjee is a doctoral student in Performance Studies at New York University working on Bengali theatre in British Calcutta. He is a director, actor, poet, playwright and translator whose work has been published and performed in both Bengali and English. His essay, "Post-Colonial Imperialism? Responding to a Report on the Work and Murder of Safdar Hashmi by Eugene van Erven," appeared in the *Drama Review* (Spring 1990). His recent adaptation of the Sanskrit play *Mṛcchakaṭikam/ The Little Clay Cart* had its off-Broadway run in July 1991.

Mary Karen Dahl is an Assistant Professor of Theatre and Drama at the University of Wisconsin, Madison. She is the author of *Political Violence in Drama: Classical Models, Contemporary Variations* (UMI, 1987), essays on political playwrights in the United Kingdom, and a work in progress investigating theatre, the state, and the individual called *Philomele's Sister: Making a Post-Political Theatre in the United Kingdom*.

Alan Filewod is Professor of Drama at the University of Guelph. He is the author of *Collective Encounters: Documentary Theatre in English Canada* (University of Toronto Press, 1987), editor of two volumes of Canadian drama, and author of numerous articles on Canadian theatre history and political theatre. He is editor of the quarterly *Canadian Theatre Review* and past President of the Association for Canadian Theatre Research.

Donald H. Frischmann has researched Mexican and Chicano theatre since 1982, and has published critical essays in Mexico, the United States,

Canada, Great Britain, and Spain. He is the author of *El Nuevo Teatro Popular en México* (Mexico City: Instituto Nacional de Bellas Artes/Centro de Investigación Teatral Rodolfo Usigli, 1990). He is also co-author of *Latin American Popular Theater, The First Five Centuries* (University of New Mexico, 1993). His current research focuses upon contemporary theatre in Mexico, with an emphasis on the Maya. He is currently Associate Professor in the Department of Modern Languages and Literatures, Texas Christian University.

J. Ellen Gainor is an Associate Professor of Theatre Studies at Cornell University. She is the author of *Shaw's Daughters: Dramatic and Narrative Constructions of Gender* (University of Michigan Press, 1991) and *The Plays of Susan Glaspell: A Contextual Study* (forthcoming from Michigan). She has published essays on modern and contemporary British and American theatre, and has written on imperialism and colonialism in the drama of Bernard Shaw and Athol Fugard.

Rhonda K. Garelick is an Assistant Professor of French at the University of Colorado at Boulder. Her essays have appeared in *Nineteenth Century French Studies* and in the *Modern Critical Views* series, and her translations have appeared in *Yale French Studies* and *Poetics Today*. She has recently completed a book-length manuscript on dandyism, gender and celebrity in the *fin de siècle*.

Helen Gilbert is a lecturer in Drama and Theatre Studies at the University of Queensland. She has published widely on Australian drama, especially Aboriginal theatre, and is co-author of *Reacting (to) Empire: Post-Colonial Drama and Performance Theory* (forthcoming from Routledge). She also writes short fiction.

Michael Hays currently teaches at Cornell University. He is the author and editor of several books in the areas of theatre history and theory. The most recent of these are *Critical Conditions* (University of Minnesota Press, 1993), and the forthcoming *Melodramatic Formations* (Cambridge University Press, 1995).

Loren Kruger teaches at the University of Chicago and is the author of *The National Stage* (University of Chicago Press, 1992), translator of *The Institutions of Art* by Christa and Peter Bürger (University of Nebraska Press, 1992), and editor of *The Autobiography of Leontine Sagan* (forthcoming from Witwatersrand University Press). She is currently at work on a book with the provisional title of "The Drama of Modernity. Plays, Pageants, and the Public Sphere in Twentieth-Century South Africa."

Josephine Lee is currently an Assistant Professor of English at the University of Minnesota. She recently completed a book-length manuscript on modern British playwrights and language theory, and is at work on a study of Asian American drama.

Robert Eric Livingston is an instructor in the Department of English at Ohio State University. He is the author of "Seeing Through Reading: Class, Race and Literary Authority in Conrad's *Nigger of the Narcissus*" (*Novel*, Winter 1993), as well as reviews and translations of literary theory. He is completing a manuscript entitled *Writing the Congo: Constructions and Deconstructions of Colonial Discourse.*

Julie Stone Peters is Associate Professor of English, Comparative Literature, and Theatre Arts at Columbia University. She is currently working on a book on the relationship between theatre and printing in Europe 1500–1900, and is the author of *Congreve, the Drama, and the Printed Word* (Stanford, 1990) and the co-editor of *Women's Rights, Human Rights: International Feminist Perspectives* (Routledge, 1994).

Michael Quinn, who, sadly, died in 1994, was Assistant Professor at the School of Drama, the University of Washington, and the author of *The Semiotic Stage: Prague School Theatre Theory* and many essays on acting, directing and dramatic literature. He was also the editor of *Theatre Survey*, the Journal of the American Society for Theatre Research.

Edward W. Said is University Professor at Colombia University. He is the author of *Culture and Imperialism* (Knopf 1993), *The Politics of Dispossession* (Pantheon 1994) and *Representations of the Intellectual* (Pantheon 1994).

Elaine Savory formerly wrote as Elaine Savory Fido. She taught at universities in Ghana, Barbados, Nigeria and the United States during the period 1972–92, and has directed and acted in performances during that period. She has written widely on African and Caribbean drama, theatre and women's writing. She co-edited *Out of the Kumbla: Women and Caribbean Literature* (African World Press, 1990), the first collection of feminist essays on Caribbean literature. Her first collection of poems, *flame tree time* (Sandberry Press, 1993), was published in Jamaica. She presently divides her time between the United States and the Caribbean. Her book on Jean Rhys is in preparation for Cambridge University Press and she is working on her first play, *spirit*.

ACKNOWLEDGEMENTS

I want to take this opportunity to express debts of gratitude for the contributions of a number of individuals to the shaping of this volume, at the same time accepting full responsibility for its final form. First, to Rick Livingston, who generously shared the names of scholars from his MLA panel on this topic, many of whom became contributors to the collection. To Michael Hays, Biodun Jeyifo, and Julie Peters for helping me locate others to join the project, and to LeAnn Fields, Timothy Wiles, and Thomas Postlewait for their invaluable suggestions on the structure and content of the book. To a number of scholars who, for various reasons, could not ultimately submit essays, but who did inform my thinking about the collection. To our editor, Talia Rodgers, who also helped identify a contributor, but who more importantly maintained a commitment to the project despite upheavals and setbacks, as well as to the efficient and thorough production staff at Routledge. And as always, to David, for prompting serious thought and providing invaluable guidance. It has been a great pleasure to work with a number of old friends and new colleagues as the contributors to this project; they deserve the true credit for its existence.

J. Ellen Gainor

INTRODUCTION

J. Ellen Gainor

The purpose of this collection is to discuss issues of imperialism and colonialism as they pertain to the theatre, to performance, to dramatic and other theory, and to dramatic texts. "Imperialism" is both a transnational and transhistorical phenomenon; it occurs neither in limited areas nor at one specific moment. Thus this volume will present examinations of a range of imperial and colonial events and periods, focusing on the unique nexus of theatrical performance as a site for the representation of, but also the resistance to, imperialism. Several other previously published collections have explored specific aspects of this dynamic. Both *Imperialism and Popular Culture* and *Acts of Supremacy: The British Empire and the Stage, 1790–1930*[1] confine themselves to British imperialism, while *The Dramatic Touch of Difference: Theatre, Own and Foreign* and *Interculturalism and Performance*[2] explore multi- and intercultural creativity, only some of which is connected with imperialism or colonialism (Fischer-Lichte 15; Marranca 22). While individual essays in scholarly and popular publications have dealt with discrete examples of imperialism and the theatre, or, more frequently, with imperialism and dramatic literature, we believe our collection brings together a topical and methodological sampling demonstrative of the burgeoning research possibilities in this field.

Within literary studies of the past decade or so, imperialism has become an increasingly central concern, and critics such as Edward W. Said, Homi K. Bhabha, Gayatri Chakravorty Spivak and others have provided theoretical frameworks through which we can explore cultural and literary production. This body of criticism foregrounds the political contexts of its objects, and highlights their status as political artifacts. However, as Nora Alter observes in her essay here, theatre studies are comparatively marginalized "within and without the academy," particularly when compared to "other forms of cultural production such as novels and films." When we consider the concerns of this volume, such imbalance seems particularly ironic, given the strategic political and cultural force of theatrical production within a community or larger geographical region. This irony is especially notable when we juxtapose the flexibility of theatre to the limitations of printed texts, which for economic, educational or other reasons may not be widely accessible, and which, for many readers, are experienced privately or only in small groups.[3]

The theatre has always been a locus of political force; the authors represented in this collection are all addressing in some way the questions of why the theatre was selected within a culture or by an artist for the depiction of imperial and colonial concerns, and how the theatre was utilized as the disseminator of a dominant ideology and/or the place for colonized revolt. The impact of live performance for an audience cannot be underestimated, and in earlier historical moments and still for many parts of the world, theatrical performance can be the primary conduit for lessons of vital social and personal import.[4] Writing here on Aimé Césaire, Robert Eric Livingston calls theatrical spectacle "a site for the active transformation of culture," and reading theatre as this kind of political artifact is equally important for all the contributors.

One of the distinctive features of this collection is its demonstration of theatre as a vehicle for the promotion of as well as the revolt against empire. Essays by Michael Hays on Victorian melodrama, Rhonda K. Garelick on the 1900 World's Fair, and Alan Filewod on governmentally supported Canadian theatre reveal how performance served to reinforce the imperial policies of England and France. Essays by Sudipto Chatterjee on Bengal, Donald H. Frischmann on the Yucatan and Chiapas, and Elaine Savory on the Anglophone Caribbean depict how colonial cultures generate new theatrical forms by negotiating between indigenous performance modes and imported imperial culture. Nora Alter on Thich Nhat Hanh, Mary Karen Dahl on post-colonial dramatists in England, Loren Kruger on post-colonial performance in South Africa, and Robert Eric Livingston on Aimé Césaire present specific examples of resistance. While Josephine Lee focuses on dramatic language in Ireland as a point of colonial contestation, Helen Gilbert explores theatrical costuming in Australia as a marker of imperial and patriarchal discourse. Both Michael Quinn and Edward W. Said show how an individual author – Peter Karvas and Jean Genet, respectively – responds to prolonged colonial engagement. And Julie Stone Peters provides a theoretical exploration of recent critical engagements with interculturalism, anthropology, and imperialism in the theatre.

While there are many other points of commonality among the pieces than those I have just mentioned,[5] taken as a whole, these essays gesture toward the global implications and incidence of the conjunction of imperialism and theatre. While we cannot be exhaustive, we hope we are not perceived as tokenist in the effort to touch upon as many areas, peoples, and moments as possible within the constraints of a single volume. The basic structure of colonialism, with its imbalance of power and potential for cultural manipulation, may be a common denominator for many locations and periods, but individual dynamics are distinctive and resist homogenizing critical dicta. Furthermore, the nuances of each colonial situation present opportunities for a range of analytic strategies to be brought to bear on theatrical artifacts from each locus. Thus this collection hopes to provide a sample of critical approaches for future scholarship in this field. From primary field research to more distanced theoretical inquiry, the essays demonstrate the legitimacy and potential of varied discursive strategies to reveal the relationship between the theatre and its culture. Similarly, the essays highlight the range of performative possibilities, including dance, pageants, ceremonies, and proscenium drama that we can conceive as theatre. Within the larger context of colonial and post-colonial studies, the essays participate in the ongoing debate on the continuity of culture before and after decolonization, and may provide new dimensions for this dialogue.

NOTES

1 John M. MacKenzie, ed., *Imperialism and Popular Culture* (Manchester: Manchester University Press, 1986); J. S. Bratton *et al.*, eds., *Acts of Supremacy: The British Empire and the Stage, 1790–1930* (Manchester: Manchester University Press, 1991).
2 Erika Fischer-Lichte, Josephine Riley, and Michael Gissenwehrer, eds., *The Dramatic Touch of Difference: Theatre, Own and Foreign* (Tübingen: Narr, 1990); Bonnie Marranca and Gautam Dasgupta, eds., *Interculturalism and Performance* (NY: PAJ Publications, 1991).
3 Of course, particularly in highly industrialized urban areas, theatre may also be financially inaccessible to many; however, the kind of strategic political engagement of interest here is rarely a feature of such theatre, or, if it is, arrangements are often made to make the work accessible to the communities that might otherwise not witness it.
4 African communities' use of theatrical performance to teach "safe sex" practices in the effort to combat the spread of AIDS, and the juvenile prison system's use of theatre to help young inmates confront their personal histories as part of rehabilitation in some sections of the United States are just two current examples.
5 Other organizational strategies might be geographical, temporal, generic, etc.

1

VIETNAMESE THEATRE OF RESISTANCE

Thich Nhat Hanh's Metaphysical Sortie on the Margins

Nora M. Alter

The whole of this contradiction – revolutionary anti-colonialism; the most advanced socialist political practice in the most backward peasant economy; the direct, historic, prolonged combat between socialism and imperialism; the utterly unequal balance of forces – was condensed in the Vietnam War.

Aijaz Ahmad

No scientific instrument can verify the existential nature of life in this story.

Thich Nhat Hanh

Few of the recent studies about the Vietnam war, even those dealing explicitly with protest theatre, mention, let alone analyze, protest plays written and produced by the Vietnamese. This omission is unfortunate in light of the exceptionally rich theatrical tradition of Vietnam, and in particular the use throughout its history of theatre as a cultural–political tool and weapon, most recently in the struggle against European and American colonialism and imperialism. Both part of a larger tradition of global protest thought and writing and also a unique contribution in its own right, Vietnamese theatre both offers itself to and yet also resists incorporation by Western audiences. As such, it remains a response on the margins. As put by the Vietnamese filmmaker and theorist Trinh T. Minh-ha in *When the Moon Waxes Red: Representation, Gender and Cultural Politics* (1991):

The margins, our sites of survival, become our fighting grounds and their site for pilgrimage. Thus, while we turn around and reclaim them as our exclusive territory, they happily approve, for the divisions between margin and center should be preserved, as clearly demarcated as possible, if the two positions are to remain intact in their power relations. Without a certain work of displacement . . . the margins can easily recomfort the center in its goodwill and liberalism; strategies of reversal thereby meet with their own limits.

(Trinh 1991, 17)

1

During the Vietnam war the National Liberation Front and Viet Cong were able to draw on the long history of Vietnamese theatre to develop extensive culture–drama programs, which had itinerant groups of performers travel from one hamlet or village to the next, educating the people, spreading the word of communism, and calling for resistance against the South Vietnamese and the United States armies. This form of oral interaction stressed both visual and verbal messages and could change its thematic content from day to day, adapting it to current events. It was thus an especially flexible and effective type of theatre for a rural, often illiterate or preliterate and largely pretechnological society.[1] Its power – actual or potential – lay in part in its recognition by the Joint US Public Affairs Office (JUSPAO) as a major medium for spreading enemy propaganda. Indeed, in general, JUSPAO seems to have given more credit to the power of fiction than was generally admitted either to or by the general public. It had an ordinance which specifically prohibited playwrights from being granted passes to travel to Vietnam. (See Moeller 360.) JUSPAO was so concerned about the impact of North Vietnamese and Viet-Cong theatre troupes that it began to imitate them, promoting several theatrical performing groups siding with the South Vietnamese and the Americans. Among these, the Van Tac Vu Cultural Drama Teams engaged in "cultural seed planting" and served "as a uniquely credible means of communication between the government and the people in a rural society where word of mouth and face-to-face discussion remain the major means of communication."[2] Clearly the theatre played an important role on both sides in Vietnam, and any full account of the history of that conflict ought to reserve a place for it. In a moment I will be looking at a Buddhist play that attempted to negotiate the space between these competing ideologies, staging an ostensibly neutral space in their interstices, between margin and center. In the words again of Trinh, "On the one hand, truth is produced, induced, and extended according to the regime in power. On the other, truth lies in between all regimes of power" (Trinh 1991, 30). In the case of the play in question, the attempt was made to find a truth not merely between, even beyond, the ideological positions of North and South Vietnam but also between, and beyond, the positions of East and West, "Third World" and "First," "theatre" and "fact." But first a few more preliminaries.

There are several explanations for the neglect of Vietnamese protest theatre. Two lie no doubt not only in the difficulty of dealing with the live-performative aspect of theatre generally but also in the marginalized institutional status of theatre studies both within and without the academy.[3] A third reason may be found in the general neglect of any kind of non-American representations of the Vietnam war – films, novels, poetry – within most Vietnam war studies.[4] A fourth, perhaps more immediately relevant to my topic, surely results from the specific nature of the

Vietnamese performances, which were rarely recorded in writing. Instead they favored the oral form that could easily change according to shifting external events and internal conditions: where they were being performed and for whom. To that extent they may seem to come close to the tradition of Western (political) cabaret and agit-prop, sharing with them also a certain collective spirit. It is important, however, not to leap too quickly into comparisons that might deny Vietnam theatre its specificity. However, *The Path of Return* both encourages comparison and slips away from it – its path of protest is always marginal, always "other." Its construction is that of a type which, in a different context and text, Trinh has called "the inappropriate/d other." (See Trinh 1986/87.) In any case, the plays in question were rarely the product of a single author but instead manifested the ongoing work-in-progress of an ensemble. A final explanation of neglect is related to the fact that few of the war plays have been translated or performed outside of Vietnam, and unless one has had the rare chance to have seen and heard them directly in Vietnam, any discussion of their performances can only be imaginative speculation. It is with this caveat in mind that I propose to take a closer look at a play that a Vietnamese Buddhist monk wrote against the war, a play located at various kinds of margins – theatrical and religious, as well as social and political.

Thich Nhat Hanh's *The Path of Return Continues the Journey* was published in English translation in 1972, with a foreword by Daniel Berrigan. (See Nhat Hanh 1972.) The publisher, Hoa Binh (Peace) Press, was linked to the Jesuit Thomas Merton Life Center. Born in 1926 in Dalat, Nhat Hanh became a novice monk at age 16. After studying literature and philosophy at Saigon University, he went on in 1961 to study philosophy of religion at Princeton and lectured on Buddhism at Columbia two years later. He returned to South Vietnam, where he was already one of the most popular poets in the early 1960s, and took a leading role, through various writing and publishing activities, in several Buddhist social and political movements. Adopting a position on the war opposed to both North Vietnamese Communism and the repressive, US-backed Vietnamese Government in the South, Nhat Hanh attempted to synthesize European Existentialist philosophy with Buddhist pacifism. He outlined his political, literary, philosophical, and religious convictions in a short Preface, "A Buddhist Poet in Vietnam," to some of his explicitly political poems which appeared, in his own translation, in the *New York Review of Books*, June 9, 1966. (See Nhat Hanh 1966.) This Preface made it impossible for him to return to Vietnam, because of the subversive nature of his argument; in his own words: "I risk my life publishing these poems. Other Buddhists who have protested the war have been arrested and exiled and now they are being killed" (Nhat Hanh 1966, 36).

To my knowledge, *The Path of Return* is one of a tiny handful of plays to have been translated into English during the Vietnam war. This exceptional circumstance is quite significant. On the one hand, the publication of a political message in the land of the enemy is often problematic, even when that message adopts the fictional or, in this case, quasi-fictional form of a play. One cannot help wondering what sort of "Western" or "American" limitations and restrictions were imposed – unconsciously if not consciously – during the process of translation on its political content. To be endorsed by one of the leading Jesuit anti-war demonstrators in the US must have further informed the thematic and ideological orientation of the translation. On the other hand, the English translation was clearly authorized by Nhat Hanh himself. (As we have seen, he could easily have translated this play, too, as he had his political poetry six years earlier.) What matters most for our purposes here is to interpret *The Path of Return* as it is presented to an English-speaking readership.

The Path of Return, similar to Berrigan's own quasi-documentary play, *The Trial of the Catonsville Nine* (1969), is based on a "true story": in this case, the self-immolation of a young nun and social worker, Sister Mai, and the killing of four young men (a fifth was badly injured). Nhat Hanh's play adds two additional figures (also based on fact): Vui, "a young girl student of the School of Youth for Social Service [SYSS], Saigon"; and Lui, "a young woman teacher [and] political prisoner just released from jail," who was also part of the SYSS. Both were murdered "during a terrorist raid on the School by a group of unknown persons" (Nhat Hanh 1972, 6). They appear as talking, visible ghosts in the play. But before it narrates its central story, explicitly Vietnamese in origin, the play, as it is presented to an American audience or reader, introduces a framing device in the form of a statement by Berrigan which serves as proleptic commentary on the main plot. This statement, elliptically entitled " . . . Their Speech Is All of Forgiveness . . . ," is signed with a facsimile of "Dan Berrigan, S.J.": thus it conveys at once a sense of existential authenticity and familiarity (the reproduced signature and the nickname) and also official sanction or legitimation (The Society of Jesus). This framing is completed by an equally significant, anonymous closing statement on the final page, where, blocked out separately, one finds a call for contributions to the Vietnamese Buddhist Peace Delegation – with an address in Paris. Both parts of this "frame" (along with an additional sub-framing at the onset, about which more later) contribute a definite tone of commitment to what at first sight may be a relatively mild political statement. The larger "frame" makes it clear that the play has, in part, a distinctly pragmatic goal: to raise money for a Vietnamese peace organization. In a written text, this call for money might not appear controversial or dangerous today, and likely did not result in any censure at the time. But it is important to note that, a few years earlier, the earliest performances, in 1968, of Peter Weiss' *Viet Nam Discourse* in Germany were closed numerous times because, directly after the show, collections were taken for the Viet Cong. *The Path of Return* also tried to raise money in a foreign country for a peace mission officially considered as "subversive" in that country. One may also note the irony that the two ends of the frame are attributed, respectively, to an American citizen (Berrigan), and to a committee in France, so that two imperial powers seem uncannily to embrace/contain the Vietnamese core play. It is within these boundaries, for better or worse, that a resisting, colonized, and imperialized voice is left "free" to speak.

It is also striking to find that the properly "Vietnamese" text also is preceded by yet another framing device: a page-long statement, also elliptically titled, "Love Enables Us . . . ." It, too, is undersigned with a facsimile hand-written signature (in Western script), this time: "Nhat Hanh," which suggests that his statement was written explicitly for the American version. Nhat Hanh's statement of intent clearly serves two purposes, corresponding to the two distinct aspects of his play (aspects that are part related, part contradictory): first, it constitutes a third-person factual reference to the murder of four students/workers of the SYSS on the bank of the Saigon river in 1967; second, quoting the author's own paradoxical words, it conveys the claim to "guarantee" not only the truth of the murder story (which however doesn't really need such a guarantee since it is supposedly so well-known, albeit less in the US than in Vietnam) but also the authenticity of the story of what ostensibly happened afterwards, posthumously, to the four dead students and the self-immolated nun Mai. This push toward a certain kind of documentary truth or verisimilitude impacts on the problem of representability, as we will see later. In any case, this second part of the truth, the author freely admits, is a lived (read: poetic or fictional) rather than scientific (read: historical) truth. Certainly it is produced and moved less by any conventional Western principle of dramatic conflict but by "love" (as is the entire play itself), and promises to lead hermeneutically to ever higher levels of "love," if only one is willing to join the author on his imaginary boat, and row together with him. Vocabulary, images, and the thematic formal principle of "love" set apart this "play" from the Western Vietnam protest theatre.

We shall follow the author's invitation and, as the play proper begins, join him and his characters on the sampan. They are just getting ready to row with their bare hands. And this rudimentary physical act of rowing, along with some other small gestures, is virtually all the action that will take place on the boat and in the play. What follows is a fragmented retelling of the circumstances of the deaths of the characters, as related by them, and a long, sometimes poetic but repetitive discussion of the meaning of life in general as well as of specific manifestations of war and violence. Much of that conversation, led by the nun Mai, is devoted to philosophical and/or moral considerations that preach understanding and forgiveness – even (indeed especially) forgiveness of those who kill "us." It is in this context, then, that the Buddhist themes of love and tolerance are most evident. To quote one of the characteristic concluding statements: "Let us hope that our earthly lives, as well as our death, have sown the seeds of tolerance and love" (Nhat Hanh 1972, 27).

Thus summarized, the play cannot be fit easily into the rubrics of traditional Western theatre. At the very least it is marginal to them, in the sense that it has no acts, no scenes, little or no dramatic or conceptual progression of any type. Rather, it resembles a collective poem recited by several voices, something that in the West could be qualified as a "performance" (i.e., a kind of dramatic monologue collectively recited), but questioned as "theatre." Needless to say, any definition of theatre *qua* genre or medium is a matter of cultural opinion, and, to be appreciated fully in its own terms, *The Path of Return* must be contextualized within the Vietnamese culture and hence the Vietnamese concept of "theatre." This genre or medium consists of four major types: the more traditional forms of Cheo and Tuong, and the more modern ones of Cai Luong and Kich Noi. (See Mackerras.) From what can be deduced from its text, and particularly from the role of the sampan, *The Path of Return* jibes best with the category of Cheo, which means "a boat play."

Cheo was an especially popular traditional form of theatre for and by the people, with performers often singing the text while floating in a boat down the river, and it can legitimately be called "popular culture," in a way that little Western theatre still can. Cheo performers would address the people along the river's banks directly, somewhat like performers of Street Theatre, and invite them to join the performance. There were no entrance fees. But the Cheo is not a subsidized State theatre. It was and is an independent form, often serving, as part of this traditional generic norm, to oppose the authorities in power, whoever they might be. In that sense, formal and oppositional, Cheo appears to illustrate Augusto Boal's recommendation, in *Theatre of the Oppressed* (1974), for political theatre generally, even though it was developed for an entirely different historical context: "All the truly revolutionary theatrical groups should transfer to the people the means of production in the theatre so that the people may utilize them. Theatre is a weapon, and it is the people who should wield it" (Boal 122). To be sure, the pacifist Nhat Hanh would presumably object to this rather militant metaphor to describe what he was about in *The Path of Return*.

The river on which Mai's sampan is floating has both a literal–physical and a symbolic–metaphysical meaning in this larger context. Literal–physical because it obviously refers to the common generic venue of the Cheo boat plays: the rivers on which performers actually move from village to village to offer their performance in a land heavily dependent on river travel. One has the impression that *The Path of Return* was initially intended to be performed on a river boat – the sampan in the story. But the river also refers metaphysically to the symbolic river mentioned in Nhat Hanh's framing statement: "Is there a river that separates the two sides, a river which no boat can cross? . . . I will show you that there is a river, but there is no separation" (Nhat Hanh 1972, 5). Here, again, one confronts in its dominant poetic, quasi-mystical mode, the use of a theme often alluded to in Western protest plays: the real (geophysical) and yet illusory (ideological) separation between the two Vietnams, South and North, and perhaps between the two armies in conflict, or even between the two continents or two ideologies – a real separation that Western (especially European) playwrights sometimes denounce, while acknowledging, but more generally accept and further legitimize (mainly in American plays). For Nhat Hanh, this is a purely illusory separation that Buddhism is set to dispel. We shall see that this difference in outlook is also projected onto the different treatment of more concrete aspects of war in general and this one in particular. Finally, the river both distinguishes and yet articulates life and death. In a uncanny sense, the voices on the sampan are messages from the dead and fictional to the living and real audience or reader.

The roots of *The Path of Return* in the Cheo tradition also account for other peculiar features of the play that might be otherwise unexpected, even inexplicable. For example, the reiterated invocation of the power of sutras (the main intertextual reference is the *Prajnaparamita Sutra* (first recorded between AD 400 and 600), which is alluded to so often as to indicate that it, not the play at hand, is the crucial text to study) likely results from the association of the Cheo with religious celebrations as well as from the playwright's personal Buddhist convictions. Actually, sutras like the *Prajnaparamita* are intended not to be read so much as memorized and embodied, for the purpose not merely of meditation but also practical application, by the seeker of enlightenment or "Bodhisattva." This means literally "enlightenment-being" – the Buddhist ideal. The enlightenment in question is not personal merely but also that of others, with the ultimate goal being nothing less than the full enlightenment of a Buddha for everyone. Which helps explain the character, lines, and role, in *The Path of Return*, of Sister Lien in particular. Not only is she, both in the play and in real life, a teacher in the School of Youth for Social Service, but she refers often to the *Prajnaparamita*. Now according to this sutra, the concept of Bodhisattva is overdetermined. It is part of an elaborate sign-system or semiotic that appears to contain contradictory elements but with the goal of purification from appearances and contradictions. Thus, for example, the sutra informs us that "The word 'Bodhisattva' is a word for . . . the purity of views, of Delight, of craving, of arrogance, of Adornment, of mental satisfaction, of Light, and of physical happiness. It is a word for the purity of visual forms, sounds, smells, tastes and touchables" (*Prajnaparamita* 1973, 184). There would seem to be two main consequences of this doctrine for staging any play in accord with it, and *The Path of Return* specifically. The first is formal, the second thematic.

Formally, playwright and viewers must cooperate to realize that although we are of course seeing and hearing someone and something on stage and/ or in the text, nonetheless this someone and something is always to be grasped, conceptually if not actually, as a part of an intricate process aimed at higher or deeper truths than what is merely visible and audible. The precise location of these truths is problematic. Presumably, they lie not so much "outside" the performance or text, in the sense of being a wisdom that is strictly "transcendent," as a viewer imbued with Western religious values might assume. Nor are these higher truths strictly "immanent," either. Rather, as resolutely "marginal" to all such binary categories, they are to be grasped, somehow, as both transcendent and immanent, and yet neither. It is in this sense only that they are "metaphysical." Which is to say, perhaps most precisely, they are part of a single "path": a "continuing path of return" in and around the Bodhisattva ideal. This ideal is represented not only by certain set dialogues and/or monologues (the distinction is moot in this conceptual world) in *The Path of Return* – as a part "religious," part "theatrical" artifact – but also by its structure as a variation of its generic norm of Cheo.

Finally, in this context, there is the question of the *thematic* point of the reiterated intertextual references to the *Prajnaparamita Sutra* for *The Path of Return*, specifically as an anti-war play. One of the central teachings of the sutra is that the Bodhisattva, while travelling on his/her path to the "Buddha-field" (i.e., the realm in which a Buddha teaches and brings sentient beings to spiritual understanding), has no ultimate reason to be fearful of anything or anyone. A section of the sutra entitled "Five Places Which Inspire Fear" (Vietnam during the war had at least five such places) reads:

a Bodhisattva should not be afraid if he finds himself in a wilderness infested by robbers. For Bodhisattvas take pleasure in the wholesome practice of renouncing all their belongings. A Bodhisattva must cast away even his body, and he must renounce all that is necessary to life.
(*Prajnaparamita* 1958, 139)

At one point in *The Path of Return*, Sister Lien says: "Our country will be destroyed and our people will suffer even more than they already have. The cycle must be completed" (Nhat Hanh 1972, 18). The specific problem for interpreting *The Path of Return* as political theatre, is that, in terms of its ultimate message – namely, such radical pacifism even while being raped and murdered – it can do little more than continually refer to its master text or sutra. But, by so doing, it would seem radically to forfeit its own *raison d'être* – both generically, as staged event, but also politically, as anti-war and anti-imperialist play. On the other hand, one also gets the sense, reading Thich Nhat Hanh's own remarks in 1966 about his writings, that, even though he is obviously a committed Buddhist monk, he is also willing to instrumentalize his religious convictions for specific purposes of protest. His historical analysis of the religious situation in Vietnam was this:

> Catholicism came to Vietnam with the French, and the Catholic leaders backed by the United States were suspect from the first; the Buddhist tradition is closely linked with nationalism and it is unthinkable to the broad mass of people that the Buddhists would betray them to a foreign power.
>
> (Nhat Hanh 1966, 37)

Be the accuracy of this claim as it may, the consequences for his works (an analysis which might have given Berrigan pause) was clearly pragmatic in his own mind:

> when I write them I feel I am trying to speak very simply for the majority of Vietnamese who are peasants and cannot speak for themselves; they do not know or care much about words like communism or democracy but want above all for the war to end so they may survive and not be maimed or killed.
>
> (Nhat Hanh 1966, 36)

The translation of *The Path of Return* might therefore be read as offering a glimpse, for English speakers (who likely have not internalized the sutras), of the mentality of an "inappropriate/d other," which is traversing a path that is always going to appear just beyond Western patterns of political and theatrical understanding. In its inappropriateness from the point of view of exclusively Western categories, even if it depends on them in part and in the end, this path strives to remain inappropriated for as long as possible.

Another leitmotif in *The Path of Return*, one which functions in dialectical relation to its rather heavy-handed and repetitious allusions to its master text, is provided by a few humorous and light dialogues, no doubt inspired by the bawdy tradition and standard stock comic figures of the Cheo. More interesting and significant for our purpose is the centrality of a female figure: the wise Mai. That centrality of a woman, too, is provided by the Cheo model.[5] But it also reflects the fact that the theatrical groups in the areas controlled by the Viet Cong were composed of women.[6] In the play the sampan – real and metaphysical – is steered by Mai with the intent to reach two other martyred young women, who were murdered. Thus it is the women who serve as anchors in the audience's physical reality, or, to change the metaphor, as the two polar points between which the males move and interact, in life and in death, in fiction and in reality. Men, by contrast, may sometimes be coaxed to make some profound statements (especially if they have advanced Buddhist training), but they can also act and talk in rather silly fashion; so, for example, Tho (one of the four male SYSS graduates depicted) says that one of his "dead" comrades "is a little devil, but a lovable little devil . . . . I don't know whether he really was all that bright or not" (Nhat Hanh 1972, 7). The overriding gender hierarchy may also have been normal or expected in a Cheo play; but it does acquire a certain potentially subversive quality when matched against the male-dominated might of the US forces in Vietnam, and against the reduction and degradation of women to service jobs, prostitution, or victims of rape – not only in real life but as Vietnamese women are (re)presented in the Western Vietnam protest plays. Unwittingly, perhaps, but effectively, Nhat Hanh's Vietnamese protest play thus offers a certain gender resistance to some of the most prevalent stereotypes on the American and European protest stage.

In other ways, too, the choice of the Cheo as the paradigmatic theatrical form is, almost in and of itself, always already a form of protest, opposition, or resistance. For Cheo, though one of the oldest theatre forms, has rarely been recorded in writing. Performed "for the simple people," it has eluded written appropriation, including that by the Vietnamese elite influenced by and/or educated in foreign cultures. Something of an exception willy-nilly, simply by virtue of the fact that it was published and translated at all, nonetheless *The Path of Return* resists total appropriation as best it can, in order to remain inappropriate/d as long as it can.

The other traditional form of Vietnamese theatre, the Tuong (often performed in the Chinese language), rests on a strong Chinese foundation; and the two modern forms, especially the Cai Long, originated as part of the French influence, starting with adaptations of French classics such as Molière or Racine. The Cheo alone could be seen as a properly Vietnamese theatrical form, a uniquely national product standing for the (hypothetically unified) Vietnamese people and against the colonial or modern imperialist powers: France, England, the United States. Simply by adopting the Cheo form, Nhat Hanh formally articulates the ongoing war against the Americans in Vietnam with the long history of resistance to other invaders of Vietnam.

However, despite the differences in form, some similarities with Western Vietnam war protest theatre exist. The most obvious convergences or similarities between *The Path of Return* and the Western protest plays are those grounded in the spectacular nature of a single shared image, shown or implicit: the scene of self-immolation. Particularly important is the fact that these scenes appeared in houses, apartments, and bars around the world, including in the United States.

Vietnam has been called "the first television war." The pictures of Vietnam, "brought into the living room" – at once mediated and immediate – were not only removed from the prior experience of the viewer's own social and visual context, they also referred out to a context that was unknown, that could not be checked or verified from independent sources. To a significant extent, "Vietnam" itself was a pure visual image, disguised as truth. And all the various sub-images were also basically selected, controlled, and (re)produced by the Western mass media.

The first really powerful image to shake the Western world, to momentarily crack through the chain of mediatized simulacra, was the filmed self-immolation of the Buddhist monk, Thich Quang Duc. He burned himself in front of reporters on June 9, 1963. Exactly three years later to the day, ironically enough, Thich Nhat Hanh would publish English translations of his anti-war poems in the *New York Review of Books*, making impossible his return to his native country. It was Thich Quang Duc's action, and its representation in American living rooms and around the world, not the deaths of US servicemen, that sparked the first organized demonstration against the Vietnam war, in August 1963.[7] Thich Quang Duc's dramatic (some said ultimate) form of protest was repeated at various times during the following years: a total of eight Americans immolated themselves between 1965 and 1970 (an act of protest recently repeated at the Amherst College campus during the Gulf war). To be sure, one may never know how many Vietnamese were to follow Quang Duc into the flames. His immolation became perhaps the purest, most "auratic" referent of spectacularization.

The impact of Thich Quang Duc's immolation was international; the same image was mechanically reproduced in many of the Western Vietnam war protest plays, either directly or, as interestingly, in displaced forms. In Günter Grass' *Max* (1969), it is a dog who replaces a human, and in Peter Brook's *US* (1966) a butterfly is burned. Explicit depiction and/or allusion to Quang Duc's suicide appears in Amlin Gray's *How I Got That Story* (1979), and in both Armand Gatti's *V comme Vietnam* (1967) and in his compatriot André Benedetto's *Napalm* (1967). The theatrical tactic common to all these otherwise quite different plays is the attempt to despectacularize the highlighted central image of the burning monk in order to breathe into the entire performance the spirit of an ostensibly authentic vision of the truth: the horror of war that the other media had, consciously or unconsciously, occulted. The interaction between all-too-familiar images and live actors is supposed to produce effective political protest, beyond all the aesthetic fascination and attraction/repulsion, which strives to counteract the process of reification and commodification whereby any image – here the image of a burning monk, but all other mediatized pictures of the war – eventually become inert, interchangeable goods in the memory of the public, in its visual imaginary. Because of its live nature, theatre turns representations into a live experience that, although still mediated in some ways, gives off the strong appearance of the Real. This appearance, in turn, can produce a new or renewed feeling of immediacy and, it is further hoped, the urge to act accordingly, in this case in protest against war. It is in this sense that one may understand Hannah Arendt's claim in *The Human Condition* that theatre is the "political art par excellence" (Arendt

187–88). Since it cannot itself be reproduced without distortion to its live aspect, or at least has resistance to reproduction built into itself *qua* genre, theatre (re)produces the unique kernel of an originary event, before being swallowed up by its simulacra: in this case, a real living human burning in protest, and not (just) a sensational Western photograph. It goes without saying that the authenticity and effectivity of even this horrific image can only be ephemeral when it is (re)staged, before being eventually absorbed by commodified indifference.

But in all these Western attempts at inserting the referent back into the image no comparable attempt was made to understand the social context and motivations behind the immolation itself. The fact that it was a *Buddhist* monk, for instance, is important on TV mainly for its visual effect: the flaming orange of the gown in the interstices of the orange and yellow flames. What is completely occluded now is the religious referent and meaning behind both act and image. What is captured by the media is transformed from a sacred rite, with a complex and deep history, into yet another spectacular Western image, seen by Western eyes. For these eyes, what is visible is necessarily individualized and subjectified. Ironically, such extreme human suffering and self-sacrifice is virtually incomprehensible in the West except in these privatizing terms, and hence may forfeit not only its cultural specificity but its potential political force. A fundamental problem for attempts to articulate theatre with colonialization and imperialism is that these attempts take place on the turf of an increasingly global economy of capitalism that, almost by definition, profoundly resists its representation in any cultural practice for any length of time. (See Jameson.) In any case, it is not living theatre but television (among other technologized mass media) that is among the most powerful tools in the colonization of the so-called "Third World." American television and its images in particular are disseminated throughout the world, in the hegemonic attempt to "colonize the global unconscious." In terms of techno-culture, the flow from developed to underdeveloped nations is a one-way street.[8] This is the problem faced by all playwrights, but by few more than "Third World" intellectuals like Nhat Hanh, who took recourse to several strategies of resistance.

The printed copy of *The Path of Return* contains six interspersed woodblock prints entitled "Visage," including the cover illustration of a Vietnamese woman's face. Produced by Vo-Dinh, also the translator of the play, these are quasi-abstract (re)presentations relating to the events surrounding the self-immolation of Phan Thi Mai, a real person and now a central character in the play. Nhat Hanh centers his play on this woman who immolated herself, yet this act is said to have occurred in an atmosphere of evidently peaceful resignation, as taught by the sutras. Death, even the most terribly painful, is here part of an existential, even ontological, process of rebirth and reincarnation – which is somehow supposed to be grasped as an act of love and of effective resistance against violent death dealt by the "other." An attempt is made, in other words, not only to connect the action of self-immolation to a much larger philosophy of life and death but also to a specific political agenda. Following Michael Taussig, one might say that theatre intends to reinvest familiar images with "magic," so as to force them to become "original once again" (Taussig 31). In such a reiterative spirit (the title asks us to imagine continually that a path of return *continues* a journey, which, precisely as a path of *return*, would seem not to need to continue), the character of the ghost of Mai describes the experience of her self-immolation as follows:

> I stood on the balcony and looked at my own body enveloped in flames. Yes, I think I even smiled although my eyes were full of tears. All the people around me were weeping . . . an Army captain arrived and wanted to examine and confiscate my charred body.
>
> (Nhat Hanh 1972, 19)

She attempts to wrest back a counter-image of death from that image commodified, and polluted by the Western mass media. So that we might be "moved" again, "touched" again, and in this case, hopefully, induced to send a financial donation to Paris.

But let us look more closely at how the "others" are represented in the text. One sees the reverse of what takes place in many of the American plays, which commonly have only Americans with speaking roles on stage. In Western protest plays, Vietnamese are mostly silent shadowy figures (but not lively ghosts as in *The Path of Return*), whose identity (North or South) is at best ambivalent and ultimately insignificant, since for Americans "any dead Vietnamese is a Viet Cong," as a well-known US Army saying went. In Nhat Hanh's play, by binary contrast, the people or "strangers" who have killed the Vietnamese social workers, and who are presumably still alive in real life, are not represented, are only evoked in a verbal description. When the killers are described (and it is left to a director whether or not the death scene is to be reenacted on the stage), their true identity (national and racial) is left seemingly ambiguous: "a group of armed men . . . some wore black clothes, some uniforms. One of them had a raincoat and another a poncho. Some wore military caps and bullet belts. I know who they were" (Nhat Hanh 1972, 14). The problem, however, is that "*we*" don't know who the killers are. ("Black uniforms" hints at Viet Cong, whereas "ponchos" at Americans.) Arguably, this ambiguity is intended by the playwright. Perhaps it is "we," the Americans, who are responsible, and "we" cannot see "ourselves" on stage, except metaphorically. Although, had the play been performed in South Vietnam in 1972 (equally unlikely), it would have been the Viet Cong who would be implicated; performed in the North, it would have been the South Vietnamese and Americans. (To repeat, in the list of characters the murder in 1967 of the two women, Vui and Lien, is depicted

13

only as having occurred "during a terrorist raid . . . by a group of unknown persons.") This refusal in *The Path of Return* to name the killers thus functions as what might be called a "structured textual gap" which must be filled in semantically and politically by all possible audiences differently. This semiotic or hermeneutic gesture, this refusal to represent directly, is related perhaps to certain Buddhist meditation practices which require making the mind "blank." This certainly distinguishes Nhat Hanh's play from all Western Vietnam protest plays, where the enemy (whether Vietnamese or American) is clearly identified, sooner or later, and all trace of ambiguity lost. The problem for this particular play, however, at least as effective political theatre, is that the idea of not being bound by physical appearances, another central tenet of Buddhism, may be ineffective in a genre that, for better or worse, relies as heavily as it does on mimesis and visual representation. Obviously, the specific *staging* of this play could make the referents clear, but only thereby destroy its metaphysical integrity and commitment. And here we reach, in my opinion, a central contradiction of *The Path of Return*, but also arguably of the ability of this genre to respond to imperialist aggression in anything more than a conceptual mode especially for a Western readership or audience. Based, as we have seen, in a largely oral tradition of performance, the play in a sense demands to be staged, *not* read. Yet its metaphysical reluctance, even refusal, to represent *anything*, including the agents of imperialist aggression *and/or* militant opposition to it, threatens to turn the play into an artifact that cannot be staged, *only* read. The overdetermined nature of this fundamental contradiction is apparent in the simultaneous refusal either to represent the killers or to assign responsibility for their acts, but also in the metaphysical and ideological presumption that life and death are essentially interchangeable – not merely on stage but elsewhere, cosmically even. Finally, there is the concomitant impossibility to have dramatic conflict in this quasi-theological system, including to put it on stage. At one point a character says "How can I see you if you do not have a body?" (Nhat Hanh 1972, 13). How indeed? This may make some sense when reading or meditating, but the problems of staging may be all but insoluble. One of the remarkable things about political theatre is its ability simultaneously to provoke and to elude censorship, precisely because its written text, which appears fixed and innocuous, can actually become quite subversive, and even transformative when staged. Whether that could have occurred with this particular Vietnamese protest play is a question that cannot be decided.

While the victims in *The Path of Return* do not blame the (American?) soldiers for killing them – soldiers are only carrying out orders – what they *are* chided for is their ignorance. When the play does come to speak explicitly of the American presence in Vietnam, it is in terms of a culpable ignorance. For, it is implied, ignorance is something that can be corrected. But how can responsibility for one's actions or the actions of one's group or class be taken – in this world infused with the sutras, in which the very distinction between life and death is always already problematized, if not actually moot? But even this is not the whole story. In more practical terms, and somewhat surprisingly in the light shown on reality by the sutras, Americans *are* blamed, to some extent, for their chauvinistic prejudice and their unwillingness to find out what is actually going on in Vietnam.

> The American knew absolutely nothing about Vietnamese history and culture or the truth of the conflict in which he was playing a part. He was certain of only one thing: the V.C. was his enemy . . . . He could hate the V.C. only because he really did not know what the V.C. were.
>
> (Nhat Hanh 1972, 24)

And then, in a related twist, Americans *are* actually blamed in one other sense as well. This is the Buddhist–Existentialist version of the American phrase "I have seen the enemy and it is us." For Nhat Hanh pities the Americans in their ignorance. "Who really kills them? Their own fear and hatred and prejudice" (Nhat Hanh 1972, 25). Nonetheless, to repeat, we never see these Americans on stage, and see only one of them in our mind's eye as readers. Not only is American imperialism under- or un-represented, it seems it *cannot* be represented, in this play at least, except in this extraordinarily oblique and indirect way.

What then becomes the function of "theatre" and its relation to a very specific war, in a very specific country, at a very specific time? What can be theatre in an underdeveloped country, a country under violent seige everyday, a country whose very existence is continually threatening to disappear? Before the war, as one character in the play, Hy, former head of the Performing Arts Committee, puts it: "art was used as a means for rural reconstruction and social development. We used poetry, painting, music and theatre to serve the people" (Nhat Hanh 1972, 11). And here we return to the problem of the function of art and culture vis-à-vis imperialism, especially in a country indelibly, perhaps permanently marked by the necessity of resistance to it: a resistance manifesting itself militarily, politically, and economically as well as religiously, culturally, and theatrically. On the one horn of the central dilemma of the articulation of theatre and imperialism, it is important not to *reduce* overdetermined problems to any one of these, themselves overdetermined aspects of domination and resistance around the world. On the other horn, with regard specifically to art, Nhat Hanh himself seems to suggest, as Buddhist, what the Communist Gramsci noted in the 1930s when attempting to resist Fascism: when "cultural functions predominate," "political language becomes jargon," and "political questions are disguised as cultural ones," and as such they become "insoluble" (Gramsci 149).

Recalling a key question from the play "How can I see you if you do not have a body?" it can be said that, however disembodied this "theatre" may be, its very existence *may* suggest that it is possible during a global crisis, to forge a *community* of response and resistance to war across national and linguistic borders and peripheries – an artistic protest more or less independent of other forms of protest and yet in solidarity with them. Which brings us back, at the end of this essay, to the fact that the Vietnamese play has a foreword by Berrigan, who himself tried to forge some sort of international resistance community, and desired fervently that theatre be instrumental in this project: "The religious resistance in this country cannot help but take into special account, with a special gratitude, the Vietnamese Buddhist movement. Spiritually speaking we are the closest to them" (Nhat Hanh 1972, 3). Thus there is forged a metaphysical – if not also physical – articulation of cross-cultural peace movements, a virtual transcendence of the Western imperial death machine. For Berrigan, "We Americans cross the great waters with our techniques of death, supersonic instruments of appetite . . . to smell out and destroy the least lurking evidence of life . . . . 'Let it all come down!' is the manic whine of the Machine" (Nhat Hanh 1972, 4). So it is, in this text at least, that imperialism *is* linked to the machines of war after all, and *is* then resisted, by the imagined moral superiority of a technologically inferior "other," who turns out, however, to be "our" true friend: the friend, that is, not of all Americans, or of humanity at large, but of the embattled peace movement, in all *its* technological weakness and in all *its* moral strength.[9] In other words: unlike television and the television war, in all their moral weakness and technological strength.

NOTES

1 Of course, one may always argue about the label "theatre," but here I am taking it in its loosest definition as a performance where actors are playing out roles. For a relevant discussion of the complexities of the definitions of theatre and performance, see Schechner.

2 See the statement of purpose published by JUSPAO and reprinted in the *Drama Review* 13:4 (Summer 1969).

3 Obviously this observation opens up on a much larger problematic of the fate of theatre and theatre studies in general. Books such as this one participate in an ongoing effort to establish theatre in its own (relative) right in the field of theory and criticism, and as a cultural text just as worthy of attention as other forms of cultural production such as novels and films.

4 Again, while it is not the point of this essay, it is worth mentioning that many writers and intellectuals around the world protested against the war in Vietnam. But this was essentially "America's war" and the perspectives on it have too often been reduced to an exclusively American problematic. This is perhaps nowhere more obvious than in the fact that the number of deaths of U.S. servicemen (*c.* 58,000) comes readily to mind but the exact number of Vietnamese killed (well into the millions) is not known.

5 "Indeed, one of the features of cheo characterization was the special place it

gave to women. The main characters were female, and . . . the male roles were more or less disgraced" (Mackerras 3).

6 "A great many of the communist culture–drama organizations are totally female. During the performances they costume themselves as men." JUSPAO report, " 'Them' – Seen by Us," reprinted in the *Drama Review* 13:4 (Summer 1969).

7 The first organized demonstrations against American involvement in Vietnam took place in Aug. 1963, during the annual commemorations by American pacifists of the Hiroshima–Nagasaki atomic bombings. . . . In New York the action was inspired by the self-immolation of the Buddhist Thich Quang Doc.

(Zaroulis and Sullivan 12)

8 From the standpoint of the Third World, a good deal is wrong with the "old," and still prevailing, order. In terms of news and news coverage, the overwhelming majority of world news flows from the developed to the developing countries and is generated by four large transnational new agencies – AP, UPI, AFP, and Reuters.

(Wete 139)

9 In Armand Gatti's anti-Vietnam war play, *V comme Vietnam* (1967), the same attack on technology and machinery is mounted.

WORKS CITED

Ahmad, Aijaz, *In Theory: Classes, Nations, Literatures* (New York and London: Verso, 1992).

Arendt, Hannah, *The Human Condition* (Chicago and London: University of Chicago Press, 1958).

Benedetto, André, *Napalm* (Paris: Oswald, 1968).

Berrigan, Daniel, *The Trial of the Catonsville Nine* (Boston: Beacon Press, 1970).

Boal, Augusto, *Theatre of the Oppressed* [1974], trans. Charles A. and Maria-Odilia Leal McBride (New York: Theatre Communications Group, 1985).

Brook, Peter, *US* (London: Calder & Boyars, 1968).

Gatti, Armand, *V comme Vietnam* (Paris: Seuil, 1967).

Gramsci, Antonio, *Selections from the Prison Notebooks of Antonio Gramsci*, ed. and trans. Quintin Hoare and Geoffrey Nowell Smith (New York: International Publishers, 1971).

Grass, Günter, *Max* [original title *Davor*, 1970], trans. Leslie A. Willson and Ralph Manheim (New York: Harcourt Brace Jovanovich, Inc., 1972).

Gray, Amlin, *How I Got that Story* [1979], in *Coming to Terms: American Plays and the Vietnam War*, ed. James Reston, Jr. (New York: Theatre Communications Group, Inc., 1985).

Jameson, Fredric, *The Geopolitical Aesthetic: Cinema and Space in the World System* (Bloomington and Indianapolis: Indiana University Press, and London: BFI, 1992).

Mackerras, Colin, "Theatre in Vietnam," *Asian Theatre Journal* 4:1 (Spring 1987).

Moeller, Susan D., *Shooting the War: Photography and the American Experience of Combat* (New York: Basic Books, 1989).

Nhat Hanh (Thich), "A Buddhist Poet in Vietnam" [*New York Review of Books*, June 9, 1966], reprinted in *The First Anthology: 30 Years of the New York Review of Books*, ed. Robert B. Silvers, *et al.* (New York: NYRB, 1993).

———— *The Path of Return Continues the Journey*, trans. and drawings by Vo-Dinh, with a Foreword by Daniel Berrigan (New York: Hoa Binh Press, 1972).

Astasahasrika Prajnaparamita: The Perfection of Wisdom in Eight Thousand Slokas, trans. Edward Conze (Calcutta: Asiatic Society/Biblioteca Indica, 1958).

The Short Prajnaparamita Texts, trans. Edward Conze (London: Luzac & Company Ltd., 1973).

Schechner, Richard, *Between Performance and Anthropology* (Philadelphia: University of Pennsylvania Press, 1985).

Taussig, Michael, *Mimesis and Alterity: A Particular History of the Senses* (New York and London: Routledge, 1993).

Trinh T. Minh-ha, *When the Moon Waxes Red: Representation, Gender and Cultural Politics* (New York and London: Routledge, 1991).

Trinh T. Minh-ha (ed.), *She, the Inappropriate/d Other*, special issue of *Discourse* 8 (Fall–Winter 1986/87).

Weiss, Peter, *Viet Nam Discourse* [1967], trans. Lee Baxandall (New York: Atheneum, 1970).

Wete, Francis N., "The New World Information Order and the US Press," in *Global Television*, ed. Cynthia Schneider and Brian Wallis (New York: Wedge Press, 1988).

Zaroulis, Nancy, and Gerald Sullivan, *Who Spoke Up? American Protest Against the War in Vietnam 1963–1975* (New York: Rinehart & Winston, 1984).

2

MISE-EN-(COLONIAL-)*SCÈNE*
The Theatre of the Bengal Renaissance
Sudipto Chatterjee

You see before you, as it were on a stage, two actors, the Anglo-Saxon and the Hindu – and believe me, it is a sublime, a solemn, a grand, a wondrous Drama they are destined to act.

Michael Madhusūdan Dutta[1]

On October 6, 1835 (some historians claim the year to be 1833 or even 1831), Nabin Candra Basu, a Calcutta-based Bengali *bhadra lok*[2] or *bābu*[3] of a high order, organized the various spaces available in his mansion. A play based on the popular eighteenth-century Bengali poem *Vidyā Sundar* by the poet Bhārat Candra (1712–60) was staged on that evening. Performed before a mixed audience of more than a thousand drawn from the Hindu and Muslim as well as European communities, the play ran from 12 midnight till 6:30 in the morning. Many historians mark this as the first Bengali play on a Calcutta "stage," although it was done environmentally and the audience was required to follow the actors to the various places where scenes from the play were enacted.

About four decades prior to this a similar lone effort had been made to perform a play in Bengali. On that occasion, the person making the effort was not a Bengali, not even an Englishman, but a Russian violinist – Gerasim Stepanovich Lebedeff. Lebedeff had arrived in Calcutta in 1787, after a two-year spell in Madras, and spent the next ten years of his life there. In 1795, he decided to give vent to his other artistic ambition – theatre. He rented a house and soon began the work of converting it into a theatre. By this time Lebedeff must also have finished translating the two English plays he chose to perform for his theatre: Paul Jodrell's *The Disguise* and *Love is the Best Doctor*. On November 27, at least 200 Calcuttans witnessed the first Western-style Bengali play ever to be staged. It is hard to ascertain whether any subsequent performances of *The Disguise* ever took place. What is certain is that after this point Lebedeff's career in Calcutta took a sudden blightful turn, when he fell victim to politics in the company ranks and the influential natives turned against him in fear of company castigation. In December, 1797, Lebedeff decided to leave India, never to return. There would be no theatre in Bengali for about three decades until Nabin Basu's Śhyāmbāzār Theatre. Lebedeff had, knowingly or otherwise, activated an apocalyptic clock that started ticking in a patient countdown with a promised climax that was to happen almost eighty years later with the foundation of the National Theatre in 1872. The endeavors of Lebedeff and Basu represent the two disparate factors – the foreign and the native, the Anglicist and the Orientalist – that would eventually determine and define the hybrid character of Bengali theatre.

Between 1795 and the last quarter of the nineteenth century, Bengal witnessed what was termed, even in its own time, a "Renaissance." This one period of Indian history brought about the most radical changes the sub-continent had seen since the time of the first Islamic invasion. The Bengal Renaissance was the outgrowth of the grafting of a foreign culture onto that of a more-than-willing native culture. For the Bengalis their response to what was imposed by the British was a search for a cultural identity that could, at some level, set them on a par with their European overlords. It is in the wake of this endeavor to assume/regain a respectful self-identity that, in the 1840s, several theatres were spawned in the native quarters of Calcutta. Concentration of wealth in the hands of the *bābu*s and the rise of a Western-style educated middle class provided the right moment of pollination for the budding of a Bengali theatre. Wealth of the *bābu*s meant both leisure and availability of patronage; growth of the middle class meant surplus creative energy seeking channels of expression. Close contact with the British inspired both classes to create their own theatre in the European mold. With the coming of economic, political and social stability – with a mean being struck between traditional Bengali culture and the *bilāti* (i.e. British) cultural imports – a system of patronage was born that was to keep Bengali theatre alive for some time.

Bengali newspapers started voicing the need for native theatres very early in the first quarter of the nineteenth century. But other than Nabin Basu's exalted effort, the only other theatrical enterprise in the 1830s was *Bābu* Prasanna Kumar Tagore's Hindu Theatre (1831). But this theatre concentrated, by general consensus among the organizers, on producing plays in the English language – not only English plays but also English translations of Sanskrit plays. The trend of English plays enacted by native actors continued in the *bābu*-theatre circuit of the 1840s. The one achievement the natives could be proud of during this decade was the appearance of a Bengali, Vaiṣṇav Caraṇ Āḍhya, as Othello in a professional English production of the Shakespearean play at the Sans Souci Theatre, one of the few professional European theatres in the white quarters of Calcutta, in 1848 (Mukherjee 6). Āḍhya, or Auddy as he was better known was probably the first person of color to play the tragic Moor.

With the turning of the 1850s, however, an enormous amount of theatrical activity suddenly overwhelmed the cultural scene of native Calcutta. The growth of the urban gentry under the English was not the only reason for the rapid development of the Bengali theatre in the 1850s. A burgeoning new urban middle class was helping the cause tremendously, not simply by coming to see the plays but also by supplying a good number of actors. But it was in Joyrām Basāk's efforts that this impetus finally found true results, when in 1857 he produced the first noteworthy original play in Bengali – *Kulīnkulasarvasva* by Rāmnārāyaṇ Tarkaratna (1828–86). The play, a scathing social satire on the polygamous practice of the *kulīn* group of brahmins, turned out to be a very successful production. However, the trend of performing translations of Sanskrit plays continued even after *Kulīnkulasarvasva*.

The question arising at this point is: why so many translations? And if translations, why Sanskrit plays? Lebedeff had observed during his stay in Calcutta "that the Indian preferred mimicry and the drollery to plain grave solid sense, however purely expressed . . . " (Ghosh, A. 17). Why were the descendants of the same Indians now ready to measure up to the classical loftiness of the Sanskrit theatre? Why was Sanskrit drama reinvented for a Bengali palate in the middle of the nineteenth century after centuries of oblivion? To find out more, we need to return to a point made more perfunctorily above. A process of cultural rediscovery was indeed in swing as the natives searched for a self-identity that could take them beyond the humiliation of being ruled. Taking the cue from the scholarship of the British orientalists and the work of institutions like the Asiatic Society of Bengal (established 1784) and the Royal Asiatic Society in England (established 1823), several members of the Bengali literati had become serious and proud scholars of Indian antiquity. This scholarship is reflected in the regularity with which Sanskrit plays were being translated.

Under Warren Hastings (Governor of Bengal, 1772–74, and Governor-General of India, 1774–85) the British East India Company realized for the first time that it was necessary for them to know their subjects before ruling them – that *power* could not come without *knowledge*. The arrival of William Jones in 1783, and the genre of scholarship that he launched, began the period of sympathetic colonialism which replaced Robert Clive's policy of exerting brute imperialistic power. Under the leadership of Jones, the Asiatic Society became the foremost British orientalist institution. Soon to come, under Earl Wellesley (Governor-General 1798–1805), who followed in the footsteps of Hastings, were the Serampore (corruption of the Bengali Srirāmpur) Mission and Fort William College, both established in 1800. One must not forget, however, that sympathetic colonialism was pragmatically attuned to the job of ruling the colony. The difference between "the glory that India was" and "the mass of decadence" it had turned into was something the British never allowed themselves to forget; they propagated this unfailingly among the native bourgeoisie. The respect with which the Western orientalist scholars approached their subjects was seldom free from desires of domination. This ambiguously respectful attitude was compensatory justification for the essentially appropriative act of ruling the orient, the now classical strategy of legitimizing colonization, the great project of civilizing barbarians: "We are ruling you, but also, we are giving you a knowledge of what you were; hence, our presence in your land is justified, because we are (also) showing you the light of knowledge." But sympathetic colonialism, directly or indirectly, gave the Bengali intelligentsia clear and open access to materials they would use continually to fashion a sense of cultural inheritance that would infiltrate all modes of cultural expression, from language to literature to art to music to the theatre.

The projects undertaken by Fort William College involved a good number of Bengalis and inspired them to come closer to the English and their culture. The contact deepened with the gradual conversion of Indian society into a quasi-capitalist outfit, the perpetuation of which led to the birth of a Bengali intelligentsia. The new-born intelligentsia of Bengal came forward with great enthusiasm to learn the culture of their colonizers. This new intelligentsia or the *bābu* class received the guarantee of a long life with the establishment of the Hindu College in 1817. A strong base had been built for the growing class, because now they could rightfully educate themselves and their children in the *bilāti kāidā* (superior/foreign way), which was now highly fashionable and desirable for climbing the social ladder. With the natives so blindly eager to receive Western instruction, the time could not be more fitting for English education to be brought to India. The Anglicists, in the mean time, had overwhelmed their Orientalist opponents in the Company ranks. That victory was spelt out, in one of the clearest statements ever made on the business of British presence in India, by Thomas Babbington Macaulay in his celebrated Educational Minute of February 2, 1835, when he professed to create a class of Indians who would be interpreters and "Indian in blood and color, but English in tastes, in opinions, in morals and in intellect" (de Bary 49). The assertive victory of the Anglicists over the Orientalists in 1835 allowed the intelligentsia to imbue their fashioned Indianness with the progressive hue of Westernization. Anglicist policy gave the natives an instrument to think with – namely, the English language and the command of it – the instrument that the colonizer had used so far to keep himself away from the natives. It would now be used to create (and maintain, if not increase) another kind of distance, this time between the English-educated native and his own native identity. The educated native had somewhat lost his innate "native-ness" through contact with his colonizer. This yawning gulf between native and native-ness was further enlarged by the Anglicists. This inevitably resulted in a binary vision on the part of the colonized. With one eye he saw the yoke of colonialism on his shoulders; with the other he regarded the intricate web of now inseparable connections he had developed with the master to whom he owed his present state of being. The onus of striking a mean, of being at once native and accultured with the "other," was on him. The paradox was irreducible. The native had to invent a new identity for himself. This new identity, essentially a paradigm of hybridity, was fashioned out of the binary strains of Sanskritic *revivalism* and *Westernization.*

It is this revivalist theme that is reflected in the penchant the early movers of the Bengali theatre had for Sanskrit texts. The propensity for producing plays in English, however short lived, was an expression of the flip side of the dual desire: Westernization. And when the tenets and principles of Western drama started influencing Bengali theatre more palpably, this rather strong inclination for both Sanskrit texts and subjects continued to thrive and find various avenues of expressing itself even in the midst of the Western-style theatre that was adopted by the Bengalis. Translating from the repertoire of extant Sanskrit plays was the first step the Bengali literati took towards an indigenous theatre after a few solitary efforts like those of Nabin Basu and, earlier, that of Lebedeff. The literati were confronted with two compelling factors in their desire to refashion a compensatory national identity. While on the one side there stood the great tradition of Sanskrit theatre and its plays (like Kālīdāsa's *Sakuntalā*[4]) and theoretical treatises (like Bharata's *Nātyaśāstra*[5]) and their need to be translated and/or emulated, on the other side there was the example of colonial English theatres of Calcutta, their plays and mostly their proscenium stage whose mode of production the natives thought was a good idea to follow. It was mainly in response to the theatrical activities of the English that the Bengali *bābu*s started presenting their own plays. Obviously, the two initial impulses were either to imitate or create their own, and, as a corollary to that, translate. We have already mentioned the trend among the Bengali *bābu*s of performing Sanskrit plays in English, but there were some translations of Western plays into Bengali as well, mainly Shakespeare.

We can safely bracket the Sanskrit/Orientalist period of the Bengali Theatre between 1831 and 1859. Most of the original Bengali plays that were written during this period followed the tenets of Sanskrit drama. Till 1860 only a meager thirty-five plays had been published in Bengali, of which eleven were translations from Sanskrit, five original but mythological (in the Sanskrit style), one translated from English, thirteen on social problems and five miscellaneous. By 1867, however, the total had risen to a healthy eighty-two; a good number of new plays had been added, but the pattern was still the same: Bengali versions of Sanskrit (and a few English) plays, Sanskrit imitations and a barrage of social problem plays, mainly farces. But towards the end of this period one can see the rivalry between Sanskrit drama and its Western counterpart stiffening.

This competition between Sanskrit and European drama is very similar to the competition between the Orientalist and Anglicist rivalry in the ranks of the Company administration. The theatre of the Bengali intelligentsia, too, had phases structurally similar to the Orientalist and Anglicist phases of the colonial administration. Ironically, in its Orientalist phase most of the productions mounted were in English, while the Anglicist phase saw the rise of theatre in the Bengali language. Also, one must note that the Orientalist phase of the theatre of the Bengali literati touched ground around the time Anglicist philosophy had gained almost total control over Company administration. One must, of course, remember that neither of the two periods is mutually exclusive of each other. That they did overlap and mingle can best be seen in the way in which an "Indian" set of terms was made to stand in for the various appurtenances of Western theatre the Bengali stage was emulating. Very specific and context-bound terms[6] were freely appropriated from the Sanskrit theatre and *jātrā* in order to indicate parts of a Western-style theatre whose English terms the Bengalis did not always find convenient to use. These "translations" of terms, equivalencies, were pulled out of context, at times their actual meanings bent around to signify objects they were never meant to indicate. The following is a list of some equivalencies the Bengali theatre used in the nineteenth century (most of these terms are still being used today):

Sanskrit term	Actual meaning	Equivalency for
abhinaya	codified gestures	acting
nṛtya	dramatic dancing	dance
nāṭaka	one form of drama	drama
janāntike	thinking aloud	aside
raṅgabhūmi	performance space	proscenium stage
prekṣāgṛha	theatre house (generic)	Western-style auditorium
rūpaka	a form of drama	metaphor
swagata	to him/herself	soliloquy

These are but a few of the many other examples that illustrate this phenomenon of converting equivalents into equals, obscuring passages between cultures and homogenizing history to refashion a national identity.

This *re*fashioning was closely following a prescription, a text, or several texts, created by foreigners (often collaborating with natives), both in and outside India, both Orientalists and civil servants (and many Orientalists were civil servants and vice versa). This text, in turn, was being deconstructed and reconstructed by the Bengali literati after assimilation with what was native to the soil to form a final performance text for the new society. Within the first half of the nineteenth century Bengali literature suddenly became a force to reckon with. A tremendous amount of writing was being done in Calcutta, creative as well as journalistic. Books were flooding the market as were newspapers and periodicals. The energy of this Bengal Renaissance was of such magnitude that the ill effects of imperialism were not considered seriously by the Bengali intelligentsia and even ignored in favor of English superiority in the excitement of learning and performing the new text. During the first half of the nineteenth century the Bengali intelligentsia, in general, regarded the colonial situation rather myopically, as a socio-economic set-up that best served their interests; the questions of self-rule and independence would not gain real ground until the birth of nationalism in the latter half of the century. The *bābu* society was more interested in finding an independent social and/or cultural voice rather than political independence.[7]

Consequently, a socio-cultural *mise-en-scène* emerged out of the Bengal Renaissance, demonstrating its multifarious workings: (1) its *text* (composed of the colonial social structure, its behavioral requirements from the natives, and the Western Orientalist's discoveries of the Indian past which circumscribed the native's own national identity); (2) the process of *catalysis/rehearsal* (the raging debates on social and educational issues, the major social changes upsetting the traditional socio-cultural order and other such instruments-of-change in social structure); and (3) its *performance* (best reflected in the copious literary output of the writers in the Bengali language, especially in the numerous periodicals that were being published in the vernacular). Bengali theatre, in the context of this large *mise-en-scènic* superstructure, performs a metonymic function and works like a play-within-a-play. It is both emblematic as well as a product of a larger *mise-en-scène* of the social order. As a result we find the two structures – the macro and the micro – feeding and informing each other. The reasons are not far from obvious. Mimesis – to mime, to mimic – is at the base of theatre just as it is also one of the components of imperialist power. Homi K. Bhabha defines the colonial subject's "desire" for mimicry as one for a "reformed, recognizable Other, as a subject of a difference that is almost the same, but not quite" (Bhabha 126).

Jean-François Lyotard proposes a useful definition of *mise-en-scène*. He suggests:

> [M]ise-en-scène consists of a complex group of operations, each of which transcribes a message written in a given sign system (literary writing, musical notation) and turns it into a message capable of being inscribed on human bodies and transmitted by those to other bodies: a kind of somatography. (88)

What Lyotard calls "a given sign system" can also be called, in a more limited sense, the written or, more accurately, the codified text that is merely suggestive of a possible transcription or transference into a more palpably physicalized text through somatographic transmission. And when that possibility of somatographic transmission turns into reality the process of what we generally identify as rehearsal has begun. The process of rehearsal can also be called a process of catalysis: the acceleration or causing of a chemical change by the addition of a substance that is not permanently affected by the reaction. The chemistry of the change that happens during rehearsal occurs on the body of the stage or social actor. What remains "not permanently affected" is the written/codified text securely nested in the realm of the readable codes at a unimedial level of the script. A rehearsal then is a phenomenon that bounces off the codified text; it is a preparation for the performance text that eventually emerges. It is, therefore, an essentially semiotic exercise, a decoding and a subsequent recoding of signs interpreted from the codified text at a multimedial level. Richard Schechner, offering a definition of the rehearsal process, talks about the interpretive function of rehearsal:

> [T]he rehearsal is a way of selecting from possible actions those to be performed, of simplifying these, making them as clear as possible in regard both to the matrix from which they have been taken and the audience with which they are meant to communicate. (183)

The catalytic process of rehearsing then is a system of communication that molds the written text/script and pushes it towards the final performance text.

Questions can, of course, be raised about whether there can be a final performance text at all. However, for the time being we shall consider the performance text as finite (if not final). The performance text, in effect, adds more meaning to the original written text. Very often the reverberation of one performance text is felt in the next production of the same written text. Of course, this reverberation – one may also call it legacy – may be followed either in conformity/observance or disavowal/repudiation in subsequent productions. However, what is important is that this allows the cycle of the *mise-en-scènic* structure to roll on inexorably.

This inexorable renewal of the *mise-en-scènic* structure is of particular importance in the colonial context. Looking at colonialism from this perspective allows us to see not only the theatricality of how political, especially colonial, power is exercised but also to find ways to read the texts hidden behind the colonizers' mask. It allows us to explore the plethora of issues moving between what is shown and what is believed, what vacillates between the cultures of the colonizer and the colonized, between mimesis and alterity. It is important to examine the myriad forms and structures that the hybridized society of the colonized (as that of Renaissance Bengal) assumes and rejects while evolving into something that is a distinctive cultural formation in its own right.

The colonial *mise-en-scène* begins with the Motor/Idea which is "what India should be." The Written Text/Script that stems out of the Motor/Idea is "Orientalism and British Rule" and all its appurtenances and effects which include the responses and collaborative activities of the native elite. Consequently, the Text/Script of this massive colonial *mise-en-scène* responds to the desires of the colonized as well as the power of the colonizer. Like a script evolving in a workshop situation, it emanates from a discourse that, in turn, is emerging out of a collusion/fusion between the colonizer and the colonized. The colonial Catalysis/Rehearsal then is a process of transcribing the Western mode of using knowledge that would make the native bourgeoisie absorb the Western mode of thinking into its fold and thus reinforce the colonizer's presence in the colony. The success of the training, the colonizer hoped, would set off a chain reaction among the natives that would keep reinforcing the cause of the colonizer relentlessly. Charles Trevelyan, a civil servant, confirmed the belief that the influence of an English educated native upper class would ensure the permanence of all the changes that Western education had introduced in India: "Our subjects have set out on a new career of improvement: they are about to have a new character imprinted on them" (quoted in Niranjana 30).

In 1859, a very important personage, a brilliant "subject" bearing all the imprints of the "new character," appeared on the scene of Bengali theatre: Michael Madhusūdan Dutta. In the same year he wrote *Śarmiṣṭhā* and translated Rāmnārāyaṇ Tarkaratna's Bengali translation of *Ratnāvalī* (by Śrīharṣa) into English, and thereafter went straight into translating his own *Śarmiṣṭhā* into English. Dutta was, very soon, expressing the need for more original plays in Bengali that would "call onto the field a host of writers who will discard Sanskrit models and look to far higher sources for inspiration" (Dutta, Introduction, 76). Dutta's "far higher sources" comprised Shakespeare and the Elizabethans as well as the classical dramatic theories from the Greeks down to Dryden and Racine. Dutta read and spoke not only English and Latin but also French, Italian and, probably, Hebrew and Greek along with Sanskrit and several Indian languages. He was also acutely aware of the differences between European culture, the culture he tried all his life to make his own, and Bengali culture, the one that he was born into. And in *Śarmiṣṭhā* one can see Dutta struggling to strike a mean between his dual cultural propensities. The play abounds with instances of allegiance to Sanskrit aesthetics[8] while striving, at the same time, to be Western in structure and conflict. A comparative examination of his *Śarmiṣṭhā* in the original Bengali and its English translation (done, of course, by Dutta himself) is sure to leave the bilingual reader questioning which one is the original. The following excerpt is from Dutta's English version of the play, where Princess Sermista (Dutta Anglicized the name in his translation) talks of her woes:

> Have I not myself *wantonly woo'd* calamity to darken my path? Have I not like a *bedlamite* mixed *worm-wood* and gall with the honied draught Destiny gave me to drink? How cans't thou curse Destiny? How cans't thou call her cruel?
>
> (Dutta 707, my italics)

The words and phrases I have highlighted adequately reveal Dutta's fondness for the English language. While "wantonly woo'd" sounds distinctly

Elizabethan, "worm-wood" recalls Hamlet's madness, and "bedlamite," an outrageous anachronism, refers to the Hospital of St. Mary of Bethlehem, an eighteenth-century asylum for the insane in London!

Nevertheless, what is most important in Dutta's *Śarmiṣṭhā/Sermista* is the inherent search for an equilibrium that could justify artistic creativity in a society that was grappling with two identities. And it is this singular keynote of trial and error that makes Dutta's quest emblematic of a rehearsal for a larger and eventually more mature operation: the theatre of the Bengal Renaissance. His writings stand as the best paradigms of the kind of hybridity that the *mise-en-scène* of the Bengal Renaissance generated. And hybridity is also a political strategy whereby the colonized subject gradually develops for himself an independent voice that, whatever its original components, at some point of time begins to make itself heard, begins to perform itself. For "hybridity," according to Homi K. Bhabha,

> unsettles the mimetic and narcissistic demands of colonial power but reimplicates its identifications in strategies of subversion that turn the gaze of the discriminated back upon the eye of the power.
>
> (Bhabha 173)

Michael Madhusūdan Dutta was writing at a time when vast transformations were being wrought upon human society globally. Europe was changing with the winds of democracy and capitalism initiated by the bourgeois. It was these winds that shaped Dutta's sensibility. He was witnessing (and wishing) the rapid decline of a feudal order and from its ashes the rise of a revolutionary bourgeoisie. Only, in his case, the feudal order was a rather young one, a decadent *bābu* society that came into being in the wake of Lord Cornwallis' (Governor-General 1786–93) Permanent Settlement Act and the *zamindāri* system of absentee landlordism.[9] *Kṛṣṇākumārī*, his third and most mature full-length play, draws its storyline from Tod's *Annals and Antiquities of Rājasthān*. But, instead of playing up the expected orientalist melody of "the glory that India was," Dutta chose to metaphorize what he saw in his society. Instead of upholding a pretentious veneer of Hindu nationalism he portrayed a Rājput world that was a gloomy arena of lust, tyranny, political intrigues, conspiracy, treachery and greed. Dutta was not writing from a Bengali point of view alone; he was aware of the last attempt of resurrection the European feudal system made through Napoleon and the Metternich system. The revolutionary thought of the European bourgeoisie of the previous century – Rousseau, Voltaire, Diderot, Robespierre, and others – was embedded in his mind quite deeply. He must have been aware of the work of Goethe, Schiller and Lessing. In fact, the endings of Lessing's *Emilia Galotti* and *Kṛṣṇākumārī* are strikingly similar; in both plays fathers end up murdering their daughters to save them from infamy. Like his European predecessors, Dutta was revolting against a feudal order too; hopelessly caged in the *bābu* set-up his eyes were set on a democratized national theatre.

Kṛṣṇākumārī is about the struggle of several Rājput princes for Princess Kṛṣṇākumārī's hand, and the terrible lengths to which they are willing to go. It is not hard to understand why *Kṛṣṇākumārī* was never performed by the *bābu*s who commissioned it. With *Kṛṣṇākumārī*, Dutta had dared to bite the hand that fed him. He must have been aware of the risk he was taking, since while giving finishing touches to *Kṛṣṇākumārī* he cautioned a friend: "Mind you, you all broke my wings once about the farces; if you play a similar trick this time I shall forswear Bengali and write books in Hebrew and Chinese!" (Dutta 574). True enough, after the play got a cold shoulder from his *bābu* patrons, Dutta delved deep into something that was indeed as foreign as Hebrew and Chinese to Bengali literature: epic poetry. What we see in Dutta's writings is a kind of creativity that legitimizes hybridity as a valid form of artistic expression. In Dutta, the two major components of the Bengali theatre – the Orientalist/Sanskrit and Anglicist/Western tenets – were first integrated as a valid and independent entity. The written text for the performance of the theatre of the Bengal Renaissance had run its first full course with Dutta under *bābu*-patronage.

The second course would begin with the arrival of the democratized public theatre in 1872. By this time, Bengali theatre had completed its journey away from the clutches of the *bābu*s and orientalists to the democratic level of the ticketed theatre, which soon became professional under the leadership of Girish Chandra Ghosh[10] and his friends Ardhendu Ṣekhar Mustāphi, Amṛta Lāl Basu and others. By 1867 Ghosh had formed a *jātrā* troupe at Bāgbāzār that mounted a production of Dutta's *Śarmiṣṭhā*. Calling itself the Bāgbāzār Amateur Theatre, the troupe chose Dutta's Western-style play only to perform it in the *jātrā* style that had been abhorred by both the British and the *bābu*s. The question remains: why? Some scholars believe that sheer economic necessity prompted Ghosh and his friends to settle for jātrā. The young men did not have the money to put up a Western-style production that only the *bābu*s could afford (Rāy Caudhurī 31) but, at the same time, they had good reasons to think in terms of professionalism. For one, they felt a frustration with the amateurish state of Bengali theatre. Along with that was the wish to escape the control of the whimsical *bābu*s and connect with a larger audience. The sprawling mansions of the *bābu*s had no place for the riff-raff of Calcutta's black quarters and yet they, formidable in numbers, were the people who flocked to see *jātrā*s. A combination of all these reasons made Ghosh and his band reach out for a professional outfit.

Son of a clerk at a British counting-house, Ghosh was brought up by a wet-nurse from a very low Hindu caste. Although a school drop-out, he never stopped educating himself. A social rebel from the beginning, he shed, under his nurse's guidance, all vestiges of *bābu*-hood he had inherited by birth. This spirit of rebellion tempered his sensibilities when it came to theatre. His theatrical talents developed under two opposing influences: the traditional folk performers who populated the black quarters of North Calcutta, and Mrs G. B. W. Lewis, the American actress/proprietress of Theatre Royal in white Calcutta. Ghosh knew and revered Mrs Lewis. While the first influence was a conduit to his own traditions, the second opened to him a door to the vast resources of Western drama. No wonder, then, that Ghosh, with the desire to attract a bigger audience looming large in his mind, would try to combine the two cultural elements.

When the Bāgbāzār Amateur Theatre succeeded commercially with *Sadhabār Ekādaśī* and then *Līlābatī*, both by Dīnabandhu Mitra, it decided to throw off the amateur's garb and look for a permanent stage. With the help of borrowed money they built a stage in a *bābu* patron's residence in north Calcutta where *Līlābatī* opened in 1871. At this time, Ghosh temporarily left the company when a member proposed that the group be called the National Theatre. He felt that the time was not right to call their theatre "national." He was to rejoin the theatre later in the same year only to make it his own. The next play of the National Theatre (without Ghosh), again on the premises of a *bābu*, was *Nīldarpaṇ*, a poignant protest-play addressing the atrocities meted out to the indigo-plantation farmers by British administrators and their collaborators the native landowners (the *zamindārs*) – a portrayal of the inhuman conditions that led to the Indigo Rebellion in 1860. *Nīldarpaṇ*, serious and political in content, was a very different play, especially considering that the social problem plays written during the period were mainly slapstick satires. One must, however, note with consternation that *Nīldarpaṇ*, like the stream of *darpaṇ* plays it came to inspire,[11] was produced in the safety of urban limits and came long after the Indigo situation had eased. This blurs the line between the educated native's opposition to and collaboration with the imperial administration (Mitra was a dedicated Civil Servant) and draws attention towards the ambivalent attitude of the native literati towards the colonizer.[12] This also indicates that the Bengal Renaissance (its theatre included) was basically an urban educated society's response to colonialism. Did Ghosh see through this? Could this then be the reason why he thought it unfit to bestow the meaningful epithet, "national," on the first professional Bengali theatre company? Or did he, like Madhusūdan Dutta, feel that "we have not yet got a body of sound classical dramas to regulate the national taste" (Dutta 561), which is why it would be unwise to lend the term "national" to this fledgling effort? However, the fact remains that *Nīldarpaṇ* succeeded in launching the first ever commercial theatre company in Calcutta on December 7, 1872.

The attitude of the Bengali bourgeoisie towards this new theatrical enthusiasm that had started to go beyond the *bābu*'s mansion lost its unanimity when the public theatre invited women to play the female parts. Interestingly, Lebedeff had staged his Bengali plays with "performers of both sexes" as early as in 1795 and so had Nabin Basu in 1835. As women from respectable households were not allowed to appear on stage, a wave of controversy arose when prostitutes were brought in to act. Newspapers that had previously championed the cause of the public theatre now volte-faced, doubting even its commercial viability. But the public theatre in Bengal had come of age. Not only did women, in the face of severe opposition, now start playing female characters, but the doubts about the commercial possibilities of the public theatre soon dissipated and the companies grew numerically and financially. One reason for their success was that the companies, in order to attract more audiences, kept the prices of the tickets affordable. But the other more important reason was that they managed to incorporate a few elements of *jātrā* into their productions.

Although audiences did flock to the theatres, during the initial phase of the public theatre there was a paucity of new plays. Dinabandhu Mitra, Michael Madhusūdan Dutta and Rāmnārāyaṇ were still the most prominent dramatists until Ghosh appeared on the scene. Ghosh confessed later to a friend that he decided to write plays "out of sheer necessity" (Rāy Chaudhurī 35). His forced transformation into a playwright was a stroke of good fortune for Bengali theatre since it was his huge dramatic corpus that finally gave to Bengali theatre what Dutta had earlier called "a body of sound classical dramas to regulate the national taste."

The question of "national taste" dominated Ghosh's thinking. He wrote in 1900, defending the role and position of actor in a conservative society:

> [I]f we in the theatre can explain to [the society] . . . that the discipline of the actor is, like all other disciplines, expressive of the nation's civilization – only then will the actor win the respect he deserves, the prize of his life-long striving, the fruits of his single-minded dedication from a civilized society.
>
> (Ghosh, G. C., Vol. 3, 840–41)

To make the theatre "expressive of the nation's civilization" was a lofty aim, much loftier than what could be achieved by simplistic and vainglorious historical dramas, blindly religious mythological plays, socio-satiric farces and social tragedies. Ghosh dreamt of a theatre that went far beyond the humdrum; stage-reality to him was more a reality of the mind, a commentary on the quotidian state of being. He searched constantly for metaphors that evaluated the socio-historical moment he was living in. A metaphoric representation was, for him, an enrichment of the real. He did not have much respect for realistic social plays.

However, social drama was a very important element in the professional Bengali theatre of the nineteenth century. In fact, Bengali social drama has always closely followed the development of Bengali society. The genre of social drama in Bengal came as a natural outgrowth of the plethora of issues that dominated the mutating social psyche of nineteenth-century Calcutta. The socio-cultural ideals that ruled over the mind of the European bourgeois – tenets and models of social drama in Victorian England, the drama of Scribe and Dumas, satires and the comedy of manners that were tools for social criticism in Europe – were also feeding the Bengali theatre's strong predilection for creating a theatre with a strong social message. Consequently, the social plays of the time betray the anxieties of a society undergoing very rapid, perplexing and not altogether comprehensible changes under a foreign administration that was radically *re*writing their lifestyle. This is exposed abundantly in the vast number of social plays that were written at that time, from Dīnabandhu Mitra's *Nīldarpaṇ* (1860) to Girish Ghosh's reluctantly written *Praphulla* (1889) and *Balidān* (1905), both of which were successful not only at the box office but were also destined to have an enduring effect on Bengali theatre.

But Ghosh's historical and mythological plays were actually commenting indirectly on the social situation. As a result, although a large majority of his plays are set in different times or in ethereal worlds, they are simultaneously rooted, by metaphoric extension, in the contemporary. Aesthetically Ghosh's feet were on two rocking boats at the same time: Western dramaturgy and Indian aesthetics. His entire corpus, in that light, is a continual act of balancing cultures. The scope of this essay does not allow any lengthy discussion of Girish Ghosh's works.[13] However, we shall look at a few of his representative plays.

Ghosh was always busy packing his plays with socio-political significance, always trying to blend instruction with amusement. In *Śrībatsa-Cintā* (1884) Ghosh expressed the need for a violent political upheaval. Utpal Dutt believes that it is the French Revolution that he is talking about in *Śrībatsa-Cintā*, where the macrocosm of the gods is integrated with the human world. As a result of a struggle of supremacy between Śani and Lakṣmī, King Śrībatsa is forced to make a choice between Lakṣmī, the goddess of wealth, and Śani, the destructive god. Śrībatsa's state is run by merchants and his obvious partiality is for Lakṣmī. The enraged Śani himself, in the form of a brāhmin, becomes the agent provocateur of a mass rebellion. The revolution destroys the city and the king and queen are forced to escape. Thereafter Śrībatsa and Cintā, his queen, are forced to come to terms with poverty, as we learn that the very same merchants whom Śrībatsa had tried hard to keep appeased have unpatriotically sold the throne to a foreign ruler. An easy-to-decipher metaphor for the Bengali audience that knew the story of how Mir Jāfar, the Nawāb of Bengal's prime minister, sold out to Robert Clive during the historic Battle of Palaṣi in 1757!

In 1890 Ghosh wrote *Caṇḍa*, returning once again to the theme of revolution and political intrigue. This time he uses the same source Dutta used for *Kṛṣṇākumārī*, Tod's *The Annals and Antiquities of Rajasthan*. In this play Ghosh attempts something in the line of *Julius Caesar*, deliberately violating historicity in order to bring out the universality of the theme. He makes this intention evident in the very first scene, when he brings in Prologue and Epilogue as two characters who engage in rhymed repartee. While Prologue is decided on presenting a resolutely structured historical play, Epilogue promises mischievous interventions and begs for forgiveness in advance. Hereafter, the complicated plot – packed with family feuds, rapacious political intrigues, thwarted romance, attempted rape, tyranny and rebellion – begins to unfold rapidly. Here again Ghosh displays an uncanny ability to analyze dictatorial regimes, a lesson he must have learnt from observing the situation in his own country, and he does not attempt to hide his intention of drawing parallels at various levels. Raṇamalla, the King of Rāṭhor, imprisons a protester on the following ground (Act III, scene i):

> Quick, quick, quick!
> Put him behind bars, make sure none of his
> Treasonous words are heard by anyone. Whoever cries,
> "Oppression, there's oppression in this kingdom," is
> An insurgent – according to the principles of politics.
> (Ghosh, G. C., Vol. 3, 458)

Many characters in *Caṇḍa* speak lines that could easily be termed "seditious" and/or "treasonous" by the British Government. In Act III, scene v, for example, Girish plants a call for a revolution against the play's "foreign" regime in the words of a patrician of Chitore:

> If your Excellency would order it so, the citizens of Chitore
> Would all rise up in flames; young and old,
> Boys and women, all would take up arms to finish off
> The oppressive enemy of the land . . . .
> (Ghosh, G. C., Vol. 3, 467)

Caṇḍa narrowly escaped proscription on account of being a historical play, but *Sirāj-Ud-Daulā* (1905), *Mir-Qāsim* (1906) and *Chatrapatī Śivājī* (1907), being more explicit than *Caṇḍa*, were all banned by the Dramatic Performances Control Act. On February 29, 1876, Lord Northbrook, Governor-General of India, had promulgated an ordinance. A bill was passed by the Viceroy's Council in December, 1876 to make the ordinance an act despite strong opposition and severe criticism from the native literati. According to this act, all plays needed police sanction prior to public performance. The *Amrita Bazar Patrika*, an English newspaper with an Indian name, immediately declared in a patriotic editorial: "Indians cannot continue for long to bow to the orders of the King of England" (Rāhā 31). But on March 4, 1876, the police raided the Great National Theatre and arrested eight members while a performance was in progress. The play being performed, *The Police of Pig and Sheep*, was a satirical burlesque on Mr Hogg and Mr Lamb, the Commissioner and Assistant Commissioners of Calcutta Police, respectively, written by Amṛta Lāl Basu specifically to criticize the Dramatic Performances Control Act. The play was proscribed for being "obscene" and Basu was sentenced to one month's imprisonment.

While *Caṇḍa* and *Chatrapati Śivajī* were plays set in pre-British India, *Sirāj-Ud-Daulā* and *Mir-Qāsim* were directly about how the British came to rule Bengal. Thus, the latter were banned with good reason on the part of the Government. Ghosh's dramaturgy in these two plays is exemplary. Here he was not trying to create a metaphor, the metaphor was the subject itself. Sirāj was the last free Nawāb of Bengal, who waged and lost the Battle of Palāśī against Clive more due to treachery in his own camp than chivalry on his opponent's side. The story of Mir-Qāsim, Sirāj's successor, on the other hand, was that of a titular head who watches his kingdom being ravaged as his power to save it diminishes faster than the movement of time. Both plays presented history with such uncanny accuracy and patriotic fervor that it became difficult for the British administration to ignore them; both plays were, thus, deemed politically provocative and, consequently, proscribed.

Ghosh still remains one of the best translators Shakespeare has had in the Bengali language. His *Macbeth* (produced 1893) is undoubtedly the finest Bengali version of the play to date. No doubt, it was a tough project to undertake. He confessed later that he had prepared for sixteen or seventeen years before he produced the play. While producing it, Ghosh went all the way in paying due respect to the European tradition which the play represented. But *Macbeth* lived through only ten performances and died an untimely death. The reason behind this audience disapproval could have been that Shakespeare was too foreign for the Bengali audience and, as a result, failed to touch them. However, when elements of Shakespearean drama – for instance, its strong character delineation or its conflict-based larger-than-life action – were silently applied to indigenous plays, they were well received. In other words, the blind respect for everything Sanskrit and/ or Shakespearean had, within a span of fifty years, given way to a firm basis for an indigenous aesthetics that occupied a middle ground between the foreign and the native. Girish Ghosh's theatre epitomized the Bengal Renaissance's journey away from the small world of *bābu* leisure to the much wider audience of urban Calcutta. His plays represent the performance text that the larger *mise-en-scène* of the theatre of the Bengal Renaissance begot. But in being so it also became a new written text for the next phase, the new *mise-en-scène* that would emerge in the next period.

This brings us back to the question of the non-finalizability of written texts. A written text is meant to be changed during rehearsal, on its way to the performance space. Similarly, Bengali theatre in the age of Girish

Ghosh – a performance text that came out of the theatre of the *bābu*s – was very different from where it started, to say the least. It became quite something else, going far beyond the prescribed colonial (Orientalist and/or Anglicist) parameters that the *bābu* theatre worked within, by embracing a wider audience and its preferences as its ingredients. And having attained its own autonomous status as valid artistic/performative articulation, this new theatre of the last quarter of the nineteenth century was necessarily responding to, as we have noted in the work of Girish Ghosh, the larger socio-political situation, begotten by the imperialist set-up that circumscribed it – the *mise-en-*(colonial-)*scène*. What transpired thereafter is another story.

NOTES

NB: Spellings of Indian/Bengali names have been generally spelt (with phonetic signs) according to principles of Sanskrit/Bengali spelling and/or Bengali pronunciation. There are, however, a few exceptions with certain words where Anglicized versions of Bengali names have been retained for the sake of expedience and authorized or normative preference. All passages translated from Bengali sources are by the author. *Acknowledgements:* Dr Richard Schechner for his candid criticism, Mrs Arati Mukerji for her patient prodding and Gargi for being there when needed most. This essay is dedicated to Utpal Dutt, whose untimely passing marks the end of an era in Bengali theatre.

1 Michael Madhusūdan Dutta (1824–73) wrote some of the earliest and best original plays in Bengali and also gave to Bengali literature its own blank verse, sonnet and epic. Dutta also wrote original essays and poems in English, along with translations of his own plays as well as those by contemporaries. This quote is from an early essay entitled *The Anglo-Saxon and the Hindu,* written in 1854.
2 Literally "civilized person," for which "gentry" could be a close equivalent.
3 The etymology of the word is obscure. It is suspected that the word became a signifier of social status only in the eighteenth century. Initially an address indicating the person to be a landowner, by the end of the century it had became an honorific prefix and suffix to denote the economically privileged.
4 Translated into English for the first time by William Jones, in 1789, *Sakuntalā* is probably the most important achievement of the classical Sanskrit theatre and Kālidāsa its most noted playwright.
5 A Sanskrit treatise and book of codes on theatre and dance written by Bharata probably in the first or second century.
6 Spelt *yātrā* in Sanskrit but pronounced *jātrā* in Bengali. It is a three-sided open folk-theatre form with audience members sitting on all three sides. *Jātrā* plays depend heavily on music, songs and lyrical dialogue; no attempt is made to be realistic, the acting is very often high strung and the plays sentimental.
7 See J. H. Broomfield's essay for a persuasive analysis of the Indian elite's early response to British imperialism.
8 Since, unlike Western drama, plot is not the driving force in Sanskrit drama, the efficacy of a given play rests mainly on how the predominant *rasa* (emotional flavor) finds expression. As a result, Sanskrit drama abounds with instances of

poetic diversions in the text that are often unrelated to plot, but in line with the mood. Dutta's play contains many such instances. Dutta also uses a number of conventions from the Sanskrit drama; for instance, the character of the *vidūṣaka* (jester).

9 Promulgated in 1793, the Permanent Settlement Act was designed to regularize tax collection in such a fashion that the East India Company's Treasury would never be in lack. This system made the landowners solely responsible for paying taxes (giving them sweeping disciplinary rights over the peasants). The Act also required landowners to pay their taxes on a timely basis, which put them under pressure, often forcing them to adopt extreme extortionist measures. One of the results of this system of land-lordism was the creation of the idle-rich class, the *bābu* bourgeoisie, who lived in the city and drew their income from the villages only to pay taxes and spend it on luxuries.

10 Girish Chandra Ghosh (1844–1911) was not only one of the pioneering producers for the professional Bengali theatre, he became one of its greatest director–actors. He was also a fine lyricist–composer, a revered regisseur and the first great Bengali playwright, having written more than forty plays in a theatrical career that lasted almost four decades.

11 The two most important *darpaṇ* plays that followed *Nīldarpaṇ* were Mir Maśārraf Hossain's *Jamidār-darpaṇ* (1873), on the atrocities of landlords on peasants, and Dakṣiṇārañjan Caṭṭopadhyāy's *Cā-Kar-darpaṇ* (1875) which dealt with the conditions of the indentured laborers in the tea estates of North Bengal.

12 See Ranajit Guha's essay.

13 See Utpal Dutt's monograph for an insightful study of Ghosh's drama.

WORKS CITED

Bhabha, Homi K. "Of Mimicry and Man: The Ambivalence of Colonial Discourse." *October*. No. 28 (Spring). London, 1986.

Broomfield, J. H. "The Regional Elites: A Theory of Modern Indian History." *Modern India: An Interpretive Anthology*. Ed. Thomas E. Metcalf. London: Macmillan, 1971.

de Bary, William Theodore (Gen. Ed.). *Sources of Indian Tradition*. Vol. II. New York: Columbia University Press, 1958.

Dutt, Utpal. *Girish Chandra Ghosh*. New Delhi: Sāhitya Ākādemi, 1992.

Dutta, Michael Madhusūdan. *Madhusūdan Rachanābalī*. Ed. Kṣetra Gupta. Calcutta: Sāhitya Sangsad, 1982.

Ghosh, Ajit Kumar. *Bānglā Nātakèr Itihās*. Calcutta: General Printers and Publishers Pvt. Ltd., 1985.

Ghosh, Girish Chandra. *Giriś Racanābalī*. Ed. Debīpada Bhaṭṭāchārya. Vols. 1–5. Calcutta: Sāhitya Sangsad, 1972.

Guha, Ranajit. "Neel-Darpan: The Image of Peasant Revolt in a Liberal Mirror." *The Journal of Peasant Studies*. Vol. 2 (No. 1). London, 1974.

Lyotard, Jean François. "The Unconscious as Mise-en-scène." *Performance in Post-modern Culture*. Eds. Michel Benomou and Charles Caramello. Madison: Coda Press, 1977.

Mukherjee, Suil. *The Story of the Calcutta Theatres*. Calcutta: K. P. Bagchi & Company, 1982.

Niranjana, Tejaswini. *Siting Translation: History, Post-Structuralism and the Colonial Context*. Berkeley: University of California Press, 1992.

Rāhā, Kiranmay. *Bāṅglā Thieṭār* (translated into Bengali from English by Kumār Rāy). New Delhi: National Book Trust of India, 1985.

Rāy Chaudhurī, Subīr (Ed.). *Bilāti Jātrā Theke Swadèsī Thieṭār.* Calcutta: Jadavpur University, 1972.

Schechner, Richard. *Performance Theory.* Philadelphia: University of Pennsylvania Press, 1988.

3

POSTCOLONIAL BRITISH THEATRE

Black Voices at the Center

Mary Karen Dahl

the substantive challenge awaiting those who would break the alternating current of racism between problem and victim status lies in the possibility of representing a black presence outside these categories. This reintroduction of history is not a minimal aim. Racism rests on the ability to contain blacks in the present, to repress and to deny the past.

Paul Gilroy
There Ain't No Black in the Union Jack

The postcolonial space is now "supplementary" to the metropolitan centre; it stands in a subaltern, adjunct relation that doesn't aggrandise the *presence* of the west but redraws its frontiers in the menacing, agonistic boundary of cultural difference that never quite adds up, always less than one nation and double.

Homi K. Bhabha
"DissemiNation: Time, Narrative, and the Margins of the Modern Nation."

If the subaltern can speak then, thank God, the subaltern is not a subaltern any more.

Gayatri Chakravorty Spivak
The Post-Colonial Critic

BY WAY OF INTRODUCTION

The large-scale absorption of commonwealth immigrants – it is sometimes claimed – has significantly contributed to the economic, political, and social strains that post-Suez Britain experiences as it struggles to preserve pride of place in the world economy. And at least since John Osborne's Jimmy Porter, the stress marks and fracture lines that accompanied the empire's break-up have provided matter for Britain's theatre. John Arden brought the troops' violence home to England in *Serjeant Musgrave's Dance*. Howard Brenton's *Romans in Britain* drew parallels between Caesar's imperialist ventures in England and British actions in Northern Ireland. In *Destiny*, David Edgar traced links between British soldiers' racism in India and the rise of the National Front in England.

Written by white British authors, these examples appropriately enough address the impulses and abuses of the makers and executors of imperial policy: statesmen, generals and footsoldiers. They continue the focus on the imperial center, even though their implied subject is the (formerly) colonized peoples. When I began looking for voices speaking directly from "the postcolonial space," I found a significant body of work based not only in the former colonies, but (as Homi K. Bhabha implies) in the heart of empire itself. The empire is striking back, and – although some are reluctant to take the call – it's phoning *from* home.

Key dates tie the development of black British theatre to the postcolonial era. In 1956 Trinidadian Errol John won an Observer drama award and Royal Court mainstage production for *Moon on a Rainbow Shawl*, his play about working-class blacks living in Britain. In 1981 Hanif Kureishi's *Borderline* brought characters representing British Asians to the stage, again at the Royal Court. Today a partial list of British playwrights who have roots in the former colonies and whose work has recently been staged in the United Kingdom would include Felix Cross, Harwant Bains, Michael Ellis, Tunde Ikoli, Jackie Kay, Hanif Kureishi, Mustapha Matura, Maria Oshodi, Caryl Phillips, Winsome Pinnock, Jacqueline Rudet, Zindike – each of them an immigrant or child of immigrant parents. They address challenging and complex issues: the erosion of cultural traditions, the conflicts between first- and second-generation immigrants, the pull of assimilation, violence, racism, discrimination, and poverty. The playwrights speak from a variety of economic, cultural, and gendered positions, and the plays have been staged in establishment and alternative venues from the Royal National Theatre and the Royal Court to Soho Poly, Riverside Studios, Battersea Arts Centre, Oval House and Drill Hall, as well as in community and cultural centers around the country.

To describe in all its complexity the territory that is articulating itself with British culture is beyond the scope of this essay. But rapidly expanding new sources of information make it clear that energetic development continues despite deep cuts in public funding. Yvonne Brewster sketches the history of performance and publication of plays by and about Britons of African and Afro-Caribbean descent in her ground-breaking collections *Black Plays* and *Black Plays: Two*. The 1991 *Bloomsbury Theatre Guide* has general historical entries on Black and Asian theatre, and entries on numerous individual writers. Lizbeth Goodman devotes a chapter to black companies in her study of feminist British theatre, and the strength and variety in women's writing is apparent when reading though another first, an anthology of *Six Plays by Black and Asian Women Writers* edited by Kadija George. The Minorities Arts Advisory Service (MAAS) quarterly *Artrage* keeps the reader current with feature articles and a calendar of events. The Cultural Diversity Unit of the Arts Council of Great Britain and the Theatre Museum in Tavistock Street provide policy overviews and archival material. The sense of growth and change is perhaps captured most imaginatively in the imagery (as well as the reality) of a new computer database developed jointly by New Playwrights Trust and the Black Audio Film Collective with the support of the Black Writers Association. It is updated regularly and sold under the title *Black Writers Directory.*

In these few pages my objective is to begin clearing a space within which to visit with those producing this multifaceted theatre. Today I'm not interested in reading against the grain, looking for imperial traces in some (it would be implied) less politically conscious creator's work. Here I'm the outsider. But because scholarly attention may be part of the package government grantors and private funders buy, any approach by one not of the immediate viewing community raises ethical questions. My work engages in what John Solomos calls "the politics of racism": I must strive towards the "self-critical awareness that research can have both intended and unintended political consequences" that he demands (13). This awareness led to the design of a more permeable analytic style that places theatre workers' views alongside mine. Institutionally privileged by my status as an American academic to ask questions and publish my observations, I am experiencing that privilege most materially in the responses my inquiries receive from the makers of black theatre.

Clearing a space entails several preparatory moves. Neither British nor black, I am driven by my topic into a series of not-so-academic clarifications. I live in a former colony, the United States, that now is itself a neocolonial world power. A third-generation member of a family of (mostly) Norwegian immigrants who followed earlier waves of settlers and joined in displacing the continent's indigenous peoples, I acknowledge that history to ground my notion of "immigrant" and "settler" and to open up these terms, making them vulnerable to interrogation.

CLEARING GROUND

The necessity for interrogating the categories used in making my approach rose out of a Euro-British colleague's flat rejection of my description of the black theatre I was thinking about as "postcolonial." It was, he said, "immigrant drama." What did that mean? Certainly the correction follows usage in the academy, where a book analyzing British postcolonial literature would deal with texts from Australia, New Zealand, Canada (the old Commonwealth) or Trinidad, Barbados, Kenya, India, Bangladesh, Ghana, Nigeria, etc. (the NCWP or new Commonwealth and Pakistan). I have chosen to address writers who were born in Britain: Can the one term, immigrant, simply displace the other, postcolonial? Are both terms irrelevant to any discussion of the black British? What history informed this potential revision of my title (if not my topic)? Was it the same history the playwrights would tell? Pursuing that question led me to focus on three playtexts, Hanif Kureishi's *Borderline*, Jackie Kay's *Chiaroscuro*, and Maria Oshodi's *Blood, Sweat and Fears*, each of which contributed to the resolution I eventually attained.

What does being black in Britain mean? Asking the question, I immediately bumped into one of the many barriers English speakers stumble over when they assume they share a common tongue. Unlike in the United States, in the United Kingdom the term "black" includes individuals of both African and Asian descent. It can refer to someone who is Afro-Caribbean, Pakistani, Indian, or Chinese. Or, in the words of a prizewinning general information book, *Black and British*, it means "anyone in Britain who is not 'white'" (Bygott 6). "Asian" refers to those tracing ancestry to India, Pakistan, or Bangladesh, rather than to China or Japan (Walby 37). As in the United States, some activists prefer more specific forms of naming, claiming their individual ethnicities en route to asserting their rightful place in British society. Such insistence on variety and specificity within a community clumped together as the other, the "not white," has tactical value, although other activists see the move as splintering an already small community that together needs to resist attempts to demonize and dispossess it (Anthias 140–56).

Politicization of the vocabulary that articulates race and ethnicity hardly surprises any American who learned through the 1960s. What is less evident is the valence of the term "immigrant." Francesca Klug points out that a comprehensive history of immigration to Britain would necessarily refer to Romans, Normans, Vikings, Angles and Saxons (17). Bygott notes that Berbers and Moors accompanied the Roman Imperial Army, and speculates that some may have settled in Britain as early as 2,000 years ago (9). His reminder in a book aimed at a general-information audience seems calculated to counter the notion that blacks are newcomers to England. The necessity for such reminders suggests contemporary misconceptions about and hostility toward the British black presence. And indeed, Paul Gilroy, John Solomos, Floya Anthias and Nira Yuval-Davis, among many others, persuasively argue that the racism that helped to justify colonialism continues to shape immigration controls and domestic policy governing education, race relations, police practices, and public assistance programs.[1]

These critiques of the cultural and political landscape in the United Kingdom provide another significant frame of reference as I approach the plays and those who produced them. The following discussion circulates through scholarly and theatrical representations of postcolonial Britain, juxtaposing formal academic analysis against performative responses to social and political themes.

THE RACIALIZATION OF IMMIGRATION POLICY

In *Black Youth, Racism and the State*, John Solomos summarizes the government actions that codified a more general process through which immigration came to be seen in terms of race, and black settlers were constructed

as an alien presence disturbing the English peace. He notes that, throughout the postwar period, although "the 1948 British Nationality Act
confirmed the rights of colonial subjects to enter and seek employment,"
"coloured" immigration was construed as a "problem." Policymakers from
both the Labour and Conservative parties anticipated difficulties for the
economy, employment, housing, and in the white population's response to
the black presence (30–32). They passed a series of measures from the
1962 Commonwealth Immigrants Act to the Immigration Act of 1971 that,
although ostensibly aimed at all migrants from former British territories,
actually "took away the right of black Commonwealth migrants to settle in
Britain." These Bills (along with the various regulations that govern
immigration) comprise "what was popularly seen as a 'White Britain
Policy'" (40). The 1981 Nationality Act further limited black settlement.
(Klug reviews policy changes, 17–20.)

As immigration was being brought under ever stricter controls, a new
kind of racism was also taking shape. Paul Gilroy describes the development as "primarily concerned with mechanisms of inclusion and exclusion." Enoch Powell was the official who shocked his government
colleagues by presenting racist views publicly in April 1968. Even as
Britain's borders closed, Gilroy reports, Powell and the like-minded wrote
and spoke of "the enemy within, the unarmed invasion, alien encampments,
alien territory and new commonwealth occupation." Use of these metaphors to describe black settlers kept the image of migration in play and
interpreted immigration as a process that displaced an indigenous white
population. Gilroy writes: Britain's "national decline is presented as coincid-
ing with the dilution of once homogeneous and continuous national stock
by alien strains." That national decline will be remedied if blacks can be
expelled. Repatriation may be an extreme formulation of this way of
thinking, but Thatcherism's populist (as opposed to patrician) conservatism absorbed Powell's views. The continuity ensures, in Gilroy's words, that
"black settlers and their British-born children are denied authentic national
membership on the basis of their 'race' and, at the same time, prevented
from aligning themselves within the 'British race' on the grounds that their
national allegiance inevitably lies elsewhere." That is, with the former
colony (45–46).

The hostility contained in the metaphors of aliens within and the reality
of borders closing shapes Hanif Kureishi's *Borderline*, a project with Joint
Stock Theatre Group that was directed by Max Stafford-Clark and staged at
the Royal Court in November 1981. The playwright had two audiences in
mind for the piece, he recently told me: the Asian community in places
Joint Stock planned to tour the production, and young Asians he hoped to
attract to the Court.[2] The play addresses those populations directly by focus-
sing on matters of immediate importance to them. It portrays the community of Southall at the very time when the Nationality Act was being

discussed. As one character, a British Asian activist named Yasmin, says, "the Tories are working towards giving us only guest-worker status here. With no proper rights" (14). Other characters include legal settlers like Amjad and Banoo, who came from Pakistan before immigration policies changed; their British-born children; and Ravi, who has recently entered Britain illegally. Many conflicting strategies for living in England are considered and enacted, although the action closely follows two young people as they decide how to honor their Asian heritage in Britain. Will Amina marry the man her father selects and remain homebound like her mother? Will Haroon leave the neighborhood, become a lawyer, and change the system from within (14)? What approach will make Britain habitable (37)?

Kureishi's play demonstrates that Gilroy's "mechanisms of inclusion and exclusion" are more than a way of speaking. The border separating white and black is militarized; territories are held and defended. If you cross the boundary, you may be attacked. Amina's father, Amjad, bought a house in white territory (14); his neighbors beat him, and his wife, Banoo, rarely ventures onto the streets. "It's the bricks and stones through the window," she explains (8). White hostility encircles the neighborhood, and the siege produces reactive violence. Amina observes, "We're afraid to leave the area. People want revenge for all that" (42–43). Deportation policies, energized by anger toward now unwelcome legal immigrants, produce systemic violence. Haroon's father uses the threat of deportation to guarantee cheap labor for his restaurant (25). Pakistani exploitation of Pakistani is predicated on the differential status British immigration policy has constructed. The oppressed do the work of the oppressors. In these circumstances, demonstrating against collaborators seems inevitable (32), and protecting territory against enemy invasion is logical (16). The play climaxes as young Asian activists mobilize against a fascist meeting that is scheduled to take place in their neighborhood (37).

Locating a position from which to attack the system that the play represents challenges those who would dismantle it. Two favorable responses to the production in the mainstream press suggested enticing pitfalls on the way to choosing a stance. In the *Times Literary Supplement*, reviewer David Nokes astutely described *Borderline* as "a portrait of a community under threat." He found "running through" the play "the fear of violence and intolerance that will compress all its subtle distinctions into one stark antithesis." But his formulation, attractive as it is, produced a message that came apart in my hands. Subtle distinctions will be lost through fear. The Asian community is the likely sufferer up to this point in the sentence. But the image of a stark antithesis must refer to a white perspective. The diverse community of Asian individuals will become the stereotypical black antithesis that occupies Powell's nightmares and must be expelled from the white homeland. Pushing on through the contradiction, I elaborated the message: The external threat will actually produce the alien that racist discourse and behavior desire as their object. This will be a tragedy for the Asian community and impoverish the white community as well.

The apparent instability of perspective is striking because the playtext presents many different Asian responses to living with English racism, but the production at the Royal Court surely was not only "about" Asians. It was also about spectators, many of whom were members of the dominant white culture. Nokes's remark implicates the spectator without locating responsibility for "making Britain habitable." It seems to straddle Asian and white points of view, without acknowledging where one leaves off and the other begins. It passes over an opportunity to distinguish and reinforce the many standpoints from which institutionalized racism could be addressed.

A critic's remark written under deadline pressure can bear the weight of only so much analysis. But this one brings the review to a point and has a disturbingly familiar effect: it endows racism with primary agency. The production, in contrast, strives to locate agency elsewhere, in individual decisions and community action rather than in an external or anonymous dynamic of prejudice. It does this in various ways: as indicated above, by staging different views and acts of resistance; by putting the British Asian community centerstage; by using theatrical conventions designed to encourage spectators to think critically; and by changing the composition of the Court audience.

Kureishi primarily stages postcolonial views of the postimperial center. A journalist named Susan is the only white character whose role extends through the entire play. According to the playwright, she represented not only well-meaning white commentators on Asian affairs (or, I would add, American academics writing about black Britons), but also all of the Joint Stock Group – actors, writer, and director included – who were going into and trying to understand Southall as a community. For him, the character served to underline the importance of position and how investigators shape, even create, their subject as they study it. Otherwise, with two minor exceptions, white Britain is represented referentially through the Asian characters. Bullying neighbors, fascist thugs, men who expose themselves to a middle-aged mother, friends who came to the neighborhood to watch Churchill's funeral with Amjad before he moved across the border-line exist only as they are talked about by Asian characters. The focus stays on the community and its perceptions of its relations with white Britain. Significantly, however, some spectators could not forget the larger context. Kureishi remembers that it was in audience discussions after performances of this play that he first encountered what have become common criticisms of his depictions of British Asians. Members of the community protested at having arranged marriages and intergenerational conflicts exposed to view in a potentially hostile political environment controlled by white Britons.

On another level, however, following Joint Stock custom, a multiracial cast doubled roles and played characters of races and ages other than their own. White actor David Beames, for example, played the Asian characters Amjad and Anwar, as well as a white neighbor. The effect is complex. At the very least, it opens a gap between performer and character that spectators can read in their own ways. Nokes, for example, found, "The effect of this racial impersonation is to emphasize the play's conviction that the barriers of race are less rigid than those of attitude." The *Bloomsbury Theatre Guide* reports that members of the Asian community criticized Kureishi for using white actors to portray Pakistani characters. I find it makes white culture present at all times even as the play represents Asians struggling to live productively within and against it.[5]

In this context, Irving Wardle's praise for the production was unsettling. Reviewing for *The Times*, he discovered no resounding message for Asian or white spectators, and praised the dramaturgy that makes effective scenes, draws fine characters, and "has no axe to grind." The stress he lays on the absence of polemic as the basis for his favorable evaluation is interesting for two reasons. First, Kureishi's notes to the playtext (published in full as the production's program) clearly assert the play's origins in interviews the company conducted with Asians. The Joint Stock method grounds the theatrical event in the world beyond. The production brings voices from Southall into the theatre at Sloane Square. As a first-time occurrence, at the very least these voices shift theatrical space. Second, at the conclusion of the play, the Asian characters born in Britain reassert their commitment to living there. After her father dies, Amina's mother returns to Pakistan. Amina chooses to live alone in England. The politics of the choice seems clear in the context of general calls for repatriation and attacks on "aliens within." Blacks are British, and only the means of living together are in doubt. Yasmin ends the play by telling Amina to leave the lights on, "so people know we're here" (43). Her assertion flies in the face of spectators who manage to watch the play and erase its political implications. Refusing to issue prescriptions is not the same as refusing politics.

The play puts spectators in that postcolonial space supplementary to the metropolitan centre proposed by Homi K. Bhabha. Its action comprises many individuals redrawing "frontiers in the menacing, agonistic boundary of cultural difference." The indeterminacy of the solutions offered, the multiplicity of voices speaking and positions staged never quite resolve. The play closes without closure, with no expectation of learning who or what will make the nation whole (when was it so?) or bring the doubles into singularity (were that desirable). Even the Joint Stock practice of doubling roles, and using actors of one age or race to represent characters with other attributes, adds layers without adding up. Postcolonial Britain, as Bhabha writes, is "always less than one nation and double" (318). This state of affairs may discomfit those who desire global settlements. But those who thrive on discontinuity, debate, and discovery will find individual agency in the possibilities difference opens to view.

POSTCOLONIAL IDENTITIES

In 1978, Margaret Thatcher recapitulated Enoch Powell's justification for restricting immigration.

> People are really rather afraid that this country might be rather swamped by people with a different culture . . . the British character has done so much for democracy, for law, and done so much throughout the world, that if there is any fear that it might be swamped, people are going to react and be rather hostile to those coming in.
>
> (*Daily Mail* 31 January 1978; quoted in Bhat 14–15)

From my perspective, the invocation of a homogeneous English culture or a singular British character must be viewed ironically. The United Kingdom includes Irish, Welsh, and Scottish nations, which the authors of *The Empire Writes Back* remind us are sometimes considered "the first victims of English expansion" (Ashcroft *et al.* 33). The English suppression of Celts, especially the Irish, has a racial dimension (Anthias and Yuval-Davis 43–45). Certainly the redistribution of political and economic power during Thatcher's years in office strengthened the image of internal colonialism: the imperial center, London, and "home" countries grew richer, while outlying regions, Northern England, Scotland, Wales, and Northern Ireland grew poorer (Riddell 158–61).

The resistance to the poll tax that brought Thatcher's reign to a close originated in Scotland (Anthias and Yuval-Davis 43), but those who might independently describe their particular collectivity as unwilling British subjects are often reluctant to combine forces. Because the "internally colonized" participated in England's imperial ventures, it is "difficult for colonized people outside Britain to accept their identity as post-colonial" (Ashcroft *et al.* 33). It may be hard for ex-colonial citizens living in Britain to accept as well. Yet, as postcolonials from abroad have spread out over the kingdom(s), they have given birth to new generations of children whose primary identifications may combine Nigerian or Trinidadian with Welsh or Scots. These British subjects, with their intercut, sometimes crosscutting postcolonial cultures, present the clearest rebuttal to Thatcher's vision of a discernible, singular, British character. Yet that vision has staying power, and the experience of being born black in the United Kingdom was summed up for me by one young woman very simply: "I'm tired of being asked where I'm from."

That question captures the constant pressure on members of visible minorities to locate themselves in relation to "the British character." Even when asked in the friendliest of tones, it taps into the pervasive assumption that blacks are alien and must explain their continued presence. In this environment, self-articulation is a permanent necessity. Jackie Kay, a black poet raised in Scotland, affirms that need in her first play, *Chiaroscuro*:

four black women of different heritages tell the stories of their names and reenact moments from their common history as friends. Yomi is Nigerian; Aisha, Asian. Beth's father is from the Caribbean, her mother is white (65).[4] The orphan Opal has no knowledge of her parents. Their sexual orientation differs as well: Beth is comfortable being a lesbian; Opal wrestles with coming out; Aisha won't articulate her desire for Beth; and Yomi resists the very idea that women loving women could be "natural."

For these characters, claiming their rights involves managing sometimes oppositional identifications. Kay exploits the characters' multiple positions to stage arguments circulating in the black community. Can Asians share in the label "black"? Does the Afro-Caribbean community privilege "pure blood"? Do some in the black community assume that those of mixed parentage face less discrimination in white society (70–71)? How does homophobia within the community strain their common effort to resist racism?

By staging disputations publically, Kay asserts the social and political value of defining a postcolonial presence at the metropolitan center. The scene ending the first act in the published text is exemplary: the performers reenact sharing a meal. The characters' heated conversation exposes deep divisions among the friends and leaves Aisha with dirty dishes and a room full of "horrible air." The quasi-realist enactment of strong emotions invites spectators to identify with one or more of the positions articulated. A lighting cue signals a change; the actor playing Aisha declares "that bit is over," and acknowledges its difficulty: "It was too near the bone." The performer's admission creates an opening for spectators to become complicit with her. They may acknowledge their own discomfort observing the scene or the pain of similar arguments with friends. In another change, the actors take percussion instruments, and join in a song. The lyrics describe the alienation they each felt "yesterday": "we believed the mirror held only one face." Now they have met one another, and they "have to find a place to say/those words we need to utter out loud/those words we need to hear/because there is nothing like fear." They need a "meeting place," literal and figurative, so that they will not "separate again" and the world seem "empty of others" (72). The intermission follows; during the break, spectators can carry on the dinner debate alone or with others. They can attempt to clear the air, bridge rifts, and carry on the search for one another that the song describes.

Meetings around tables, onstage, in foyers – all may provide physical and emotional space where fear can speak out loud and find relief. The text constructs theatrical performance as one of those meeting places. Act II opens with Opal *peering into her imaginary mirror (the audience)*. "It's you again," she says. "I had a good break without you" (73). The line is consistent with the character's ongoing struggle to reconcile her internal and external images. But it also constructs spectators as others whose gaze she fears. Kay says: "We wanted a wide range of people to constitute the audience: black and white, gay and straight." Such an array reproduces different combinations of the conflicting positions staged through the four characters. Spectators both reflect Opal to herself, and threaten her secret self with discovery. But discovery is to be desired – in the course of exposure, attitudes change.

The significance of the processes staged becomes clearer when the production is placed in context. It opened at Soho Poly 19 March 1986, played fringe venues in London, and toured the country. Joan-Ann Maynard, who workshopped and directed the script for Theatre of Black Women, remembers it as "ahead of its time." Plays with "those sorts of issues attached" had not previously been done. It appealed to her own conviction that "Theatre's all about challenging people's assumptions and preconceptions." She recalls: "the play certainly did that – some people loved it and some people absolutely hated it" (cf. Goodman 133–34; 260). Maynard, now Artistic Director for Black Theatre Co-operative, describes the play as formally innovative as well. The text moves quickly among different performance modes – realistic dialogue and acting style, direct audience address, and sung poetry. Kay credits Ntozake Shange as an inspiration (in Davis 83), but even so, Maynard comments that when the play was written, "that kind of form was not generally done" in Britain. For the director, working on the play "was a way of trying to find a different way of putting text onstage – a different form in fact for black plays," and she notes that British playwrights searching for a distinctive black form still gravitate toward a similar "abstract mixture" of elements.

Interestingly, the published playtext has not been produced, although it incorporates changes Kay made based on her dissatisfaction with the performed play. My comments are based on the printed version not only for the reader's convenience, but out of respect for what the act of revising suggests in relation to this particular script. According to her notes to the text, Kay devised a situational metaphor based in her earliest image of the play as "an elaborate déjà vu" and decided that the "four women had invented themselves and together they made up the play." Rather like the playwright working through revisions, "They all see the play, the journey, as part of a painful and enjoyable process that they have to go through, and which they've been through already." Performing, like writing, embodies subjectivity. "Each of the characters tells the story of her name. She is also searching for another name. She is in flux, reassessing her identity, travelling back into memory and forward into possibility." Kay stresses "how difficult communication is in a racist and homophobic society." But communication and honesty are critical: "In order to change we have to examine who we say we are and how much of that has been imposed." Strenuous, sustained effort is required: the play repeats again and again. "The more these four characters perform this play the closer they get to who they are" (in Davis

82–83). Understanding does not come in one hearing; articulation is not perfect on the first attempt. The effort must go on. Or momentarily taking up Spivak's interpretation of the subaltern: one who speaks has become part of the elite and is subaltern no more. Kay's text indicates the extensive personal and political activity that must take place if such a shift is to occur.[5]

SMOKE AND MIRRORS: DATA THAT DISCRIMINATE

Attention to color has been a consistent feature of public discussion and policies on immigration. But the attention seems disproportionate relative to the actual numbers of black immigrants compared to white. Thus, for example, Solomos argues that, even though settlers arriving from the Irish Republic, Europe, and white Commonwealth countries outnumbered them, during the 1950s it was the smaller number of newcomers from the West Indies, India, and Pakistan that was perceived as problematic (30–31). Gilroy observes: "The word 'immigrant' became synonymous with the word 'black' during the 1970s" (46). By 1992 Anthias and Yuval-Davis describe this trend as institutionalized in government data-collection:

> On the one hand, the differentiation between those Third-World immigrants with British and commonwealth nationalities and others, especially from other Third-World and other "non-White" (to use the [Labor Force Survey] term) nationalities, is becoming more and more blurred. . . . Meanwhile EEC nationals, who are not included in the official statistics on settlement in Britain, have a virtually automatic right to immigrate and settle in Britain. (These are the same statistics which have been used in the past to point to the possibility of being "swamped" by waves of immigrants and to the heavy burden of extra numbers on the labour market and the Welfare State.) (51–52)

In addition, tiered systems of rights (including the tiered immigration system that the 1968 Immigration Act concept of patriality codified) have increasingly restricted not only who can settle in Britain, but the level of social services that will be delivered to any individual. Strategies designed to limit services delivered to temporary workers (holding limited visas) or to track down and expel illegal immigrants in practice target all people of color and effectively discriminate against black Britons. Officials have been granted increasingly extensive powers to investigate and detain suspected illegal immigrants (see Bhat 270–71). In addition, "in order to have access to health and welfare services, proof of eligibility, based on legal settlement here, may be required. This is practiced mainly on people with certain accents and skin colour" (Anthias and Yuval-Davis 52; also Bhat 277).

Policies that encourage health-care workers (for example) to single out individuals who appear to be non-white and poor and question their right to care may be part of an ill-defined system of discriminatory practices with far-reaching consequences. The mechanisms and implications of such an informal system are suggested by Maria Oshodi's *Blood, Sweat and Fears.* Her protagonist is a young man named Ben who works in a fast-food restaurant (the Star Trek Cafe) while he studies to become a chef. He has Sickle Cell Anemia, and the play recounts his struggle to come to terms with what the playwright calls an "invisible disability."[6]

The plot follows a relationship between Ben and a co-worker, Ashley. They fall in love; Ashley determines to make Ben face his condition; he resists. His uncle used the illness to justify his own slothfulness, so Ben will not accept that he is legitimately disabled (122). Ignoring the disease, however, puts Ben in situations that trigger the painful crises that immobilize, even hospitalize him. Can Ben acknowledge the disease without giving in to debilitating definitions of himself as a victim?

Negotiating a position of agency for one who has a disabling condition requires acknowledging complex societal and institutional forces that play upon the individual "patient." Here the average citizen's ignorance about the disease provides one motive for concealing it. When the manager of the restaurant learns Ben has Sickle Cell Anemia, he fires him because he thinks any illness involving the blood must be AIDS. The institutions that conduct research and give care play even more immediate roles in the patient's construction of their illness. Oshodi's play suggests that medical practice replicates and concentrates the biases of society at large.

This is most evident in the limited knowledge medical personnel exhibit about the illness as they interact with Ben. When she was researching the play, "the medical profession seemed completely ignorant about the multiplicity of ways Sickle Cell Anemia could affect its victims," Oshodi told me. Low interest in the population that the disease affects, low budgets for research, and inadequate training were mutually reinforcing factors contributing to this ignorance. But rather than mounting a polemic detailing these causes, Oshodi achieves her critique through casting and stylistic choices.

After a pain crisis puts Ben in bed for a week, for example, Ashley insists he go to the hospital. The doctor addresses Ben's file and the medical student who accompanies him, not Ben. His dialogue is composed of uncommunicative grunts and technical terms. When Ashley asks questions, he mutters or answers too quickly. She finally inquires about being tested to make sure she does not carry the trait that produces sickle cell in children. The doctor responds, "there's always termination" (114).

Oshodi says she was "determined not to mention race." Instead, the doctor and student were to be played by white actors, establishing the racial difference. Language would communicate a class difference between white professionals and black working class. Our sympathies would be directed toward the working class: Oshodi made the professionals "parodic," and "kept Ben and Ashley in a state that spectators could identify with." Doubling characters would suggest the association between class and race in society at large. David Sulkin, who directed the May 1988 premiere by Harmony Theatre at Battersea Art Centre, realized the desired effect: one white actor performed the doctor and cafe manager; another, both medical student and Ben's teacher at college.[7]

The strategies that Oshodi chose cross racial lines and draw spectators at no risk from the condition into Ben's and Ashley's plights. I flinched at the doctor's callous assumption that Ashley could abort a child rather than avoid conceiving one at high risk from Sickle Cell Trait by having a simple blood test. He was questioning her intelligence, self-discipline, and right to control her own body while asserting that the children she would bear were expendable. Similarly, while the text never forgets race, it never draws Ben solely in terms of color. The fast-food restaurant satirically presents the contemporary American "go-getter" ethic; Ben's disability means he must work harder, run faster, to succeed in a system most of us know. Finally, Oshodi treats sickle cell disease in such a way that it can suggest another level of struggle:

> I hoped that the play wouldn't just reach people who were suffering from this thing but would be a metaphor for all sorts of other conditions or even a comment on people generally and the way you try and integrate quite difficult painful parts of yourself and learn to live with that as an aspect of yourself that you can't escape or deny.

The play includes me as a reader/spectator, but in a very important way, it is not *for* me. Oshodi did not "assume" a black audience, but she did "intend it to reach" black audiences. That intention was literal. The Harmony Theatre production toured arts centers in London and around the country. A national network of support groups for individuals who have Sickle Cell Trait was one of Oshodi's resources while she researched the play. Each group maintains public education programs (including outreach to schools), and the network contributed significantly to the Harmony production's finding (sometimes bussing in) their target audience, especially in the smaller communities the production toured.

Judging from the number of fundraising events and black celebrities speaking out about the disease, Oshodi believes that the black community has become more aware and involved in fighting the disease since she wrote the play. Additionally, soap operas with national distribution have featured characters with Sickle Cell Anemia so that information about the illness has entered more generally into popular discourse. Despite this increase in awareness (or perhaps because of it), interest in her play "has never flagged." Shortly before our conversation in October 1993, she had signed an agreement for another professional production to be mounted in the spring of 1994.

As this new production suggests, the play still speaks to critical concerns. But these are not limited to health issues. The medical profession is only one of many visible elites defining the "other" in Britain (as elsewhere). The play uses the instance of treating a specific illness to invoke less identifiable, but pervasive, discriminatory practices shaping black life. Ben's determination not to have his "disability" known can be seen as his need to push against the weight of decades of language and decisions that have attempted to solve the "problem" of the black British by construing them as victims. His struggle to define himself in/against that history refutes the very notion of victim. And the play as a whole moves to redress the power imbalance by addressing spectators (black or white) from an/other position.

A SUMMARY IS NOT A CONCLUSION

To summarize the situation in the United Kingdom as I have come to understand it: Hegemonic political and popular discourses combine diverse groups representing diverse cultures into a single category, the "not white," which is perceived as "alien" and designated "immigrant" although an increasing proportion of those who trace their descent to the ex-colonies must of necessity (owing to changes in immigration laws) be born in Britain. Taken as a whole, this group is a comparatively small part of the British population, yet its presence in Britain is an issue, while the presence of EC nationals (for example) is not. These attitudes are tied up in the colonial heritage. The racism that enabled imperial ventures and slavery is now directed at people of color in Britain, whether or not they trace their lineage to England's former territories. From a certain perspective, this elision between all individuals of color further undermines the moral, historically-based claim of individuals from the ex-colonies to live and work in Britain.

In answer to the question posed earlier, as I look at black British theatre, I will not put aside the term postcolonial. Notions of "settler" and "immigrant" must accommodate the motive, the past precipitating impulse of the immigrant, and the history of imperial policies that first granted, then withdrew their right to freely settle at the empire's center. Those born in Britain claim both the rights and the betrayal. Changing the terms of my project ignores their heritage. I have neither the right nor the desire, in Gilroy's words, "to repress and to deny the past" (12).

Even the designation "black Briton" resonates with imperial history. At Eastbourne on 16 November 1968, Enoch Powell claimed that "The West Indian does not by being born in England, become an Englishman. In law, he becomes a United Kingdom citizen by birth; in fact he is a West Indian or an Asian still" (quoted in Gilroy 46). By reasserting the importance of an individual's heritage, Powell reasserted the colonial past. He hinted at (re)patriation – even for those born in Britain – as a solution to the black presence, and implied segregationist policies. He implicitly gestured towards some undefinable notion of culture, some essential "Englishness" to which these "others" cannot have access. Readers who pause for a moment and hear in their heads the rousing orchestration for Gilbert and Sullivan's refrain "For he is an Englishman," or imagine the soccer fan chanting "England, England" that Bill Buford describes to chilling effect in *Among the Thugs* (82; 300) will glimpse the forces that shape my respect for the myth he invoked.[8] As long as cultural difference is seen as deeply threatening to the English way of life, cultural praxis must be one field where the fate of the nation is contested. Certainly a new generation of black British theatre workers are already on the field of play. Their tactical command of theatre's disciplines, and their diverse strategies are, I believe, producing visions of culture and of the new Britain that – like their histories – will not be contained, repressed, or denied.

NOTES

1 Different, but related, arguments apply to US immigration policy. See, for example, Bill Ong Hing, *Making and Remaking Asian America Through Immigration Policy 1850–1990*. Stanford: Stanford University Press, 1993. Political analysts are already predicting that border control will be a flashpoint in California's next gubernatorial election.

2 Page numbers refer to Kureishi, *Borderline*. Kureishi's comments are paraphrased from my notes of our telephone conversation.

3 Limited space prevents my elaborating the problems these differences suggest.

4 Page numbers refer to Davis, *Lesbian Plays*. If not otherwise indicated, comments by Kay are personal correspondence; comments by Maynard are from my notes of our telephone conversation.

5 Spivak and Bhabha give different answers to the question "Can the Subaltern Speak?" See Spivak's essay of that name in Cary Nelson and Lawrence Grossberg (eds). *Marxism and the Interpretation of Culture*. Urbana: University of Illinois Press, 1988. 271–313.

6 Page numbers refer to the published text. Oshodi's comments are from my notes of our telephone conversation unless otherwise indicated.

7 Other casting choices send other social and political messages. Oshodi says Yvonne Brewster's 1990 production at Riverside Studio cast a black actor as the doctor, who then used a "cut glass accent" to suggest the class difference and raise questions about assimilation. An Asian actor played the restaurant manager.

8 When a portion of the letters approving Powell's 21 April 1968 "rivers of blood" speech were sampled, D. Spearman reports that a vast majority of the justifications offered (1,128 out of 1,444) were framed as "fears for British culture." Summarized from "Enoch Powell's Postbag," *New Society Race and Immigration Reader*, IPC Magazines, 1968, 14, by Anthias and Yuval-Davis, 56.

WORKS CITED

Anthias, Floya, and Nira Yuval-Davis (with Harriet Cain). *Racialized Boundaries: Race, Nation, Gender, Colour and Class and the Anti-Racist Struggle*. London: Routledge, 1992.

Ashcroft, Bill, Gareth Griffiths, and Helen Tiffin. *The Empire Writes Back: Theory and Practice in Post-Colonial Literatures*. London: Routledge, 1989.

Bhabha, Homi K. "DissemiNation: Time, Narrative, and the Margins of the Modern Nation." In Homi K. Bhaba, ed. *Nation and Narration*. London: Routledge, 1990. 291–322.

Bhat, Ashok, Roy Carr-Hill, and Sushel Ohri (eds). The Radical Statistics Race Group. *Britain's Black Population: A New Perspective*. 2nd edn. Aldershot: Gower, 1988.

Buford, Bill. *Among the Thugs*. New York: Vintage-Random, 1993.

Bygott, David. *Black and British*. Oxford: Oxford University Press, 1992.

CCCS (Centre for Contemporary Cultural Studies). *The Empire Strikes Back: Race and Racism in 70s Britain*. London: Hutchinson with CCCS, University of Birmingham, 1982.

Davis, Jill (ed.). *Lesbian Plays*. London: Methuen, 1987.

George, Kadija (ed.) *Six Plays by Black and Asian Women Writers*. London: Aurora Metro Press, 1993.

Gilroy, Paul. '*There Ain't No Black in the Union Jack*'. Chicago: University of Chicago Press, 1991.

Goodman, Lizbeth. *Contemporary Feminist Theatres*. London: Routledge, 1993.

Kay, Jackie. *Chiaroscuro*. In Jill Davis, ed. *Lesbian Plays*. London: Methuen, 1987. 58–84.

Klug, Francesca. "'Oh to be in England': The British Case Study." In Nira Yuval-Davis and Floya Anthias, eds. *Woman – Nation – State*. New York: St Martin's, 1989. 16–35.

"Kureishi." *Bloomsbury Theatre Guide*. Eds. Trevor R. Griffiths and Carole Woddis. London: Bloomsbury, 1991.

Kureishi, Hanif. *Borderline*. Royal Court Writers Series. London: Methuen, 1981.

Nokes, David. "Anthem for doomed youth?" Review of *Borderline* by Hanif Kureishi. Joint Stock Theatre Group. Royal Court, London. *Times Literary Supplement* 4 December 1981: 1427a.

Oshodi, Maria. *Blood, Sweat and Fears*. In Yvonne Brewster, ed. *Black Plays: Two*. London: Methuen, 1989. 93–142.

Riddell, Peter. *The Thatcher Era*. 2nd edn. Oxford: Blackwell, 1991.

Solomos, John. *Black Youth, Racism and the State*. Cambridge: Cambridge University Press, 1988.

Spivak, Gayatri Chakravorty. *The Post-Colonial Critic*. Ed. Sarah Harasym. New York: Routledge, 1990.

Walby, Sylvia. "Post-Post-Modernism? Theorizing Social Complexity." In Michele Barrett and Anne Phillips, eds. *Destabilizing Theory*. Stanford: Stanford University Press, 1992. 31–52.

Wardle, Irving. Review of *Borderline* by Hanif Kureishi. Joint Stock Theatre Group. Royal Court, London. *The Times* 6 November 1981: 18e.

Interviews and correspondence

AyibaNwaah VII, Nana. Black Writing Development Volunteer, New Playwrights Trust. Telephone conversation. 17 June 1993.

Blackman, Peter. Arts Council of Great Britain. Telephone conversation. 8 June 1993.

Burton, Gillian. Publicist, Riverside Studios. Personal conversation. July 1992.

Kay, Jackie. Written correspondence. 19 October 1993.

Kureishi, Hanif. Telephone conversation. 14 May 1994.

Maynard, Joan-Ann. Artistic Director, Black Theatre Co-operative. Telephone conversation. 28 October 1993.

Oshodi, Maria. Telephone conversation. 31 October 1993.

4

ERECT SONS AND DUTIFUL DAUGHTERS

Imperialism, Empires and Canadian Theatre

Alan Filewod

Imperialism, considered as both an ideological construct and an historical experience, has been the defining condition in the development of the public enterprise that manifests the idea of Canadian theatre. The fundamental notion of Canada as a nation-state has been discursively framed by historical complicity in two expansionist empires, of Great Britain and the United States.

The historical consciousness of the British Empire – of which Canada was both a product and a complicit part – has for the most part vanished from Canadian political and social life, but the experience of Empire remains inscribed, often invisibly, in the material conditions in which Canadian culture is practised. This is particularly true of the theatre, which has developed as a public enterprise in this century because of cultural policies that have their origin in Victorian and Edwardian notions of art and empire.

"NATIONAL IDENTITY" AND THE ZOOMORPHISM OF EMPIRE

If we accept that empires expand the national narratives of the centre and destabilize those of the satellite, we can locate the perennial question of Canada's unresolved "identity" in the interstice of empire and nation. Canada is a country that may contain several nations, however defined, but whether it is in sum a nation is a question of ongoing contention. Cultural praxis – the interconnected realms of cultural policy, material conditions and artistic practice – has been predicated on the idea of the unresolved nation (or the undefined "identity") but the fundamental assertion of nationhood that underlies it has been largely accepted as a natural truth.

Canadian theatre (as the term is commonly understood) has been formed by imperial experience not simply because Canada was a Dominion of the British Empire but also because it is a product of liberal Victorian state-making. The history of Canada as a colonial/post-colonial culture has been one of renegotiating the principles of nineteenth-century liberalism

A PERTINENT QUESTION

MRS BRITANNIA: — "Is it possible, my dear, that you have ever given your cousin Jonathan any encouragement?"

MISS CANADA: — "Encouragement? Certainly not, Mama. I have told him we can *never* be united."

Figure 4.1 "A Pertinent Question." Originally published in *Diogenes*, 1869

inscribed in the very idea of the nation. One of the consequences of this experience has been that Victorian zoomorphic determinism has been materialized in the theatre as a public enterprise in Canada. The perennial obsession with national "identity" in Canadian post-colonial (or particularly in this case, post-imperial) nationalism may be seen as an anthropomorphic fallacy which projects human psychological characteristics as a requisite for nationhood.

The ideologies of Canadian nationhood evolved gradually and (for the most part) peacefully, from what late Victorian observers termed "colonial nationalism" to a modern pluralist statism. In the period from 1867 to 1914, English-speaking nationalists of the new Dominion of Canada promoted imperialism (and its corollary, Imperial Federation) as an ideological construct to legitimize their ethnic and class vision of what a nation-state should be. The commonly expressed rhetoric of the empire as "a vaster Britain," of the Dominions as sibling "sisters" and "daughters" of the crown, offered the new Canadian state a legitimizing national sentiment in the anthropomorphic terms of nineteenth-century racialism. Accepting the zoomorphic determinism of Victorian "race-science," nationalists spoke of the country's "evolution" into "maturity." Canadian nationhood was configured epicenely as both male and female, son and daughter, in this rhetoric. In poetry, popular cartoons and dramatic pageants, Canada was frequently personified as a young woman coming of age, submissive but robust, loyal to her mother and wary of her "cousin Jonathan." In political and social analysis, national traits were more commonly projected in terms of masculinity. The colonial Dominions were frequently represented as young men, ready, as Richard Jebb wrote in 1905, "to put on the armour of national manhood – in no metaphorical sense" (Eddy and Schreuder 169). Charles Mair, the playwright whose *Tecumseh*, published in 1886, is one of the most revealing representations of Canadian colonial imperialism, looked to the day when the Dominions would assume the responsibilities of adulthood:

> Then shall a whole family of young giants stand "Erect, unbound, at Britain's side – " her imperial offspring oversea [*sic*], the upholders in the far future of her glorious tradition, or, should exhaustion ever come, the props and supports of her declining years.
>
> (Mair 80)

Mair's projection of Canadian nationhood is embodied in *Tecumseh* in the character of Lefroy, a Byronesque poet whose quest for natural genius in the Upper Canadian bush is interrupted by the American invasion of 1812. Lefroy learns from the British General Brock that natural law finds its outward form in the monarchic principle, when Brock tells him that

> The kingly function is the soul of state,
> The crown the emblem of authority

58

And loyalty the symbol of all faith.
Omitting these, man's government decays –
His family falls into revolt and ruin.

(Mair 162)

Lefroy also learns from the Shawnee chieftain Tecumseh that nature must be defended against the perversion of American materialism. Tecumseh dies at the hands of the invaders who seek, in Mair's imperialist terms, to rewrite the history of British North America by inscribing the republican and materialist narrative of "America" retroactively on the land. His death legitimizes the proto- (anglo) Canadians as the natural guardians of the land, and Canadian manhood finds mature expression in a race of armed poets. Mair's proposal of Canada as a projection of Great Britain into the new world was profoundly ethnocentric and racist: the aboriginal peoples who survived Tecumseh's death he saw as degenerate remnants who had failed their historical destiny, and the French Canadian contribution to the war of 1812 he erased utterly. His inability to integrate Native Indians and Québécois into his vision of empire reveals one of the major fallacies of the late-Victorian imperial narrative (the other fallacy was that like many Canadians, he believed Kipling's sentimentalism and assumed that Britain was committed to maintaining the Empire as a trans-national political body).

That *Tecumseh* never saw a fully mounted production may be a fairly obvious consequence of the New York syndicates' control of Canadian playhouses in the late nineteenth century, but Mair seems not to have tried very hard to secure a production. True, his imperial ideology would have seemed naive in Britain and his anti-Americanism would have been offensive to American producers. But Mair's deliberate choice of an arch literary model for his drama seems to have ensured that its failure to attain the stage would prove its anti-American polemic by confining it to a literary ghetto of "worthy" (validated by allegiance to Shakespearean form and diction) but unproduced Canadian plays while dozens of coarse melodramas rolled over the border. The dialectic of poet/soldier typified a common imperial masculine role, but Mair's choices in and around *Tecumseh* reproduced the gender ambivalence already noted. Like the winsome young Miss Canada who assures her mother Britannia that she and her vulpine "cousin Jonathan" will "never be united" in J. W. Bengough's anti-annexionist cartoon of 1869, Mair wrote his play as a chaste defence against penetrating Americanism (Bengough 27). So long as the play was untouched by professional producers, its virtue remained intact and its thesis validated. The ambivalence of gendering (as defined by the stereotypes of the day) reflects the instability of the post-colonial artist who seeks "identity" in the discursive mirror of the imperial parent.

59

IMPERIAL GENEALOGIES

Theatre historians tend to reorder material in terms of sequential chronology, itself an iteration of human biological experience. By doing so, we centre those events which construct genealogy, and decentre others as less significant. This type of construction enables historians to submit that the years from 1890 to 1920 saw little in the way of "indigenous" Canadian theatre because few Canadian plays were produced on professional stages. Orthodoxy (reiterated, for example, in the *Oxford Companion to Canadian Theatre*) points to the Little Theatre movement and the founding of Hart House Theatre after the First World War as the origins of an active tradition of professional "Canadian" theatre defined by the criteria of professional artists performing Canadian plays. This narrative proposes that the American monopoly completed its life cycle and was followed by the "birth" of the Canadian drama that it had retarded.

Against this narrative we must consider the problem of synchronicity. By extending our field of meaning of what drama "is" we find that there were very active dramatic traditions that coincided with the American syndicate and occasional British tours. One example of this is the tradition of grandstand patriotic pageants produced annually at the Canadian National Exhibition (CNE) in Toronto from 1887 to 1943 by the fireworks firm of Hand & Teale. Although such pageants confront theatre historians with numerous problems of categorization, they are of particular relevance here because in them the icons of ideology function as talismanic dramatic elements which disturb the historian's traditional acceptance of canonical dramas as indexes of theatrical "maturity."

The list of Hand & Teale pageants at the CNE over six decades (found in typescript in the firm's archive) offers a compressed history of Canadian imperial affinities. For the first decade the pageants reproduced historic battles of empire (*The Siege of Pekin* in 1887, followed in 1888 by *The Siege of Sebastopol*), with occasional subjects apparently chosen more for their spectacular possibilities than their ideological relevance (*The Fall of Ninevah* in 1892). But as the century closed with a wave of imperial expansion, the pageants became more timely, often functioning as a form of popular reportage, such as the 1900 *The Siege of Mafeking* – the first pageant to document a battle in which Canadian troops had been involved. For the next four decades the producer tried whenever possible to select a topical theme, whether it be *The Naval Review at Spithead* in 1910, or the Great War episodes which continued until 1921. Even as the Empire dissolved, imperial sentiment remained a popular choice on the grandstand, and imperial nostalgia took on a more urgent meaning with the outbreak of war in 1939.

In all of these pageants, the accurate quotation of iconography functioned to establish a genealogy of empire. Just as the collections of the

60

British Museum may be said to order a genealogy and hierarchy of empires, each of which validates its successor, these pageants quoted from the past to locate and affirm changing ideas of the present. In its selection of theme, the 1913 pageant of *The Burning of Rome* reproduced the popular identification of the British and Roman empires. In performance, that identification was made overt by the inclusion of contemporary military references. Hand & Teale engaged John Henderson (a British pageant-master whose letter-head billed him as author of *Under the Maple Leaf, In Far-Away Calgary* and producer of a repertory that included *Uncle Tom's Cabin* and *The Octoroon*) to write and produce the 1913 pageant. Henderson's letters to the firm show an academic interest in the archaeological details of costuming and sets. He also advised on the selection of performers, suggesting they should be drawn from the Toronto militia regiments, which, like the British Yeomanry regiments on which they were modelled, functioned as markers of class formation. For the interlude, which he described as "the Naval and Military Musical Patrols – a surprise parade," he recommended combining militia with naval cadets and Girl Guides.

No script or description of the military parade survives, but a loose sheet of "Choruses, Chant, Exclamations, Etc" lists patriotic verses for the Musical Patrol:

> Three Cheers for the Red, White and Blue.
> Three Cheers for the Red, White and Blue.
> Hail Columbia's brave Star Spangled Banner.
> Three Cheers for the Red, White and Blue.
>
> Three Cheers for the Red, White and Blue.
> Three Cheers for the Red, White and Blue.
> Hail Canada – The Jewel of our Empire.
> Three Cheers for the Red, White and Blue.

The layering of imperial signifiers in this song, and in the pageant as a whole, suggests that the burning of Rome was little more than a grandiose pretext for parading imperial sentiment, and the reference to the American flag can be taken as a gesture towards the many American tourists who attended the CNE. But beneath that gesture is a more ambivalent one. The pageant is a display of affinity to an *Empire*, which acknowledges the gaze of another, increasingly powerful *empire*, at a time when Great Britain had completed the withdrawal of its military and naval garrisons from Canada in acknowledgment of American military primacy in the new world. In that sense, *The Burning of Rome* upholds the majesty of Empire with a detectable nervousness. By 1913 the anglophone Canadian ideal of Imperial Federation had effectively disappeared, and cultural critics were already exploring the relation of imperialism and the elusive "national identity."

IMPERIAL LEGACIES

The image of the loyal son took on a parodic verdigris as the ideology of imperialism was secularized after the First World War, but the zoomorphic trope that equates national "growth" with a maturation from dependent infancy to autonomous adulthood is still very much part of the rhetoric of Canadian nationhood. The prevalence of anthropomorphism as the defining metaphor of nationalism can be seen in numerous references to Canada's "coming of age" at various points in the country's history, and by the federal government's practice of celebrating Canada Day as "Canada's Birthday." Such practices reinforce the state's powers to control the terms of nationalism by reinforcing the relationship of the government and the citizens as familial: the government serves as the parents of the "Canadian family," and like parents, enforces unity. The question at hand is how an ideological metaphor has come to be inscribed in the material conditions by which culture is institutionalized.

The answer lies in the dialectic of colonialism in Canada, and in the fact that by the end of the nineteenth century, theatre in English-speaking Canada was largely an American enterprise. The theatre was perhaps one of the first economic sectors of Canadian society to have been penetrated deeply by American capital, and consequently it was one of the first sectors to resist that penetration. The theatre of the Edwardian era in Canada was extremely busy but, as contemporary critics noted vehemently, not very Canadian: the touring circuits were owned or controlled by American booking agencies. Nationalist critics argued that such control would necessarily impede the development of Canadian drama. One of the most vociferous was B. K. Sandwell, who in a series of articles and addresses to business clubs, argued that American control of the theatre jeopardized Canadian cultural development, while exposure to British drama would encourage it:

> It is possible that at no distant date we may have quite a lot to say about the running of the Empire; and we cannot understand the Empire without understanding the people of the British Isles and their conditions and problems. The British drama is the drama of our own people, of our brothers and fellow subjects. The American drama is an alien drama . . . .

> (Sandwell "Adjunct" 102)

The formative role of British experience has continued to shape the notion of Canadian theatre. When Sandwell attacked the American commercial stage, he proposed a remedy in the form of civic repertory theatres along the British model. Through the first decades of the century, the argument in favour of public subsidy was invariably linked to the proposition of a national theatre, again following recent British developments. In the Canadian case, however, the national theatre idea was not merely a defence against degraded commercialism, it was a defence against degraded *American* commercialism. Consequently, the class assumptions of the British national theatre debate (which sought to unify class difference in a transcendent national ideology reinforced by the canon) were grafted onto the proposal of a youthful and distinct Canadian theatre, which would thereafter carry with it the assumption that the theatre and drama would (in the words of the Royal Commission on National Development in the Arts, Letters and Sciences 1949–51) stand as "not only the most striking symbol of a nation's culture but the central structure enshrining much that is finest in a nation's spiritual and artistic greatness" (Canada vol. 1, 193).

The development of cultural policy in the mid-century can be seen as an attempt to legitimize an ostensibly decolonized vision of the mature state. In 1949 the Liberal government of Louis St Laurent invited Vincent Massey to chair a Royal Commission with a brief to survey the state of Canadian culture and make recommendations regarding cultural policies. Massey's credentials were widely known: in his youth he had championed the cause of Canadian playwriting at the University of Toronto's Hart House Theatre (which his family foundation had built), and he was one of the first anthologists of Canadian drama. His nationalism was based on profound cultural allegiance to Great Britain, reinforced by his deep loyalty to the monarchy and friendship with King George VI, his close affiliations with Oxford, his diplomatic service as High Commissioner to Britain, and his term as Governor General of Canada. More than any other person, Massey had the power and opportunity to give material form to the ideology of the imperial family. In his memoirs he made the point that

> It is significant that movements in Canada such as the Dominion Drama Festival, and the Shakespearean Festival at Stratford, have very close connections with England. Although New York, a great theatrical centre, is so near, it is to London that we have turned for experience, expertise and training in the sphere of drama.
>
> (Massey 198)

For two years the commission travelled across the country, hearing from hundreds of groups and individuals. These hearings reinforced Massey's belief that Canadian national culture had to be "cultivated" so that "Canadians – French- and English-speaking – can find true Canadianism" (Canada vol. 1, 271).

Given the conjunction of these two principles – British experience and "true Canadianism" – it was inevitable that Massey's chief recommendation was a Canadian refinement of a British prototype, although the government waited for six years before following his advice and establishing the Canada Council (on the model of the British Arts Council). The founding of the Canada Council is normally seen as a watershed in cultural history, a move·which superseded the immaturity of the colonized past and established the conditions for the adult future. The Massey *Report* itself proposes this view with its reference to "this young nation, struggling to be itself" (Canada vol. 2, 11). In his presentation to the commission, Sandwell referred to Canada's "extreme youth as a single and self-conscious community" (Canada vol. 2, 1) and to the "unripe state of national culture." Hilda Neatby, an eminent historian and one of Massey's appointees to the commission, wrote of Canada as "a young country, only recently aware of its own increasing maturity among the nations of the world" (Canada vol. 2, 211).

Despite the prevalence of this trope, it may be more useful to look at the founding of the Canada Council from the opposite perspective, which posits the founding of the Council as the material realization of an imperial vision first pronounced at the turn of the century. The issue is not just one of the acceptance of state patronage as a principle, but of the notions of culture the state saw fit to patronize and the institutional structures it established for that purpose. In its own operations and policies, the new Canada Council embodied an elitist concept of culture which had not changed in substance since Vincent Massey's student days at Oxford.

POST-IMPERIAL RECURSIONS

Throughout the twentieth century the signifiers of imperial experience were gradually eradicated in Canadian life but in the arts its substance was reinforced. In English-speaking Canada the professional theatre funded by the Canada Council unabashedly relied on the "experience and expertise" of British directors, designers and actors. By the late 1960s, the vision of the Massey report had been realized insofar as English Canada boasted a dozen or so civic theatres. Their dependence on British experience, so welcomed by Massey, would in the ensuing decade be the site of renewed post-colonial anxiety. Fifty years earlier critics had identified American popular drama as the factor that retarded Canadian playwriting; in the 1970s, in a Canada deeply implicated in the new American empire, American drama was no longer a threat to the notion of an elite theatre (although it was the site of controversy in broadcasting and film distribution). In the theatre, the once-liberating force of British culture was now perceived as the colonizing agency. The polarity of Canadian/American had now been superseded by the new antitheses of Canadian and "international"; and the call for increased "Canadian content" in the theatre was a threat to the class assumptions inscribed in the civic theatre network. The large theatres in the 1950s and 1960s had a dismal record of producing new work, and when challenged, responded in terms that suggest the continuing instability of Canadian nationality. Even as the Liberal government was promoting the Centennial year of 1967 as a post-colonial coming-of-age,

Eddie Gilbert, the artistic director of the Manitoba Theatre Centre, justified his lack of interest in Canadian playwriting with the comment that

> I don't see how a play can be Canadian. I mean, what is a Canadian play? Is it a play written by a Canadian, is it a play written in Canada? What happens if a Canadian writes a play in Bermuda? Is that a West Indian play or a Canadian play? The whole issue seems to me to be a total red herring.
>
> (Chusid 14)

Two years later, Gilbert's successor at MTC, Kurt Reis, used the same rhetorical strategy to answer a similar criticism:

> Frankly, I don't think there is any way to suddenly cause good Canadian plays to appear. What does the phrase mean? Does it mean the author was born in Canada? Writes in Canada? Writes about Canada? Once visited Canada?
>
> (Hendry 13)

Such attitudes, which displaced the responsibility for developing new playwrights to small non-funded theatres, played a major role in defining the temper of the great surge of creativity and reorganization in the theatre of the 1960s and 1970s. Commonly referred to as the "alternative theatre movement," this reconstitution of the theatre profession was the result of many interconnected historical factors. In the post-colonial context it was a nationalist revolt against the perceived dominance of an imperial model which expressed itself as "international." At the same time it revealed the changing terms of nationalism. The alternative theatre was heavily influenced in its formative stages by the American experimental theatre: in terms of cultural ideology and theatrical techniques, companies such as the Living Theatre, the San Francisco Mime Troupe, Bread and Puppet and the Open Theatre gave the post-war generation the artistic vocabulary to repudiate the model of culture institutionalized in the civic theatres. Politically, this generation was closely aligned with its American and European counterparts (in fact, the new Canadian theatres included many American war resisters), and it expressed itself in similar ways. In the 1969–70 season in Toronto the most popular plays showed the strong affinity between Canadian and American counter-culture politics with local productions of *Dionysus in '69*, *Hair*, Paul Foster's *Tom Paine* and Rochelle Owen's *Futz*. Within two years the new force of nationalism had asserted itself with unprecedented creative energy: by mid-decade dozens of new small theatres had produced hundreds of original works. Many of them followed the example of Theatre Passe Muraille, which from 1972 began exploring the application of collective creation to localist history and culture.

This new nationalism may have accorded with federal policy but it also met with strong resistance. The provincial and federal arts councils were caught in a bind: on the one hand they promoted new work but on the other they had an enduring investment in the idea of "showcase" culture, which apportioned the greater share of public funding to "world-class" institutions such as the Stratford Shakespearean Festival (which because of its reputation and size was frequently identified as the *de facto* national theatre) and the National Ballet; such institutions normally turned to Great Britain for artistic expertise, and commonly hired British directors. But the appointment of Robin Phillips as artistic director of Stratford in 1974 was the first in a series of controversies regarding preferential hiring of British directors that marked the decade. Perhaps for the first time in Canadian theatre, a British artist was opposed as alien when in its inaugural issue, *Canadian Theatre Review* editorialized (with perhaps more bravado than accuracy) that "no other country in the world has a foreigner running its 'national' theatre" (Rubin 5).

The new theatre movement of the 1970s was the expression of a nationalist generation that came to the theatre after the founding of the Canada Council and which perceived public subsidy as a right. The new theatres that survived the decade were institutionalized out of their underground beginnings by the cultural policies of Pierre Trudeau's Liberal government, which encouraged nationalism and provided easily obtained grants through job-creation programs. Many of the theatre companies that began with these grants turned to the Canada Council for support when the original programs lapsed; invariably those that survived the decade did so by tempering their original radicalism to meet the institutional demands of the arts councils. The signal example is that of the Toronto Free Theatre, founded in 1971 as a radical company to present new works free of charge; by the end of the decade it was one of the largest of the new generation of theatres, with prices to match; by the end of the 1980s it had merged with its former nemesis, the bourgeois CentreStage, to form the Canadian Stage Company, one of the three largest civic theatres in the country. In this way it was the alternative theatres that finally realized the vision of the Massey Commission by establishing a network of civic companies that balanced obligations to the "world" repertoire (still largely British and American) with a proven commitment to Canadian playwrights. But just as the theatres of the 1970s challenged institutional culture as colonized, so were the confidently "Canadian" theatres of the 1980s challenged in turn; now the terms of colonization had more to do with gender and ethnicity than with imperial affinities.

By the end of the 1970s, the nationalism that inspired the new theatre movement no longer seemed adequate, except in Quebec. And even the rise of Québécois nationalism and separatism merely confirmed the collapse of the essentialism of the Trudeau years; in terms of the theatre, Quebec and (English) Canada were obviously separate. Outside of Quebec, nationalism no longer seemed to define cultural difference; in fact it seemed to obscure it. The change can be measured in the shifting values of key words: in 1974 the terms "native" and "indigenous" meant "Canadian" as opposed to British or American; by 1984 they had acquired a much more specific value (pertaining to aboriginal peoples) which challenged the very meaning of "Canadian" as it was understood only a decade earlier.

The adoption of multiculturalism as a national theory and policy was intended as the final stage of repudiating the imperial tradition, in part as a response to changing demographics, and in part to constrain the separatist tendencies of Quebecois nationalism. The doctrines of bilingualism and multiculturalism promoted by federal governments since the 1960s attempted to replace the defining signifier of the principle of nationhood. In the fundamental relation of nation and state, multiculturalism serves the same purpose for today's governments as imperialism did for yesterday's, by defining the conditions of national distinctiveness and imbuing the state with a national mission. The fact of official multiculturalism, however, had little impact on the theatre, which as an institution continued to reflect the actual distribution of wealth and power in Canadian society. In the 1980s the cultural assertions of previously silenced and marginalized communities began to destabilize the official meaning of "multicultural" and showed the nationalism of the 1970s to have been the artifact of a particular segment of Canadian society. So too were the cultural enterprises that legitimized that nationalism.

The Liberal ideology of the Trudeau years needed an active, nationalist theatre as one of the proofs of its vision of Canada as a true federation which was post-colonial in the technical sense of the term: a culture that had moved beyond colonial signifiers to "true Canadianism." The Progressive Conservative government of Brian Mulroney that followed Trudeau had as a result of its own ideological program exposed that vision as a post-imperial stage of unresolved colonialism. Mulroney's attempt to complete Trudeau's failed mission to obtain Quebec's agreement on a constitutional accord resulted in ongoing negotiations with the ten provinces as well as aboriginal groups in which it became clear that "Canada" was still an unstable construct that defied consensual definition, and which could quite conceivably break apart. At the very least, if the prospect of an independent Quebec recognized that Quebec had achieved nationhood but not autonomy, then this forced the question of whether English Canada might be considered a nation as well, although a majority of its population had been steeped in the Liberal principle that defined Canadianism as the historical marriage of two founding cultures.

In the renegotiation of federalism there appeared to be the potential for a post-national state, and as cultural minorities found renewed opportunity to express their experience (and win the rhetorical status of nationhood, as was the case of the First Nations), funding programs in the arts gradually opened to accommodate them. Still, cultural policies continued to favour the monumental showcases of "national" as opposed to "community" importance. In 1992, the Stratford Shakespearean Festival was still the most heavily subsidized theatre in the country.

The two major developments in Canadian theatre in the 1980s suggest a shift in perception, from an acceptance of the arts as a public enterprise to the notion of "the culture industry" as a business "sector" in a nation-state defined as a "competitor" in a world marketplace. The development of entrepreneurial commercial theatre, particularly with Canadian productions of Broadway and West End "mega-hits," has created a marked disparity between public and private sectors in the theatre. As the theatre business becomes more lucrative, the subsidized theatres – the large civic companies as well as the small "community" based companies – have been forced to justify themselves in business terms defined by "popular" hits on the order of *The Phantom of the Opera*. In this the Canadian experience parallels similar developments in the United States and Great Britain – with the familiar complication that the commercial theatres invariably rely on imported West End or Broadway repertoires. By 1993 a few multi-national production companies (based in Britain but routed through New York) had so successfully reconfigured the terms of theatrical success that when the Mirvishes, owners of the Royal Alexandra Theatre and Canadian franchisees of *Les Misérables*, opened their neo-Edwardian Princess of Wales Theatre in May 1993, the Toronto *Globe and Mail* rhapsodized in a lead editorial that the theatre's inaugural production of *Miss Saigon* "heralds Toronto's arrival as a major theatrical centre" (27 May 1993). Contrasting the recent surge of imported "mega-musicals" with the "small, subsidized theatre-as-therapy" that had characterized Toronto theatre, the *Globe* claimed, erroneously, that musicals such as *Miss Saigon* were "done without a dime of public subsidy." In the *Globe*'s analysis, the intersection of international (or "world class") repertoire and entrepreneurial capitalism eliminates the need for public subsidy, and exposes the products of publicly funded theatres as provincial and elitist. No mention is made of the fact that the template productions of *Cats*, *Les Misérables* and *Miss Saigon* were developed by heavily subsidized theatres in Great Britain. In effect, the *Globe*'s argument restates the historical position of the colony which abrogates responsibility for risk venture to the imperial powers.

The second development to reconfigure the relationship of artistic development and economics is that of the Fringe festivals, which began in Edmonton in 1981 and by 1992 had become annual events in seven Canadian cities. The festival programs typically feature several dozen participating companies selected on a first-to-apply basis; after paying a small initial fee, the companies keep their entire box office. The Fringe festivals market new work and talent in a competitive arena where reputations can be made quickly and success is measured mainly in terms of box-office popularity. In effect the Fringe functions as an entry-level trade show for the theatre industry. Significantly the success of the Fringe festivals coincides with the decline of initiative funding for new theatre companies. The Fringe template provides entry into the profession in manner analogous to the make-work projects of the 1970s, but its neo-conservative acceptance of market economics has meant that the criteria of evaluating success have moved entirely to the realm of statistics (so many plays performed on so many nights, so many tickets bought).

These two developments, at both ends of the theatre's financial spectrum, disprove a fundamental assertion of the Massey report, that a professional theatre must be a public enterprise. But they do so by reconstituting the same theatrical conditions that Massey criticized. The commercial theatres continue the enterprise of the touring syndicates of a century ago, and the Fringe festivals effectively strip the artists of professional status: they earn only what they make at the box office and therefore rarely make a living at their art. Massey, like many others, believed that public funding would diminish, if not eradicate, those conditions from the theatre.

In the theatre then, the power of market economics shows the notion of public funding to have been an ideological strategy rather than the realization of a national imperative. In the ideology of the nation-as-market, the simple existence of any form of professional theatre, regardless of origin or content, is enough to satisfy those who see the arts as nothing more than a showcase of national "maturity." The existence of a profitable commercial theatre has repeatedly been used to justify reduced subsidies by the conservative governments of the 1980s and 1990s. For the Mulroney government, the most overtly pro-American and continentalist in history, the expressions of nationalism (and of cultural difference) that seem to result from public subsidy were seen as an embarrassment. To the government mind of the 1990s, the arts are increasingly irrelevant to "true Canadianism." If the assumptions of the Massey report derive from the imperial traditions of Great Britain, the assumptions of public funding in the 1990s tend to conform to the ideological priorities of the United States in its imperial aspect of "America."

Like so many of the other national narratives that are the historical products of late nineteenth- and early twentieth-century state-making, "Canada" has become a decentered text, and in consequence the cultural enterprises that legitimized the state have been exposed as artifacts rather than essential principles. If the experience of the Canadian theatre shows that enterprises that legitimize the state lose their centrality (and too often their funding) when they are no longer needed, that merely restates an historical principle all too familiar to students of East European theatre.

The developmental patterns of Canadian theatre and drama in the twentieth century can be read as the expression of a post-colonial impulse that failed to transcend the contradictions of colonialism. The desire for essential nationhood may in the end be little more than nostalgia for the sense of historical certainty that imperial colonialism provided. If so, "Canadian identity" (or to use its more recent signifier, "national unity") can never be achieved: it is nostalgia for a perpetually reinvented past.

NOTE

This essay is drawn from and revises an earlier article, "Between Empires: Post-Imperialism and Canadian Theatre," published in *Essays in Theatre/Études Théâtrales* 11, 1 (November 1992). I wish to thank Harry Lane and Ann Wilson for their helpful comments.

WORKS CITED

Bengough, J. W., ed. Doug Fetherling. *A Caricature History of Canadian Politics* [1886]. Toronto, Peter Martin, 1974.

Benson, Eugene and L. W. Conolly, eds. *The Oxford Companion to Canadian Theatre.* Toronto: Oxford University Press, 1989.

Canada. *Report of the Royal Commission on National Development in the Arts, Letters and Sciences 1949–1951*, 2 vols. Ottawa: The King's Printer, 1951.

Chusid, Harvey. "Nationalistic Labels Stifle Development." *The Stage in Canada/La Scène au Canada* May 1967: 9–18.

Eddy, John and Deryck Schreuder, eds. *The Rise of Colonial Nationalism.* Sydney: Allen & Unwin, 1988.

Henderson, John. *The Burning of Rome/Nero* t.s., 1913. Hand Fireworks Company archive, Milton, Ont.

Hendry, Tom. "Regional Theatre Works." *The Stage in Canada/La Scène au Canada* November 1969: 10–14.

Mair, Charles. *Tecumseh, A Drama, and Canadian Poems.* Toronto: The Radisson Society of Canada, 1926.

Massey, Vincent. *What's Past is Prologue: The Memoirs of the Right Honourable Vincent Massey, C.H..* Toronto: Macmillan, 1963.

Rubin, Don, Stephen Mezie and Ross Stuart. "Aside: An Editorial Viewpoint." *Canadian Theatre Review* 1 (1974): 4–5.

Sandwell, B. K. "Our Adjunct Theatre." *Addresses Delivered Before the Canadian Club of Montreal: Season 1913–1914.* Montreal: The Canadian Club, 1914: 95–104.

——— "The Annexation Of Our Stage." *Canadian Magazine* November 1911: 22–26.

5

CONTEMPORARY MAYAN THEATRE AND ETHNIC CONFLICT

The Recovery and (Re)Interpretation of History

Donald H. Frischmann

The objective of this essay is to demonstrate that drama is an increasingly popular means by which contemporary Mayan artists consciously work to "recover reality" for themselves and their communities; i.e., "to change the reality that is, to recover the reality that was, the lied about, hidden, betrayed reality of the history of America" (Galeano 15). To these ends, Mayan artists stage (re)interpretations of key historic episodes pivotal in the imposition and perpetuation of the indigenous colonial situation. Such works achieve meaning for their indigenous audiences partially through the use of prophecy as rooted in the oral tradition. My focus will be two representative plays: *The Inquisition, or the Colliding of Two Cultures* (1988–91) by Carlos Armando Dzul Ek, which examines the milestone 1562 Inquisition at Maní, Yucatán; and *Dynasty of Jaguars* (1992) by Chiapas' literary and theatre collective Sna Jtz'ibajom (The Writers' House), which explores ancient Mayan history and conflict, and the Spanish military conquest; pertinent historical and other background information precedes my discussion of each.

My interest in these authors' work results from a conviction that it is significant in artistic, social, cultural, and political terms – both within its immediate context and the broader context of contemporary Latin American theatre. While the Maya have practiced forms of ritual drama since ancient times, contemporary performance groups such as Dzul Ek's Sac Nicté (White Flower) and Sna Jtz'ibajom are quite unique. Despite – and perhaps because of this uniqueness, both have achieved wide acceptance and popularity in, and increasingly beyond their regions and states; they have also proven to be seedbeds for a few new troupes, founded by former collaborators.

My repeated and close contact with Mayan theatre and ritual drama began in January 1986 as an anthropologist friend in Mérida introduced me to Yucatec Mayan dramatist/bilingual teacher Carlos Armando Dzul Ek. After a few visits to Dzul Ek's home in Oxkutzcab and regular correspondence, a close friendship began to develop. He subsequently lectured twice at Texas Christian University and has been a guest in my Texas home. He and his family have equally accommodated my wife and me in Oxkutzcab on many occasions, also including us on the touring truck or bus when Sac Nicté heads out to perform.

My relationship with Sna Jtz'ibajom literary and theatre collective began in 1989: I received a call from Robert Laughlin, the group's long-time friend and advisor, to see if a July engagement in Austin could be extended to Fort Worth. I convinced Texas Christian University to bring them in, and since that first encounter our professional and personal relationship has strengthened. This has been partially due to my visits to their San Cristóbal de las Casas, Chiapas workshop, and their subsequent Fort Worth stage appearance and lectures in October, 1992.

For the record, the Maya of Yucatán and Chiapas are not the same. Differences include languages spoken, dress, and food; additionally, Mayan Catholicism tends to be much more orthodox in Yucatán than in Chiapas. Yucatecs also tend to be more open to outsiders and more bilingual (Yucatec Mayan/Spanish), whereas Tzotzil and Tzeltal Mayan communities in Chiapas tend to be more closed, culturally conservative, and more monolingual in their respective Mayan language. Finally, Chiapan Maya suffer human rights abuses perpetrated by landlords and state security police much more than their Yucatec counterparts,[1] thus perpetuating inter-ethnic and class conflict in the region.

ETHNIC RESISTANCE, CARNIVAL, AND CONTEMPORARY MAYAN THEATRE

While numerous native American ethnic groups have been driven into oblivion during the past 500 years, indigenous peoples as a whole have not disappeared from the Americas' nor Mexico's cultural map,[2] nor have they ever been a passive, static colonial other. New Spain/Mexico, prior to and following Independence, has been repeatedly shaken by indigenous rebellions which have now extended into 1994.[3] This is not surprising, if we take into account the characteristics of Latin America's indigenous colonial situation: ethnic discrimination, political dependence, social inferiority, residential segregation, economic subjection, and juridical incapacity. And since Independence from Spain, indigenous peoples have faced internal colonialism: they lost their lands, were forced to work for strangers, were integrated against their will into a new monetary economy, and fell under new forms of national political domination; colonial society became national society itself (Stavenhagen 269–72).

During the past century, strained, neo-colonial relations with the white and mestizo overclass resulted in the Mayan rebellions dubbed the *Caste Wars* of 1847–53 (Yucatán) and 1867–70 (Chiapas). Several dramatic performances are linked to the manifest social drama of those years (Turner 300).

In Yucatán, "a good theatrical performance" was observed in rebel Mayan territory during 1849–50, which included "song and dance" and whose theme was "the Spanish invasion and conquest" (Carrillo y Ancona 261). We may reasonably assume that this work had an anti-colonialist perspective, based on the geographic and historic context. In 1965, eminent Mayanist Barrera Vázquez observed that this was still the only known reference to a theatrical work performed by the Peninsula's natives dealing with a modern historical theme (12).

In Chiapas, Mayan Carnival has been a principal vehicle for the ritual, dramatic representation of ethnic conflict: the Caste Wars and each large-scale incident of such conflict since the Spanish conquest have become conflated into its ritual performances. Bricker observes that "the ritual of Carnival *is* historical drama, but drama which treats the history of ethnic conflict in symbolic terms. What is important in ritualized ethnic conflict is not the order of historical events, but the message communicated by their structure," which is the division of people into two groups: the Conquerors and the Conquered (133–35).

This is achieved in part through what Vansina terms the "telescoping" or foreshortening of historical time in folklore, which has two major results: the overlapping or conflation of human or divine protagonists and events based on shared archetypal qualities, and the elimination of those protagonists or events who have lost relevance for a society. While temporal distortions are also found in non-indigenous folklore, in the Mayan case they are consistent with a traditional cyclical notion of time (Vansina 102, Bricker 3–9). This theory has strong implications for the temporal distortions found in the Yucatec Mayan work *El Auto de Fé o Choque de Dos Culturas.*

The two contemporary works which we examine in this essay either coincide with, or consciously conform to, Western theatrical tenets, strategically appropriated by contemporary Maya through different means. First of all, Sna Jtz'ibajom's international contacts have attracted outside directors and consultants who are interested in sharing their technical expertise with the group. This has led for example to Ralph Lee's yearly participation with the group as guest director; he has also shared his mask-making skills with them, resulting in some very striking stage effects.[4]

Secondly, Mexican school teachers are routinely trained to engage their students in some form of theatre performance for holiday observances; in many cases, however, neither teachers nor students have ever actually seen a non-scholastic play performed. This gap is precisely the point at which theatre undergoes a process of transculturation or cultural syncretism, freely incorporating whatever elements the author, director, or artists deem desirable. For example, bilingual teacher/dramatist Dzul Ek once told me: "We don't know exactly what theatre is supposed to be like, if we should sing, or if we should dance, so we just do whatever we want." This results in an inseparable blend of contemporary Mayan worldview and age-old indigenous performance modes (ritual and historic drama, social and political satire, dance) with Western theatrical structures (drama, comedy, farce). In the case of Dzul Ek and Sac Nicté, the latter have been internalized through teachers' training and scholastic performances, exposure to urban regional theatre (particularly Teatro Herrera),[5] and, more recently, to international cable television's incursion into Mayan Yucatán.

THE INQUISITION, OR THE COLLIDING OF TWO CULTURES

Historical studies by non-indigenous authors,[6] and elements of the oral tradition of Maní, Yucatán, inspired the creation of *El Auto de Fé, o Choque de Dos Culturas* (*The Inquisition, or The Colliding of Two Cultures*)[7] by Dzul Ek. The author's stated purpose is to bolster Mayan historical consciousness regarding the infamous 1562 Inquisition at Maní, or as the Spaniards called it, *El Auto de Fé de Maní* – the "Maní Act of Faith."

Figure 5.1 Gonzalo González, Dolores Góngora, Carlos Armando Dzul Ek, and Julián Colonia of Sac Nicté prepare to perform *El Auto de Fé* . . . in Maní, Yucatán, June 1991
Photo: D. Frischmann

Regarding this historic episode, most contemporary scholarly studies (all by non-Mayan authors) concur on the following: Diego de Landa, Spanish Franciscan Provincial of Guatemala and Yucatán, and other friars orchestrated a several months' long campaign of terror. Yucatec Mayan leaders were publicly humiliated, and perhaps as many as ten thousand alleged Mayan "idolaters" were brutally tortured in the Maní churchyard; 158 died, at least 13 committed suicide to escape the torture, and many more were left crippled. Landa's objective was not only to decapitate Mayan leadership (particularly the locally reigning Xiu dynasty) and assert the power of the Franciscans, but also to effect a religious and cultural holocaust; to this end, most Yucatec hieroglyphic codices and a large number of other cultural–religious artefacts were incinerated in the presence of the overpowered Maya. All of this was carried out with the cautious approval of the Spanish civil authorities who also feared Landa's wrath, particularly Diego de Quijada, Yucatán's *Alcalde Mayor* (Governor).[8]

While the preceding is one pre-text for *The Inquisition . . .* , a second pre-text was the oral version as related by the elders of Maní, who concurred with most of the above with one important exception: the identity of the Maya's chief defender. Oral tradition has it that the Maya were represented at the 1562 Inquisition by King Tutul Xiu; however, trustworthy historical documents[9] reveal that Tutul Xiu was the Lord of Uxmal who moved the seat of his kingdom to Maní in 1420 – that is, 142 years prior to the 1562 incident! His successor by four generations, Kukum Xiu, actually surrendered to conquistador Francisco de Montejo, and submitted to baptism in 1548 symbolically assuming his godfather's name "Francisco de Montejo Xiu"; he was allowed to continue his rule as Governor of Maní province though now as a Spanish subject (Clendinnen 54). Nevertheless, he too was victimized by Landa in 1562, and in a letter to the King of Spain in 1567 he denounced the Franciscans' having "tortured, killed and put us to scandal" (Clendinnen 101–2).

I believe that historical telescoping has occurred here, and that Dzul Ek consciously or subconsciously capitulated to popular, oral versions of history, rejecting turncoat Kukum Xiu in favor of Tutul Xiu as the 1562 representative of his people. An archetype – which we might call Cultural Hero/Defender – therefore leaps forward in time by four generations in the popular mind, thus eliminating an unworthy ancestor from collective historical memory.

Furthermore, the author's profession as bilingual educator[10] and his ethnic worldview have had a profound impact on the casting of Tutul Xiu. Landa and Tutul Xiu are unable to communicate with each other verbally and quickly become very impatient; but Tutul Xiu's final response before forced conversion begins rings of Maní's Doroteo Arango Bilingual School project as it denounces an anticipated colonialist linguistic imposition:

75

Figure 5.2 King Tutul Xiu (played by Don Luciano Tun) addresses his people in
Carlos A. Dzul Ek's *El Auto de Fé* . . . , Maní, Yucatán, June 1991
Photo: D. Frischmann

TUTUL XIU: [Also impatient] I don't understand what you say. We speak
in Mayan, we think in Mayan, we dream in Mayan, we have no reason
to speak or learn another language! (60)[11]

In several other passages the author also emphasizes the colonial
situation about to unfold; some are voiced by the Spaniards:

LANDA: Friar Francisco, take note of everything we are doing. Remember
that today is Sunday, July 12, 1562. In the name of the Holy Inquisition
and Phillip II of Spain we are carrying out this Auto de Fé. Spain will be
proud of this, and our God will not deny us a place in heaven. (60)

And once Tutul Xiu has been forced to carry the cross while leading the other accused idolators in procession:

LANDA: From now on, we shall reign in this land. We'll change their crops, their dress, their music, their dances . . .

QUIJADA: Also their religion, their language, their ways of thinking and also their names. We'll show them that we Spaniards are a superior culture, and we'll make them despise their own culture. Our conquistadors will see to that, and also that they obey our laws. (61)

The response offered by Tutul Xiu's soothsayer underlines the overly optimistic – and therefore ironic – nature of the Spaniards' objectives:

SOOTHSAYER: They can't force us to change everything, our dress, our customs, our language! The years and the centuries will pass, and we'll show them that we'll never change! (61)

The truth actually lies somewhere in between; the Spaniards' expressed intentions have never been completely realized, and many cultural impositions were simply strategically appropriated by the Maya into their own cultural system. With regard to religion, Farriss points out that there was a "gradual shift in emphasis from the old, risky, and increasingly dysfunctional (because necessarily secret) idolatry, which itself was becoming infused with Christian elements, to the less obviously syncretic worship of saint-deities in the churches." Additionally: "The shift would have received a major push from Fray Diego de Landa's vigorous campaign against paganism." By the end of the colonial period "the old gods no longer had a separate identity" (312–14).

However, Hispano-Christian colonialism was never able to completely control the forms of worship autonomously pursued by the tenacious Maya. To the present day, the Christian Gods are frequently honored along two parallel, and at times intersecting tracks as orthodox Catholic ceremonies combine with age-old indigenous rituals.[12]

Having witnessed the icons of his age-old culture go up in flames, Tutul Xiu's final words ring of prophecy, and hope in the face of old, and new colonialisms:

TUTUL XIU: We may think that you have defeated us; however, some day you will suffer the consequences, because we were born free, free like the air we breath, free like the birds that fly! And when that comes to pass, our Gods will protect us, and we shall once again walk down our pathway! (62)

The oral tradition as related by Maní's elders indeed tells of cataclysmic events to come, of when the world's only remaining waterhole will be the *cenote*[13] at Maní. The evil oppressors will once again wage war on the Maya in order to gain control of this precious resource; however, the Ancestors –

frozen in stone in the cenote's cavernous entrance since their initial defeat by the Spaniards – will rise up and defeat the oppressors, with the aid of the Plumed Serpent God, Xkukil Can.[14] Tutul Xiu's final words are therefore, not merely an attempt to retain some hope and dignity in the face of defeat; instead, they represent the firm belief, rooted in Mayan prophecy, that the persisting colonial situation will indeed be broken, but not without bloodshed. All of this will come to pass in Maní, the Mayan *Tuch Lu'um* or World's Navel.

DYNASTY OF JAGUARS

While The Writers' House[15] scripts exist within the written domain, their content is generally derived from the oral tradition. *Dynasty of Jaguars* (unpublished, 1992)[16] departs however from this pattern; its treatment of ancient and Conquest-period Mayan history is based almost exclusively upon written accounts, as follows: Act I: the historical study *La Batalla del Sumidero* by Belgian anthropologist Jan de Vos; Act II: an unidentified edition of the *Popol Vuh,* sacred Mayan Council Book; and Act III: *A Forest of Kings* by North American anthropologists Linda Schele and David Freidel, supplemented by talks given to the group by Schele in Copán, Honduras in 1992.

Figure 5.3 Albina López Gómez, Juan de la Torre López, and Isabel Juárez Espinosa of Sna Jtz'ibajom performing *Herencia Fatal* in San Juan Chamula, Chiapas, during the Fiesta de San Juan, June 24, 1991
Photo: D. Frischmann

This emphasis on written sources results in part from the writers' friendship with De Vos and Schele, and English-literate Francisco Alvarez' role as principal scriptwriter. As a result, Acts I and III are faithful to current scholarship regarding the history of Mayan peoples and their neighbors the Chiapanecs. Through this unusual, international circuit, The Writers' House has directed this long forgotten, yet newly uncovered data back into indigenous communities for the nativistic purpose of recovering reality. As Clifford points out, "twentieth-century identities no longer presuppose continuous cultures or traditions. Everywhere individuals and groups improvise local performances from (re)collected pasts, drawing on foreign media, symbols, and languages" (14). Today's Maya – exposed to international travellers just outside their doorsteps, and watching international television next to the home altar – certainly fit Clifford's observation.

In *Dynasty of Jaguars*, The Writers' House adopts an anti-colonialist stance vis-à-vis Spanish conquest and domination. The play also promotes a position of pacifism, in light of recently uncovered evidence that armed conflict among ancient Mayan kingdoms was instrumental in the ninth-century collapse of Classic Mayan civilization. The ultimate message is one of "unity" and "peace" amongst all peoples as necessary conditions for ethnic, and human, survival.

Central to Act I of *Dynasty of Jaguars* is De Vos' well-documented study which effectively debunks a legend born probably in the sixteenth century among the now vanished Chiapanec ethnic group. This legend recounts how thousands of Chiapanecs leaped to their death into the Sumidero Canyon rather than surrender to the Spanish in a 1534 battle. De Vos hypothesizes that this legend perhaps reflects indigenous attempts to somehow glorify their people's defeat. The legend was subsequently inscribed by seventeenth-century Spanish historians into official historical discourse and perpetuated as historic truth to this day (17–21).

The Chiapanecs seem to have been a very aggressive people who probably emigrated from the Mexican Central Plateau in the sixth century; they maintained a reign of terror over neighboring Zoque and Tzotzil Maya, and were perhaps the fiercest warriors in all of New Spain (De Vos 22–24). Their unwillingness to make allies, coupled with the treason of sell-out indigenous leaders such as Don Diego Nocayola (36–38), gave the Spanish a decisive advantage against them. In the play, Nocayola is cast as a complete sell-out to the Spaniards' liquor, religion, dress, and a share of the gold he took from his people as colonial Collector of Tribute. Additionally in the play, the torturers of captured rebel leader Sanguieme[17] are Tzotzil Maya from Zinacantán, who ally themselves with the Spanish for purposes of revenge; representatives of the Inquisition give their blessing as Sanguieme is burned alive. Despite Sna Jtz'ibajom's strong Tzotzil membership, the authors believed it important to publicly recognize Sanguieme as a true indigenous hero in the early resistance and struggle against Spanish colonialism; this becomes clear in Act II, as shaman Matawil directs his Tzotzil apprentice, Ch'ok, to gather up Sanguieme's still warm ashes and cast them into the river so that his soul may rise to heaven:

CH'OK: I'm afraid, teacher. Not of the Spaniards or Nocayola, but of the spirits of these Chiapanecs; they were never friends of the Maya.

MATAWIL: Oh, Ch'ok! For a long time, none of our peoples were friends to each other! That's why it was so easy for the Spaniards to conquer us.

CH'OK: But Matawil, what do you seek in coming to conjure up the souls of those who hated our ancestors?

MATAWIL: Do you want me to tell you? Our ancestors and those of these heroic warriors were one and the same! We all are born of the same dream of Junab Ku, true creator God. [. . .] That's why I've brought you here, so that our most ancient history may be revealed to you. Now that our world is enslaved, it's the only way to save our gods and our souls. [. . .] This is no time for bitterness. The stars have shifted. We must learn to unite our peoples' thoughts and actions.[18]

Ch'ok finally obeys, and from the water vapor which rises from the river the sacred Mayan Vision Serpent appears; Ch'ok then goes into a dream state to which the spectator is privy. This vision sequence presents several *Popol Vuh* episodes which affirm the superiority of wit over brute force, as we see hero twins Ixbalanqué and Hunahpú defeat the evil Lords of Xibalbá, following their rebirth from ashes; also, the primordial Jaguar beings are recognized as progenitors of all Mayan peoples.

Act III explores the history of the ancient Mayan kingdom of Yaxchilán, particularly the seventh-century succession of rule from Pacal Balam (Shield Jaguar) to Kuk Balam (Bird Jaguar) – not his firstborn, but a younger, more capable son by a latter wife who was apparently a foreigner of high rank; this was a strategic move meant to broaden the kingdom's many alliances (Schele and Freidel 270). Matawil explains how envy destroyed the peace:

MATAWIL: In this way they had peace, because the kingdoms remained united until Shield Jaguar's death. Then began the wars which continue up until our days. [. . .] Many were envious of Bird Jaguar and tried to topple him. But he knew how to defend himself.

But Bird Jaguar allows himself to be controlled by rampant desires of empire, which ultimately lead him down a self-destructive path:

KUK BALAM: Bah, there is no army stronger than ours! We are invincible! Besides . . . I must obtain slaves and tribute to build temples and palaces! Yaxchilán will be grander, and I shall be the emperor of all kingdoms!

Bird Jaguar is subsequently captured and is about to be put to death, when Ch'ok's vision abruptly ends. The shaman's apprentice has, however, been witness to the beginning of the end of Classic Mayan civilization: All over the Mayan world – present-day Chiapas, Yucatán, Campeche, Belize, Guatemala, and Honduras – history ceased to be recorded between the late 700s and the early 900s; Yaxchilán's last inscription (AD 808), commissioned by Bird Jaguar's son and successor, speaks of war. Current scholarship has it that the Great Mayan Collapse resulted in part from growing military competition between Late Classic ruling lineages, resulting in endemic warfare with neighboring kingdoms (Schele and Freidel 379–83).

In the concluding scene, shaman Matawil wraps up his apprentice's lesson with a specific charge:

MATAWIL: [. . .] Peoples must work together if they wish to live in peace.

CH'OK: Oh, that's very difficult. How could they be united, if they have different gods, different languages and customs?

MATAWIL: Only the names change. The Great Creator Spirit never changes. Peoples must learn to live in peace. Great calamities will come if they do not. [. . .] Many will be killed, and others will die of strange diseases. They will lose their lands and culture. They will suffer for nearly 500 years, or longer, if they do not learn to live together. [. . .] They must be worthy and prudent, and learn to unite to demand justice. [. . .] The jaguar twins [Ixbalanqué and Hunahpú] overcame death through wit and wisdom, not brute force.

CH'OK: I understand you, Grandfather! What should I do so that our peoples may survive in peace?

MATAWIL: If you plan for just one year, sow corn; if you plan for one hundred years, plant a thousand trees; but if you plan for one thousand years, educate your children, and may they educate their offspring! [. . .] It's in your hands, Ch'ok, since you possess the spirit of resistance. [. . .]

CH'OK: Great Jaguar Sun! When these bad years pass, don't allow our peoples to continue weeping! (He cries then looks up decidedly toward the audience) We shall never die! [THE END]

Ch'ok thus represents each and every spectator of this play, as we witness together these powerful lessons of history. Both this play and *The Inquisition* end with a similar glimmer of hope in a different future order; in *The Inquisition*, this hope is rooted in prophecy as handed down through oral tradition. In *Dynasty of Jaguars,* the words of the elderly shaman Matawil mirror actual pre-Conquest prophecies regarding impending disaster and subjugation, while hope in a new order lies entirely in human hands: the Maya, and all peoples, must learn to live together, control destructive envy, and educate their children accordingly if justice is to be achieved. Negative examples abound: Chiapanec self-isolation, Nocayola's selling out, and Bird Jaguar's unrestrained empire building; but there are as many positive examples: Sanguieme's resistance, Ixbalanqué and Hunahpú's use of wit rather than force to overcome evil, Shield Jaguar's peace-keeping alliances, and finally, elder Matawil's words of wisdom: "Educate your children . . . ."

In conclusion, Sac Nicté and Sna Jtz'ibajom neither patiently nor passively await the fulfillment of ancient prophecies, despite the persisting Mayan cyclical notion of time reflected in their works. Instead, they have assumed an active yet peaceful role as artists and writers whose pathway has been that of recovering and (re)interpreting historic episodes which were pivotal in the imposition and perpetuation of the persisting indigenous colonial situation. This is important for the indigenous communities, as well as for wider audiences, as I believe such work is capable of building a bridge of understanding, ever more essential in these times of world-wide inter-ethnic warfare and renewed conflict in Chiapas State.

Yet the indigenous neo-colonial situation persists at the threshold of the twenty-first century – despite the work of human rights organizations, social scientists, Mayan intellectuals, the Catholic church, and others to create consciousness and bring about change in the region before a new crisis occurred. In the midst of writing this, I ask myself: Who will ultimately spur positive change – armed peasants, well-prepared Mayan intellectuals and artists, or both? It becomes obvious that guns speak louder than art in today's world and mass media. Nevertheless Dzul Ek, Sac Nicté, and the writers of Sna Jtz'ibajom press forward, confronting reality head on, and reminding themselves and others on the threshold of the new millennium that Mayan culture is still proudly and very much alive.

NOTES

1 See for example Amnesty International's *Mexico: Human Rights in Rural Areas*, London: 1986.
2 According to the 1990 national census, Mexico's indigenous peoples numbered 6,411,972, or 7.9 percent of the total population (divided amongst 56 ethnic groups). Yucatec Mayan speakers (of at least 5 years of age) remained numerically second only to Nahuatl speakers, numbering 713,116 and 1,199,092 respectively. In Chiapas, the Tzeltal Maya, the sixth largest ethnic group, numbered 258,835, and the Tzotzil Maya ranked seventh, at 232,423. Source: Instituto Nacional de Estadística, Geografía e Información, *La Población de México en 1990*, Aguascalientes: INEGI, 1992.
3 For an extensive listing of native American resistance movements throughout the Americas from 1510 to 1941, see Munro S. Edmonson, *Nativism, Syncretism, and Anthropological Science*, New Orleans: Tulane University Middle America Research Institute Publication No. 19 (1960): 186–88.

4 Lee is artistic director of Salem, New York's Mettawee River Company; like Sna Jtz'ibajom, Lee's own itinerant troupe deals primarily with folktales.

5 On this uniquely Yucatecan theatre, see Donald H. Frischmann, " 'Cholo' habla del Teatro Regional," *Novedades de Yucatán* Suplemento Cultural, 15 and 21 March 1987: 1 and 6–7.

6 Data was primarily extracted from the newspaper publications of Luis Ramírez Aznar, highly respected historian and cultural journalist residing in Mérida.

7 Of the fifteen or so works created and performed by Dzul Ek and Sac Nicté, this is the only one which director/dramatist Dzul Ek has written down to date. Given the emergent quality of Sac Nicté's oral, improvisational approach, however, the text from which I quote reflects no particular performance, but rather constitutes a virtual, or literary text that only approximates many actual performances. Furthermore, Sac Nicté's overwhelmingly oral approach underlines Fabian's observations that "performance [is . . .] not merely enactment of a preexisting script; it is making, fashioning, creating" (13).

8 See for example Inga Clendinnen, *Ambivalent Conquests: Maya and Spaniard in Yucatán, 1517–1570*, Cambridge: Cambridge University Press, 1987; and Luis Ramírez Aznar, *Auto de Fé: Maní*, Mérida: Dahemont, 1986.

9 The Xiu Family Papers; see William Gates, trans. and notes for Friar Diego de Landa, *Yucatán: Before and After the Conquest*, New York: Dover, 1978, 121–26.

10 Dzul Ek is founder/director of the Escuela Primaria Federal Bilingüe Doroteo Arango, which he founded simultaneously with Sac Nicté in 1978; this is the only bilingual school (Yucatec Mayan/Spanish) servicing Maní's overwhelmingly bilingual Mayan population.

11 My English translations are based upon the author's published Spanish-language version. In performance, however, the Mayan characters speak in Mayan, and the Spaniards speak in Spanish, just as they would have during an initial encounter; this linguistic format works perfectly well for Sac Nicté's largely bilingual audiences.

12 For example, the Dance of the Pig's Head honors the Christ Child every January 2 in Oxkutzcab, and the Dance of the Beheading of the Turkeys honors Santa Inés on January 21 in Dzitás.

13 From the Mayan *ts'ono'ot*, designating a sinkhole in the limestone slab which extends over the entire Yucatán Peninsula; such openings allow access to subterranean streams, the primary source of fresh water to this day.

14 A summary of the prophecies, as retold by Dzul Ek, February 1993; for a somewhat different version, see: Allan F. Burns, *An Epoch of Miracles*, Austin: University of Texas, 1983: 37–38 and 244–57.

15 For a detailed account of Sna Jtz'ibajom's development as a literary and theatre collective, see Donald H. Frischmann's essay "New Mayan Theatre in Chiapas: Anthropology, Literacy, and Social Drama" in *Negotiating Performance: Gender, Sexuality and Theatricality in Latin/o America*, eds. Diana Taylor and Juan Villegas, Durham: Duke University Press, 1994: 213–238. On the women of Sna Jtz'ibajom, see Miriam Laughlin, "The Drama of Mayan Women," *Ms.* July/August 1991: 88–89 and Cynthia Steele, " 'A Woman Fell into the River': Negotiating Female Subjects in Contemporary Mayan Theatre", in Taylor and Villegas, op. cit. 239–256; see also Patrick Breslin, "Coping with Change, the Maya Discover the Play's the Thing," *Smithsonian* August 1992: 78–87 and Sienna Craig and Maccluff Everton, "Maya Dreams," *Summit* Fall 1993: 60–69.

16 *Dynasty of Jaguars* was guest-directed by Ralph Lee, of Salem, New York's Mettawee River Company. In the area of theatre, Sna Jtz'ibajom has focused upon creating Spanish-language scripts, and spontaneously translating them

into Mayan Tzotzil when performing for such audiences. The performances in Spanish are for wider audiences, which they have indeed reached in San Cristóbal, Mexico City, and in several university and other venues across the United States. I have translated the passages which I quote in this essay from the original Spanish.

17 The name of the rebel leader was recently recovered thanks to De Vos' discovery of eyewitness indigenous testimonies of the 1534 rebellion and massacre from the Archivo General de Centroamérica, Guatemala (De Vos 148–51). While De Vos' book remains unknown to most of Chiapas' indigenous population, The Writers' House's utilization of this data in public performance effectively constitutes one example of their recovering reality for indigenous audiences, one small but significant step toward decolonization, particularly in light of their positive presentation of Sanguieme as a symbol of resistance.

18 All translations from this work are mine.

19 I express my appreciation to Prof. Carlos Armando Dzul Ek, his family, and members of Sac Nicté: *Dios botic!* Also, to Sna Jtz'ibajom and Dr Robert and Miriam Laughlin: *Kolaval!* Finally, to Dr Teresa Marrero Frischmann for her informed editing of this essay: *¡Gracias!*

WORKS CITED

Barrera Vázquez, Alfredo. *El Libro de los Cantares de Dzitbalché.* Mexico City: Instituto Nacional de Antropología e Historia, 1965.

Bricker, Victoria Reifler. *The Indian Christ, the Indian King: The Historical Substrate of Maya Myth and Ritual.* Austin: University of Texas, 1981.

Carrillo y Ancona, Crescencio. "Disertación sobre la Literatura Antigua de Yucatán." *Boletín de la Sociedad Mexicana de Geografía y Estadística* (1871): 257–71.

Clendinnen, Inga. *Ambivalent Conquests: Maya and Spaniard in Yucatán, 1517–1570.* Cambridge: Cambridge University Press, 1987.

Clifford, James. *The Predicament of Culture.* Cambridge, Mass.: Harvard University Press, 1988.

De Vos, Jan. *La Batalla del Sumidero.* Mexico City: Katún, 1985.

Dzul Ek, Carlos Armando. *El Auto de Fé o Choque de Dos Culturas. Tramoya* 33 (October–December 1992): 57–62.

Farriss, Nancy. *Maya Society Under Colonial Rule.* Princeton: Princeton University Press, 1984.

Galeano, Eduardo. "The Blue Tiger and the Promised Land." *Report on the Americas* (North American Congress on Latin America, Inc.) 24(5) (February 1991): 12–17.

Schele, Linda and David Freidel. *A Forest of Kings.* New York: Wm. Morrow, 1990.

Sna Jtz'ibajom and Francisco Alvarez. *Dinastía de Jaguares.* San Cristóbal de las Casas: unpublished ms., 1992.

Stavenhagen, Rodolfo. "Classes, Colonialism, and Acculturation: A System of Inter-Ethnic Relations in Mesoamerica." *Masses in Latin America.* Ed. Irving Louis Horowitz, New York: Oxford University Press, 1970: 235–88.

Turner, Victor. *On the Edge of the Bush: Anthropology as Experience.* Tucson: University of Arizona, 1985.

Vansina, Jan. *Oral Tradition: A Study in Historical Methodology.* Trans. H. M. Wright. Chicago: Aldine, 1965.

6

ELECTRIC SALOME

Loie Fuller at the Exposition Universelle of 1900

Rhonda K. Garelick

INTRODUCTION: AN AMERICAN IN PARIS

In the year 1900, short, plump, 38-year-old Loie Fuller from Fullersburg, Illinois was the undisputed queen of the Paris World's Fair. Wrapped in enormous silk veils, Fuller performed her famous *danses lumineuses* in a specially built theatre, the only American included in the section designed as a patriotic showcase for the most Parisian entertainment available: Montmartre-style cabaret. But Fuller was not exactly a foreigner. She had been living in France for nine years by this time, and had become perhaps the most famous cabaret dancer in Europe. Many of the most influential writers and painters of the 1890s took Fuller as their subject. Whistler and Toulouse-Lautrec painted her; Pierre Roche sculpted her in marble; Mallarmé wrote a celebrated essay about her; and Massenet granted her unrestricted rights to use his music in her performances.

But Fuller was a very unlikely sensation as a dancing girl. She had come to France after a very minor career in American cabaret theatre, with virtually no formal dance training. She was too old, too heavy, too plain, and known publicly as a lesbian. Fuller never relied upon the motif of heterosexual seduction traditionally present in cabaret dance, especially in the popular North African and "Oriental" style dances that dominated cabaret stages in Paris at the turn of the century.

The most famous of all the tremendously popular "Oriental" veil dances was, of course, Salome's Dance of the Seven Veils – for it was during this era that the phenomenon known as "Salomania" raged. The fin de siècle's fascination with the biblical princess was sparked by, among other things, Flaubert's novel *Salammbô* (1862), Mallarmé's dramatic poem *Hérodiade* (1864), Gustave Moreau's *Salome* paintings (1876), and the famous passages of *A Rebours* (1884) in which Huysmans' hero Des Esseintes contemplates Moreau's paintings. Salomania touched virtually every aspect of popular and "high" culture, from Symbolist verse to theatrical parodies, from night club reviews to department store fashions for women.[1]

Of all the performers of the Dance of the Seven Veils, without question the most celebrated was Loie Fuller. We know that Fuller had long been exposed to, and aware of, such Orientalist entertainments. In 1886, Fuller appeared at New York's Standard Theater in a review called "The Arabian Nights," which featured fourteen different Oriental dance numbers, including the "Veil of Vapor" dance, done with clouds of steam instead of fabric veils (Sommer 55). She was also on intimate terms with all of Paris's artistic avant-garde through which she would naturally have been exposed to many versions of Salome. And by 1900, Fuller had toured the music halls of Berlin, London, New York, and, of course, Paris, all of which regularly featured "Oriental" reviews.[2]

But while Fuller's veil dances owed much to the Oriental "belly dance" (prominently featured at the World's Fair), they actually involved no "belly" at all. They did not tantalize; and they did not *un*veil any parts of her body. The press accordingly dubbed Fuller the "*modern* Salome," because her veil dances relied so much on technology, lights, and elaborate stage machinery of her own invention. This reworking of an Orientalist myth would prove to have a very charged place at the Expo of 1900.

THE WORLD'S FAIR OF 1900: BACKWARD AND FORWARD IN TIME

"All that interests the French about the Empire," Prime Minister Jules Ferry once lamented, "is the belly dance." And it was true that, despite the enormous increase in France's empire, the general public at the turn of the century seemed uninterested in its country's conquests.[3] This lack of interest, especially on the part of the bourgeoisie, greatly concerned the officials of the Expositions Universelles of 1889 and 1900, since a major purpose of both Fairs was to promote awareness and acceptance of the Empire, and to ally it in the public imagination with the excitement of modern scientific advancement. Advances in technology, had, of course, tremendous importance in the so-called "new imperialism" of the second half of the nineteenth century. Steamships, railways, the telegraph, and electricity had all contributed significantly to Europe's conquest of the tropics; but the public, while adoring such items as Edison's lightbulb, did not appear to comprehend their usefulness in colonialism.

The Fair of 1900 was a particularly aggressive extravaganza celebrating two main themes: technological wizardry and colonial expansion. In fact, one of the Fair's goals was to use "progress" to entice more French citizens to become colonizers. The glorification of technology centered here on the miracle of electricity. Crowds marvelled at the mechanically propelled walkways and the many tricks of lighting and sound that created the magical panorama and stereorama displays. Spotlights in dazzling colors bathed the exhibitions. "At night," wrote journalist Paul Morand:

the searchlights sweep the Champs de Mars, the fountains shimmer in cyclamen tints and fall in showers of green and purple light . . . . Electricity is accumulated, condensed, transformed, bottled, . . . it is the scourge and the religion of 1900. (65)

The main site of the Fair's colonial promotion was the Parc du Trocadéro. Here, 50,000 square meters were divided into two main sections, one devoted to foreign-owned colonies, and the other to French holdings. On the French side, nineteen pavilions represented all the nation's colonies and protectorates. Temples, palaces, pyramids, and huts featured scenes of "native life," using live actors as well as electrical *trompe l'oeil* effects. At the Algerian display, for example, a "stéreorama mouvant" recreated a sea voyage to Oran. Passengers would board a boat that lurched and swayed as a "sea breeze" wafted by, and rotating panorama disks depicted the approaching Algerian coastline. When they "arrived," visitors could enjoy an Algerian café, complete with musical entertainment, and young women performing the *danse du ventre*.[4]

Most of the technologically advanced colonial displays employed one very simple marketing strategy: the use of a commodified female sexuality to suggest the attainable, voluptuous charms of the colonial landscape. Since the Fair exhibitors were as familiar as Jules Ferry with the drawing power of the *danse du ventre*, colonial dancing women provided much of the "authentic" entertainment at these exhibitions. These women of color also worked as waitresses in native-style cafés and restaurants, and also simply as background scenery, paid by the Fair Commission to walk around the grounds in scanty costumes. The most acclaimed of the Fair's many belly and veil dancers were those in Algeria's all-female Ouled-Nail troupe, who entertained onstage with their famous "mobile bellies," and offstage simply by strolling through the crowds in their revealing costumes.

It is hardly necessary to explain here the well-known formula by which imperialism came to be viewed as the inevitable sexual conquest of supine, feminized parts of the world by the virile, civilizing force of Europe. What is relevant for my argument is the fact that among the many artifacts on display at the World's Fair's colonial exhibitions – costumed dolls, native artwork, musical instruments, etc. – there were nearly always attractive, indigenous women, the *almées*, the *bayadères*.

And so spectators at this Fair could board one of the futuristic electric walkways in order to be transported backward in time, to performances designed to vaunt the ancient seductive charms of veiled dancing girls. The striking nature of such combinations of advanced technology and "ancient" entertainments of the East – the modern West and the antique Orient – was a frequent theme in the journalistic reports of the Exposition Universelle.

RHONDA K. GARELICK

A MODERN SALOME: FULLER AT THE EXPO

In 1900, Loie Fuller – dubbed "The Electricity Fairy" – was adopted as the World's Fair's emblem, an idealized representative of the Exhibition's heavily promoted mixing of "ancient style" colonialist entertainment and modern technology.

Fair officials commissioned the noted architect Henri Sauvage to build the *Théâtre Loie Fuller* on the "Rue de Paris," a strip of recreated cabaret theatres placed at the Porte Binet, the Exhibition's main entrance. Fuller's theatre was, therefore, among the very first attractions that most visitors encountered upon entering the imposing gates. Fuller was also, as I have mentioned, the only American to be included in this ultra-Parisian cabaret section.

Like all other exhibitions on the Rue de Paris, Fuller's theatre operated as a concession. The Fair Commission paid for the construction of the theatre (which was later torn down with most of the other Fair pavilions); and, in return, Fuller paid the French government 25,000 francs for the privilege of performing in it, keeping all box-office proceeds in excess of that amount (Ministère du commerce 16). Inside this theatre, Fuller danced her version of "Salome" along with the rest of her repertoire, most of which relied similarly upon elaborate use of veiling, drapery, and impressive electrical effects.

The logical path of fairgoers entering through the Porte Binet led from the Rue de Paris, through the Champs de Mars, site of such travel-based attractions as the "Cinéorama,"[5] onto the Quai d'Orsay, past the displays of European commerce, arts, agriculture, and navigation, and over the Pont d'Iéna to the Trocadéro's huge colonial displays. In other words, the Fair was laid out so that the majority of visitors moved from the domestic, light-hearted charms of Parisian cabaret, cinema, and puppetry, through a technological fantasy of global travel, past displays of European artistic and economic accomplishment, and then on to an expansive, festive display of the just extension of these domestic successes: the imperial conquest of Africa and Asia. Curiously, Fuller, in her little theatre, commented on and encapsulated the entire project.

THE BACKDROP AND THE BODY: A DIFFERENT KIND OF VEIL DANCER

> out of the New World has sprung an artist who resuscitates the spectacle out of which paganism was created . . . Loie Fuller, who is the soul of antiquity reincarnated . . . the secret of the past.
>
> (Marx 7–8)

Combining veils and flowing robes borrowed from the classical dance of antiquity with colored electric lights mounted on rotating platforms, Fuller

88

Figure 6.1 Loie Fuller in early, hand-painted costume
Photo courtesy of Bibliothèque nationale, Arsenal division, Paris

seemed to exist in two eras at once.[6] And her repertoire was as well suited as her costumes and lighting to the Exhibition's goal of melding ancient and modern worlds. The themes of her pieces leapt from the pagan to the biblical, from the Oriental to the journalistic, including titles such as: "The Dance of the 1,000 Veils," "A Thousand and One Nights," "The Snake Dance," "The Fire of Life," "Ave Maria," and "Radium," a dance based on Pierre and Marie Curie's discoveries.

And while her veils and Orientalist themes allied Fuller with the colonial *bayadères* who performed on the other side of the Exhibition park, her performances did not take place against any specifically oriental backdrop, since Fuller deliberately suppressed all decor. She did not recreate a colonial site such as those seen in the Fair's colonial pavilions, for among Fuller's many remarkable innovations for theatre, one of the most radical was her discarding of all conventional scenery.

Traditionally, cabaret dance revues of this period revolved around a theme, often an "exotic" or Orientalist motif which depended upon elaborate backdrops, props, jewels, and costumes. Rejecting these trappings entirely, Fuller draped the stage and its floor in black velvet and plunged the theatre into total darkness before her dances began. Early in her career, she had used silk costumes upon which she painted her own designs, combining costume and scenery (fig. 6.1). But by the time she first performed her Dance of the Seven Veils in 1895, Fuller had dispensed with the painted fabrics as well, choosing instead to form the dozens of yards of silk that she wore into the very designs she had once painted upon them. And so, instead of wearing a costume painted with lilies, or butterflies, for example, Fuller would transform her entire body into those objects. She would accomplish this by manipulating large batons that were sewn into the material, sculpting the silk into enormous winged or floral patterns in the air, over her head (fig. 6.2). By creatively wielding these batons – for which she held a patent – Fuller could shape the silk around her into countless images, transforming costume into figure, merging dancer with scenery. Fuller's choreography marked, in fact, the moment when modern dance began to supplant the nineteenth century's more narrative, decorative forms of dance.

Fuller's innovations in the use of theatrical space and backdrop effectively removed the veil dance from any specific sense of geography, replacing such details with form, light, and movement. At the same time, however, Fuller did not entirely eradicate the *concept* of geographical locale. Camille Mauclair seems aware of this ambiguity in Fuller's work, writing that "Loie Fuller tears us away from the conflicts of ordinary life, and leads us to the *purifying landscapes* of dreams" (106; my italics and translation). Mallarmé also appears sensitive to Fuller's suppression and evocation of place, and in a review essay on her performances wrote:

Figure 6.2 Fuller in patented costume, featuring sewn-in batons
Photo courtesy of Bibliothèque nationale, Arsenal division, Paris

the frenzied dancer . . . acquires the virginity of an *undreamt city* . . .
Fuller's sorcery *institutes a place* . . . soon we will see the disappearance –
as of an imbecility – of the traditional stable or permanent decor that is
constructed in opposition to choreographic mobility . . . the stage itself
is unleashed . . . exhaled in the play of a veil. (309; my italics and
translation)

Both Mauclair and Mallarmé intuited Fuller's proximity to the very backdrops she had rejected. The images of purifying dream landscapes, and
virginal, undreamt-of cities partake quite manifestly of the kind of paternal-
ist, feminizing, and Orientalist vision of the colonies which fueled and
justified imperial expansion. Rather than freeing her entirely from the
concept of "place," Fuller's dances instead transformed her into place
and occupant at the same time; and so it is fully consistent that she
performed in a pavilion that bore only her name. While the Ouled-Nail
troupe performed their veil dances in the Palace of Algeria, Loie Fuller
performed hers in the Loie Fuller pavilion, detached from any specific
country. Transforming her body into the only scenery, Fuller took the
theatrical space upon her own person. The fictive space she inhabited as
Salome and all her other incarnations was her own body. Fuller used
performance to turn herself from occupant of a theatrical space into the
space itself, "instituting a place," as Mallarmé wrote.

THE "NATIVE," THE VITRINE, AND THE PHOTOGRAPH

A word needs to be said about the depiction of Oriental women in general
at the World's Fair of 1900. By the end of the nineteenth century, images of
colonized women were a commonplace in all forms of French entertainment. Malek Alloula has analyzed France's prurient fascination with these
veiled women in *The Colonial Harem*, a study of the countless photographs
of North African women that flooded France during this time. Alloula
compares the women photographed to "butterflies and insects that
museums of natural history and taxidermists exhibit in their glass display
cases" (92).

In its own exhibitions of colonized women, the World's Fair partook of a
similar "display case" motif, setting up tableaux in which the women
became objects in *vitrines*, available for inspection. Often the "native"
women were kept behind windows. The *Hachette* guide to the Fair tells
us that in the Moroccan pavilion, for example, the women are only visible
through "petites fenêtres de harem, étroites, et mystérieuses" (272). Some
of the women displayed at the Fair lived in the Trocadéro's recreations of
colonial sites, known as "native villages." "Village" women, imported from
their home countries to add authenticity to the Fair, were paid to live their

daily lives in public. They tended to their children, cooked meals, and wove cloth in full view of European passersby. A striking example of this phenomenon appears in the following extract from the *Figaro* guidebook to the Fair, which describes a "native" Algerian village. Once again, the women are noticeably enframed by windows:

> Let us cross the threshold of Babel-oued, here we are in the Rue de la Kasbah. The steep path snakes around . . . behind the barred doors and windows pass the shadows of mysterious veiled women . . . . We pass huts where belly dancing, sword dancing . . . restaurants proudly displaying Arab cuisine, laughter, shouts and songs . . . all form a multi-colored tableau, most animated and alive. (88; my translation)

The guidebook invites the European spectator to consider the theatrical appeal of the setting; the visitor is entering a new world apart: "let us cross the threshold." The women, supposedly glimpsed in their daily life, are visible only through their veils and behind doors and windows. Like the taxidermist's butterflies, these women are images under glass to be admired as scientific oddities, part of a cleverly recreated world in miniature. They move about as mere shadows in this realm, as simulacra of themselves, visible only *through* or *between* obstructions. Partially hidden by the windows' bars, the *algériennes* become peep-show attractions, even though they are supposedly glimpsed at home. The Fair's technological gaze turns the colonial woman into a cinematic ghost in a display case, blurring the boundary between the technologized body and the "natural" or "native" body.

CHOREOGRAPHY, INVENTIONS, AND COLONIAL SUBTEXTS

Loie Fuller's art took as its starting point the encounter between the Orientalist mythology of the veiled woman and the scientific, cinematic commodity into which the World's Fair transformed this motif. While Fuller's veils and silks recalled the costumes of Oriental dancing girls, she was very unlike those highly eroticized entertainers, for onstage she had no "natural" body at all. Fuller suppressed her physical outline entirely, recreating her shape through her various coverings. She showcased those created shapes, and never her own female figure, for her art lay in the technological reshaping and replication of the body.

Fuller's most ingenious inventions in stagecraft featured mirrors and lights which duplicated or displaced her dancing form. One such invention – for which she held a patent – involved an arrangement of mirrors which formed a small, octagonal room in whose center Fuller would dance. Rows of lights were placed at the interstices of these mirrors, with the result that Fuller's dancing body was reflected all around her (fig. 6.3). The multiple

Patent No. 533,167

Figure 6.3 Patent drawing for the mirror room

reflections gave the appearance of a small crowd of identical dancers in a self-enclosed mirrored room, a microcosmic harem. Malek Alloula has analyzed the frequent motif of replication in photographs of colonized women, and notes how often the veil winds up suggesting an endless reproduceability, the women's status as interchangeable, duplicate bodies:

> The veil is a sort of perfect and generalized mask . . . it instills uniformity . . . . It will be noted that whenever a photographer aims his camera at a veiled woman, he cannot help but include in his visual field several instances of her. As if to photograph one of them from the outside required the inclusion of a *principle of duplication* in the framing. (11)

Fuller's use of technology onstage may be read as an enactment of the *process* of colonial gazing as Alloula describes it here. Instead of many women melding into one, one woman turns herself into many. That is to say that the process of mirroring or duplication at work in Fuller's glass-enclosed chamber reveals itself plainly. Rather than inviting the spectator into a technologically recreated harem which disavows its fictitiousness, such as those depicted on postcards and in the colonial exhibitions, Fuller staged the process of the harem's creation.[7] The audience watched as the reduplication of the veiled woman occurred.

If those World's Fair dioramas, panoramas, cabarets, and "native villages" that showcased dancing colonized women seemed subtly to resemble

94

scientific or commercial display cases, Loie Fuller's pavilion featured a woman who danced inside an actual glass box, a *vitrine* into which she proudly stepped each night. In placing herself inside a glass case (and one of her own creation), Fuller literalized and played with the scientific voyeurism of the other spectacles of veiled dancers. Within her display case Fuller, her body obscured by yards of fabric, would transform herself into butterflies and lilies. In so doing, she was effectively revealing the apparatus of production that was normally suppressed. Fuller's performances showcased more the technologized dancing girl *industry*, than the dancing girl herself. Returning to Alloula's analogy, one could say that Fuller played both the butterfly and the taxidermist.

Another variation on the "display case" theme was Fuller's famous patented glass pedestal, upon which she danced nightly at the World's Fair. By lighting the pedestal from below, Fuller managed to create the illusion that she danced with no stage beneath her feet, mysteriously suspended above the stage – a bodiless vision of changing color and form.

In nineteenth-century depictions of colonial women, not only was the woman generally an encased, anonymous creature, she often appeared to be entirely solipsistic, a languid narcissist unaware of those gazing upon her (fig. 6.4). Once again, Loie Fuller managed to use her stagecraft to gesture toward this common motif, while at the same time distancing herself from it. This is especially evident in another one of the patented devices that she

THE DRESSES OF THE "KHANDS" ARE VERY VALUABLE, AND THE JEWELS ARE OF GREAT IMPORTANCE.

A WEALTHY ALGERIAN LADY IN HER HOME, SMOKING A "NARGILA" AFTER HER BREAKFAST.

Figure 6.4 Nineteenth-century commercial photograph of harem woman
Photo courtesy of Bibliothèque nationale, Collection des Estampes, Paris

used at the World's Fair. The device consisted primarily of a wall of transparent glass mounted at the front of the stage. With the auditorium kept as dark as possible, and the stage brightly illuminated, the glass would seem to disappear, becoming invisible to the audience. For the dancer, however, the glass acted as a mirror. As she danced, Fuller saw, not the audience, but only herself reflected in the glass. The audience knew it was watching Fuller watching herself. She danced before their gaze without acknowledging it, in what could be read as a self-conscious revision of the auto-erotic poses so often seen in paintings and photographs of colonial women.

Even Fuller's colored lights were a technologized reinterpretation of the traditional *bayadère*'s appeal. Onstage, the enormous white silk veils in which she draped her body acted as a screen for dozens of jewel-colored spot-lights that projected intricate designs upon the fabric. Special panels in an overhead lantern projector (that Fuller had invented and built) accomplished this effect. The panels were made from slides of molded glass which had been handcut by Fuller. Then, using pigment dissolved in a special gelatin concoction (also of her own invention), Fuller would paint abstract designs on the glass, and have the designs shone directly upon her veils. The result was that colored designs of light tattooed her face and body in constantly shifting patterns – a modernized, electrical version of the *tatouage* that North African women used to embellish their faces and bodies.

While the Fair's colonial exhibitions employed the most advanced tech-nology available to create the impression that visitors had been transported to another world, Fuller used her own technology to do the reverse: with her mirrors and lighting tricks, she transported *herself* to another place. Whether dancing in a mirror-lined cubicle or floating suspended over the stage, Fuller dismantled and toyed with the scenario of the colonized dancing women. Instead of the spectator's relying upon technology in order to espy the primitive eroticism of an Oriental *danseuse*, the dancing woman in this case manifestly appropriates technology to render herself spectacle. While Fuller narcissistically dancing before her own reflection recalls the languid poses of those Oriental girls dancing in supposed ignorance of the spectator's voyeurism, it does so very self-consciously.

The desired effect of the colonial dance performance is the recreation of the colonizing gaze that only penetrates one way, never acknowledged or returned by its object. Fuller opened up this model, and played with its assumptions. Without scenery, or conventional costumes, and with tech-nology employed in acknowledgement rather than an obfuscation of theatrical artifice, her performances laid bare the trappings of colonial spectacles. While she may not have been able to see the audience through her glass box of mirrors, Fuller had built and patented it, and in placing her heavily veiled body inside it she seemed to reveal the device of the colonial, objectifying gaze.

What then is the relationship between Fuller's technological reinterpretation of the veil dance and the imperialism of the World's Fair? To explore this question, it will be necessary to return to her status as a foreigner, as an American at the Expo. And because the turn of the century represents such a charged moment in global imperialism, and in European–American relations in particular, I would like first to consider the place of the United States at the World's Fair.

AMERICANS AT THE EXPO

In the months preceding the Exposition's opening in April of 1900, the United States began expressing disgruntlement with the Fair Commission. The Americans wanted twice as much exhibition space as they had been allotted by the French. They were also lobbying for space in the Trocadéro, since victory in the 1898 Spanish–American war had left the United States with something of a small empire – a fact which alarmed the French.[8]

Alfred Picard, director of the Exposition, at first rejected America's demands for extra space, with an ironic phrase that quickly became famous. Explaining the scarcity of exhibition space, Picard compared his Commission to a young woman granting sexual favors: "Même la plus belle fille du monde ne peut donner que ce qu'elle a," he said (quoted in Moynet 91). But the most beautiful girl in the world can sometimes find a little more to give, and despite his initial refusal, Picard eventually doubled the exhibition space given to the US, and even allowed them a small colonial exhibition at the Trocadéro.

This episode, and Picard's famous remark, suggest the United States' unique place in the French imagination. The young, newly imperialist country was imposing enough to reverse the usual sexual metaphor of France's colonialism. While France was an inseminating, virile force in the Edenically feminine regions of Morocco, Algeria or Indochina, it was a beautiful girl flirting with a suitor when it came to the US. The United States, perhaps feeling its imperialist oats, elbowed its way into the World's Fair, gaining ground that it had originally been denied. The fact that part of the territory gained was in the Trocadéro, and meant to flaunt American colonial conquests, only reinforces the event's imperialist subtext. The former colony was now a colonizer, and intended to show off its new status. The US Pavilion at the Fair wound up being one of the grandest and most technologically advanced. A building with a rotunda resembling the US Capitol's, the Pavilion provided such advanced mechanical luxuries as typewriters and telegraphs for use by American businessmen.

A HYBRID OF NATIONALITIES

Loie Fuller's performances at the Fair offered a curious mixture of nationalities. As a performer on the Rue de Paris, she was coded as "French" entertainment. As a Salome figure, she clearly relied upon conventional forms of Orientalism, thereby allying herself with such colonized places as Algeria and Morocco. But at the same time, Fuller's status as an American was widely recognized. She was seen as an inventive, mechanically astute Yankee, a businesswoman; and this persona jibed well with the image of America as an unromantic, even desexualized, but highly efficient place.

Although recognized as a lesbian by the worlds of art, music, and literature, Fuller was, at the same time, viewed as a kind of sexless and spritely maiden aunt from America. Unmarried, she traveled all over Europe with her aged mother. Offstage she dressed haphazardly in dowdy clothes, wore little round spectacles, no makeup, and kept her hair in a tight bun. The fact that her American-accented, ungrammatical French never improved during all her years in France only reinforced Fuller's offstage image as an endearing but uncultivated matron whose real appeal lay in her scientific abilities, however dazzling she might have been onstage.

And, of course, even that dazzle bore the stamp of Fuller's American-ness. Hers was the dazzle of machinery, of technology, of Yankee ingenuity. In the French imagination, Fuller held an appeal closer to Thomas Edison's than to Josephine Baker's. "After all, the glory goes to the electrician," wrote Huysmans of Fuller's performances, "it's American" (quoted in "Loie Fuller's Glory Laid to Light"). After interviewing her, one journalist sarcastically remarked that "Madame Fuller's conversation would be of extreme interest to an electrician" (De Ménasce 1). Another contemporary review described Fuller as a "chaste dancer who lives surrounded by her family; and like a typical American, is of an extremely practical nature" (H. C. 109; my translation). (The proximity of the adjectives "chaste" and "American" is unsurprising here.)

The hybrid, or multilayered, foreignness of Fuller's performances may explain her position at the Fair's gateway. When Fuller, an unprepossessing American woman, took on the trappings of colonized women of color (the veils, the Orientalist Salome persona), and performed as a French attraction on the Rue de Paris, she suggested a defusing of the American imperialist threat, while subtly promoting French colonialism. For Fuller appeared to be, as I have said, a particularly unthreatening and unsexual presence in whose choreography "the traditional art of ancient oriental civilizations [was] extenuated by science" (Mauclair 44; my translation). She was "chaste" and small, "sweet and gentle," noted for her "admirable naivete" and "magnificent innocence" (anonymous press clippings; Rondel collection). In so prominently showcasing this American woman, the French World's Fair Commission could appropriate her Yankee ingenuity. In adopting her as the Fair's emblem, France could use Fuller's techno-logical dazzle to augment its own version of "progress." And if American technology had won a small but disturbing colonial empire, on the Rue de Paris at least, the lone American was touted as a uniquely French treasure, "la fée éléctricité" herself. Fairies, of course, are not fully sexualized women; and the erotically sanitized nature of Fuller's veil dances enabled her to gesture toward colonialism while not competing with the French. The Orientalist subtext of her dances was defused of any lubricity, thereby keeping a safe distance from the traditional Gallic versions of the veil dance.[9]

And so while science extenuated her traditional art, Fuller's status as adopted Frenchwoman extenuated her Americanness. Enjoying her thirty-minute performances, audiences could marvel, on several levels, at a perfect blending of the "new world" and the old. Fuller could point toward a happy melding of the United States (the new world) into a European context, suggesting a slight easing of recent political tensions between the countries. She could represent the union of the "new" world of technology that the French so wanted to vaunt as their own, with the "old" world of the tropical *bayadère*. And consequently, she could represent the civilizing beauty of France's imperialism, in which "new" civilization merged with the ancient east. Performing virtually at the Exhibition's entrance, Fuller provided safe amusement that, nonetheless, suggested the imperialist pageant to come.

LOIE FULLER, DONALD DUCK, AND STYLES OF IMPERIALISM

But such an interpretation does not exhaust the potential significance of Loie Fuller's unique status at the World's Fair. Certainly, Fuller subtracted both the Oriental decor and the eroticized body from the veil dance, becoming in essence, a PG rendition of an X-rated fantasy, a proto-Disney image of the dancing girl. And this kind of whitewashed version of the colonial *bayadère* definitely suggests a defusing of America's inchoate imperialism. But Fuller's "innocent" performances did not blot out or dismantle all traces of an imminent US empire; and the key to their subtext of peculiarly *American* imperialism may be found in a subtle stylistic distinction.

The difference between Fuller's veil dances and those usually seen in cabarets, as well as all others at the World's Fair, lies in the presence or absence of history and ethnography. In Fuller's performances technology superseded the historical specificity in which French colonial dances seemed steeped. And such a distinction may, in fact, conform to differences in styles of imperialism in the US and France.

Ariel Dorfman has examined cultural manifestations of various imperial styles in *The Empire's Old Clothes*, particularly in the chapter which reads Jean de Brunoff's *Babar the Elephant* series – stories of an African jungle elephant who becomes "civilized" in France – against Walt Disney's cartoon forays into "colonial" landscapes. Dorfman concludes that the Babar stories offer a kind of geographical and historical specificity, despite their sugar-coating

– a "parallel, ideal history." "Babar's history," writes Dorfman, "is none other than the fulfillment of the dominant countries' colonial dream" (25).

When Donald Duck and Mickey Mouse visit the tropics, however (to find adventures in "Foola Zoola" or "San Bananador"), they do so without the annoying encumbrance of any history at all. Dorfman points out that, although de Brunhoff avoids mentioning individual countries' names, Babar moves from a recognizable African jungle to a recognizable Parisian household; and moments of loss and colonial violence are included in the stories. Disney's characters, on the other hand, float around in caricatured parodies of Third World countries, enjoying harmless good times, totally avoiding any issues of colonial struggle:

> [Disney] . . . can exercise his commercial and linguistic domination in less colonial and more indirect ways than de Brunhoff could . . . . Just as Disney plunders . . . literature, reshaping it in his average North American image, so he proceeds with world geography. He feels no obligation to avoid the caricature, and rebaptizes each country as if it were a can on a shelf, an object of infinite fun. (24)

Dorfman sees the United States' image as a good-natured and innocent country as a crucial factor in the success of its economic imperialism. "America has been interpreted time and again as a domain of innocence," he writes:

> [Americans] only felt comfortable if other people assented to the image they had of themselves as naive, frolicsome, unable to harm a mouse . . . the US managed [to become a global empire] . . . without its people losing their basic intuition that they were good, clean and wholesome. Its citizens never recognized themselves as an empire . . . . (201–202)

In Disney's cartoon parodies of Third World nations Dorfman sees a desire to erase all historical and geographical detail, as well as responsibility, and a desire to replace these elements with the power and appeal of modern science. "[Disney's] response to the misfortunes of the past is a benign modernization of the untamed world, the application of . . . technology" (29). For Dorfman, the Babar books recall France's sense of a responsibility to *govern* and *know* the countries it had colonized, a desire to absorb and master the history and customs of its extended empire. America's empire, which never really became *colonial*, developed economically and technologically, and was, accordingly, devoid of the sense of historical specificity and cultural duty that France clearly had. In Dorfman's reading, Americans have always wanted to play Donald Duck in "Chiliburgeria," innocently searching absurd new lands for fun and profit, always disavowing any imperialist greed.

Dorfman's vision of the US as an imperial power obscuring its politics with proclamations of innocence holds true even for the US of 1900, thirty years before Disney drew his first cartoon. By the turn of the twentieth century, the United States was well on its way to gaining its eventual place as a global power, having already demonstrated its expansionism on the North American continent, justifying the Monroe Doctrine as divinely decreed, a policy purified by God's word.

This kind of self-professed American purity was already visible in Loie Fuller's image in France generally, and at the World's Fair specifically. Fuller was "unsexual," technologized, and highly commercial – she even sold lamps and dolls fashioned in her own likeness in the lobby of her theatre. Nearing forty and lacking any formal training, she had succeeded in France through her determination and her practical genius, embodying much the same American "spirit" that got the United States its enormous pavilion at the Fair, over the objections of French officials.

When Fuller, clad in her silken veils, waved her batons under the colored spotlights, she was "pure" and "chaste" in the minds of her audience, a performer people brought their children to see.[10] In this way, she was an unthreatening introduction to the less pure, more disturbing veiled women across the fairgrounds at the Trocadéro, women now living under French dominion. As a Rue de Paris entertainer, Fuller also functioned as an appropriated or "Frenchified" American at a time when the United States was beginning to look rather imposing. But finally, Fuller exhibited a uniquely American aspect, a quality that remained and persevered despite both her adopted French status and her appeal as a *bayadère manquée*.

Loie Fuller was a one-woman industry, a household name, known simply as "La Loie" to an entire generation of Europe; and she accomplished all this by technologizing her body and turning a traditional, Oriental art into a mechanical feat. Her body hidden, even dematerialized under the veils, Fuller was the ghost of America's future at the World's Fair. More than America's Philippines exhibition at the Trocadéro, more than the grand Congressional-style pavilion on the "Rue des Nations," with its impressive telegraph machines, Loie Fuller hinted at the America to come. Amazing audiences with her inventions on a stage stripped of decor, hawking her memorabilia in the lobby, she was an Electric Salome, subtle symbol of the historically detached, technologized, and commercial imperialism that her own nation would make its trademark.

NOTES

1 For discussions of the Salome rage in the 1890s, see Françoise Meltzer, Helen Grace Zagona, Bram Dikstra, and Nina Auerbach.

2 See, for example, Huysmans' *Croquis parisiens* for a colorful account of colonialist revues at the Folies-Bergère.

3 During the last fifteen years of the nineteenth century France increased its

territories in Africa and Indochina from one million to 9.5 million square kilometers; the colonized population increased from five million to fifty million (Girardet 80).

4 For more on the technologically recreated worlds of the Expo, see my essay "Bayadères, Stereorama and Vahat-Loukoum: Technological Realism in the Age of Empire," in *Realism, Gender, and Sexuality.*

5 This attraction used ten cinematograph screens to create an "aerial tour" of the world.

6 The Greek robes later became the trademark of one of Fuller's most gifted dancing students: Isadora Duncan.

7 Writing of the shift from nineteenth-century, Orientalist dance performances to early modernism, Randy Martin observes:

> If nineteenth-century ballet tended to displace women's labor onstage onto the prior image of an exotic Other that could not carry the weight of intention and hence could not work, the women who inaugurated modern dance could restore this relation of act and meaning. The work of Loie Fuller, Isadora Duncan, Ruth St. Denis, and Maud Allan provides an image of agency that had previously been denied women on the stage.
>
> (Martin 108)

8 As a result of President McKinley's imperialist campaign against Spain, the Americans now controlled the Philippines, Puerto Rico, and Guam; they had also recently annexed Hawaii. Looking then like powerful new participants in global imperialism, the United States worried the French, who feared that American competition or even aggression in the French-controlled Caribbean.

9 Since the heavily erotic *danses du ventre* of the 1889 World's Fair had offended certain government officials, the 1900 Fair Commission was under orders to enforce "decency codes." However, theatres on the Rue de Paris enjoyed special artistic freedom on account of their "gallic" nature. The French considered their own popular culture to be inherently slightly provocative, and had no intention of inhibiting it. Accordingly, the Fair Commission simply warned Rue de Paris theatres to advertise clearly their level of "gallicity." Although Loie Fuller could have made use of such license, she never needed to (Picard 114).

10 Fuller also gave the first matinee performances ever seen at the Folies-Bergère. The Folies' management felt that her innocent dances would make a good afternoon show for the wives and children of the middle-class men who so loved its more "gallic" nighttime attractions (de Morinni 212 and Rondel Collection).

WORKS CITED

Alloula, Malek. *The Colonial Harem.* Trans. Myrna Godzich and Wlad Godzich. Minneapolis: University of Minnesota Press, 1986.

Auerbach, Nina. *Women and the Demon: The Life of a Victorian Myth.* Cambridge, Mass.: Harvard University Press, 1982.

De Ménasce, J. "Loie Fuller." Press clipping. Rondel Collection, Bibliothèque de L'Arsenal.

de Morinni, Clare. "Loie Fuller: The Fairy of Light," in *Chronicles of the American Dance: From the Shakers to Martha Graham.* Ed. Paul Magriel. New York: Da Capo Press, 1984: 203–220.

Dijkstra, Bram. *Idols of Perversity.* New York: Oxford University Press, 1986.

Dorfman, Ariel. *The Empire's Old Clothes: What the Lone Ranger, Babar and other Innocent Heroes do to our Minds.* New York: Pantheon Books, 1983.

Figaro: Guide Bleu de Figaro à l'Exposition de 1900. Paris: Le Figaro, 1900.

Garelick, Rhonda K. "Bayadères, Stereorama, and Vahat-Loukoum: Technological Realism in the Age of Empire," forthcoming in *Realism, Gender, and Sexuality.* Eds. Margaret Cohen and Christopher Prendergast. Minneapolis: University of Minnesota Press, 1995.

Girardet, Raoul. *L'Idée coloniale en France de 1871 à 1962.* Paris: La Table Ronde, 1972.

Hachette: Guide Pratique du Visiteur. Paris: Hachette, 1900.

H. C. Review article. *Revue encyclopédique.* February 1893. 107–109.

Huysmans, Joris-Karl. *Croquis parisiens.* Paris: Éditions Marcel Valtrat, 1981.

"Loie Fuller's Glory Laid to Light." *Chicago Tribune* 8 January 1928.

Mallarmé, Stéphane. *Oeuvre complètes.* Paris: Gallimard, 1945.

Martin, Randy. "Dance Ethnography and the Limits of Representation." *Social Text* 33 (1992): 103–23.

Marx, Roger. "Loie Fuller." *Les Arts et la vie* May 1905.

Mauclair, Camille. *Idées Vivantes.* Paris: Librairie de l'art ancien et moderne, 1904.

Meltzer, Françoise. *Salome and the Dance of Writing: Portraits of Mimesis in Literature.* Chicago: University of Chicago Press, 1987.

Ministère du commerce et de l'industrie. *Compte des Recettes et des Dépenses: Exposition Universelle Internationale de 1900 à Paris.* Paris: Imprimerie Nationale, 1909.

Morand, Paul. *1900 A.D.* Trans. Rollilly Fedden. New York: William Farquhar Payson, 1931.

Moynet, G. "Le Pavillon national des États Unis." *L'Encyclopédie du siècle.* Tome 2. Paris: Montgredien et Cie., 1900.

Picard, Alfred. *Rapport général administratif et technique.* Paris: Exposition Universelle, 1900.

Rondel Collection on Loie Fuller. Press Clippings. Bibliothèque de l'Arsenal, Paris.

Sommer, Sally. "Loie Fuller." *Drama Review* 19, 1 (March 1975): 53–67.

Zagona, Helen Grace. *The Legend of Salome and the Principle of Art for Art's Sake.* Geneva: Droz, 1960.

7

DRESSED TO KILL

A Post-Colonial Reading of Costume and the Body in Australian Theatre

Helen Gilbert

[T]he empty garment, without head and limbs . . . is death, not the neutral absence of the body, but the body mutilated, decapitated.
(Roland Barthes, *The Responsibility of Forms*)

While the body gives existence to clothing, as Barthes argues, clothing also gives the body presence, particularly on stage where even nakedness becomes a costume of sorts. Theatre practitioners have of course long recognized that the theatrical subject is indelibly marked by costume, but critics and audiences seem less willing to scrutinize the textuality of clothes and fabrics, especially in naturalistic theatre where they are barely noted unless something does not quite fit, literally or figuratively. What is judged inappropriate or incongruous then becomes significant in terms of Barthes' idea of the "aberrant message which '*surprises*' the code" (*Rustle* 94), but in general dress operates to naturalize particular representations – or rather fabrications. Jane Gaines' critique of film as a medium in which costume, paradoxically, is designed to "recede" at the same time as it "registers" (183) can be aptly applied to much contemporary theatre practice wherein costume delivers as self-evident particular gender, racial, social, and national identities and then recedes into the background as mere cloth- ing, a mood-setting device for the verbal text. From a political standpoint, then, any garment is a problematic signifier because the paradox of its transparency conceals a rhetorical power which is nonetheless expressed through the materiality of clothing as part of the *mise-en-scène*, and in its relationship to the body as the most localized site of ideological struggle. This essay's exploration of costume in Australian theatre examines the ways in which such rhetorical power has been exercised in a country historically constituted within and by imperial and patriarchal discourses. By illustrating the key role of particular kinds of dress in constructing, consolidating and/ or contesting various concepts of national character on our stages, I hope to develop an "epistemology of the wardrobe"[1] which emphasizes how the marginalized might de-sign costume for strategic purposes.

Because its power is literal as well as symbolic, clothing has a number of important functions in the processes of imperialism. A brief look at Shakespeare's much discussed colonial paradigm, *The Tempest*, indicates that Prospero maintains his position of authority not only through language but also by sartorial fiat, a strategy designed to achieve full effects in performance. Predictably, he discards his magic robe only when he can don another powerful costume: his rightful attire as Duke of Milan. Caliban, in contrast, is clothed in a coarse gaberdine cloak which confers low social status, signifies alterity, and functions as a comic device when he is mistaken for a monster of the Isle. In a text that deploys costume in the interests of the colonizer, Prospero's garments become an object of desire for the oppressed, as suggested by Stephano and Trinculo's fascination with the glistening apparel which Ariel sets as a trap. Although Caliban himself is not fooled by this "trumpery," for he at least can distinguish between mere adornment and the vestments of power, it nonetheless prevents the trio from overthrowing colonial rule; and because he has merely exchanged one master for another, Caliban is forced to carry the clothes – a strong visual image for "wearing the blame." His failed insurrection can be directly related to his inability to appropriate his master's clothes as successfully as he appropriates his language by learning "how to curse" (I, ii 363). Historically, most performances of *The Tempest* have certainly depended on costume to subordinate Caliban as the "missing link" in the evolutionary chain,[2] a predictable tactic given that his language is frequently far too eloquent to do the trick. The theatrical clout of this kind of visual characterization is incidentally illustrated by Trevor Griffiths' observation that one early twentieth-century production which attempted to represent Caliban more sympathetically seemed to flounder because of the difficulty of playing against costume (175).

The larger historical picture shows that clothing was used throughout the empire to instigate similar hierarchies of power. Military or police uniforms, for example, not only signalled authority but in many instances actually conferred it, a point amply if ironically illustrated in colonial Australia by the recruitment of Black trackers as policemen who were then empowered to discipline Aborigines. Western-style civilian clothing, on the other hand, patrolled certain important borders: it delineated "civilized" from "savage," self from other, and Christian from heathen. Wearing indigenous dress thus became a gesture of recalcitrance on behalf of the colonized but tantamount to barbarism in the case of the European because it threatened to dissolve boundaries; hence the implied criticism when someone "went native."[3] The conative aspects of clothing – that it encourages people to act in prescribed ways – are clearly at work here. The idea that "clothes make the man" [*sic*] underlies discourses which marginalize traditional clothing as a risible sign of difference and explains efforts by imperial powers in many countries to mobilize dress as a means of acculturation of the racial other.

Studies of colonial and post-colonial literatures have paid scant attention to the role of costume as a site of negotiation or struggle, perhaps because such criticism's general failure to extend its purview beyond the predominantly language-centred genres of fiction and poetry leads to undue emphasis on the written text. Post-colonial theory does, however, offer a number of concepts which can be fruitfully applied to a reading of costume that focuses on politics rather than aesthetics to investigate how institutional authority is invoked or countered through vestimentary codes and performative devices such as cross-gender and/or cross-race dressing. Outlining how clothing functions to establish and maintain a powerful identity for the self while securing the textual capture and containment of the colonizable other is a major aim of my discussion. The parallel project is to identify ways of resisting this capture, a task at least partly addressed by rewriting, or in this case remodelling, the epistemological frameworks which shape representation. Helen Tiffin's contention that post-colonial literatures are "constituted in counter-discursive rather than homologous practices" (18) begs us to consider the ways in which costuming on our stages has not simply involved transplanting European codes and fashions but formulating a complex, sometimes ambivalent, response to their underlying assumptions. The hybrid forms that result from such repatterning provide a key for unlocking imperialism's master wardrobe and dismantling the vestiges of its power. As Homi K. Bhabha argues,

> [i]f the effect of colonial power is seen to be the *production* of hybrid-isation rather than the hegemonic command of colonialist authority or the silent repression of native traditions, then an important change of perspective occurs. It reveals ambivalence at the source of traditional discourses on authority and enables a form of subversion, founded on that uncertainty, that turns the discursive conditions of dominance into the grounds of intervention. (97)

Hybridization or "contamination" – to use Diana Brydon's deliberately polemical term – allows the creative potential of cross-cultural contact to emerge without homogenizing differences (Brydon 196). This strategy, particularly evident in contemporary Aboriginal texts, suggests that mixed-dress codes operate as a form of cultural negotiation, often through comedy and parody, even while they indicate detribalization and acculturation.

Any discussion of theatrical costume inevitably raises questions of gender, in part because dress is one of the main signifiers by which we (mis)identify gender, and also because "dressing up" to perform has been cast as a feminine activity in Western culture despite strong traditions of male transvestite theatres on the Greek and Elizabethan stages. In much post-colonial theory, gender has been the under-theorized term, particularly in analyses of settler literatures which tend to ignore the ambivalent position of white women, who are necessarily complicit in some of the processes of imperialism but deprivileged by others. Feminist analyses, on the other hand, are apt to produce critiques divorced from rather than inflected by critiques of colonialism. Some critics have drawn parallels between the condition of women interpellated by the discourses of patriarchy and the marginalization of the indigenous subject in the imperial situation, but, as W. D. Ashcroft points out, "the amount of genuine cross-fertilisation between the two [critical approaches] is scant" (23). Hence, as well as investigating some of the costuming devices which have functioned to forge images of national stereotypes – usually white and male – I am concerned to map out the "intersecting marginalities" in and through which a feminist post-colonial wardrobe might be assembled.

What post-colonial theory does not adequately explore is the gap between text and performance, an important site of intervention for the colonized. How something is worn can signify as much as what is worn. Thus far my discussion implicitly recognizes that wearing certain clothing is a political act, which, though inseparable from the costume itself, is by no means always collusive with its normative sartorial codes. I am interested here in the iconoclastic possibilities of performance and the sometimes disjunctive relationships between the actor and his/her clothing as mediated by the role. Non-naturalistic techniques such as Brecht's alienation effect offer ways to prevent the seamless application of clothing to the performer/character, suggesting that its race and gender connotations are highly arbitrary. Focus on how costume is worn also explains the effectiveness of parody and masquerade as ways of subverting imperial/patriarchal codes.

The ambit of this essay is extensive; therefore discussions of particular texts are necessarily limited. I do not set out to give a comprehensive account of costume but rather to develop a critical framework for its deployment as a decolonizing strategy in Australian performance texts, and, by implication, those of other post-colonial countries. The title of my paper, "Dressed to Kill," is intended to evoke the literal and metaphoric power of the colonizer, and the intentional nature of an enterprise which has decimated indigenous cultures and disenfranchised other marginalized peoples. However, such a title also alludes to "dressing up" as empowerment, an oppositional strategy whereby the subjugated not only appropriate the vestments of authority but find ways of fabricating their own.

MYTHS, HEROES, AND ANTI-HEROES

Since the late nineteenth century when Antipodean participation in British imperial wars first began, one of our most enduring and revered national characters has been the uniformed (boy) soldier immortalized in the Gallipoli myth. Like his bushranging prototype, the "Aussie digger"[4] was ambivalently constructed in the nexus of imperialist and nationalist

Figure 7.1 Typical Anzac celebrations beneath monument to the "Aussie Digger"
The Man from Mukinupin, Royal Queensland Theatre Company, 1989
Photo: Fiora Sacco

discourses: on the one hand he represented loyalty to the mother country and a willingness to defend England's interests; on the other, he became the "custodian of nationhood" for a country anxious to give itself a "heroic, legendary core" (R. White 130). Fetishized on stage as well as in film as a symbol of masculinity and mateship, the digger's uniform was invested with distinct, albeit sometimes contradictory, traits. Its khaki colours and rakish broad-brimmed hat pinned up on one side showed affinities with the habit of an idealized bush proletariat and suggested a certain larrikinism[5] even while packaging the Australian as an exemplary soldier type – broad-built, strong, skilled at survival, and, crucially, disciplined enough to outgrow the moral turpitude of his convict heritage. The conflicting codes of the digger myth, as Richard White points out (136), are still embodied in Anzac Day celebrations which feature two very different forms of (theatrical) display: full military dress parades and solemn rituals in the morning followed by drunken brawls and gambling in the afternoon, the latter in some ways functioning to splinter the vestimentary codes of the former.

What is particularly interesting about the longevity of the Anzac myth are the ways in which its conflation of imperial and anti-imperial discourses approves the basic military agenda of the British Empire but critiques its specific strategies, thus providing the perfect alibi for Australian defeat: betrayal by the parent culture. This narrative trope, which reached its apotheosis in such films as Peter Weir's *Gallipoli* (1981), also appears in a number of contemporary (anti)war plays, recycled and adapted to fit the contingencies of the post-Vietnam era. The reluctance of these texts to confront Australia's own colonizing activities in the Asia-Pacific region reflects the dilemma that intervention in Vietnam posed to a country which has relied heavily on a military past for images of national identity. The result is often a figural displacement of military and economic aggression onto Americans, who, decked out in full Uncle Sam regalia, provide sitting targets for burlesque and parody, while the Australians, more obviously "dressed to kill," usually maintain the probity embodied by the digger uniform. Barry Lowe's *Tokyo Rose* (1989) exemplifies this trope by constructing the Australian soldier as an innocent abroad seduced by the "stars and stripes" of his more powerful allies, while Rob George's *Sandy Lee Live at Nui Dat* (1981) partly deconstructs the myth of our blamelessness. Both plays foreground the Uncle Sam figure in ways which suggest that although the anxieties exposed, repressed, contained, or displaced by American/Australian contrasts are manifold, their cathectic topoi seem to indicate an urgent imperative to resist the effects of colonization and neo-imperialism, or, as P. R. Stephensen put it in 1936, to precipitate the "de-Pommification" and "un-Yankeefying" of Australian culture (89, 98).

If, as Robert Kroetsch contends, decolonization involves "unhiding the hidden" and "speaking the unspeakable" (44), a post-colonial analysis of our most celebrated national hero must ask not only what his costume dresses up for cultural consumption but also what is thus marginalized, obscured or erased by its sartorial signifiers. The mythopoeic project of constructing a (male) Australian identity vis-à-vis British, American, and, more lately, Japanese "invaders" camouflages a deep disquiet about more subtle challenges by racial and/or sexual others to the vested interests of imperial patriarchy in this country. Jill Shearer's *Shimada* (1986) enacts precisely this anxiety through an emphasis on cross-gender and

Figure 7.2 Symbolic "Uncle Sam" and Vietnam peasant costumes
Sandy Lee Live at Nui Dat, Stage Company, 1981
Photo: David Simmonds, Festival Centre

110

Figure 7.3 Billy in homemade Geisha costume as entertainer for the POWs
Shimada, Royal Queensland Theatre Company, 1990
Photo: Chris Ellis

cross-race dressing which problematizes the ideals of masculinity and racial superiority that undergird authorizations of the Anzac as a national icon. The play dramatizes current economic tensions and past military conflicts between Australia and Japan. Its most striking visual feature is the recurring image of the Australian boy soldier, Billy, dressed in a homemade Geisha costume which marks his role as entertainer in a Japanese prisoner of war camp. As a transvestite figure Billy actualizes fears of emasculation that necessarily shadow military constructions of masculinity which attempt to "expel anything infantile, female, or homoerotic" and project it onto a feminized enemy other (S. White 128). As the dressmaker and costumier who fits Billy with the clothes for his role and who later dons the kimono after Billy is killed during a performance, his fellow inmate, Clive, is also implicated in this symbolic castration. The Geisha role, overtly constructed by the Japanese guard, Shimada, and then forced upon successive prisoners, foregrounds gender as a costume that functions to signal defeat; henceforth, the Australians' primary task is to resist cross-dressing.[6] Women's clothes, so carefully excised from their constructions of the soldier hero, are here exposed as the spaces on and through which the men are sorted from the boys. Metaphorically, then, war enacts a sexualized battle, the outcome of which determines who'll wear the pants and who the dress. In the context of orientalism and the historical gendering of the Orient as

111

feminine, the spectre of Japanese victory over the Australians looms as a doubly degrading "dressing down."

The force of ambivalence which energizes representations of the colonizer/colonized binary emerges through a complex interplay of fear and desire in *Shimada*. Although its war narrative functions as a tacit warning against the effects of Japanese economic and cultural neo-imperialism, the text, especially in performance, exhibits an active fascination with the theatrical conventions of Noh and Kabuki, and a desire to enliven its own predominantly naturalistic semiotic codes with the richly evocative costumes of the Samurai, the Wisteria Lady, and the Geisha. The play's fantasies of cross-dressing are also deeply inflected by homoeroticism, which Shearer takes pains to align with the Japanese by stressing Shimada's pleasure in the visual display of the transvestite figure and highlighting his final sadistic annihilation of this soldier-temptress. But given that the Geisha is commonly the object of the western male imperial gaze, the orientalized Billy must also be acknowledged as a strong locus of homoerotic desire for his fellow soldiers. This impels a closer look at the concept of mateship which has been a cornerstone of the Anzac legend since its inception. That such male bonding is revealed as (psycho)sexual as well as social supports my earlier assertion about military discourse's

Figure 7.4 Noh and Kabuki influence as figured through the Samurai *Shimada*, Royal Queensland Theatre Company, 1990
Photo: Chris Ellis

112

strategic erasure of the feminine. More complex metaphorical transfers inform the specific construction of the boy hero whose function as an idealized figure is predicated as much on sexual innocence as on fighting potential. He can assert his manhood *and* operate as a locus of male homosexual desire only if he remains untouched by woman's castrating otherness. The real subversion effected by the Geisha costume in *Shimada* must then rest on an audience's recognition of its sexual taint. Billy himself is poignantly aware that this costume vitiates the Gallipoli myth, as indicated by his desperate efforts to divest himself of the kimono lest he die "done up like some tart" (20).

If Shearer equivocates in her exploration of the Anzac legacy and attempts to preserve some aspects of the myth even while deconstructing its masculinist textures, Louis Nowra is more acutely aware of what kinds of histories are occulted in constructions of the soldier-hero as a national emblem. One of our most important contemporary playwrights, Nowra exhibits a deep interest in imperialism and consistently sets out to unveil its military, cultural, and economic faces through vivid metaphorical images and highly resonant dialogue. Because his early plays were mainly set outside Australia and in remote historical periods, some theatre critics tagged them as costume dramas and failed to give them the critical attention they deserve. Such tags refuse to recognize the agency of clothes in mediating power relations and tend to assume that costume merely "blends straggling physiological signifiers so that they contribute to character" (Gaines 193). As Kelly suggests, however, Nowra's theatre has always offered to the interpreter prepared to embark on parabolic readings a mirror in which white Australians might see themselves clothed as colonizers of Aboriginal peoples and/or colonized subjects of a transplanted feudal system which gives lie to our myths of egalitarianism ("Mirror" 440).

Inside the Island (1980) provides a direct and sustained challenge to the fetishization of the military uniform that underlies Anzac mythology. Although set on an outback wheat property in New South Wales two years before the First World War, it is, as others have pointed out, Nowra's Gallipoli play (McCallum; Kelly "Lest We Forget"). Unlike Weir's film, which Nowra views as a "homoerotic sprinting contest" (Interview 122), *Inside the Island* paints a savage and confrontational yet not entirely unsympathetic portrait of the soldier figure. The plot is relatively simple: a cricket match played by a group of raw recruits stationed outback for military exercises disintegrates into an orgy of manic violence when the soldiers go mad as a result of having eaten ergot-poisoned flour given to them by the matriarch of the wheat farm, Lillian Dawson. Even before this mayhem erupts, the play's burlesque comedy fractures the integrity of the military uniform by subverting its sartorial codes. Sergeant Collins, who by his own admission joined the army not out of any sense of patriotic duty but because the coal mines closed down,

Figure 7.5 Mrs Dawson examines the armoury of cricket
Inside the Island, Nimrod Theatre, 1980
Photo: Peter Holderness

provides the most obvious butt for visual satire, especially when the insignia of his authority is undercut by a mere accessory – a sock puppet he dons in a bumbling effort to entertain Mrs Dawson's adolescent daughter, Susan. Private Higgs, the weakling stumbling under a bag of flour while taunted by the workmen, is also part of a deliberately composed series of images that deflate the heroic status of the soldier figure and expose the "latent hostility and aggression" masked as "bonhomie" by the mateship myth (Kelly, "Lest We Forget" 107). A closer look at the equipment assembled for the cricket game is illuminating in this respect. Featured is a protector, which Mrs Dawson aptly labels a "piece of masculine boasting" (61), after poking at it with her umbrella in puzzlement for some time. More than just a humorous gag, the protector suggests the competitive violence which underpins a number of sports in phallocentric culture, and which, particularly in cricket, is disguised by obsessive rituals and dress codes. The play makes a further point by clothing its players in khaki shorts and singlets instead of the customary whites which have functioned for centuries in far-flung reaches of the British empire to signal/produce gentlemanly demeanour and good sportsmanship (read "civilized" values) in this quintessentially colonial game. The soldiers' attire is of course partly a mark of disrespect for the Anglophile Mrs Dawson and the imperial power she represents, but it also underscores the links between the battlefield and the sports arena as testing grounds of national and imperial identities.[7] More disturbingly, the military garb presages the devolution of the cricket match into a brutal and bloody battle that turns the killing glance of the soldiers towards women, children and ultimately themselves while the colonizer retires to England relatively unscathed.

The fabrics of the Anzac myth disintegrate completely in the second half of *Inside the Island* as the recruits' clothes become sullied by acts of rape, murder, and self-mutilation, and the aggressive homoeroticism repressed or displaced in other Australian war narratives clearly emerges in images of soldiers dancing together in a Dionysian frenzy. But the play's particular strength lies in an ability to conjure the pain of a number of imperialist wars while eliding the fate of the tortured soldiers with that of the Aborigines whose camp ground was usurped some decades beforehand to build the cricket pitch. The soldier's uniforms, dusty and white with contaminated flour, play a crucial role in establishing Aboriginal spirits as part of this text's representational field by recalling what Kelly has labelled that "quintessentially Australian colonial method of land clearance" – poisoning ("Apocalypse" 73). That some soldiers' hands and feet turn black suggests further resonances between their horrific experiences and the genocide of Aboriginal peoples. In the nightmarish vision that ensues as these hybridized spirit-like figures wander despairingly over the blazing landscape, boundaries between black and white, victor and vanquished, civilized and savage, are blurred in a genuine post-colonial moment which ruptures the colonizer/colonized binary and sketches out the trajectories of racial and class violence. After such a vivid apocalyptic moment, it is impossible to reconstruct images of the military from the Anzac template alone. The play underlines this point in a final tableau which extends the idea of the soldier-puppet through the dazed figure of the Sergeant, who, in a soiled uniform with socks covering his diseased hands, sits alone on a charred bench, staring at the carnage.

While *Inside the Island* relocates the killing fields of Europe (and Vietnam) firmly in our own backyard, Nowra's earlier play, *Visions* (1978), enacts the tale of Australia's colonial history somewhat more elliptically. Set in Paraguay in the 1860s, this text details the catastrophic effects of cultural imperialism when Madame Lynch, a Parisian courtesan married to President Lopez, determines to impose her version of "civilized" culture on the country. The play, quite specific in its construction of costume as a colonizing tool, presents the magnificently attired Lynch as "dressed to kill" in more ways than one. Put simply, she sets out to refurbish Paraguay's unpretentious wardrobe with Parisian *haute couture*. But Nowra is just as concerned to intervene in the processes of imperialism as to locate them; hence, as the superstructure for domination is put in place through a series of "cultural" events and military maneuvers, so too are the mechanisms of subversion. Notably, Lynch's concept of refined European entertainment, the *bal masqué*, devolves into Latin-American street carnival, making her own gown look somewhat ridiculous when she is obliged to dance with a local militia man dressed as a seven-foot rabbit. This abrogation of the privilege of European costume/culture and its subsequent appropriation to fit marginalized local experience parallels what Ashcroft, Griffiths and Tiffin define in *The Empire Writes Back* as the characteristic linguistic strategies of post-colonial literatures (38).

Carnivalesque disruptions of Lynch's sartorial power redouble as the play progresses and her obsession with clothes proves not only selfish and stupid but self-destructive. Ironically, only the *bal masqué* costumes get packed when Lynch and Lopez flee the city in panic as their military adversaries close in. Although we never actually see what happens to her finery, the mix up of luggage wagons adumbrates what Lynch most abhors: the spectacle of "those barbarians parading around in [her] clothes" (49). Even her attempt to maintain a thin veneer of "civilization" by staging a play in the swamps to lift the troops' morale is undercut. With solely the *bal masqué* wardrobe to dress the actors from, the performance is inevitably coded as a burlesque circus featuring sword-swallowers, acrobats, strongmen and jugglers, and of course the colonized Juana (standing by metaphorical extension for the country itself) as the mouthpiece/puppet of the colonizer. As a vision of Paraguay's future should the Lynch-Lopez coalition win, this anti-masque not only exposes Lynch's quest to bring culture to the "barbarians" as a not-so-elegant farce but also replays the tropologies

Figure 7.6 "Dressed to Kill": Madame Lynch with maid and Lopez's sisters
Visions, Paris Company, 1978
Photo: Branco Gaica, Currency Press

of the new world vision enacted in the masque scenes of *The Tempest*.[8] What Lynch doesn't sufficiently attend to, here and throughout the action, is costume's potential for subversion: the paradox of its specificity *and* versatility make it an extremely unstable power base because it threatens to become absurd when unsuited to the occasion, and/or counteractive if seized by the colonized and worn differently. Nor does she realize that her power (like Prospero's) is inherently theatrical: having the key to the costume cupboard gives her some control over representation but by no means accounts for the complex negotiations that occur between actors, audiences and the *mise-en-scène*.

Working through Pierre Macherey's theories of literary production, Kelly describes Nowra's theatre as making explicit the idea of the text as a "haunted work" which leads back to the histories informing it ("Nowra" 51–52). For the purposes of this analysis, it is possible to regard clothes as haunting devices that aid a text's counter-discursivity. In such a model, rather than simply indicating a reality which might be decoded in structuralist terms, the warp and weft of costume functions as the woven surface on which are negotiated signifiers of past and present, of person and place, and by implication, of self and other. The colonial dresses and uniforms which visit Nowra's work, and which in later plays like *The Golden Age* (1985) carry strong resonances of convictism,[9] can thus be seen to make visible the absences implied in dominant constructions of (military) history. Nowra's real iconoclastic achievement is a theatre that enacts conflicting visions of national identity rather than simply buttressing well-worn mythologies.

IMPERIAL PATRIARCHY AND GENDER DIFFERENCE

Though less remarked upon, a number of plays by Australian women show a similar concern to intervene in the discourses of imperialism, and, in particular, to insert the dimension of gender more fully into accounts of colonial experience. Early twentieth-century women's texts approach this subject ambivalently, at once enacting complicity with, and resistance to, the hegemonic practices of imperial patriarchy. Henrietta Drake-Brockman's *Men Without Wives* (1938) is a case in point, for it attempts to expose the oppressions and hardships women endure in the settler situation, but clearly stresses their reproductive obligations to empire and displaces anxieties about male/female relationships onto the landscape and/or the indigenous other. In this text, the chief contrast between the two women who face the challenge of settling the outback finds pictorial representation in initial images of their costumes: Ma Bates, the hardened bushwoman, wears the stockman's hat, shirt and trousers while Mrs Abbott, newly arrived from the city, sports a series of elegant, if unsuitable, dress ensembles. Although Ma Bates' costume confers some degree of authority thus allowing her access to the mateship circle, the play takes pains to militate against the masculinizing effects of this "trousers role" and, by establishing that she doesn't in fact "wear the pants," to dissipate the threat that the cross-dressed woman poses. Despite her attire, or perhaps even because of it, Ma fits the stereotype of the idealized bushwoman, rough and tough on the exterior but feminine at heart, as indicated when one of the men offers her a cigarette: "What d'yer take me for? I ain't one of yer flash barmaids. Joe, he don't fancy women what smokes. Unladylike, he calls it!" (5). Visual emphasis on Ma and her daughters sewing reinforces her deftness at feminine tasks and, by dint of metatheatrical reference to costume construction, suggests that her masculine behaviour is indeed role-play. A preoccupation with dressmaking also characterizes Mrs Abbott, and although her skill is described as a "stuckup bit of play-acting" (29), this "metaphor of the woman as 'actress'" actually links the destinies of the two women (Dunstone, "Another Planet" 72). That Mrs Abbott's masquerade is marginalized by both sexes while Ma's is not suggests a widespread anxiety about women whose disruptive potential is located not so much in an ability to usurp masculine power but to feminize its sites of construction. Hence the implied criticism in the comment: "She's got lots of time to get dolled up for yarding and branding. Or for killing. Dressed fit to kill, eh?" (28). The suggestion that Mrs Abbott won't go far in the outback until she learns better dress sense is something of a reprimand, but what is really at stake in the play as a whole is the economic and cultural survival of the (male) settler, and, by extension, of the constitutive bases of imperialism itself, for without woman's proper sexual and social contribution, the integrity of the colonizing enterprise risks being undermined by that ultimate threat: miscegenation. The moral and physical decay seen to accompany such hybridization is potently imaged in Ma's warning that without wives white men in this harsh and forbidding environment "go black within twenty years" (62). Women's overtly constructed costumes (roles) therefore function to save men's skins ("real" costumes), and the female body becomes the physical terrain on which colonial expansion is mapped symbolically and literally through reproduction of the imperial self. Within this paradigm, a woman needs one crucial item which is conspicuously absent from the wardrobes of both the cross-dressed insider and the fashion-conscious outsider in *Men Without Wives*: a maternity dress. Ma Bates can get away with her trousers role because she has already produced several offspring; Mrs Abbott, the play suggests, had better get out her scissors and start sewing a bit more sensibly.

The fate of the woman who doesn't learn to adequately manipulate the many costumes she must wear is poignantly expressed in Betty Roland's *The Touch of Silk* (1928), which details the plight of a young Parisian war-bride who, having married an Australian soldier, finds herself stranded in an outback community in the 1920s. In its first act, set in a drapery and millinery department, the play quickly establishes the importance of clothing as a focus for social interaction among the townswomen while at the same time highlighting its seductive appeal to men. Costume also becomes a site of contestation when the Frenchwoman, Jeanne, commits a serious faux pas by suggesting that her mother-in-law's rose-bedecked hat would look better trimmed with a feather. This contrast between European *chic* and Australian *démodé*, while making visible the central oppositions of the narrative, reveals more than a hint of the cultural cringe that Michael Gow investigates in his 1987 play, *Europe*. Jeanne's status as a disruptive outsider is clearly coded by a certain panache about the way she wears her clothes, a superior appreciation of fine fabrics, and, once again, by the significant absence of a maternity dress. That she constructs her femininity through an aesthetic sexuality rather than through motherhood (or spinsterhood) causes considerable envy and anxiety and is deemed inappropriate for a bush town that defines itself in opposition to the metropolitan centres of Australia, and, beyond that, of Europe. Tragedy seems almost inevitable when, during a devastating drought, Jeanne spends her last six pounds on silk lingerie instead of helping her husband, Jim, to save their farm, thus precipitating the chain of events that leads to his manslaughter of the salesman who tempted her to such wilful extravagance. In the end, sadly, Jeanne becomes the sacrificial victim who must pay for her (sartorial) excesses by taking on the mantle of the adulteress so that Jim, thereby provided with an acceptable excuse for his actions, can be released from jail. Although condemning the mean-spiritedness of a community which marginalizes difference in an effort to displace internal tensions onto an external other, this text, in its depiction of the relationship between Jeanne and Jim (Europe and Australia), reveals a deep ambivalence towards the outsider and tends to specify gender as the cause of the split subjectivities that mark post-colonial identity. As Phillip Parsons points out, Jeanne (Europe) is "the wound [Jim] carries within him," the cause of his shell-shock which, though imaged in terms of war, "is the symbolic statement of the divided self" (xv). The illicit and corruptive "touch of silk" is thus Jeanne herself; like the "black velvet" of the Aboriginal woman, her destabilizing sexual/cultural alterity cannot be tolerated by an insular and misogynist colonial culture.[10]

A number of contemporary women playwrights countervail the historical strictures of female costumes through non-naturalistic styles of theatre that expose the constructedness of all roles. A recent example is Alma De Groen's award-winning play *The Rivers of China* (1987), which figures androgyny – iconized firstly by an unsexed body in bandages and then by the gender-neutral hospital gown – as the "impossible referent" that calls into question relationships between gender, costume, and imperialism, in a narrative about the Frankensteinian reconstruction of a modern-day Sydney man infused with the mind and spirit of colonial writer, Katherine

Mansfield. A more common strategy has been to focus on the theatricality of costume itself, a tack that encourages the disruptive potential of role-playing and constructs a wardrobe which defines female identity as fluid, adaptable, and discursive, restlessly seeking a home within the dislocations of marginality but never quite becoming anchored. Dorothy Hewett's drama is exemplary in this respect, not only because of her focus on the multiple roles women play in society, but also because she frequently utilizes theatre as a self-reflexive art form that draws attention to the ideological assumptions which traverse representation itself.

Among her works, *The Man From Mukinupin* (1979) concerns itself most directly with our legacy of imperialism. Set around the period of the First World War in a "wheatbelt town east of the rabbit proof fence" (4), the play masquerades as a lighthearted romantic musical but gradually strips itself of that guise while penetrating the respectable veneer of a community that has long obscured from its collective memory an unpalatable history: the genocide of its Aboriginal peoples. Hewett foregrounds costume on a number of levels. Firstly, cliched dress functions as a signifier of out-rageous theatricality: witness the fashionable robes of the ageing Shakespearian diva, Mercy Montebello; the black dress and veil of the Dickensian Widow Tuesday; the ever-opening raincoat of the town Flasher; or the colourful garments of the Misses Hummer, presenters of the play and themselves remnants of a bygone era of showbiz. The text divides its characters into two distinct groups: the daytime townspeople, synonymous with white Australian society; and the nighttime revellers, aligned with the oppressed Aboriginal culture. Costume is used to signal whether a character belongs to the light or the dark side of town and to distinguish between the two groups since both are played by the same actors. This doubling technique sets up an immediate paradox: despite the differences signified by their clothes, once two characters are introduced by the same actor, each carries traces of the other throughout the action, a process which thwarts the formation of an unproblematically delineated character. Such strategies can be linked, once again, to Bhabha's idea of the ambivalence of the colonial subject: the performance produces characters which are "less than one and double" (103), which is to say that represent-ing one always signifies the other's partial presence in both senses of the term.

An emphasis on dressing and undressing on stage further historicizes costume and alienates it from the body even while underlining the arbitrary meanings assigned to certain styles or garments. In Brechtian terms these strategies outline how gender is mapped across the theatrical subject through socio-cultural inscriptions on the performing body.[11] Polly Perkins, for example, is deemed to have become a woman when Miss Clarry, town dressmaker and ex-wardrobe mistress, overtly constructs the teenager's new status by dressing her up in a "beaded pink georgette" with

Figure 7.7 The dressing-up of "Pretty Polly Perkins"
The Man from Mukinupin, Royal Queensland Theatre Company, 1989
Photo: Fiora Sacco

a lengthened hem (18). Hewett's parodic treatment of the "fabrications" of theatricality is not merely humorous but also tactical. Notably, the symbology invoked in the dressing up of "pretty Polly Perkins" is questioned when, in a parallel scene, Touch of the Tar, her unacknowledged half-caste sister and sole survivor of the Aboriginal massacre, seizes the costume of the colonizer and, looking just like Polly (the parts are doubled), sashays down the streets of Mukinupin, all "dressed up to kill" (92). The threat of miscegenation is here potently imaged through Touch of the Tar's mimicry. Later when she marries Harry Tuesday, shell-shocked war hero and twin brother of Polly's sweetheart, Jack, her wedding ceremony foreshadows her sister's but undercuts the ostentatious display of the approved sacrament with simple bush rites shaped from the (mis)appropriated lines of *The Tempest*. This scene enacts another type of anti-masque which fractures the utopian vision of its prototype through the insistent presence of racial alterity, and also undermines the canonical status of Shakespeare's text by a process of dispersive citation. Hence Hewett's costumes, like Nowra's, can be viewed as "haunted" or shadowed by multiple ghosts, not least of which are those passed on through theatrical traditions themselves.

In drawing attention to its own sites of enunciation, *The Man from Mukinupin* presents costume as ideologically constructed and therefore capable of being changed. That theatre provides such sites of intervention is potently illustrated when, during a performance of "The Strangling of Desdemona," Jack leaps on stage screaming "Murder, bloody murder" and knocks down Othello, evoking a standing ovation from the townspeople (29). The play's metatheatricality resists the textual closures of imperial (stage) history and enacts what Bill Dunstone calls a "crisis in reception" that problematizes the audience's role in the production of meaning because a split gaze is required to follow the many overlapping images ("Performance and Difference" 79). And if the text bespeaks a need for reconciliation between the feminine and the masculine, the light and the dark, the Aborigines and white Australians, it also offers performance as a means to rapprochement. "In the theatre," as Miss Clarry says with tape measure and pins in hand, "everything is possible" (19).

CONTEMPORARY ABORIGINAL THEATRE AND THE COSTUMES OF SURVIVAL

Aboriginal theatre, developed over the past two decades, poses the Australian stage's most trenchant challenge to the hegemony of imperialism. Prominent on the political agenda of this drama is a concern to problematize axiomatic ways of viewing the Aborigines and hence to intervene in object-signifying processes that have circumscribed representations of native peoples in our culture since "history awarded semiotic control to the invaders" (Goldie 60). Like recent feminist works, this theatre aims to expose the ways in which clothing has been mobilized in the interests of the powerful and to sketch its strategic possibilities in decolonizing marginalized cultures. A number of Aboriginal plays first bring costume into focus by scrutinizing its function at the moment of invasion. Robert Merritt's *The Cake Man* (1975) makes an explicit point of showing how images of the indigene have been captured and contained by the imperial gaze when the protagonist, a tribal Black who has been shot, awakens and literally steps into the shoes of a stereotype after he discovers a pile of European clothes, and eventually, with some comic experimentation, puts them on to re-name himself "[t]he Australian Aborigine . . . made in England" (12). The subsequent narrative details just what becomes of this culturally commodified tourist attraction in the modern era. Whereas Merritt makes his point through the indigene's self-parody, Jack Davis, Australia's best known Aboriginal playwright, levels his satire directly at the colonizer. In *Kullark* (1979), a play which spans 150 years of Aboriginal history, the whites' "civilizing" gesture of clothing the natives is presented as a farce when a botanist comes away from first contact looking decidedly *outré* in his underwear after he is forced to offer his shirt and trousers to a group of Aborigines. At the same time, the affective power of this costume is clearly recognized through the fear and mistrust it evokes in one of the Aboriginal woman. In each play, European clothing does not bring the particular level of civility (read subjection) desired by the invader but functions as a wayward signifier which might provoke white audiences to shift their perspectives – to see themselves as the other of their others.

In a further subversive maneuver, *Kullark* encodes the (near) naked body of the Aborigine as a costume which evokes fear and desire in the colonizers who, determined to militate against the threat of racial difference, decapitate the renegade Black, Yagan, and skin him to souvenir his tribal markings. The stripping metaphor implied here suggests that the mutilated black body functions for the whites as a fetishized object and a focus for racial paranoia. Significantly, Yagan's mutilation is detailed (by a white man) not enacted, so while exposing the colonizers' barbarity on a narrative level, the play avoids the trap of voyeurism. What we do see on stage represents the ritually marked body quite differently: as a theatrical costume which potently images elements of a recuperated indigenous culture. This motif is fully developed in Davis' *The Dreamers* (1982) through the recurring visits of a tribal dancer who, by permeating the play's otherwise naturalistic account of a modern-day urban family, grounds the action firmly in Aboriginal history and epistemology through his links with the Dreamtime, "the constant supplementary signified of all Aboriginal narrative" (Muecke 98). Davis amplifies the decolonizing power of the body's ritualized costumes in *No Sugar* (1985) through a corroboree that gives Billy, the black "politjman," the opportunity to shed his uniform, de-sign his body with *wilgi*,[12] and join in a communal ceremony, thus transgressing the tracker/informant roles assigned to him within the hierarchical structures of the Aboriginal mission.[13] In a recent production in Perth, the visual impact of this scene was strengthened when, before the dust of the corroboree ground had settled, Mr Neville, Chief Protector of Aborigines, walked tentatively across it in a three-piece suit that marked his presence as incongruous, invasive and ultimately illegitimate. Later, the

Figure 7.8 Ritually marked body of the Aboriginal Dancer
The Dreamers, National Theatre Company, 1983
Photo: Geoffrey Lovell

civilizing intent of government-supplied clothing was further subverted when during the Australia Day celebrations staged especially for Neville's inspectional visit, the natives disrupted the spectacle (presented as a military-style drill) by singing their own version of the national anthem.

Resisting the colonizer's clothes is an ongoing project for many of Davis' Aboriginal characters, and the guise of the co-opted tracker is exposed as but one of the characteristic costumes imposed upon Blacks by white socio-legal systems. Equally disempowering is the "cleanliness and godliness" of the uniforms provided by the mission establishments to which Aboriginal families in *No Sugar* and *Kullark* are forcefully relocated. Both texts' emphasis on the mission as a place which uses clothing to discipline and sanitize the body of the indigene points to the intersecting oppressions of Christianity, Western government, and imperial medicine. It is not surprising, then, that the garb of the hospital patient, although not explicitly iconized, haunts Davis' works, notably in *The Dreamers* where Uncle Worru seems marked for death from the moment he first enters the corridors of the white hospital, an institution which is troped as an anathema to the well being of Aboriginal culture.[14] Condemnation of the black body's annexation by the anatomizing gaze of medical science is paralleled in Aboriginal theatre by a critical focus on the actual physical capture and containment of the racial other, imaged in that most prominent of colonial costumes in Australia: the prisoner's uniform. As a signifier of colonization, the incarcerated convict has multiple associations with imperialism in this country, but the specific links between imprisonment and subjugation of indigenous peoples should by now be inscribed in our psyches since the prolonged inquiries of the late 1980s into Black deaths in custody and recent charges of institutionalized racism in the police forces of most states. In performance texts, an important sartorial response to this oppression has been to mobilize the symbolic agency of the Aboriginal flag by fabricating costumes that foreground its black, red, and gold markings, or, more specifically, by featuring Aborigines dressed in land-rights T-shirts to mark the stage as a politically charged space. A case in point was the 1988 performance of Davis' *The First Born* trilogy[15] which made an express visual protest against two hundred years of white imperialism by dressing its actors in T-shirts inscribed with the two main counter-bicentennial slogans: "Don't celebrate '88" and "We survived."

The costumes of survival for the contemporary Aborigine are nowhere more vividly drawn than in Jimmy Chi's hit musical *Bran Nue Dae* (1990). With a great deal of parodic humour and incisive social comment, the play charts a simple love story and picaresque road-movie style search for an Aboriginal homeland in the melting pot of Australian culture. Chi, who claims Aboriginal, Chinese, Japanese, and European ancestry, proposes a hybridized vision of life and theatre in general, and of post-colonial identity in particular. The play's emphasis on theatricality not only claims the stage

126

as a crucial space for representing Aboriginal subjectivities but also allows for the effective subversion of imperial authority through the visual excesses of the carnivalesque, here mobilized primarily in opposition to the proselytizing activities of the church and the multiple oppressions of the law. First in line for satirical treatment is the head of the Perth mission school, Father Benedictus, who, while upbraiding the boys for theft and gluttony after they break into the school tuckshop, cuts a ridiculous, larger than life figure in his platform shoes, overall mitre, and cassock embroidered with cherry ripe bars. Benedictus' expulsion of Willie from the "Garden of Eden" proves to be an ironic release for the young Aboriginal protagonist who then undertakes an epic journey north to his homeland in the company of his irascible Uncle Tadpole and two "white" hippies, Marijuana Annie and Slippery. The high points of the journey are iconized in further sartorial subversions, notably when Tadpole "whites up" his face and joins a white-gloved chorus in a vigorous song and dance routine that mimics a city traffic policeman, and, more pointedly, that exceptionally racist theatrical practice: the (black and white) minstrel show. Shortly afterwards, white judicial systems are again the butt of satire as the travellers encounter two khaki-clad northern cops, played by Aborigines in shorts and bare feet with ill-fitting shirts stretched over huge paunches. The authority of these uniforms thus abrogated, they are quickly commandeered by the marginalized for additional comic effects when the police do a cakewalk style strut through the chorus, and while the more ominous aspects of incarceration are never entirely absent from this scene, it is presented as a ritual initiation into Aboriginal culture and one of its common vicissitudes. A final road-stop routine features tribal Blacks who appear in loincloths for the ritual goanna hunt. Although these costumes mark the travellers' entry into Aboriginal territory, they offer less an authentic or essentialized concept of Black identity than a recognition, through self-conscious parody, of the ways in which Aborigines have been looked at in the discourses of theatre, film, and especially, tourism.

The multi-racial town of Broome which is the travellers' destination shows that contemporary Aboriginality wears many guises. Willie's young sweetheart, Rosie, lead singer in a country and western band, proves to be literally a knockout when her dazzling white and silver outfit causes him to fall in a faint. Other costumes appropriated from white culture are similarly celebrated *and* lampooned when a congregation of Pentecostals led by Willie's mother, Theresa, arrives on the scene to shrive the community of its sins. In the course of the enraptured singing, dancing, and confessing that follows, it is revealed that almost everyone hides a "black" secret: Tadpole is Theresa's estranged husband and therefore Willie's father, Marijuana Annie has Aboriginal blood that she hasn't acknowledged, and Slippery is the son of Theresa and none other than Benedictus. This highly theatricalized scene re-tropes the sin of miscegenation as a sin of omission in so far as Aboriginal identities have either been denied or repressed in some manner by the institutional costumes of imperialism. As a kind of "penance," the play then makes a point of celebrating a "bran nue dae" of reconciliation with further transgressive visual images: Theresa goes off with Tadpole and returns with her religious habit dishevelled after their re-union, Willie and Rosie get off their gear behind the mound to consummate their love, and Slippery puts on a land-rights T-shirt while the chorus sings "let's multiply the Aboriginal race" (77). It only remains for Benedictus to re-enter, literally cut down to size in a more demure cassock, and to admit his part in the story of hybridization before conducting the final communion rite by distributing the coveted cherry ripes of the first scene to all and sundry, including the audience.

Aided and abetted by the rhetorical power of clothes, Chi thus manages, through a rather clever sleight of hand, to situate a strong vision of harmony within both Aboriginal performance culture and the very Christian ethos that he has undermined. This ambivalent discursive emplacement is less a weakness than a testimony to the creative "contamination" which is, I have argued, one of the major energizing forces in our contemporary theatre. Ultimately Chi's text enacts its tensions and

Figure 7.9 Chorus song and dance
Bran Nue Dae, Melbourne Theatre Company, 1993
Photo: Jeff Busby

contradictions with untrammelled optimism for a future that embraces Aboriginality itself, however it might be defined, as an essential and ideologically enabling costume for the wardrobe of all colonized Australians. In this hope, utopian though it may be, *Bran Nue Dae* is indeed "a play to ease the pain."[16]

NOTES

1 Adapted from the title of Eve Kosofsky Sedgwick's book, *The Epistemology of the Closet*.

2 Griffiths discusses in depth how representations of Caliban on the British stage were inflected by imperialism.

3 A stripping metaphor is also implied here. Anthropologists assert that in the pre-colonial era the connotations of "going native" were much less loaded: Western traders and travellers simply adopted local clothes for comfort in tropical countries (Von Ehrenfels 399).

4 I use "digger" and "Anzac" interchangeably in this discussion although the former suggests more a legendary construction than the figure who actually participated in the particular battle at Gallipoli that led to naming Anzac Day as an important time of remembrance.

5 Playful rather than destructive mischief.

6 See Garber for an interesting discussion of how crises of nationalism and sexuality are troped on the transvestite figure in David Henry Hwang's *M. Butterfly* (234–66).

7 Sporting uniforms have also played a key role in packaging male Australian identities at home and abroad. For a detailed account of the role of sport in Australian drama, see Fotheringham.

8 David Malouf's *Blood Relations* (1987) enacts an even more direct Australian reworking of *The Tempest*'s masque in a carnivalesque magic show layered with irony and apocalyptic overtones. Prospero's vision of the fruition of marriage is disrupted firstly by a dance which is featured as homoerotic display and then by a recitation of Caliban's "This island's mine . . . " speech by the Aboriginal character.

9 *The Golden Age*, like all of Nowra's works, repays a sartorial reading. The traumas that the lost tribe of convicts endure at the hands of "civilization" can be traced not only to the differences their language encodes but also to their inability to fathom complicated dress etiquette. In addition, their humiliation and ultimate demise are expressed through costume codes as they are forced to discard their colorfully patchworked forest rags to become fettered in the uniforms of the lunatic asylum. On another level, the elision of convict and soldier uniforms is effected when the forest people's incarceration is paralleled by images of Francis' confinement in a European prison during the war.

10 Sandra Clark argues that love of fine clothing links two of the most fruitful themes of misogyny: women's lustful natures and their economic extravagance (157).

11 For this analysis, I am indebted to Elin Diamond's excellent work on reappropriating Brechtian theory for a theatre-specific feminist criticism.

12 Specially prepared paint for ceremonies.

13 For further discussion of the functions of the dancer and the dance in contemporary Aboriginal drama, see Gilbert.

14 Written in consultation with Davis, Sally Morgan's *Sistergirl* (1992) does feature

the hospital gown as a marker of colonization while at the same time subverting its authority through parody.

15 Composed of *No Sugar, The Dreamers*, and *Barungin* (1988), the latter written specifically as a bicentennial project about Black deaths in custody.

16 As advertised in the program notes.

WORKS CITED

Ashcroft, W. D. "Intersecting Marginalities: Post-colonialism and Feminism." *Kunapipi* XI.2 (1989): 23–35.

Ashcroft, Bill, Gareth Griffiths, and Helen Tiffin. *The Empire Writes Back: Theory and Practice in Post-Colonial Literatures.* London: Routledge, 1989.

Barthes, Roland. *The Responsibility of Forms: Critical Essays on Music, Art, and Representation.* Trans. Richard Howard. New York: Hill & Wang, 1985.

———. *The Rustle of Language.* Trans. Richard Howard. Oxford: Basil Blackwell, 1986.

Bhabha, Homi, K. "Signs Taken For Wonders: Questions of Ambivalence and Authority Under a Tree Outside Delhi, May 1817." *Europe and Its Others.* Ed. Francis Barker *et al.* Colchester: Essex University Press, 1985. 89–106.

Brydon, Diana. "The White Inuit Speaks: Contamination as Literary Strategy." *Past the Last Post: Theorizing Post Colonialism and Post Modernism.* Ed. Ian Adam and Helen Tiffin. Calgary: Calgary University Press, 1990. 191–203.

Chi, Jimmy and Kuckles. *Bran Nue Dae.* Sydney: Currency, 1991.

Clark, Sandra. "*Hic Mulier, Haec Vir*, and the Controversy over Masculine Women." *Studies in Philology* 82.1 (1985): 157–83.

Davis, Jack. *Kullark* and *The Dreamers.* Sydney: Currency, 1984. Revised edn.

———. *No Sugar.* Sydney: Currency, 1986.

———. *Barungin.* Sydney: Currency, 1989.

De Groen, Alma. *The Rivers of China.* Sydney: Currency, 1988.

Diamond, Elin. "Brechtian Theory/Feminist Theory: Towards a Gestic Feminist Criticism." *The Drama Review* 32.1 (1988): 82–95.

Drake-Brockman, H. *Men Without Wives.* Sydney: Angus & Robertson, 1955.

Dunstone, Bill. "'Another Planet': Landscape as Metaphor in Western Australian Theatre." *European Relations: Essays for Helen Watson-Williams.* Ed. Bruce Bennett and John Hay. Perth: Centre for Studies in Australian Literature, 1985. 67–79.

———. "Performance and Difference in Dorothy Hewett's *The Man From Mukinupin.*" *New Literatures Review* 19 (1990): 72–81.

Fotheringham, Richard. *Sport in Australian Drama.* Melbourne: Cambridge University Press, 1992.

Gaines, Jane. "Costume and Narrative: How Dress Tells the Woman's Story." *Fabrications: Costume and the Female Body.* Ed. Jane Gaines and Charlotte Herzog. New York: Routledge, 1990: 180–211.

Garber, Marjorie. *Vested Interests: Cross-Dressing and Cultural Anxiety.* New York: Routledge, 1992.

George, Rob. *Sandy Lee Live at Nui Dat.* Sydney: Currency, 1983.

Gilbert, Helen. "The Dance as Text in Contemporary Australian Drama: Movement and Resistance Politics." *ARIEL: A Review of International English Literature* 23.1 (1992): 133–47.

Goldie, Terry. "Signifier Resignified: Aborigines in Australian Literature." *Kunapipi* X.1/2 (1988): 59–75.

Gow, Michael. *Europe* and *On Top of the World.* Sydney: Currency, 1987.

Griffiths, Trevor R. "'This Island's Mine': Caliban and Colonialism." *The Yearbook of English Studies* 13 (1983): 138–80.

Hewett, Dorothy. *The Man From Mukinupin*. Sydney: Currency, 1979.

Interview: Louis Nowra, Stephen Sewell and Neil Armfield talk to Jeremy Ridgman. *Australasian Drama Studies* 1.2 (1983): 105–23.

Kelly, Veronica. "A Mirror for Australia: Louis Nowra's Emblematic Theatre." *Southerly* 41 (1981): 431–58.

———. "Apocalypse and After: Historical Visions in Some Recent Australian Drama." *Kunapipi* IX.3 (1987): 68–78.

———. "Lest We Forget: Louis Nowra's *Inside the Island*." *Louis Nowra*. Ed. Veronica Kelly. Amsterdam: Rodopi, 1987. 99–103.

———. "Louis Nowra." *Post-Colonial English Plays: Commonwealth Drama Since 1960*. Ed. Bruce King. London: Macmillan, 1992. 50–66.

Kroetsch, Robert. "Unhiding the Hidden: Recent Canadian Fiction." *Journal of Canadian Fiction* 3.3 (1974): 43–45.

Lowe, Barry. *Tokyo Rose*. Manuscript, 1989. University of Queensland.

Malouf, David. *Blood Relations*. Sydney: Currency, 1988.

McCallum, John. "The World Outside: Cosmopolitanism in the plays of Nowra and Sewell." *Meanjin* 43.2 (1984): 286–96.

Merritt, Robert J. *The Cake Man*. Sydney: Currency, 1978.

Morgan, Sally. *Sistergirl*. Dir. Andrew Ross. Arts Theatre, Adelaide. 17 March 1992.

Muecke, Stephen. "Ideology Re-iterated: The Uses of Aboriginal Oral Narrative." *Southern Review* 16.1 (1983): 86–101.

Nowra, Louis. *Visions*. Sydney: Currency, 1979.

———. *Inside the Island* and *The Precious Woman*. Sydney: Currency, 1981.

———. *The Golden Age*. Sydney: Currency, 1985.

Parsons Phillip. Introduction. *The Touch of Silk* and *Granite Peak*. By Betty Roland. Sydney: Currency, 1988.

Roland, Betty. *The Touch of Silk* and *Granite Peak*. Sydney: Currency, 1988.

Shakespeare, William. *The Tempest*. Ed. Stephen Orgel. Oxford: Oxford University Press, 1987.

Shearer, Jill. *Shimada*. Sydney: Currency, 1989.

Stephensen, P. R. *The Foundations of Culture in Australia: An Essay Towards National Self Respect*. Sydney: W. J. Miles, 1936.

Tiffin, Helen. "Post-Colonial Literatures and Counter-Discourse." *Kunapipi* IX.3 (1987): 17–34.

Von Ehrenfels, U. R. "Clothing and Power Abuse." *The Fabrics of Culture: The Anthropology of Clothing and Adornment*. Ed. Justine M. Cordwell and Ronald A. Schwarz. The Hague: Mouton, 1979. 399–403.

White, Richard. *Inventing Australia: Images and Identity 1688–1980*. Sydney: Allen & Unwin, 1981.

White, Susan. "Male Bonding, Hollywood Orientalism, and the Repression of the Feminine in Kubrick's *Full Metal Jacket*." *Arizona Quarterly* 44.3 (1988): 120–44.

8

REPRESENTING EMPIRE

Class, Culture, and the Popular Theatre in the Nineteenth Century

Michael Hays

The work of discovering colonial and imperialist moments in the literary products of nineteenth-century Europe and America has gone on for some time now, but with the appearance of Edward W. Said's powerful book, *Culture and Imperialism*, a larger conceptual scope and greater obligations have been allotted the critic who would engage in this enterprise. The question should no longer be *whether* there are such moments, but, rather, how these moments are fundamental to the historical development of imperialist discourse and to the production of Western culture in general, and, more importantly, how the retelling of this tale of "literary" production can move beyond merely providing further evidence of western imperialism and cultural hegemony to become a means of understanding how, for example, British imperial culture acquired its authority, and the power to impose itself both at home and in world at large.

As Said demonstrates, the best way to come to grips with these problems is to return to the cultural archive (Said's primary concern is novel and narrative fiction in the nineteenth century) to see what story it can tell us about the ways in which supposedly autonomous works of art participate in the labor of elaborating and consolidating the practice of empire by fixing and naturalizing the spatial as well as social relations that empower the imperial center, connecting it to and defining the priorities that regulate other, subordinate peoples and places. This essay is intended as a small contribution to the task that Said has so impressively set out for his readers. If I begin by reassembling some of the material from his book it is both to signal my debt to his text and to mark off the space in which this essay aims to insert a slightly different construction of the history of imperial culture in England, one which suggests that its presence is not quite so pervasive and its development less uniform than *Culture and Imperialism* seeks to claim.

The story I will sketch here highlights the difference between the triumphant tale of imperial sway Said locates in the (middle class) fiction of the nineteenth century and the somewhat different and disruptive history that emerges from a consideration of the popular theatre of the age. For it was not only the space and the voice of the colonial other that had to be elided or usurped in order to stage the discourse of empire, the political and cultural imagination of the lower classes had to be captured and made to work for the empire as well. As I will show here, traces of this process can readily be found in the cultural struggle that pitted the novel and "literature" against the popular theatre and drama early in the century. If, as Said suggests, the discourse of empire pervades the art of the end of the century, this becomes possible only when internal cultural differences in Britain have finally been submerged in a unifying fantasy of the imperial adventure that can be staged for all classes to enjoy.

As I suggested earlier, Said sets aside the tendency to hunt out occasional instances of imperialist nastiness in the otherwise aesthetically fulfilling works of the nineteenth century. He baldly asserts that, by the time Conrad writes *Heart of Darkness*, there is "no use looking for other, non-imperialist alternatives, since the system has simply eliminated them and made them unthinkable. The circularity, the perfect closure of the whole thing is not only aesthetically but also mentally unassailable" (24). Despite his own sense of marginality, and despite his subversive and ironic qualification of the material of his narrative, Conrad can only see the other, that which is "non-European," through the imaginative filter of the imperial enterprise: "Independence was for whites and Europeans, the lesser or subject peoples were to be ruled; science, learning, history emanated from the West" (24).

Much of the remainder of Said's remarkable book documents the ways in which the geographic and human relations redeployed and represented in narrative works produced in nineteenth-century France and England converge with those of science and political economy to erase the possibility of imagining that there could be another way of seeing, an alternative to speaking for as well as about the rest of the world. Already in Jane Austen's *Mansfield Park* (1814) the colonial plantations owned by Sir Thomas are portrayed as a "natural" extension of the Bertram estate at Mansfield Park – the periphery that supplies the center with the money and commodities necessary for its proper functioning.

> Austen here synchronizes domestic with international authority, making it plain that the value associated with such things as ordination, law, and propriety must be grounded firmly in actual rule over and possession of territory . . . . What assures the domestic tranquillity and attractive harmony of one is the productivity and regulated discipline of the other. (87)

But however accurate and well told this tale of the imaginative intertwining of cultural production and imperial practice is, however effectively it gives "voice" to another way of speaking about the cultural condition and function of the novel, it also serves to demonstrate in its own right the principle of narrative exclusion enunciated in the opening pages of Said's text: the power to narrate – and the narrative arising therefrom – can, and inevitably does, block access to other narratives, and to other conditions and practices that may be coextensive with the socio-political, economic, and cultural imperatives that are discovered and defined by his investigation.

Said's assessment is surely correct for the late nineteenth century, but it is too monolithic in its construction of a historically continuous "British culture" – one that from the seventeenth century on is consistent in its operations and in its grasp of the objects it manipulates (52). I do not – cannot – deny that such colonizing spatializations as Said mentions appear earlier, but even as late as the 1860s the order of "British culture" was not quite so firmly and uniformly established as Said implies. Because of the extraordinary breadth of the issues with which he is grappling, and because of his focus on the novel and narrative fiction, he has been obliged to ignore the full dimensions of the *internal* struggle for cultural priority in England – the need to convince all parties that the imperial dispensation was indeed to their benefit – and further to downplay in the nineteenth century itself the way in which this struggle is instantiated in the history and dramaturgy of the popular theatre.

Interestingly enough, a suggestion of this possibility is already implicitly present in his discussion of Austen's *Mansfield Park*. Said points out that when Sir Thomas sets about re-establishing his rule over the space and the inhabitants of the estate, one of his first gestures is to forbid the performance of Kotzebue's *Lovers' Vows* that had been planned in his absence. Sir Thomas also burns all the *unbound* copies of the play found in the house. His action leaves room for us to speculate that a *bound* copy of Kotzebue's play could, presumably, take its place alongside Austen's novels in the library at Mansfield Park. There, both would be available for controlled perusal, subject to Sir Thomas's observation and interpretation, just as the characters in Austen's novel are subject to the narrator's control. The library, the physical locus for readerly knowledge (and interpretation) thus spatializes a new set of relationships. It removes from the hands of others both the task and the materials for either independent or inter-dependent construction of alternative spaces or meanings, and becomes the center of an abstract, binding order in much the way metropolitan England becomes the center of the Empire in Said's description.[1]

On the other hand, the unbound play and its separate "sides" (the individual sheets the performers of Kotzebue's play would have had in order to learn their separate parts – whether at Mansfield Park or in an actual theatre) not only suggest multiple voices and possibilities for the staging of different spaces and interpretations, but bring to mind the many-sided audience and frequently "insubordinate" performance of the lower-class public that attended the theatre,[2] thereby opening a space for the examination of the drama as a vehicle for the dissemination of a culture and politics in England that was not yet fixed within the imperial paradigm.

In other words, at the very moment it effaces the history of popular

134

performance in the name of "literature," Austen's novel reveals the traces of a quite different cultural potential – and provides the impetus for further inquiry about the subversive aspects not only of Kotzebue's play, which at the turn of the century had already been damned in England for its sexual and political frankness,[3] but, more importantly, about the popular theatre and drama in general, an inquiry that would tease out the story of the cultural colonization of the lower classes in England and would expand the story of colonial discourse found in the novels discussed in Said's text.

Of course, this essay is not the place to undertake a full analysis of the theatre and the politics of culture in the last century. My aim here is, rather, first to indicate that other cultural tales than those told by Austen were available early in the century, and, then, to add to Said's discussion of culture and imperialism by offering a supplement regarding the way in which such cultural differences can also be traced later in the popular theatre in England (and elsewhere). I want to argue for the necessity of looking at the emergence of popular drama (primarily melodrama) as a marker of and participant in the politically charged transformation of British and other European societies in the nineteenth century, societies for which the novel, as Said suggests, became both a unifying and exclusionary aesthetic icon – the verbal rendition of the spatial, linguistic, and social dimensions of "our" culture – only after an internal socio-aesthetic struggle had been won.[4]

To the degree that Said conflates the development of the novel with the development of the concept "literature" in organizing his discourse about cultural production, he is obliged to forgo telling the story of the tensions and resistances that may have operated within and against this process, however unsuccessfully, in other genres. But, just as it has become possible and necessary to read the tensions and resistances embedded in the exchanges *between* subject peoples and their ostensible masters, it behooves us to look for the traces of oppositional potential *within* what otherwise may seem to be a monolithic cultural enterprise. This is especially important if we hope to avoid the deadly possibility of unconsciously inverting the totalizing imperialist paradigm of "us" and "them" by erasing the history of internal conflict and difference that is also part of the advent of the imperial metropolis. It is also pertinent to my argument to remember that "colonial" and "imperialist" are not synonyms. The latter carries with it a history of nationalism, statism, and institutionalized racism and repression that is not coextensive with the former, and that requires its own specific analysis.

If, then, we turn to the melodrama of the early 1860s, we can do so with the sense that the discursive unity Said discovers in the age of Conrad had not only not (yet) prevailed earlier in the century, but that it was held in abeyance by an active struggle for cultural dominance, both in the public realm (forcefully manifest in the Chartist and Corn Law conflicts) *and* in the "aesthetic" realm. Indeed it is only with the plays of Robertson, Pinero and Jones, and the "modernist" preoccupations of Shaw, that what might be called "aestheticized" dramatic culture and imperialism are functionally integrated as fully as in Conrad's novels.[5] Prior to this, the project of political enclosure and cultural submersion suggested in *Mansfield Park* had yet to be completed. To get to that point, both the popular drama and its audience had to be reconfigured, included fully within the cultural politics legitimated by Austen's narrative. The drama (and its audience) had to, as it were, learn to speak differently, to accept the binding closure of the discourse and practice of imperialism instead of producing a cultural rhetoric of its own. Likewise, the "better" classes had to reconfigure their perceptions of certain segments of the lower-class public – find ways to merge them positively in the political and economic spaces of their worldly practice and in the cultural spaces open to representation in the theatre.

An interesting marker of this process, and of the resistances still to be overcome, can be found in Charles Reade's *It's Never Too Late to Mend* (1865).[6] It seems to me that this play participates in a socio-political reinscription that was also being advanced at the time in a number of other fields of cultural production: the fabulation of a new set of social models of the "nation" and its inhabitants, a picture of social integration, control, and stability which historians (Michelet, for example, in France) and early sociologists (e.g. Spencer) sought to theorize as a means of defining proper, inclusive positions for all classes (even the criminal) – a social recodification that made possible the psychological and anthropological representations of the individual and the nation that were crucial to the development of the culture of high imperialism, and to a description (and concomitant marginalization) of colonial peoples outside the national "center." Reade's play contributes to this project by enacting an idealized transformation of representative figures from these groups. Thus, it can document for us a liminal moment, a moment at which the impoverishment and abuse actually experienced by unemployed and displaced (potentially rebellious) artisans, laborers, and smallholders in England are staged as the occasion for the production of willing participants in middle-class political economy at home and the imperialist adventure abroad.

Initially, it seems that the play is merely organized around a classic "melodramatic" situation. A young man, George Fielding, is deeply in love with his neighbor, Susan Merton, but finds himself rejected as a suitor because Susan's father will not allow her to marry a man marked as he is by his failure to pay the rent on his farm. This seems especially cruel because George's mother had, years before, helped Susan's father out of serious difficulties. Of course, behind all of this lurks the villain, Meadows, a moneylender and land speculator whose name is ironically evocative of one of his primary interests. He has bought up the debt on a number of houses in the village and is anxious to foreclose whenever possible. At the very beginning of the play Meadows states his position quite clearly. "I have always put my foot on whatever has stood in my path" (20). Needless to say, he, too, is desperately in love with the beautiful Susan, and, therefore, also anxious to get George out of the way.

Meadows conspires to force George to leave his village and voyage to Australia in search of the money he needs to wed Susan, and then tricks Susan into believing that George has married someone else. Because of this Susan, after putting up great resistance, agrees to marry Meadows; but on the very eve of their wedding Fielding returns, and after some further moments of tension the play ends happily with George and Susan together and Meadows on his way to prison. In other words, the play fits our modern understanding of a rigorously formulaic melodrama. But what is of interest here is not the possibility of proving that there might have been such a formula. What matters is the way in which the formula is *used* to both figure and occult social and economic issues that, if confronted directly would no doubt have produced a far more threatening picture of the political situation in England at the time. The formulaic aspect of the play, precisely because of its familiarity, allows the audience to easily identify with the young lovers and, at the same time, understand concrete formulations of social, political, and economic inequity as parts of a *momentary* dilemma.

What then is the "historical" ground that is engaged by the generic practice of the play? If we turn to the opening scene we note that it begins with Meadows trying to foreclose on the home of Isaac Levi, an aging Jew who, like Meadows, was also a moneylender, but who now simply wants to live out his final days in the peace of his own home. This, and his treatment of Fielding, provide examples of speculation and exploitation that are not merely "melodramatic" tropes. They correspond to economic practices which, at the time the play was written, were in fact driving numbers of people off their land. Laws that allowed absentee landlords to amass extensive holdings and extract impoverishing rents from tenants had already been denounced a decade and more earlier, but with the growth of suburbs around the major manufacturing towns, the problem had gotten much worse. Indeed, at the time the play was written, land-reform agitation had been further spurred by the attempts of London landlords to appropriate common lands for building development.[7] But here the topical issue of land speculation and economic exploitation on the part of large land-holders as a group is displaced by a portrayal of the isolated evil caused by one individual in particular. Meadows' "melodramatic" cruelty places him outside the "normal" socio-economic order, in a position defined as much by literary tradition as by his specific actions: the echo of Shylock faintly preserved in the figure of the Jewish moneylender reduces Meadows' status to that of social pariah, since Levi is, in comparison, a worthy member of the world figured by the play.

This shift of focus also helps blunt the force of the complaints voiced by another character in the opening act: Tom Robinson, an old friend of George's who has been visiting from the city, gives voice to some very serious though not very well elaborated political and economic charges. England is not livable, he says:

> This very morning I heard one of your clodhoppers say, "The Squire be a good gentleman; he often gives me a day's work!" I should think it was the clodhopper *gave* the gentleman a day's work, and the gentleman gave him a shilling and made five by it. . . . Come George, England is the spot if you happen to be married to a duke's daughter: and got fifty thousand a year – and two houses and a coach . . . . But this island is the Dead Sea to a poor man. (27)

Such sentiments, when expressed in the context of Chartist and labor agitation of the recent past, had been sufficient cause for the speaker to be transported as a fomenter of criminal activity, but here they have a different effect.[8] While the mere fact that Robinson is allowed to give voice to these ideas implies their operative existence in the real world of the audience, the ultimate role they play in this drama is in fact to undermine the historical ground on which they stand. Rather than marking a confrontational situation, one which would delineate the class, economic, and political inequities in England that had been further exacerbated by the economic downturn of the late 1850s, they open the way to a transformation of the real social and economic tensions in England into a discursive unity made possible by the Empire.[9] Even before this happens, however, the truth value of Robinson's comments is diminished by our discovery that he is really a thief who has fled the city in order to avoid arrest. The fact that the play shows such malcontents are "criminal" and also under surveillance no doubt served to reduce the anxiety of the "better" parts of an audience that would surely object to the politics implicit in his lines. Nonetheless, they have been introduced into the play, just as Meadows' land speculation has; class divisions, political and economic conflict upset the small world on stage, and by the end of the first act the original social nexus of the village has been thoroughly upset.

If the play implicitly asks whether England could be the politically and economically fragmented and oppressive place suggested by these characters, the answer to this question is also already available in the situation and the characters present at the close of the act. "England" is not just the space occupied by these individuals or this village. Australia is proposed to George and to the audience as an extension of the English domain, a territory of promise for energetic workers in search of a better future – not as penal colony where lower-class troublemakers such as Robinson had habitually been sent.[10] Likewise, his discourse of resistance to social and economic exploitation will be transformed in the rest of the play, emerging finally as a positive evocation of participation in an imperial project that allows free movement between the colonies and England for all native Englishmen.

The difference between this treatment of the Australian colonies and that found in Dickens is worth noting here, since it provides some sense of the rapid transformation of their status as the need to recast the relationship between the lower classes and the colonies grew. As Hughes points out, Dickens' treatment of Magwich in *Great Expectations* (1861) shows that he retains a far more restrained view of the Australian convict (586). Since the novel is set in an earlier period, Dickens is historically justified in barring Magwich's return to England, but at the same time the novel clearly retains the idea that although transported convicts may redeem themselves through hard work, both they and the colonies remain segregated from the metropolitan center. Of course, in *David Copperfield*, Micawber willingly emigrates to Australia, but his choice and his situation are exemplary of a literary function assigned to the colonies in the industrial novel of the 1840s and early 1850s where, as Raymond Williams has pointed out, they served as a means of resolving conflict through a physical displacement of the characters to a space outside England.

Said presents Magwich in particular as yet another demonstration of the way in which the novelists he invokes make use of the colonies without ever really allowing these places formal space or presence. In contrast, Reade, in both the novel and the play, boasts of the authenticity of his representations of both the place and the practices that are available for lower-class self-transformation, a transformation that does not evict them from the metropolis, but provides them with the wherewithal to return and re-establish themselves in England as model burghers. The Empire holds out its hand here to the poor Englishman in need – George Fielding will attempt to found a new and better life by farming and prospecting for gold in the Australian colonies, and Robinson will join him later, after he spends some time in one of the new prisons where he will be disciplined by the silent and solitary system of which Foucault has written so much – and which Dickens so distrusted.

The next two acts of the play offer us further insights into both locales, but only to legitimate the roles these places play in making good fellow citizens of what would have earlier been regarded by the upper classes as potentially dangerous individuals. From the contemporary audience's point of view, the most startling of these acts was surely the second, which takes us into the new "borough gaol" in which Robinson has been confined along with Josephs, a young lad who, in the first act, had been caught stealing potatoes from Meadows. Here again it is Meadows who is the source of an injustice over which the audience will be free to weep – without ever calling the political and legal systems into question. Indeed, this is probably the most important function of the act as a whole: to allow

for a compassionate reconciliation between the audience and its counterparts on stage. We enter the prison milieu along with dear, good Susan, who
has brought gifts to Robinson, and so, with her and through her eyes,
experience the legitimation of the judicial order and the reintegration of
Robinson into society.

In the second scene of this act Robinson describes his condition as
follows:

> When I first came here I hadn't a bad heart, though my conduct was
> bad. I was a felon, but I was a man. And I had a secret respect for the
> law; who hasn't? unless he is a fool as well as a rogue. But here I find
> the law as great a felon as any of my pals. Here the law breaks the law;
> steals a prisoner's food contrary to the law and claps a prisoner in a
> black hole contrary to the law, and forces him to self-murder contrary
> to the law. So now . . . I despise the law because it is a liar and a thief. I
> loathe the law because it is a murderer. (45)

This is strong stuff. But we must keep in mind that Robinson's remarks
are also representative of the liberal penal doctrine of the time insofar as he
presents himself as someone who has been bad but is not bad of heart. In
other words, he is potentially open to self-discipline and reform – if given
the opportunity – which is precisely what the new prison system (as
opposed to the old jail regime) was supposed to offer. In effect, the play
tests this notion by pitting two figures seemingly representative of the state
against each other: Eden, the prison chaplain, and Hawes, the prison
governor. Eden confronts Hawes, saying "you have no right to reduce a
prisoner's food, nor to torment him in a punishment jacket." When Hawes
insists that he, not Eden, is master of the prison, Eden responds: "the law is
your master and mine." Hawes persists, and Eden vows he will appeal to
the Home Secretary, and if that doesn't work, to the Crown, and beyond
that to the people (in other words, to the audience of this play) in order to
see whether "the law can penetrate a prison" (44). Nevertheless, Hawes
sends Robinson to the "black hole" and causes Josephs to suffer so
horribly that he finally commits suicide. But these are solely the acts of a
governor who has failed to follow the rules set down by the state. As with
Meadows, it is the individual who is delinquent, not the order that had
made their activities possible.

This exculpation of the regime seems to me to be exactly parallel to the
public response precipitated by an event in the colonies which actually took
place somewhat later in the year that Reade's play was staged: when E. J.
Eyre, the Governor of Jamaica ordered a retaliatory massacre after some
black islanders had killed some whites during an uprising, the response in
England focused primarily on Eyre, not on the institutions that made his
regime possible. The important difference, of course, lies in the fact that
for Robinson, a white Englishman, the final result is integrative: he is

ultimately to be reunited with the social body in England, while the blacks living in Jamaica are either included in the imperium as its servants, or as "subjects" that had a theoretical right to protection from arbitrary murder, but not to socio-political equity. As Edward Said points out when he briefly discusses this incident, Ruskin, Carlyle, and Arnold *supported* Eyre's actions (as did Charles Kingsley, Tennyson, and Dickens, who for some reason Said fails to mention) while Mill, Huxley, Darwin, Herbert Spencer, and Goldwin Smith denounced Eyre as a tyrant and murderer who violated the "natural rights" of English subjects. These rights, however, did not include the "native" right to resist imperial authority.[11]

It is precisely this difference that helps explain the functional importance of the prison scenes in Reade's play. Robinson, who would have earlier been regarded as a potentially dangerous subject and, like his Irish counterparts, would have been cast away in one of the white colonies in Australia, is, here, first "reformed" and then recast as a legitimate participant in a new national order that, as we shall see, promises a new harmony of interests in England, a harmony based on a new understanding of interpersonal relations at home and a common mastery of subject peoples abroad. Henry Fawcett, a contemporary of Reade's, best sums up this wished-for new order in his *Economic Position of the British Labourer* (1865). He looks forward to a society of well-fed, well-educated citizens, with skilled artisans and peasant proprietors at the base – "scavenged for and waited upon by Negroes and Chinese."[12]

This idea seems to be the imperial, economic equivalent of the "coherent heterogeneity" that Spencer had theorized in his *First Principles* (1862) as the necessary upshot of biological evolution and as the founding principle in the progress of human societies as they move toward "the greatest perfection and the most complete happiness" (340–71, 407, 530). Even if the "nature" of this process emerges somewhat differently in the play, the goal appears to be the same. And to the degree that Robinson is successfully coerced into participation, the audience too may be convinced to set aside certain historical animosities. Artisan and lower middle class spectators can unite with their betters in appreciation of the colonial adventure that unfolds in the next act. Indeed, this seems to be one of the functional values of the play as a whole. Its unifying discourse and representation of an internally coherent England allow the members of the audience to surmount their own class differences, just as their peers were later expected to unite in "common interest" when limited franchise was extended to certain artisans and members of the lower middle class in 1867.[13]

This new cultural paradigm begins to take shape when Robinson is freed on parole as part of the "ticket of leave" program that had in fact recently been introduced in England. He is enjoined to "repent, and . . . labour with [his] hands, and steal no more" (50). After receiving a letter from Susan to

George, he sets off for Australia to build a new life. Thus, the tension produced by the violence of the prison scenes and by Josephs' death finds release both in a confirmation of the justness of the order behind the penal system and, once again, in the idea of the colonies as a place to work out one's authentic relation to the metropolitan center. Thanks to the Empire, George and Robinson will be united in their quest to become true, fulfilled Englishmen. This then becomes the core of the third act and central moment of the play: the ultimate transformation of Australia from penal colony into a land of opportunity, and the legitimation of colonial exploitation as a necessary adjunct of such opportunity, exploitation defined as a "profitable" interaction between colonials of every class and the colonized natives whom they supervise.

Reade claims to have done extensive research for the scenes in Australia and for his presentation of Jacky, the token Aborigine of the play. Nonetheless, it is obvious that he (like Isaac Levi, whom I mentioned earlier) is actually a literary artifact, a revised example of the stage Black,[14] put into play here to confirm a larger fiction of the general relation between the colonist and the colonized subject. It is Reade's *claim* that what he offers here is historically accurate that makes Jacky different from other, earlier stage figures of this type. Reade himself had, for example, included several other "Australian Blacks" along with Jacky in the play *Gold*, but none of them were focused upon as instances of the racial distinctions that found and justify colonial exploitation. They were merely useful (comic) "background," as was the stereotypical stage Irishwoman, Mary McDoggherty, who appeared with them. In the novel and in the later play, however, a new element is introduced. Jacky's presence, especially in the more tightly focused context of the second play, serves to delineate what Reade claimed was the "reality" of Australian life. He proudly announced that he had read "some thirty books" on Australia while preparing the novel, just as he had done preparatory research for the prison scenes. This new "realism" helps create a visual/spatial context that transforms characters such as Jacky from mere stock figures in the genre into authoritative ("anthropological") representations of cultural groups and their relations.[15]

Thus it is that when George reappears in the play he is accompanied by Jacky, who, needless to say, is his servant. Together they configure and justify the fundamental structures of imperial cultural relations. We see "Massa George" take on what can only be understood as 'the white man's burden' of educating Jacky – in "comic" scenes about such things as Jacky's inability to negotiate the change in temperature from the heat of midday to the chill of evening, a change that George's "friend" is apparently not able to predict: "When Jacky a good deal hot here . . . he can't feel a berry little cold a long way off . . . Jacky not white fellow" (59). From here, the play moves to a portrayal of Jacky as the stereotypical happy savage – willing to serve, but lacking mental and moral sufficiency: George comments on his "poor shallow brain" (62). But Jacky is above all *loyal*. When George gets sick, Jacky stays with him and tends him as best he can, but, of course, he doesn't do too well. Fortunately, Robinson appears on the scene just in time; it is he, not Jacky that knows how to get George back on his feet. Robinson's arrival also makes possible the introduction of more comic business demonstrating both Jacky's ignorance and an Englishman's "pluck": when Jacky threatens Robinson, he is easily put in his place by a few strong words (67).

After this series of patronizing and emphatically racist representations, the play moves on to the crucial moment when Jacky enacts the ideal role of the colonized subject. Learning that George and Robinson are in search of gold, he leads them to a nugget large enough to secure both their futures. This moment not only sets up the "happy end" the audience expects, it also gives George and Robinson an opportunity to comment further on Jacky's character. He is presented both as a savage and as "natural" man: "these poor savages have got an eye like a hawk for everything in nature" (76). Jacky is the "noble savage" who gladly reveals the existence of a great nugget, which he refers to as a "yellow stone," to his white masters, and Robinson says to George: "Here is a true philosopher. Here's Ebony despises Gold" (77). Idealism combines nicely with capital at this point to prove that the "philosophical" Aborigine *desires* to help his white master to empire and economic well-being. This is no doubt the Englishman's compensation for being cut off from nature.

What is interesting about this section of the play is that it is in fact based in real events. But those events, which had been widely publicized in England in the early 1850s, are *not* reproduced in the play. Instead of the story of an educated, native Australian who worked for a Dr W. J. Kerr, and who, after reporting the existence of a huge gold nugget, was rewarded (albeit insufficiently) with "two flocks of sheep, two saddle horses, . . . a quantity of rations, and . . . a team of bullocks to plow some land in which [he and his brother] are about to sow maize and potatoes," and instead of factual reportage on the waning of the gold boom in Australia, or the political unrest among the (white) workers there, or the anti-Chinese sentiment that had grown up around 1860 (there were about 15,000 Chinese in Australia at the time) when there was less land to prospect, we are offered Jacky.[16]

Of course, the play does not move quite so simply or directly as I have presented it. Events in the last act unfold, as did those of the first and second, in a context of "melodramatic" tension that leaves the audience no time to reflect on the possible discrepancies between known facts and the situation, the play's characters, and their actions. Jacky is quickly left behind in the final scenes of the play so that we can have a joyous reunion between George and Susan – a reunion that also brings together the various figures of the first act in such a way as to re-establish (on a new socio-economic plane) the community that had initially been disrupted by Meadow's corrupt and anti-social activities. It seems love, hard work, and moral righteousness conquer all, but their (melo)drama also functions superbly as a means of uniting all classes in the audience in their desire to further experience representations – if not the practice – of the unifying and sustaining project of empire.

Fictions of English superiority over the colonized other invert and dispel the real conditions of lower-class existence, while the image of the imperial domain provides the idea of distant land and wealth as compensation for the otherwise painful need to submit to the actual constraints – spatial, economic, and political – that define life in metropolitan England. It is not surprising therefore that the discourse of empire enters the vocabulary of the working-class movement more fully at this time, and that a (false) consciousness of national superiority impedes the development of an alternative critical analysis, while not preventing the later re-emergence of class confrontation in England. Minds as well as bodies are being mobilized for the struggles that lie ahead, and to replace those that have already fallen in England's name.[17] Indeed, it is only if we make the effort to see how this came about, only if we can seek out the cultural moments that mark the difference between individual experience and the universalizing discourse that masks, trivializes, or distorts it that we can avoid the tendency to produce equally reductive counter-discourses in our criticism, discourses that, in the name of resistance and identity formation may overlook the internal differences that are always the initial targets of cultural subjugation – and that also can provide the initial instance in the process of building new modes of (inter)cultural understanding.

NOTES

1 For further discussion of the development of this "readerly" and literary bias against the drama and performance, see Hays. As I will suggest later in this essay, not only the development of this literary bias, but the development of realism in the drama, too, seems to mark phases in the growing *emprise* of imperialist discourse in the realm of cultural production other than the novel.

2 For more information on the public in the theatre, see Nikolopoulou and Hays. That the lower-class audience was still thought to be in need of careful discipline and education as late as the 1860s is amply demonstrated by Dickens' essay of February 25, 1860 (later given the title "Two Views of a Cheap Theatre") published in *All the Year Round*.

3 The play had been castigated as an example of the tendency in German drama "to excite discontent among the lower classes of society, by representing *obscurity* and *virtue, rank* and *vice,* as close and inseparable associates," and also for its portrayal of a woman who is too independent, one who "deviates from the decorums of her *Sex*." These comments, taken from the *Anti-Jacobin Review* 3 (1799) and 9 (1801) are cited by David Simpson in his very valuable discussion of the nationalist and anti-theoretical attitudes that developed in England after

the French Revolution with regard to literary culture. See Simpson, especially 89–103.

4 Anyone familiar with the literature on the theatre and the melodrama in the nineteenth century will have noted the frequent efforts made to deny legitimacy to both, precisely by denying them the high status now accorded to the novel and to "literature" – thus also denying legitimacy to and effectively erasing the cultural expectations and desires of the audience (the lower-class public) that participated in the representational event. We, of course, have inherited this aspect of the nineteenth century cultural discourse in, for example, our learned distaste for the "bombast" and "unrealistic" situations that are understood to be the staple of the popular theatre.

5 As J. Ellen Gainor has shown, Shaw, like Conrad, is aware of the complex and destructive relationship that exists between England and its colonies. But he also enacts imperial culture in ways that are fully in accord with its projects.

6 The play is Reade's dramatized version of his novel of the same name, which carried the subtitle "A Matter of Fact Romance" (1856) and which was itself developed form his early play, *Gold* (1852, first staged January 1853). With each new version of the tale there are shifts in character and emphasis that mark the evolving context in which it appeared.

7 Perkin (106–10) indicates several such efforts. See as well Golby and Purdue, (145). The year after Reade's play appeared, the Metropolitan Commons Act (1866) was passed to prevent this kind of encroachment.

8 For some examples of the transportation of these "criminals," see Thompson (222, 226–27, 249, 513).

9 The degree to which this discursive shift succeeded in changing the story of lower-class emigraton is evident if one compares the events limned by the play with the explanation offered by a later historian of the empire. G. M. Trevelyan's confidence in the imperial discourse with which he was raised allows him to assert that:

> until the end of the Victorian era there were still large numbers of persons born and bred as agriculturalists, and desiring no better than to obtain land of their own beyond the ocean. It is only of recent years that a fear has arisen lest the English race, at home and in the Dominions, may by choice eschew the rural life and crowd too exclusively in the cities. (Trevelyan 207)

As Eric Hobsbawm later demonstrates, it was enforced poverty, the result of economic undermining of the agrarian life, rather than free choice, that was the primary cause of such emigration (Hobsbawm 181ff, 200).

10 Transportation to Australia officially ended in 1868, but had been under criticism for some years, particularly after the discovery of gold that figures so importantly in this play. On this subject see Hughes, especially chs. 15–16. A clear picture of the effort undertaken to encourage working-class emigration to Australia is provided by Clacy: "Much is done now-a-days to assist emigration, but far greater exertions are needed before either the demand for labour in the colonies or the oversupply of it in England can be exhausted" (158). At the time Reade wrote his play only the latter condition still obtained.

11 For further information on the Eyre controversy see Semmel and Workman.

12 Fawcett's comments are cited in Young (111).

13 On the Reform Act and political value of this overcoming of difference through a limited franchise as well as the resultant split between artisans and the "masses," see Hobsbawm (224), but cf. Trevelyan (203–6).

14 In addition to other sources, Reade's portrait of Jacky certainly owes something to Stowe's *Uncle Tom's Cabin*. That book's proclaimed factual basis had, in part, inspired Reade's own "realism." See Burns (131–33).

15 The historical role and the significance of this development of "realism" in the drama in the 1860s has not yet been explored in any detail and certainly merits further inquiry. The question that imposes itself here is the degree to which this shift marks the absorption of the theatre – particularly the melodrama and the audience for whom it might have embodied vestiges of resistance and difference – into the imperialist cultural project as a whole.

16 The earliest report of the discovery of the Kerr nugget, which is obviously the source of the incident in *It's Never Too Late to Mend*, appeared in the *Bathurst Free Press*, July 16, 1851. Several of the original reports have been reprinted in *Gold Fever* (39–44).

17 Foster provides further, quite interesting documentation of the development of this nationalist and racist "English" consciousness in his discussion of the impact of the Crimean War and the emergence of the anti-Irish movement in 1861 (329–46).

WORKS CITED

Baer, Marc. *Theatre and Disorder in late Georgian London*. Oxford: Oxford University Press, 1992.

Burns, Wayne. *Charles Reade: A Study in Victorian Authorship*. New York: Bookman Associates, 1961.

Clacy, Ellen. *A Lady's Visit to the Gold Diggings of Australia*. Ed. Patricia Thompson. London: Angus and Richardson, 1963.

Foster, John. *Class Struggle and the Industrial Revolution: Early Industrial Capitalism in Three English Towns*. New York: St. Martins Press, 1974.

Gainor, J. Ellen. "Bernard Shaw: The Drama of Imperialism." *The Performance of Power. Theatrical Discourse and Politics*. Ed. Sue-Ellen Case and Janelle Reinelt. Iowa City: University of Iowa Press, 1991, 56–74.

Golby, J. M. and A. W. Purdue. *The Civilization of the Crowd: Popular Culture in England 1750–1900*. New York: Schocken Books, 1985.

Hays, Michael. "From Public Space to Private Space: Staging the Discourse of the Academy." *Boundary 2* 13 (1985), 173–88.

Hobsbawm, E. J. *The Age of Capital*. New York: Scribner, 1975.

Hughes, Robert. *The Fatal Shore: The Epic of Australia's Founding*. New York: Knopf, 1987.

Gold Fever: The Australian Goldfields 1851 to the 1890's. Ed. Nancy Keesing. Sydney and London: Angus and Richardson, 1967.

Nikolopoulou, Anastasia. *Artisan Culture and the English Gothic Melodrama, 1780–1830*. Unpublished dissertation, Cornell University, 1990.

Perkin, Harold. *The Structured Crowd: Essays in English Social History*. Brighton, Sussex: Harvester Press, 1981.

Reade, Charles. *It's Never Too Late to Mend*. An edition of Charles Reade's unpublished drama with an introduction and notes by Léone Rivers. Toulouse: Impr. Toulousaine, 1940.

Said, Edward W. *Culture and Imperialism*. New York: Knopf, 1993.

Semmel, Bernard. *Jamaican Blood and Victorian Conscience: The Governor Eyre Controversy*. Boston: Houghton Mifflin, 1963.

Simpson, David. *Romanticism, Nationalism, and the Revolt Against Theory*. Chicago: University of Chicago Press, 1993.

Spencer, Herbert. *First Principles*. New York: D. Appleton and Company, 4th edn, 1904.

Thompson, E. P. *The Making of the English Working Class*. New York: Random House, 1977.

Trevelyan, G. M. *History of England*, Vol. 3 (1926). Garden City, NY: Doubleday and Company, 1956.

Workman, Gillian. "Thomas Carlyle and the Governor Eyre Controversy: An Account with Some New Material." *Victorian Studies* 18 (1974), 77–102.

Young, G. M. *Victorian England: Portrait of an Age*. London, New York: Oxford University Press, 2nd edn, 1953.

9

"THAT FLUCTUATING MOVEMENT OF NATIONAL CONSCIOUSNESS"

Protest, Publicity, and Postcolonial Theatre in South Africa

Loren Kruger

We all know where South Africa is,
but we do not yet know what it is.
                    Albie Sachs, "Preparing ourselves for freedom"

It is not enough to try to get back to the people
in that past out of which they have already emerged;
rather we must join them in that fluctuating movement
which they are just giving shape to, and which,
as soon as it has started, will be the signal
for everything to be called into question.
                    Frantz Fanon, *The Wretched of the Earth*

At a moment in South Africa's history when the euphoria generated by Nelson Mandela's release from prison (February 1990) has evaporated in the heat of an ongoing struggle for political legitimation, and when the battle over who or what South Africa is rages more fiercely than ever, the prospect of representing "the new South Africa" seems at once difficult and newly urgent.[1] The culture of apartheid may be decaying, but it is not yet dead. Although the laws underpinning racial discrimination are off the books, the laws permitting the "preventive detention" of those whose actions are all too loosely defined as "prejudicial to the safety of the state" still remain. The deformation of cultural life that is the product of educational, political, and social discrimination is very much in evidence. Official cultural institutions such as the provincial performing arts boards include only a token number of black performers, while alternative projects such as union-sponsored workshops for graphic design or township theatre groups are hampered by a shortage of funds and continual harassment.

Under these conditions, it is not surprising that alternative cultural producers, particularly the generation formed by the Black Consciousness Movement (BCM), the United Democratic Front (UDF), and the empowerment of countless community organizations in the 1970s and 1980s, continue to define themselves primarily in opposition to apartheid. In this view, culture is first and foremost a strategy of mobilization against a particular enemy: "culture is part of the national democratic struggle" (ANC 216). This sharp division of the cultural field into "our" troops and "theirs" prevailed until very recently across the anti-apartheid spectrum. Although the social democratic views of the UDF may have differed from the BCM's arguments for black solidarity across class lines, the cultural policies of both have tended to be driven by the same emphatic dichotomy between the culture of apartheid and the culture of liberation. In this respect, the claim of the African National Congress (ANC) that "the grim conditions of apartheid dictate that we cultural workers are freedom fighters first" (Masakela 252) joins Mothobi Mutloatse's Africanist assault on "European" literary models:

> We will have to *donder* [thrash] conventional literature: old-fashioned critic and reader alike. We are going to pee, spit and shit on literary convention . . . ; we are going to kick and pull and drag literature into the form we prefer . . . . Because we are in search of our true selves – *undergoing self-discovery as a people.*
>
> (Mutloatse 5; my italics)

As partisans in the global struggle against apartheid, both groups beat words into weapons, while arguing for the necessary instrumentalization of art in the interests of national liberation. Critics calling for nuance or complexity are lambasted for their alleged attachment to elitist and irrelevant literary standards as well as for their nostalgia for the imperium of European culture.

In the present context, however, as the edifice of the apartheid state begins to crack and the once-burnished image of the liberation movements is tarnished by political intrigue and sectarian violence, the opposition between oppression and liberation has lost some of its earlier clarity and the moral and aesthetic authority of protest culture is no longer absolute. Moreover, challenges to this authority cannot be simply dismissed, as they were regularly in the last two decades, as the peevish objections of academics, especially when such challenges are issued by veteran activists, such as ANC cadre Albie Sachs. Sachs's influential paper, "Preparing Ourselves for Freedom: Culture and the ANC Guidelines," was originally presented at an ANC seminar in Zambia in 1989 and published in South Africa the following year. In this paper, Sachs challenges the orthodoxy of the protest paradigm that has dominated resistance culture. Against the habit of slogans tossed at a familiar target, he argues that the notion of culture as a weapon of struggle was politically as well as artistically limited, that it represents its subjects exclusively as "angry victims" or "freedom fighters" and so remains "trapped in the multiple ghettos of the apartheid imagination" (Sachs 19), sealed off from the transformative power of "dreams and humor" (21).

In objecting to the automatic affirmation of an abstract struggle, Sachs in no way advocates a retreat from politics. On the contrary, he insists that "it is not a question of separating art and politics, but of avoiding a shallow and forced relationship between the two" (20). He argues for the representation of inner conflict and contradiction as well as collective struggle, suggesting, for instance, that a South African Sholokhov writing "And Quiet Flows the Tugela" might focus on the contradictory position of an Inkatha member rather than on the conviction of the Mass Democratic Movement (20).[2] He concludes with a plea for cultural practices that would help forge national unity in the recognition of the country's linguistic and cultural diversity and also the persistence of disputes about the relative value of its component parts (24–29).

The reaction to Sachs's paper in South Africa confirms both the impact of his intervention and the tenacity of the protest paradigm. Despite the fact that the paper was written explicitly for a committed audience, some ANC critics suggested that Sachs's critique of the excesses of the protest paradigm amounted to breaking the link between culture and struggle.[3] The Transvaal Interim Cultural Desk, in particular, drew firm battle lines between "those who support us" and "those who choose . . . to contribute to the maintenance of apartheid" and threatened to counter the latter with "all the means at our disposal (de Kok 109). Their communique moved brusquely from the "will of the people" to the "we" of the party. Despite a gesture towards artistic autonomy, it insisted not merely that culture had a political dimension (which few in South Africa would dispute), but that cultural practice was only political, that its essential value was that of an instrument in the struggle.

The debate among more sympathetic (but otherwise quite diverse) respondents to Sachs's critique of the total instrumentalization of culture focused on the question of artistic autonomy. Artists and critics, especially those defining themselves as avant-garde, applauded Sachs's critique of this instrumentalization and his defense of artistic autonomy, while criticizing him for assuming that culture directly "expresses" society. These critics argued that a consistent defense of artistic autonomy entails an acknowledgement of the avant-garde's aesthetic challenge to habitual perception and thus also of its "competition with history" rather than transparent commitment to it (Geers 43; also Younge and Morphet). Others, defining themselves as cultural workers, share Sachs's concern for the political as well as cultural ineffectiveness of old slogans, while arguing against his implication that the realist novel provides the best model or that internationally known artists such as Abdullah Ibrahim should set the tone for the grassroots.[4] In a society which grants only a small minority the luxury of leisure for art, artistic autonomy is a privilege. The celebration of avantgarde difficulty sidesteps the ongoing exclusion of most South Africans from the production and reception, indeed from the definition, of art, because it ignores the social and aesthetic prestige associated with privileged places and practices (Sitas "The Sachs Debate" 95).

What emerges in this exchange is not a simple opposition between high art and grassroots propaganda but rather a series of engagements with the articulation of culture in an as yet fragile and restricted public sphere. Culture in present-day South Africa foregrounds the question of representation and agency in that public sphere as well as the imagination of virtual public spheres not yet realized. Theatre practitioners in South Africa cannot *assume* that "the theatre of protest . . . will give way to a rich political theatre that does not depend on repetitive impoverished criticism" (Ukpokodu 49). Indeed their activities bear witness to ongoing tensions between solidarity and critique. Rather than predicting their resolution or chasing an up-to-the-minute report on the latest South African shows, my intention is to investigate the discursive and performative articulation of the paradigm that dominated South African theatre under apartheid and that continues to color this incipiently post-apartheid and perhaps postcolonial moment.

Sachs is by no means the first progressive intellectual to argue that the protest paradigm may have exhausted its potential. In a series of recent articles including "The Rediscovery of the Ordinary" and "Redefining Relevance," Njabulo Ndebele has criticized protest literature for what he calls "the hegemony of spectacle" ("Ordinary" 150). He is especially critical of the exposure and display of injustice in the abstract at the expense of the accurately caught detail of particular situations (149). Ndebele joins Sachs in arguing that the generality of protest and the immediate assent it demands from its audience not only misrepresents the actual conflicts and divided loyalties of people struggling with apartheid capitalism but also undermines attempts to build solidarity on the recognition of difference and dissent. In his view, the protest paradigm has come to substitute "posturing and sloganeering" for the rather more difficult explorations of the "methods of transformation" which may have to precede any attempts to forge unity of purpose (151).

As Ndebele points out, protest literature has often compromised its vanguardist claim by conventionally addressing its anger not to the masses who don't need to be told that they are oppressed but to a (largely white) metropolitan audience instead ("Ordinary" 148). Protest theatre, in particular, seems often more concerned to accuse its audience with the display of apartheid than to represent the lives of those who have to negotiate it. Insofar as it continues to depend on the guilty presence of the privileged spectator of apartheid, protest drama remains within the purview of a colonial encounter, offering what Fanon called the "violent, resounding, florid writing which on the whole serves to reassure the occupying power" (Fanon 239). Fanon argues that, in themselves, "stinging denunciations, the exposing of distressing conditions . . . are in fact assimilated by the occupying power in a cathartic process" (239). Although the Pretoria regime is not an occupying power in the conventional sense, its insistent claim to First World status and its continued evasion of thoroughly democratic solutions to the national question can certainly be seen as neocolonial. Moreover, the state's increasing toleration over the 1980s of certain high cultural forms of "stinging denunciations" (especially when contained in metropolitan theatres such as the Market Theatre in Johannesburg) as against its ruthless suppression (at least until 1990) of oppositional journalism or more directly political assemblies such as funerals in the townships, confirms Fanon's hypothesis that tolerance of an elite fraction of resistance culture may act as a safety valve not only for dissident colonials but for native elites as well. Seen in this light, protest drama is not yet majority theatre (Kavanagh) or theatre representing the interests, tastes, and dreams of a majority of South Africans.

Negotiating the straits between "stinging denunciations" and "national consciousness" or, to return to Mutloatse's Africanist idiom, between shitting on European conventions and "self-discovery as a people," is a tricky business in this neocolonial environment. For Black Consciousness intellectuals suspicious of manipulation by the Market yet needful of the autonomous space it can provide, the problem has been particularly acute. The audience at the Market has not been (and still is not) the assembly of the black masses invoked by Black Consciousness rhetoric, but its endorsement of protest plays has often acted as the signal legitimating the performance for Soweto audiences. One company that has wrestled directly with this problem is the Soyikwa African Theatre. Founded in the 1970s in the wake of the Soweto uprising, Soyikwa (named in honor of Wole Soyinka) began with plays in the protest mode like *Egoli* (1979) by Matsamela Manaka, which was performed at the Market and at European theatre festivals. *Egoli* portrays the effects of apartheid on mine workers in a series of accounts by different narrators linked by choral comment rather than a single story of individual alienation as in many fictional treatments of similar material.

More recently, Soyikwa has moved towards what Manaka calls "Afrocentric theatre." As his 1989 production of *Goree* indicates, however, this notion of Afrocentrism does not entail an exclusive focus on local indigenous traditions of particular ethnic groups. This strategy would stray too close to Afrikaner Nationalist policy of dividing black South

Africans by forcibly yoking them to an allegedly original tribal identity, as Zulu, Xhosa, etc., which corresponds only partly to the multiple allegiances of most South Africans. Instead, Soyikwa appeals to a global African sensibility in the pan-Africanist tradition, which has historically invoked the value of black culture as a whole in a move that might be called a "*strategic use of positive essentialism*" (Spivak 345) to counter Western culture's objectification of the exotic African primitive. Soyikwa's Afrocentrism should therefore be distinguished from the optimistic folklorism of shows like *Amabali* (meaning "stories"; Market Theatre, 1988) and *The Milkbird* (an "African opera" by Michael Williams, 1991) that claim to offer an indigenous synthesis of local and imported traditions but instead produce a sort of multiculturalist wish-fulfillment for metropolitan audiences. Soyikwa's articulation of an essentialist distinction between African and Western culture may, however, be more complicated than its founder intends.

Goree, a loosely-woven narrative in dance, music, and dialogue, was written by Matsamela Manaka, danced by Nomse Manaka and sung by Sibongile Khumalo under the direction of John Kani. It was performed at FUNDA, a center for cultural education in Diepkloof, a relatively affluent part of Soweto. Written after a trip to West Africa that included the island of Goree (departure point for the slave-ships of the Middle Passage), the piece dramatizes the encounter between a South African dancer whose search for authentic African models to replace her limited and limiting Western training has taken her from Johannesburg to London and finally to Goree, and the performer she meets on the island. The two reenact their alienating encounters with European performance traditions from ballet and classical music to Western distortions of "African dance," and conclude with a medley of African dance and music from South Africa to Senegal.

Manaka directed the FUNDA performance at those black South Africans unaware of Goree's significance in the history of the African diaspora. He argues for the need to represent to black South Africans the fact of their diaspora in the heart of their own country and to restore that country to them by celebrating the essential unity of African traditions. The enthusiastic participation (clapping, ululating, dancing, etc.) of the audience at FUNDA certainly confirms the appeal of this pan-African gesture for Soweto and suggests that invoking a transnational Afrocentrism as the source of a postcolonial national culture is not as odd as it might seem. As Fanon notes:

> Colonialism's condemnation is continental in its scope. The contention of colonialism that the darkest night of humanity lay over pre-colonial history concerns the whole of Africa. The efforts of the native to rehabilitate himself . . . are logically inscribed from the same point of view as colonialism. . . . The culture that is affirmed is African culture (211–22).

153

The affirmation of black identity may, however, be less purely African than first meets the eye. In performance, *Goree*'s treatment of the clash between African and Western traditions is less confrontational than the dialogue and Manaka's commentary imply. Any monological African identity proposed by the spare and didactic dialogue that links each dance to the next is complicated both by the use of Goree (now a tourist destination) as the site of authenticity and, in a different vein, by Nomse Manaka's and Sibongile Khumalo's virtuoso combinations of African, European, and (African)American performance forms.

Although Manaka appeals explicitly to an Africa that can ideally be retrieved intact from beneath the rubble of imperialism, his practice can more accurately be described as the invention of tradition. This does not imply the mere fabrication of a non-existent history but rather the appropriation of a "usable past" on which the idea of the nation or people might be erected (Hobsbawm 5). Or, as Veit Erlmann notes in his historical account of popular music in South Africa, "tradition has little to do with the persistence of old forms, but more with the ways in which form and value are linked" (Erlmann 10). Erlmann describes this appropriation of a usable past to fashion ethnic, even national, identity across class lines as the "situational use of ethnicity" (16). In the case of *Goree*, pan-African tradition is invoked against the ongoing dominance of neocolonial culture and also against the tribalized identity fostered by the state's "homeland" policy. The *situation* in this case combines the place and occasion of the performance, in which place is always overdetermined by occasion. The location and funding of FUNDA testifies to a tension between the aspirations of black intellectuals and the power of (predominantly) Anglo capital, as well as between the community celebration of African identity in Soweto and the subsequent performances for audiences in New York (Kruger "Apartheid" 200–205). While the intervention of metropolitan capital or cultural prestige does not resolve this tension, it does highlight the vulnerability of local practices.

This collision of different occasions and places in the "situational use of ethnicity" should alert us to the pitfalls of Africanist essentialism. Strategic or not, the Black Consciousness movement's insistence on a transhistorical African identity locks its protest against apartheid into a dichotomy between white and black, Western and African, which is as colonialist as it is illusory. It is colonialist in that it presupposes a clean-cut distinction between apartheid oppression and its consequences in the destruction of indigenous custom and the degradation of township life, on the one hand, and what Kelwyn Sole criticizes as an "idealized precolonial rural past" (Sole "Black Literature" 55), on the other. The dichotomy is illusory insofar as it confuses the considerable *affective* power of performance that reinforces "the feeling of participation by the audience and unity between them and the performers" (56) with a utopian projection of a classless black

154

community outside the theatre. This utopian projection misrecognizes the hierarchical character of precolonial society as well as the specifically class character of domination under apartheid capitalism. Furthermore, the search for a pan-African usable past paradoxically pushes Africanist companies such as Soyikwa to use English as their primary if not only medium at the expense of South African vernaculars. The effectiveness of English as a commonly used second language for most South Africans has been significantly curtailed by the state's requirement of primary schooling in the vernacular. The use of English "with a minimum of Zulu/Sotho to give 'authenticity' to the speech . . . precludes an audience of lower class semi- or nonliterate people, even if oral performance is used as a way of overcoming this problem" (Sole "Black Literature" 59).

While it is possible to overstate the case against the use of English in majority theatre since not all vernaculars are understood by all, it is also true that fluency in English remains a class privilege in South Africa. Sole's critique of the populist claims of Black Consciousness theatre does not invalidate all protest drama but it does draw attention to the economic and social strictures on the occasion of performance. It also suggests that the larger social significance of protest drama, i.e. its effect on majority audiences, cannot be simply read off the intentions of its producers. Most Soweto theatre ventures, with the notable exception of entrepreneurs such as Gibson Kente who has produced musical theatre in the townships for over twenty years, have had to rely on the Market Theatre and its liberal capitalist backers for financial support and, until very recently, had to rely on the prestige of the central and conspicuous location of the metropolitan theatre as a way of escaping the police. Focused on the exposure of the effects of apartheid, rather than on the exploratory treatments of post-apartheid plots, and performed in many cases for a metropolitan audience (whether white liberal or Black Consciousness intellectuals) protest drama has fitfully fulfilled its claim to be a "majority theatre" (Kavanagh) or at least the cultural work of a legitimate vanguard for the majority. Pressured to play the Market, groups such as the Soyikwa African Theatre have not always reached beyond the metropolitan audience of Johannesburg and have remained alienated from the popular audience-in-formation that they claim to address.

The task of majority theatre cannot be simply seen as the representation of what Robert Kavanagh calls the "fundamentally oppressed classes of South Africa" or the black proletariat (Kavanagh xv), not least because the boundaries between classes and the category "class" itself have historically been relatively rather than absolutely defined. This task is complicated first by the question of taste — many urban spectators continue to prefer the lively and spectacular musical entertainments and melodramas provided by township entrepreneurs to the talky and rather austere productions of black intellectuals (Kavanagh 189; Coplan 215) – and second by ongoing ties to rural communities and practices maintained by these spectators who themselves are not *only* urban or proletarian (Erlmann xviii, 179).[5] More modestly portrayed as a theatre with majoritarian aspirations, alternative South African theatre has attempted to refunction the occasion of theatre as a virtual public sphere. This virtual public sphere could be described as a "cultural space" (Sitas "Culture and Production"), an arena in which the theatre's fictional or what Raymond Williams has called "subjunctive" action (Williams 224) might provide a space for entertaining alternative representations, fantastic as well as serious, of South African reality that cannot (yet) risk exposure in the legitimate public arena still restricted by the state (Kruger "Placing the Occasion" 55–71).

The concept of public sphere includes not only physical space but the civic and cultural mobilization necessary to appropriate and establish such spaces and, more tentatively, the incipiently public character of the experience of exclusion from publicity. In their classic study, *Public Sphere and Experience*, Oskar Negt and Alexander Kluge argue that "fantasy is not merely an expression of alienation but a kind of unconscious critique of alienation and alienating social relations" (Negt and Kluge 67). Sachs's evocation of a space for dreams and humor (Sachs 21) and for a recognition of the salutary contradictions in the South African past and present (22) suggest that the hitherto dominant mode of agitprop or theatre of direct action might be fruitfully complemented by a theatre of subjunctive action which might bring to consciousness and public view what Kluge calls the sedimentations of incipient consciousness articulated by cultural forms (Negt and Kluge 68). Cultural forms, in this case theatrical conventions, have no intrinsic aesthetic value but draw their significance from the occasion and place of their performance and the acknowledgement (not necessarily consensus) on the part of audience and performers of the significance of the occasion and the pleasure of the performance. In the South African context, this determination of aesthetic value by the occasion of performance can mean that local producers choose to *donder* literary conventions, but it also implies that no convention, literary or rhetorical, European or indigenous, can be inherently or irrevocably imperialist or liberating.

In recent years, institutions of what might be called *dissident prestige*, such as the Market theatre, have attempted to make more ideological as well as physical space for work produced by people who had not previously habitually frequented these institutions. More recently, the Market has included more informal workshops in which local young writers present their own work alongside those of international exemplars.[6] This activity has taken place amidst ongoing attempts by unions or autonomous community groups to establish greater access not only to the consumption of cultural artifacts but also to the means of production – from theatre facilities to video and musical equipment to the training for their use (Meintjies and Hlatshwayo). The Market's contribution to this development is noteworthy but its fame should not blind us to the significance of local cultural work in community organization such as the growing union movement. We should judge this work not only by its power to mobilize the masses but also by its contribution to the "imagined community" in Benedict Anderson's haunting phrase, whether that community is imagined on a national scale or not.

Indeed, in this emerging but by no means securely postcolonial moment, a theatre grounded in local occasions and places may more effectively and more evocatively imagine a new South Africa than a theatre with emphatically nationalist ambitions. While a militantly nationalist theatre runs the risk of confusing the "we" of the party or the vanguard of the race with the will of the people, the best of the local theatre has developed out of an acknowledgment of the contradictory character of popular consciousness. In the last decade, theatre in the growing trade union movement has demonstrated the value as well as the risks of this acknowledgement. In 1981, striking iron workers in Johannesburg were arrested and assaulted by police for allegedly striking illegally. The union lawyer, Halton Cheadle, was initially unable to get consistent corroborating evidence from the fifty or more workers involved. In order to get this evidence, he set up a role-play in which one of the workers presented the manager's position, provoking responses and amendments from other workers. This reenactment of the conflict formed the basis of a play, *Ilanga le so phonela abasebenzi* (The sun is rising for the workers) devised by members of the Junction Avenue Theatre Group in collaboration with the strikers (Tomaselli 67–69; von Kotze 41–52). Although Keyan Tomaselli's account of the play identified it as "authentic black theatre" or a "medium of working class expression" and its effect on the worker-audience as "catharsis" (66), the significance of this project lies less in "catharsis" or release than in the worker-players' ability to reinterpret the events of the strike and to encourage the community of fellow-workers to recognize their own agency. It is the concrete experience of factory life and the realization that that experience merits public enactment rather than an abstract "working-class expression" that makes this possible (Sole "Identities" 79–89).

While it is certainly true that the terms of these working-class entertainments have not always been thoroughly theorized and that many continue to be the expression of grievances and in this respect "defensive combinations" (Sitas "Culture and Production" 85), they have nonetheless served as the space of cultural reproduction (89), or what I have called the site of a virtual public sphere. Despite the remarkable growth of union theatre, chronicled in part by Astrid von Kotze's account of the Durban Workers Cultural Local (DWCL), this space has remained a virtual public sphere, a space of cultural and political representation under siege. The case of *The Long March*, one of the better known DWCL productions, demonstrates the fragility but also the tenacity of this space. Conceived by Sarmcol workers and the DWCL as an historical account of the workers' expropriation since the company was established in 1920 as well as an analysis of links between apartheid capitalism and transnational corporations, the piece combined group choreography with short sharp skits, including a confrontation between a monstrously made-up Margaret Thatcher (in a papier-mâché mask) and the local Sarmcol president (von Kotze 79–100). The response of its initial audience of union members was supportive in general but critical in detail and reflected the importance of community accountability (93). The success of the tour that followed demonstrates the potentially national reach of this local story.

However much this work contributes to worker solidarity, the participants cannot assume unconditional party loyalty. On the contrary, they have had to contend not only with state surveillance but also occasionally with hostility from people whose motivation may be only barely political. Incidents such as the torching of the DWCL properties van by so-called comrades during *The Long March*'s tour of Soweto in 1986, and similar incidents that continue to dog the activities of this and other groups in the 1990s, make it unlikely that they will succumb to the kind of sentimental workerism of which they have been charged. Nor has their commitment to critical (self) representation necessarily meant an abandonment of artistic finesse. Like the "propertyless theatre of the propertyless classes" in Europe and America in the 1920s and 1930s,[7] the most effective workers' theatre in South Africa has continued to entertain its audience as well as reconstitute its history. Members of the Culture and Working Life Project (many of them workers involved in DWCL) acknowledge the limits of agitprop but argue that mobilization does not mean abandoning art:

> What we need to be asking is the following: will these times be *remembered* through our work? Will our lines like [Agostino] Neto's make Luanda come alive again? Will 1984–86 be remembered better, its tensions shown, its darkness illuminated through our plays? Or will our creative products be surface statements that need to be understood as poor products of the time? We feel that there is enough of both examples . . . and our task is to evaluate all the time our work with honesty and realism.
>
> (CWLP 102)

"Honesty and realism" entail the recognition of the "inevitability of competing hegemonic projects" but not the acquiescence to their violent resolution (103). Cultural memory depends not only on accurate documentation but also on the evocative force of subjunctive action.

One might argue that for all their emphasis on *"principled criticism,"* explicitly identified workers' theatres are primarily interested in developing solidarity and effective agency in the political and economic as well as cultural sphere. Continuing in this vein, one could suggest that the real test for a theatre with majoritarian aspirations in South Africa would be the representation of dissent. Moving from the workers' (and perhaps also workerist) theatre of the DWCL and other cultural locales of the Congress of South African Trade Unions (COSATU), I end my sketch with the African Research and Educational Puppetry Program (AREPP), founded in 1987 by theatre practitioners, a puppeteer and an ethnologist. In their work on AIDS, the company uses puppets with grey heads and variously defined features to avoid racial stereotyping, and performs to audiences in parks, schools and shopping centers, as well as rural health centers. AREPP and other groups dramatizing and disseminating health care in South Africa have something in common with state- or university-funded "theatre for development" projects elsewhere in Africa which also use performance to reach rural audiences who might be difficult to reach because of illiteracy or suspicion of centralized authority (Kerr, Eyoh). AREPP, however, receives no government subsidy, performs at urban as well as rural sites, and tends to criticize rather than affirm official AIDS policy. The government has tended to vacillate between placating white fears of an African plague and playing to homophobia in black as well as white communities. To be sure, the group's brochure (Larlham 209) focuses on heterosexual transmission and does not directly address the question of homophobia, but audiences' verbal responses and participation in postperformance surveys suggest a willingness to gain and disseminate knowledge about AIDS as well as performance skills that may be used in other contexts.

What these local projects have in common is a commitment to a theatre that is entertaining in several senses: engaging and amusing, but also able to represent concrete social alternatives. They also share a skeptical if generally cordial attitude to metropolitan institutions such as the Market or the universities. They recognize the usefulness of these institutions, but would rather not let them determine the place and thus the significance of the occasion of performance. The significance of this local theatre for a theatre with national aspirations lies in its attempt to adumbrate an alternative public sphere, in which participants may realize their potential agency, in which subjunctive action might entertain direct action without immediately enforcing it. It makes the case for the radical decentralization that Fanon sees as the necessary step if national consciousness-raising is to be democratic rather than a nationalist variant of colonial paternalism.

The recognition of the diverse ingredients of the South African nation and thus of the nation's *hybridity*, its multiple origins but also the strength of the new plant, is not to be confused with multiculturalism. Multiculturalism in the United States or Europe, in the form of the acknowledgement or promotion of distinct cultural identities of minorities, may offer an antidote to the relentless monoculturalism of European nationalism or the assimilationist ideology of the American melting pot. In South Africa, however, "multicultural can only sound profoundly undemocratic, a cue for the denial, rather than the advancement of rights" (Nixon 31). "Multiculturalism," along with "multiracialism" and the notorious "pluralism" (as in the Department of Plural Affairs, in which "plural" replaces "bantu" which replaced "native"), has been historically associated not with a liberal sense of fairness but with the segregation and underdevelopment of Grand Apartheid set out in the 1950s. President de Klerk's solicitous attention, in the name of democratic diversity in the 1990s, to Afrikaner "group rights" on the one hand, and to Inkatha demands to carry "traditional Zulu cultural weapons" on the other, is no new multicultural dispensation, but the "separate but equal" habit of apartheid as usual. By emphasizing cultural tradition at the expense of an analysis of entrenched structures of power, this dispensation promotes cultural diversity as a bulwark against universal political and economic enfranchisement.

The alternative to a multiculturalist repressive tolerance or to what Sachs calls "a picturesque collection of separate ethnic and political cultures" (25) is not a homogenous monoculture. Nor can it be an unreflecting return to a liberal or a marxist version of "the people" as *self-evident* universal subject, but rather a call for understanding the difficulty of nurturing national subjects. The hybrid character of South Africanness calls for the unflinching acknowledgment of difference not merely as diversity but as the differential relations of and to power (Nixon 32). It calls, in other words, for the acknowledgement that most South Africans remain excluded from a recognizable public sphere. The ideal route to general publicity may be universal suffrage and the implementation of a freedom charter but, until that road is travelled, the subjunctive action of theatre and other performances in virtual public spheres offers an alternative to the ongoing legitimation crisis of official publicity. Worker theatre and theatre for development do not, any more than the performance of protest in metropolitan institutions, represent a triumphant front against the old political dispensation or the universally accepted face of the new, but rather the contradictions and possibilities in the shifting currents within and between them. This enactment of and in the virtual public sphere articulates what Fanon identifies as the "fluctuating movement" of a national consciousness that is "not nationalism" but the "only thing that will give us an international dimension" (Fanon 247). It is to be hoped that the horizon of the *what* as well as the *where* of South Africa will not be sealed by the blood of the nation (as in the racialist nationalism of past and present *Europe*) but rather opened up by the entertainment of present and future public spheres.

NOTES

1 The bulk of the argument in this essay was written in 1990–91 and is intended as a historically-informed intervention in the debate about politics and culture in South Africa. Although the heat around the question of "culture as a weapon" has subsided somewhat, understanding the issues at stake is if anything more important and more difficult in a period in which historical alliances and the agents and targets of cultural weaponry are much harder to pin down. I have resisted the temptation to be strictly up to date so as to maintain historical clarity on the debates leading up to the watershed of 1990–91, which, despite some current claims, have yet to be resolved.

2 South Africans need no introduction to the conflict between the grassroots groups associated with the MDM on the one hand and the minority party, Inkatha, run as a fiefdom by kwaZulu "homeland" chief Mangosotho Buthelezi, on the other. Overseas readers, especially in the US where Buthelezi has been touted as a "moderate" African leader, should note that he was installed by the apartheid regime and that, despite his kwaZulu jurisdiction, has the support of only a minority of Zulus nationwide. In this context, Sachs's allusion to Mikhail Sholokhov's socialist realist classic *And Quiet Flows the Don* provocatively suggests that fiction might more vividly represent the popular struggle if its protagonists were frustrated members of a minority organization rather than heroes of the revolutionary vanguard.

3 See the responses collected in *Spring is Rebellious*, ed. de Kok and Press, especially the comments by Rushdy Siers, "Vampire Bats of Ambiguous Metaphors," Henry Zondi, "Our Writing is a Weapon," and the "Response to Albie Sachs" by the ANC's Transvaal Interim Cultural Desk.

4 See comments by Gerrit Olivier, "An Watter Kant van die Struggle is Jy?", Ari Sitas, "The Sachs debate: a philistine's response," and "Albie Sachs must not worry," by the Culture and Working Life Project, in de Kok and Press.

5 The distinction between proletarian entertainments and the native elite's attempt to educate black audiences has precedents earlier in the twentieth century. We should note the tension between the desire of native intellectuals such as the playwright H. I. E. Dhlomo or the composer-songwriter Reuben Caluza (his cousin) to educate South Africans into full citizenship and the syncretic tastes of the proletarianizing population of the townships from ritual practices to the African-American entertainments, as well as local urban hybridization.

6 Members of the Market Theatre Workshop, supervised by Associate Director (and Fugard collaborator) John Kani have recently arranged readings which included work by international political poets from Brecht to Neruda as well as members' own work. Although the audiences here are small (in comparison to those responding to political rallies at, say, May Day rallies), Kani has stressed the Workshop's place in the local practice of performance poety. Unlike many of the Soweto poets, however, he argued for the value of reading international "poets of resistance" as literary as well as political models.

7 For an introductory history, see Samuel. For analyses of the category of workers' theatre in the South African context, see Meintjies and Hlatshwayo, Sitas, Sole, Tomaselli, and von Kotze. For comments on the relatively unexplored common ground between workers' theatre in the European and American metropolis and in South Africa, see Kruger "Staging."

LOREN KRUGER

WORKS CITED

African National Congress (ANC). "Preamble and Resolutions of the CASA Conference." In Willem Campschreur and Joost Divendal, eds. *Culture in Another South Africa*. New York: Olive Branch Press, 1989, 214–23.

Coplan, David. *In Township Tonight!*. London: Longman, 1985.

Culture and Working Life Project (CWLP). "Albie Sachs must not Worry." In Ingrid de Kok and Karen Press, eds. *Spring is Rebellious: Arguments about Cultural Freedom by Albie Sachs and Respondents*. Cape Town: Buchu Books, 1990, 99–104.

de Kok, Ingrid, and Karen Press, eds. *Spring is Rebellious. Arguments about Cultural Freedom by Albie Sachs and Respondents*. Cape Town: Buchu Books, 1990.

Erlmann, Veit. *African Stars: Studies in Black South African Performance*. Chicago: University of Chicago Press, 1991

Eyoh, H. Ndumbe. *Hammocks to Bridges. An Experience in Theatre for Development*. Yaounde, Cameroon: Bet, 1985.

Fanon, Frantz. *The Wretched of the Earth*. Trans. Constance Farrington. New York: Grove, 1968.

Geers, Kendell. "Competition with History: Resistance and the Avantgarde." In Ingrid de Kok and Karen Press, eds. *Spring is Rebellious: Arguments about Cultural Freedom by Albie Sachs and Respondents*. Cape Town: Buchu Books, 1990, 43–46.

Hobsbawm, Eric and Terence Ranger, eds. *The Invention of Tradition*. Cambridge: Cambridge University Press, 1982.

Kavanagh, Robert. *Theatre and Cultural Struggle in South Africa*. London: Zed Books, 1985.

Kerr, David. "Community Theatre and Public Health in Malawi." *Journal of Southern African Studies* 13, 3 (1989), 469–85.

Kruger, Loren. "Apartheid on Display: South Africa Performs for New York." *Diaspora* 1, no. 2 (1991), 191–208.

———. "Placing the Occasion: Raymond Williams and Performing Culture." In Dennis Dworkin and Leslie Roman, eds. *Views Beyond the Border Country: Essays on Raymond Williams*. London and New York: Routledge, 1993.

———. "Staging South Africa." *Transition*, 59 (1993), 120–29.

Larlham, Peter. "Theatre in Transition: The Cultural Struggle in South Africa." *The Drama Review*, 35, no. 1 (1991), 200–11.

Manaka, Matsamela. "Goree and Afro-centric Theatre." Presented at the "Contemporary South African Theatre" panel, MLA Convention, Chicago, December 1990.

Masakela, Barbara. "Keynote Address" at the CASA Conference. *Culture in Another South Africa*, 250–56.

Meintjies, Frank and Mi Hlatshwayo, eds. *Staffrider* (special issue on worker culture), 8, nos. 3–4 (1989).

Morphet, Tony. "Cultural Imagination and Cultural Settlement: Albie Sachs and Njabulo Ndebele." In Ingrid de Kok and Karen Press, eds. *Spring is Rebellious: Arguments about Cultural Freedom by Albie Sachs and Respondents*. Cape Town: Buchu Books, 1990, 131–44.

Mutloatse, Mothobi. Introduction. *Forced Landing*. ed. Mothobi Mutloatse. Johannesburg: Ravan, 1981.

Ndebele, Njabulo. "The Rediscovery of the Ordinary: Some New Writings in South Africa." In *Journal of Southern African Studies* 12, no. 2 (1986), 143–57.

———. "Redefining Relevance." *Pretexts* 1, no. 1 (1989), 40–51.

Negt, Oskar and Alexander Kluge. "Public Sphere and Experience. *Selections*." Trans. Peter Labanyi. *October* 46 (1988), 60–82.

162

Nixon, Rob. "'An Everybody claim dem democratic': Notes on the 'New South Africa'," *Transition* 54 (1991), 20–35.

Olivier, Gerrit. "An Watter Kant van die Struggle is Jy?" In Ingrid de Kok and Karen Press, eds. *Spring is Rebellious: Arguments about Cultural Freedom by Albie Sachs and Respondents.* Cape Town: Buchu Books, 1990, 47–51.

Sachs, Albie. "Preparing Ourselves for Freedom: Culture and the ANC Guidelines." In Ingrid de Kok and Karen Press, eds. *Spring is Rebellious: Arguments about Cultural Freedom by Albie Sachs and Respondents.* Cape Town: Buchu Books, 1990, 19–29.

Samuel, Raphael *et al. Theatres of the Left: 1880–1935.* London: Routledge and Kegan Paul, 1981.

Sitas, Ari. "Culture and Production: The Contradictions of Working Class Theatre in South Africa." *Africa Perspective.* NS 1, nos. 1–2 (1986), 84–110.

———. "The Sachs Debate: A Philistine's Response." In Ingrid de Kok and Karen Press, eds. *Spring is Rebellious: Arguments about Cultural Freedom by Albie Sachs and Respondents.* Cape Town: Buchu Books, 1990, 91–98.

Sole, Kelwyn. "Black Literature and Performance: Notes on Class and Populism." *South African Labour Bulletin* 9, no. 8 (1984), 57–76.

———. "Identities and Priorities in Black Literature and Performance." *South African Theatre Journal* 1, no. 1 (1987), 45–111.

Spivak, Gayatri Chakravorty. "Subaltern Studies: Deconstructing Historiography." In Ranajit Guha, ed. *Subaltern Studies.* Delhi: Oxford University Press: 1984. Vol. 4: 330–64.

Tomaselli, Keyan. "From Laser to Candle. 'Ilanga le so phonela abasebenzi.' An Example of the Devolution of Theatre." *South African Labour Bulletin* 6, no. 8 (1981), 64–70.

Ukpokodu, Peter. "Plays, Possession and Rock and Roll: Political Theatre in Africa." *Drama Review,* 36 no. 4 (1992), 28–53.

von Kotze, Astrid. *Organise and Act* (Durban Culture and Working Life Publications). Durban: University of Natal Press, 1988.

Williams, Raymond. "Brecht and Beyond." In *Politics and Letters* (Interviews with *New Left Review*). London: Verso, 1981.

Younge, Gavin. "Running in the Sackrace." In Ingrid de Kok and Karen Press, eds. *Spring is Rebellious: Arguments about Cultural Freedom by Albie Sachs and Respondents.* Cape Town: Buchu Books, 1990, 80–84.

10

LINGUISTIC IMPERIALISM, THE EARLY ABBEY THEATRE, AND THE *TRANSLATIONS* OF BRIAN FRIEL

Josephine Lee

The history of English and Irish relations in the last two centuries might well present itself as a straightforward picture of England as oppressor, "rewriting" Ireland into cultural submission not only through political control, but also through the imposition of English as the language of high culture. But the project of reading cultural imperialism through language is much more complicated than it at first appears. In particular, the nineteenth-century movement to find a *"lingua communis"* for Ireland reveals that such an ideal is less of a God-given state of natural language than an unstable construct to which people give value and meaning. Nowhere is this problem more clear than in the history of the Abbey Theatre's search for a stage language. Linguistic issues that arise for the early Abbey also come back to haunt a much later play, Brian Friel's *Translations*. Both reveal the lasting ideological and political controversies surrounding language, and complicate our sense of how we can read the legacy of imperialism as inscribed within theatrical discourse.

Irish politicians and intellectuals have long recognized the importance of language; that, as Thomas Davis declared decades earlier, "A nation should guard its language more than its territories" (*Nation*, 1 April 1843; quoted in Brown 58). In the late nineteenth century, the speaking of Gaelic took on even greater symbolic weight, as various groups lobbied for the de-Anglicization of Irish culture. Douglas Hyde's inaugural address as President of the National Literary Society in November of 1892 urged "The Necessity of De-Anglicising the Irish People," and looked forward to the founding of the Gaelic League in 1893. Inghinidhe na hÉireann adopted as its goals "to discourage the reading and circulation of low English literature, the singing of English songs, the attending of vulgar English entertainments at the theatre and music-hall, and to combat in every way English influence, which is doing so much injury to the artistic taste and refinement of the Irish people" (Foster 450).

As David Cairns and Shaun Richards have suggested, the movement to cast off what was identified as English, to discard those "English" forms which had dominated Irish culture, was strongly supported by Anglo-Irish Protestant intellectuals who might otherwise have found themselves excluded as outsiders (63–5). To repudiate what was "English" as low and vulgar was also to embrace an ideal of "Irishness" as distinguished by noble and spiritualized character, a race unified by temperament rather than by actual historical origins. The notion of an essential Irish identity could unite highly contentious factions against the English colonizer as cultural "Other." Such constructs of national identity could ostensibly erase long-standing divisions along class, economic, religious, and political lines; yet it still preserved the power of the ruling class Ascendancy families. It was through promoting these ideals that Protestant Anglo-Irish writers such as Yeats found their place as nationalists, and as creators of a national art: "A country which has no national institutions must show its young men images for the affections" (*Synge* 3).

Those involved in forming the Abbey Theatre were highly conscious of their nationalist enterprise, as actor James Cousins describes:

> We talked in terms of "the movement", discussed dramatic theory and cognate subjects "off", and walked home with shining eyes and heightened colour to dream dreams of great plays in which the world should see something of the glory of Ireland, which was within and in front of all our desires.[1]

Understandably, Gaelic held the most promise as the language of a national theatre, "a Celtic and Irish school of dramatic literature" (Gregory 8–9). It offered a sense of authentic Irishness, and at the same time could be acquired by Anglo-Irish speakers, such as Hyde and Lady Gregory, as evidence of their loyalties. Lady Gregory wrote that "in the beginning we dreamed of a national drama arising in Gaelic," and Yeats voiced strong support for plays that "would be an important help to that movement for the revival of the Irish language on which the life of the nation may depend".[2]

But for a number of reasons Gaelic could not serve as the primary stage language for the Abbey. The Gaelic language had no formal history of association with theatrical presentation. There were "no Gaelic plays, no Gaelic actors, and no Gaelic audiences" (O'Leary 4). Throughout most of Ireland less than one-quarter of the population were still native speakers of Gaelic by the end of the nineteenth century (Foster 517). Various dramatic experiments made it all the more clear that simply writing in Gaelic could not magically produce a theatre closer to nationalist goals. There was no tradition of dramatic production, no indigenous form of drama originally written in Gaelic. The plays produced in Gaelic often imitated non-native forms such as farce or melodrama; some of the more successful pieces were even translated from English or other languages. Arguably, such drama was "Irish in language only" (O'Leary 10).

Importantly, many of those who held influence in the Abbey were themselves not native speakers of Gaelic, sharing Yeats's problem that "Gaelic is my national language, but it is not my mother tongue" (*Essays* 520). English, the language of the colonizer and oppressor, nonetheless remained the dominant language of the Abbey, an audible reminder that its leading playwrights such as Yeats, Lady Gregory, and Synge were also marked by their Ascendancy backgrounds. The playwrights of the early Abbey were challenged to construct a stage language that would not exclude them as ruling class, as Protestants, and importantly, as English speaking.

The plans for the Abbey Theatre called on a specific ideal of national identity.

> We hope to find in Ireland an uncorrupted and imaginative audience trained to listen by its passion for oratory, and believe that our desire to bring upon the stage the deeper thoughts and emotions of Ireland will ensure for us a tolerant welcome, and that freedom to experiment which is not found in theatres of England, and without which no new movement in art or literature can succeed. We will show that Ireland is not the home of buffoonery and of easy sentiment, as it has been represented, but the home of an ancient idealism. We are confident of the support of the Irish people, who are weary of misrepresentation, in carrying out a work that is outside all the political questions that divide us.
>
> (Gregory 8–9)

Ideally, the theatre would reveal to the audience their own essentially "Celtic and Irish" nature as "uncorrupted and imaginative," united by "deeper thoughts and emotions," not by historical allegiances. Performers and audiences would be allied against the stages of the English "Other" that were guilty not only of censoring artistic freedom, but worse, of misrepresenting Ireland as "the home of buffoonery and of easy senti-ment" instead of "ancient idealism." The plans for the Abbey Theatre promoted a particular vision of nationhood furthered through art; in a sense, the Abbey would be "carrying out a work that is outside all the political questions that divide us" by erasing the very real history of divisions *within* Ireland along lines of ethnic origin, class, and religion. George Russell (Æ) would later recall that "It was our literature more than our political activities which created outside Ireland a true image of our nationality, and brought about the recognition of a spiritual entity which should have a political body to act through."[3] Art could not only form but also disseminate images of an essential unity, smoothing over internal conflicts.

The success of the Abbey would have all to do with the need for a "true image" and a coherent rather than fragmented "spiritual entity." Thus in its crucial formative years, the Abbey's search for a new language, one that would promote an idealized cultural unity, became an aesthetic and a political concern. Assuming a natural love of verbal performance, an "audience trained to listen by its passion for oratory," the early Abbey playwrights needed to find a language that in practice could reinforce a sense of national identity. Unable to claim Gaelic, the early Abbey playwrights instead needed to construct an English which would bear Irishness as its trademark.

Synge calls for a language that has both poetic and realistic value, a goal echoed by others: "On the stage one must have reality, and one must have joy . . . rich joy found only in what is superb and wild in reality" (*Plays* ii). Lady Gregory also makes both realism and poetic "fancy" requirements for her stage speech:

> I myself consciously lift my comedies out of common life by some extravagance of idea or of language, that the imagination might play more freely and the bubble catch some radiance from fancy's prism before it breaks. Yet before that breaking one must have given the illusion of reality as the old juggler gave it at O'Ceallach's house, sending hare after hound up a silk thread.[4]

Even Yeats describes a balance between poetic diction and a naturalistic speech, asserting

> I love all the arts that can still remind me of their origin among the common people, and my ears are only comfortable when the singer sings as if mere speech had taken fire, when he appears to have passed into song almost imperceptibly.
>
> (*Essays* 223)

Claiming both "reality" and poetic "joy" as goals for dramatic language reveals a very particular strategy for constructing nationalism. Theatrical realism is less of a representation of actual events than a negotiation of a shared sense of reality; as Catherine Belsey suggests, it is "reassuring . . . because it largely conforms to the patterns of the world we know" (50–1). Thus a call for "reality" as part of a nationalist agenda can be thought of as a demand for the performance of agreed-upon truths. The theatre mirrored an idealized verisimilitude rather than any actual reality, tailoring its presentation and its language to an ideal of Irish nationhood. Any "naturalness" for the Abbey's stage language was produced through this accord. Frank Fay's comparison between the Abbey plays and English plays of the time makes such a motive clear; he distinguishes between "natural" and "poetic," "artificial" and "uninteresting," on the basis of what is "Irish" and what is "English."

> Again, the plays which are now being written in Ireland have a dialogue so lifelike that it would be ruined if made in the least theatrical in its delivery. In ordinary English plays, at any rate, people do not talk on the stage as they do in the street or in a room, whereas our dialogue allows us to talk exactly as Irish peasants talk in a cottage or on the road or in the fields. On the regular English stage, dialogue has to be made interesting; the talk of the Irish peasant is as a rule wonderfully interesting, and often even unconsciously poetic. Of course education, by making the younger generation talk "good English" would soon put an end to this gift of vivid speech, but it will take some time to accomplish that excellent object.[5]

The linguistic realism of plays written for the early Abbey, like any so-called "ordinary" speech written for the stage, sprang more out of particular ideals of community than from the faithful mimesis of real language. To call stage realism a construct, however, is not to deny its potency. Claims to authentic Irishness were measured by how successfully the play created a sense of familiarity and recognition, and convinced the audience of the playwright's first-hand knowledge of the Irish people. It is not surprising then that success for the Abbey's Anglo-Irish writers was measured in part by how audiences praised the "naturalness" of their language. Lady Gregory is mentioned as carefully transcribing "over 200,000 words of peasant speech before she wrote a line of her dialogue," and her plays were thought to have "the appearance of containing large pieces of real conversation."[6] William Boyle was likewise complimented: "The language of William Boyle's comedies is as flat as the land of Louth and Meath, from which his people were drawn," and "there is a smack of reality about every word that everybody utters."[7]

Actor Dudley Digges declared that the Abbey may have been founded in part because in the earlier Irish Literary Theatre, English actors had great difficulty with accents and dialects. But his assertion that "English voices were impossible for Irish plays"[8] was more than a practical suggestion for vocal training. It made clear that finding a particular language, and using it in the theatre, could be in many ways the ultimate act of resistance against English culture. The "Irish English" of the Abbey was no more natural for Irish actors; its unique artificiality is evident in Abbey rehearsals. Joseph Holloway describes the painstaking care Willie Fay took with the diction of his actors, "making the actors repeat over and over again those lines which did not sound quite right on the ear, until he was thoroughly satisfied with every little intonation and shade of inflection."[9] Various actors sometimes found these presumably realistic rhythms and syntax in fact quite difficult to speak. Frank Fay wryly commented of Lady Gregory that "Her dialogue used to make my teeth ache by a sort of bread and milk quality in it."[10] Synge's dialogue in particular caused difficulties; Maire Nic Shiubhlaigh remembered that

> It was neither verse nor prose. The speeches had a musical lilt, absolutely different to anything I had heard before. Every passage brought some new difficulty and we would all stumble through the speeches until the tempo in which they were written was finally discovered. I found I had to break the sentences – into sections, chanting them, slowly at first, then quickly as I became more familiar with the words.[11]

Calling for a newly "realistic" stage language was advantageous particularly for Anglo-Irish writers who needed to make claims for the essential Irishness of their plays. But careful mimesis could not in itself be enough of a goal, for a too-faithful claim for realism might in fact undo the ideal, as Synge was to discover with *Playboy*. Thus any claims for realism had to be tempered with the "poetry" marking the essentially Irish temperament. English could now be "Irish" not only because it sounded like the real speech of real peasants, but also because it reflected the spiritual, sensitive temperament that such a discourse itself marked as being truly "Irish" in nature. Thus "reality" and "joy" are not opposite qualities happily wed together, but rather manifestations of the same strategy. Paul Vincent Carroll describes the "Anglo-Irish genius" of "men who love the Irish nation passionately but who write superbly in a form of English that they have moulded to Irish requirements in beauty and art."[12] To meet these "Irish requirements" is to mold this "form of English" to echo some essential, unified, and coherent ideal of Irish character. Poetry could give the English language its own connection to an ideal of Irishness uncomplicated by actual politics; thus the language of origins, of Edenic wholeness, could become available to English as well as Gaelic writers.

In 1902 Synge predicts that the revival of Gaelic will end in "disappointment," but remains optimistic about the work of Anglo-Irish writers such as himself:

> With the present generation the linguistic atmosphere of Ireland has become definitely English enough for the first time, to allow work to be done in English that is perfectly Irish in its essence, yet has sureness and purity of form . . . . English is likely to remain the language of Ireland, and no one, I think need regret the likelihood.
>
> (*Aran Islands* 382–3)

But the success of such writers, at least in terms of nationalistic aims, was mixed. The most immediate critics of the Anglo-Irish playwrights of the Abbey were those who consistently opposed reclaiming the language of the oppressor for the oppressed. There was still strong support for a strictly

Gaelic-speaking theatre, along the lines of Frank Fay's declaration that "an Irish Theatre must, of course, express itself solely in the Irish language; otherwise it would have no *raison d'être*" (quoted in O'Leary 3). Not surprisingly, members of the Gaelic League constantly reminded the public of the inadequacies of "Irish English" for nationalistic purposes, warning of the dangers that any commercially successful Anglo-Irish theatre must pose: "Beautifully staged and performed plays in English are a danger to our hopes for self-expression in Irish – our language" (quoted in O'Leary 111). The debate over whether to use English or Gaelic haunted the history of the Abbey, even after it had long broken ties with the Gaelic League.[13]

The success of the Gaelic League and its championing of Gaelic could be measured in the guilt aroused within the hearts of even successful Anglo-Irish writers such as Yeats:

> though mine is the first English marriage I know of in the direct line, all my family names are English, and that I owe my soul to Shakespeare, to Spencer and to Blake, perhaps to William Morris, and to the English language in which I think, speak, and write, that everything I love has come to me through English; my hatred tortures me with love, my love with hate.
>
> (*Essays* 519)

Even the most Irish-sounding English betrays the goals of a "language of the tribe," not because members of the tribe cannot understand it, but because it necessarily exposes itself as adopted rather than natural. Writing in English must necessarily be fraught with a kind of irony that ruins any sense of naturalness. The terms of A. B. Walkley's praise, after a performance of the Irish National Theatre Society in London, are particularly telling. In the ears of the English critic, the English language is foreign to the Irish tongue.

> We had never realized the musical possibilities of our language until we had heard this Irish people speak it . . . . We are listening to English spoken with watchful care and slightly timorous hesitation, as though it were a learned language. That at once ennobles our mother-tongue, brings it into relief, gives it a daintiness and distinction of which, in our rough workaday use of it, we had never dreamed. But the charm does not stop there. These Irish people *sing* our language – and always in a minor key. It becomes in very fact "most musical, most melancholy". Rarely, very rarely, the chant degenerates into a whine. But, for the most part, the English ear is mildly surprised and entirely charmed. Talk of *lingua Toscana in bocca Romana*! The English tongue on Irish lips is every whit as melodious.
>
> (Walkley 146)

The impossibility of finding an original language, or even an agreed-upon substitute, shows how fragile nationalist and linguistic ideals were. In looking at the early Abbey, it becomes increasingly obvious that any formula for an essentially "Irish" English, whether sought after by play-wrights or praised by reviewers, was a political myth. The violent riots following the first performances of Synge's *Playboy of the Western World* were in part a testimony to this growing frustration. Criticism was aimed at Synge's "profane and foul-mouthed dialogue" as well as his characters as "immoral monstrosities" (Kilroy 19, 70). The anger felt was not just a matter of a few shocking expressions, but a linguistic essentialism shaken to its foundations. Members of the press, critics, and other audience members were well aware of, and in fact exploited, inflammatory issues of language, for which the word "shifts" acted as a catalyst. Attacks focused in particular on the "foulest language we have ever listened to from a public platform" (Kilroy, 66) emphasized a betrayal of the illusion of common values, both of Irish nationalism and of "good taste."

It was not, as has sometimes been suggested, that Synge was simply too "real" for his audience, too apt a mimic of the actual vices of Irish men and women. Synge in fact used "realness" as his defense: "I have used one or two words only that I have not heard among the country people, or spoken in my own nursery before I could read the newspapers" (Hogan and Kilroy, *The Abbey Theatre* 124). He reportedly even turned the issue back to the double standard of Gaelic and English: "It [the word "shifts"] was used without any objection in Douglas Hyde's 'Songs of Connaught', in the Irish, but what could be published in Irish perhaps could not be published in English?" (Kilroy, 34) But verisimilitude was not in fact the issue. What had to be censored was rather Synge's violation of the linguistic conventions necessary to sustain the ideal of Irish national character. Those involved on both sides were aware that "Truthfulness is not to be interpreted as meaning a stenographic accuracy of speech, or a mere reflection of obvious and common characteristics; but truthfulness to the tendencies, qualities, and impulses that lie hidden in the heart of the race" (Hogan and Kilroy, *The Abbey Theatre* 154). Synge's language was naturally a key target, for in its parodic tendencies as well as its profanities it denied the audience the ideals of Ireland formerly articulated by the Abbey. Synge's violation of this linguistic and political agenda damns him in the eyes of his critics: "We condemn Synge because his is not like the Ireland we know."[14]

The limited success of the Abbey playwrights at creating a "language of the tribe" does not reflect their lack of skill as dramatists; it shows rather the propensity of theatrical language itself to play out social dynamics which could not be controlled by the playwright. There could be no "pure" or "natural" Irish language, and political agendas could only ruin any attempt to create one. Any essentialist ideal of national identity demands a language which allows transparent, unmediated, immediate understanding; such an ideal all too easily must give way to doubts, and an awareness of the irony, ambiguity, and opacity inevitably present in language.

Critics have noted that in *Translations* Brian Friel responds strongly to both political questions in modern-day Northern Ireland, and to the representations of language in George Steiner's *After Babel.*[15] But Friel is also responding to the unique ways in which earlier dramatists, including the Abbey playwrights, had to negotiate the politics of creating a stage language. Like earlier Anglo-Irish playwrights, Friel is forced to create his "Irish" out of English. But although Friel has said that this play "should have been written in Irish" (Dantanus 201), it is the careful crafting of verbal action in English that makes the dynamics of the play come alive, and brings its political questions into true focus. Friel renders his stage "Irish" convincing, not so much by constructing an implicitly essentialist notion of "Irish" rhythms, syntax, and idiom, as by forcing what is behind such essentialism into sharp relief. Though Friel is firmly aware of the desire to find a "language of the tribe," he also sees that such a position cannot hold in the complex and painful political history of Ireland. His generation instead of finding words with natural and transparent meanings, find them to be tortured and problematic.

> The generation of writers immediately before mine never allowed this burden [of faith] to weigh them down. They learned to speak Irish, took their genetic purity for granted, and soldiered on. For us today the situation is more complex. We are more concerned with defining our Irishness than with pursuing it. We want to know what the word native means, what the word foreign means. We want to know have the words any meaning at all. And persistent considerations like these erode old certainties and help clear the building site.
>
> (*Aquarius* (1972) 5; Dantanus 18)

Translations, in questioning how language can express "Irishness," makes the history of the early Abbey and its idealistic aims newly relevant. The play presents a nostalgic, essentialist idea of language, but at the same time constantly undercuts this view, portraying words as complex instruments of conflicted political and social impulses. The play is not only a tragedy of cultural imperialism, where the idealized language of origins is lost through the contamination of English names. It is also a hard look at "Irish" as an idealized Edenic language, and a glimpse of ironic and parodic uses which subvert language used as symbol. Still, in the closing moments of the play, Friel comes as close as any of his dramatic predecessors to rendering English quintessentially "Irish," in ways that speak powerfully to those who are most immediately aware of this linguistic paradox.[16]

Translations opens with a glimpse of a linguistic Eden, an Irish-speaking Ireland before the Ordnance Survey.[17] The play opens in the hedge-school of Baile Beag, where the schoolmaster's son Manus is teaching the speech-impaired Sarah how to say her name and place of origin. Sarah's success, and the baptism of Nellie Ruadh's baby, open the play on a note of hope. The emphasis on *caerimonia nominationis*, the ritual of naming, foregrounds the stability and power of a society, and its power to give identity. In a more symbolic sense, it evokes the naming which takes place in Eden, where words are given magical and divine connections to things. The play thus begins with an affirmation of this culture as both natural and divinely blessed. In the hedge-school, Irish is not only an original language, but also in the intimate company of other classic languages, all in vigorous use. For Jimmy Jack Cassie in particular, the world of the hedge-school is one in which mythology – Greek and Latin as well as Gaelic – is not just language, but reality; in his Homer, the substance of words is gloriously real and present.

> JIMMY. *"Knozosen de oi osse –"* "She dimmed his two eyes that were so beautiful and clothed him in a vile ragged cloak begrimed with filthy smoke . . . "! D'you see! Smoke! Smoke! D'you see? Sure look at what the same turf-smoke has done to myself! (*He rapidly removes his hat to display his bald head.*) Would you call that flaxen hair? (385)

The security and order of this world are furthermore reflected in the language lessons of Hugh, the schoolmaster. Hugh's teaching style empha-sizes a confident link of words to meanings that even the effects of alcohol cannot blur. Thus in the first part of the play, the hedge-school suggests a kind of linguistic paradise, in which words affirm the importance and permanence of a society, and society maintains a clear and unmediated relationship between words and truth.

In comparison to the seeming solidity of this language, and the culture it sustains, English seems like a poor challenger. Doalty's *"imitation of two very agitated and confused sappers in rapid conversation"* (391) enacts English as foolish gibberish. His parody, Maire's wooden recitation of her childhood English sentence, "In Norfolk we besport ourselves around the maypoll" and Jimmy's single word "bo-som" are the stuff of comedy. English seems hardly a threat to the coherent and rich connections between the ancient language demonstrated in the hedge-school. But the stability of this linguistic Golden Age is quickly put in doubt. The mention of the "sweet smell" which foreshadows the potato blight and the Great Famine, the absence of the Donnelly twins who are presumably engaged in acts of guerrilla warfare, all signal imminent changes, internally as well as externally motivated. The new National school, where, as Bridget says, "you'll not hear one word of Irish spoken," and Maire's intentions to emigrate to America, reinforce our sense that linguistic change too is inevitable. But Hugh refuses to acknowledge these impending dangers. He ignores Maire's request to learn English, and the "Great Liberator" Dan O'Connell's political stand that "The old language is a barrier to progress," and assumes that he will be in charge of running the new National school as he has run the hedge-school. Locked into his linguistic world, Hugh disregards his own awareness that words are not fixed entities, but "signals, counters. They are not immortal. And it can happen – to use an image you'll understand – it can happen that a civilization can be imprisoned in a linguistic contour which no longer matches the landscape of . . . fact" (419). But Hugh in fact has some recognition of his own blindness to the fragility of his linguistic Eden; Irish is "a rich language," he tells Yolland, one that is "full of the mythologies of fantasy and hope and self-deception – a syntax opulent with tomorrows" (418). The saving grace of Hugh's linguistic idealism is its tragic self-consciousness, its ability to assess, even parody itself.[18]

Hugh's awareness is important, for the play is full of moments which destabilize the meanings and authority of words, and force us to be self-conscious about language. In the first scenes, Hugh's students mimic his confident language lessons. Upon his entrance, Owen also parodies his father, and his playing of "the game" takes on a more ominous tone. Although he joyfully greets the class, his expressions are touched with a somewhat patronizing irony: "Honest to God, it's such a delight to be back with you all again – 'civilized' people" (403). Owen's attitudes towards language are indeed different from the reverential, precise lessons of his father; he has been hired "to translate the quaint, archaic tongue you people persist in speaking into the King's good English" (404). His conflicted attitudes are even more evident when he translates Lancey's official declarations into Irish. Captain Lancey is indeed "a kind of military stage-Englishman" (Dantanus 197) in his linguistic inflexibility. Not only does he express himself as "the perfect colonial servant," as Yolland calls him, but he does not recognize the ridiculousness of his own bureaucratic speech, underscored by the simplicity of Owen's translation.

> LANCEY. "Ireland is privileged. No such survey is being undertaken in England. So this survey cannot but be received as proof of the disposition of this government to advance the interests of Ireland." My sentiments, too.
> OWEN. This survey demonstrates the government's interest in Ireland and the captain thanks you for listening so attentively to him. (407)

But what is perhaps more disturbing than Lancey's clear demonstration of linguistic imperialism is Owen's translation. As a contrast, Owen's version exposes the hypocrisy of Lancey's prepared speech; however, as a translation, his words simplify and soften the apparent authority of the original, leaving out allusions to "His Majesty's government" and "this part of the Empire," and substituting a more personal style of address. Owen tones down Lancey's inflammatory rhetoric, and masks its imperialistic intentions. The very "naturalness" of Owen's translation does not allow others to hear the threats implicit in Lancey's words. Both the hypocrisy of Lancey's formal declarations, and the distortions of Owen's translations, can only be evident to those who can speak both languages. As Manus recognizes, the Ordnance Survey is a "bloody military operation" in which Owen is a willing participant. The "incorrect" names and "ambiguity" will be "Anglicized"; English will now serve as the standard, the language of authority and power which will supplant Irish. The mapping will be a way of making Ireland readable to the English, and unreadable to the Irish.

> OWEN. Do you know where the priest lives?
> HUGH. At Lis na Muc, over near . . .
> OWEN. No he doesn't. Lis na Muc, the Fort of the Pigs, has become Swinefort. (*Now turning the pages of the Name-Book – a page per name*) and to get to Swinefort you pass through Greencastle and Fair Head and Strandhill and Gort and Whiteplains. And the new school isn't at Poll ma gCaorach – it's at Sheepsrock. Will you be able to find your way? (418)

With the discovery that Eden has become troubled by Babel, the problems of translation consume the play. The possibility of translation promises a fragile bridge across cultures, or a link to a past sense of origins. But the dramatic world moves progressively away from confidence in the clear connections between words and meanings, and into a fallen linguistic world of unstable and arbitrary conventions, ambiguities, and misreadings.

Ironically, the work that Owen and Yolland perform as part of the Ordnance Survey is also rooted in a kind of linguistic idealism. Although militaristic imperialism lurks behind their project, there is also the possibility for linguistic preservation as record and text.[19] Their task is to rename, to eliminate the ambiguity, opacity, and confusion of Irish place-names for English colonizers. But it is also a much more altruistic task: to find the English expression through distilling a kind of essential Irish reality, linking words to an "original" sound or meaning. Unhappily, the impossibilities of fully translating such Irishness into English become even more apparent. In the translation of Bun na hAbbann to a rather disappointing "Burnfoot," they reject any number of possibilities: Owenmore, Binhone, Bunowen. But though Owen insists that "we're standardizing those names as accurately and as sensitively as we can" (420), meaning is inevitably lost. What emerges is that not even the most careful translator can capture meaning, because meaning is inherent in the often minute and obscure differences structured within a language. The "first principles" cannot be translated, because they were conventionally rather than naturally defined. For instance, the convoluted link between "Tobair Vree" and its original significance can only be captured within that limited cultural understanding.

OWEN. I know the story because my grandfather told it to me. But ask Doalty – or Maire – or Bridget – even my father – even Manus – why it's called Tobair Vree; and do you think they'll know? I know they don't know. So the question I put to you, Lieutenant, is this: what do we do with a name like that? Do we scrap Tobair Vree altogether and call it – what? – The Cross? Crossroads? Or do we keep piety with a man long dead, long forgotten, his name "eroded" beyond recognition, whose trivial little story nobody in the parish remembers?

YOLLAND. Except you. (420)

But that there can be some "original" significance remains as the taste of Eden, the ideal for which Yolland and, albeit reluctantly, Owen yearn. It is the English Yolland who articulates the romantic ideal of an essential Irishness, "a consciousness . . . at its ease with its own conviction and assurance," and who, worried that "something is being eroded," insists on the integrity of the name "Tobair Vree." Just the moment when his argument for this integrity has become most compelling, however, Owen explodes with another incongruity: the announcement that Yolland has been calling him the wrong name all along.

The characters work towards careful and precise translation, the hope of communication between tongues, such as Owen's reassuring Yolland that "you'll decode us yet." But Friel's play does not let us rest on any confident linking of word to meaning. Rather it emphasizes a negotiation through words which are difficult, mediated, even tortured. Characters experience only momentarily the optimistic belief that linguistic differences can be bridged. Owen and Yolland, drunk with "lying Anna's poteen," celebrate a brief illusion of Eden, where they are the ultimate and absolute givers of names.

YOLLAND. A thousand baptisms! Welcome to Eden!

OWEN. Eden's right! We name a thing and – bang! – it leaps into existence!

YOLLAND. Each name a perfect equation with its roots.

OWEN. A perfect congruence with reality. (422)

Their drunken fellowship is, however, only a momentary absolution from the all-too-pervasive sense of words as problematic. Similarly the love scene between Maire and Yolland, while building the momentary illusion of relationship, at the same time emphasizes the opacity and difficulty of words. Their only common sounds are those of the place-names Yolland has learned, which Maire echoes. Through this "dialogue," they establish a sense of union, of shared world.

MAIRE. Loch an Iubhair. Machaire Buidhe.

YOLLAND. Machaire Mor. Cnoc na Mona.

MAIRE. Cnoc na nGabhar.

YOLLAND. Mullach.
MAIRE. Port.
YOLLAND. Tor.
MAIRE. Lag.
(*She holds out her hands to* YOLLAND. *He takes them*) (429)

But the same words which echo their love also emphasize its difficulty. At other points of the dialogue, they also repeat one another's words and phrases; at these moments, however, they are only aware of how far apart they are in language, and unaware of how close they are in thought.

MAIRE: The grass must be wet. My feet are soaking.
YOLLAND. Your feet must be wet. The grass is soaking. (426)

YOLLAND. I would tell you how I want to be here – to live here – always – with you – always, always.
MAIRE. "Always"? What is that word – "always"? (429)

MAIRE. I want to live with you – anywhere – anywhere at all – always, always.
YOLLAND. "Always"? What is that word – "always"? (430)

In the echoing of their thoughts we hear the possibility of communication that transcends differences, a love that is transparently felt, even through the barrier of words. But what is reinforced is that language is not in fact transcendent and universal; the repetition sounds to our English ears alone, and the "Irish" and "English" do not in fact affirm one another but intensify the incongruous distance between them. Thus each character's sudden realization, "Don't stop – I know what you're saying," is ironic as well as transcendental, coincidental as well as romantic. Their love in fact cannot escape the borders of the "tribe" created through language.

Maire and Yolland escape the social circle of the dance into a Paradise where, momentarily, only their desire for union seems to matter; similarly Yolland's wholehearted embrace of Irish suggests a desire to escape the social and political implications of language, into the realm of the aesthetic. It is Yolland who has seen Wordsworth, "out walking – in the distance," and like Wordsworth, Yolland finds his own poetry in the "common life" of Irish peasantry, experiencing "a sense of recognition, of confirmation of something I half knew instinctively" (416). But Yolland can read his newly adopted language only selectively; he misses not only the irony and complexity of words, but the danger inherent within them. For example, he cannot feel Manus's rage, as Manus recounts with disgust: "I just shouted something stupid – something like, 'You're a bastard, Yolland.' If I'd even said it in English . . . 'cos he kept saying 'Sorry-sorry?' The wrong gesture in the wrong language" (432). But Yolland's lack of knowledge can shield him only temporarily. No one in the play can escape into an aesthetic, apolitical space. Yolland must be read as political; as an Englishman and a gentleman, he can exist in no other capacity other than as imperialist, either in Bombay or in Ireland. Although sympathetic, he is also culpable; it is his sudden absence which precipitates the final tragic events of the play.

The last act of the play seems to destroy all hopes for shared understanding or translation; the situation deteriorates into misunderstanding and confusion, and English and Irish abandon the project of translation for non-verbal acts of aggression. Each of the earlier events is now given its dire consequence. The careful collaboration between Yolland and Owen is parodically distorted, as Lancey and Owen name the official list of towns that will be evicted and destroyed if the missing Yolland is not found. Sarah's symbolic failure to respond to Lancey's interrogation, and the death of the newly-named baby, grimly answers the play's opening hopes of perfect congruence between speech and social identification. A horrified Owen recognizes, too late, the impact of the collision between English and Irish that he has helped to bring about, and must suffer the guilt of his own consciousness, that as his father tells him, "To remember everything is a form of madness" (445). Maire learns from Hugh that the "always" she prizes so dearly "is a silly word." Jimmy Jack alone remains in the world of perfect "images" and myths that characterized the Eden of the hedge-school, but he too speculates on the potential problems of marrying Athene, the impossibility of a union "outside the tribe." The final moments of the play focus on Hugh's realization that he is witnessing the fall of his own Eden. Lacking a post in the new school, his only job may be to teach the despised "plebeian" English to Maire.

The play's last act not only forecasts the troubles for Ireland ahead, but it also seems to destroy any hope of shared language. Yet in the final moments of the play, Friel sets up Hugh's poignant speech to be a transcendent moment, one which commands an emotional rather than ironic reading. Hugh's closing speeches appeal again to a desire for linguistic unity, not from his empty classroom or from a sleeping Jimmy, but from an English-speaking audience waiting for some resolution. Hugh recalls his own moments of nationalist feeling, a moment from the 1798 Uprising where political ideal and practical hope fused together in an ordered vision of the world and its words: "Everything seemed to find definition that spring – congruence, a miraculous matching of hope and past and present and possibility." When the first flush of youthful patriotism faded, he recalls, there is a desire for return: "And it was there, in Phelan's pub, that we got homesick for Athens, just like Ulysses. The *desiderium nostrorum* – the need for our own. Our *pietas*, James, was for older, quieter things" (445). Hugh's words articulate in English – clearly, unambiguously, and powerfully – the desire for national unity which does not die with Irish as a language. The play ends with Hugh's final translating of Ovid; though stumbling, he persists, linking the decline of the Gaelic culture with the fall of ancient empires, "kings of broad realms and proud in war." The ending both mourns the death of great civilizations and great languages, but at the same time reminds the audience in the present that the "images of the past embodied in language" can be renewed and translated. Here it is English words that can express ancient history, and modern Irish hope and desire for a link with the past, transparently. In his speeches – to the sleeping Jimmy and to an audience on a gradually darkening stage – Friel's English becomes a language of Irish unity, which reminds that audience of every great country's *desiderium nostrorum* – the need for our own."

In modern Ireland, language embodies the conflict that is the end result of imperialism: a country torn within itself, seeking to unify against the Other that is also itself. Neither the Gaelic League nor the early Abbey Theatre could find a language that would suit their political purposes; what they created instead were memorable performances of their own desires which, with time, come to replace historical truth. Friel's final image also begins to erase Ireland's all-too-real political divisions with a poetic ideal of unity, the "reality" and the "joy" of a uniquely Irish endeavor. *Translations* ultimately still works as nostalgic tribute to the necessity of ideals of essential Irishness, prompting its audience to believe that, as Hugh says, "it is not the literal past, the 'facts' of history that shape us, but images of the past embodied in language . . . we must never cease renewing those images; because once we do, we fossilize" (445).

NOTES

1 James H. and Margaret E. Cousins, *We Two Together* (Madras: Ganesh, 1951) 67; qtd. in Hogan and Kilroy, *Laying the Foundations* 11.
2 Lady Gregory, *Our Irish Theatre* p. 167, and W. B. Yeats, *Beltaine* (February 1900) p. 4; quoted in Maureen Murphy, "Lady Gregory and the Gaelic League," in Saddlemyer and Smythe, *Lady Gregory, Fifty Years After* 159.
3 George Russell, "The Coming of Age of the Abbey," *Irish Statesman* (Dublin), 5 (2 January 1926) 517–19; Reprinted in Mikhail 136.
4 "Lady Gregory's Strenuous Effort to Found National Theatres and Quell Mobs Dissatisfied with Plays" a clipping dated April 1913 from her American cutting book, unidentified; quoted in Ann Saddlemyer, "The Glory of the World and the Peasant Mirror," in Saddlemyer and Smythe, *Lady Gregory, Fifty Years After* 313.
5 Frank Fay, "Some Account of the Early Days of the INTS," manuscript lecture; Mikhail 74.
6 Yeats, "Irish National Drama: Five Years of Progress. Mr. W. B. Yeats Interviewed", *Cambridge Daily News* 25 May 1910: 2, and Lord Dusany, *My Ireland* (London: Jarrolds, 1937); Mikhail 99 and 146.
7 Andrew Malone, "The Rise of the Realistic Movement," in *The Irish Theatre, Lectures delivered during the Abbey Theatre Festival, 1938* ed. Lennox Robinson (London: Macmillan and Co. Ltd., 1939) 94, and *Freeman's Journal* 26 April 1905; quoted in Clarke 163.

8 Dudley Digges, condensed from the *Recorder: Bulletin of the American Irish Historical Society* (New York), 10 (1 July 1939): 15–18; Mikhail 32.

9 Joseph Holloway, *Impressions of a Dublin Playgoer*, manuscript diary; quoted in Clarke 54–6.

10 Frank Fay, Letter to Maire Garvey, 3 June 1909; quoted in Clarke 154.

11 Maire Nic Shiubhlaigh, *The Splendid Years* (Dublin: James Duffy and Company, Ltd., 1958) 42–3; quoted in Clarke 158.

12 Paul Vincent Carroll, "Can the Abbey Theatre be Restored?" *Theatre Arts* (New York), 36 (January 1952); Mikhail 189.

13 One such playwright is Paul Vincent Carroll, who describes "the deplorable policy" of the later Abbey "to submerge criminally the Anglo-Irish achievements on which the Abbey was built, and replace them by an insane policy of purely Gaelic culture, expressed through the medium of the native language, of which the majority of the Irish people know little and care less." Mikhail 189.

14 Walter Starkie, *Scholars and Gypsies: An Autobiography* (London: John Murray, 1963); Mikhail 111.

15 See especially Dantanus and Pine.

16 Seamus Heaney comments that the figure of Sarah, and her troubled loss of language at the end of the play is particularly significant:

> It is as if some symbolic figure of Ireland from an eighteenth-century vision poem, the one who confidently called herself Cathleen Ni Houlihan, has been struck dumb by the shock of modernity. Friel's work, not just here but in his fourteen preceding plays, constitutes a powerful therapy, a set of imaginative exercises that give her the chance to know and say herself properly to herself again.
>
> (*Times Literary Supplement*, 24 October 1980)

The tone of Heaney's review contrasts strongly with the favorable but more guarded remarks of British and American critics, who found the play "a vigorous example of corrective propaganda: immensely enjoyable as theatre if, like much else in Ireland, gleamingly tendentious" (*Sunday Times*, 28 September 1980), or unduly "obsessed" with language (*New York Daily News*, 15 April 1981), or "a manifestly uneven piece of theater" (*New York Times*, 15 April 1981).

17 The Ordnance Surveys of Ireland, begun in 1824, were set up as civilian organizations, to formalize the boundaries of land and properties for tax purposes. However, as Friel suggests in his play, such operations also had a military basis. For further information, see W. A. Seymour, *History of the Ordnance Survey* (Folkstone: Dawson, 1980).

18 Friel's stage direction is that "*as the scene progresses, one has the sense that he is deliberately parodying himself*" (416).

19 For a more sympathetic view of the Ordinance Survey as linguistic preservation and scholarship, see John Paddy Browne, "Wonderful Knowledge: The Ordnance Survey of Ireland," *Eire-Ireland: A Journal of Irish Studies* 20 (1985): 15–27.

WORKS CITED

Belsey, Catherine. *Critical Practice*. London: Methuen, 1980.
Brown, Malcolm. *The Politics of Irish Literature: From Thomas Davis to W. B. Yeats*. Seattle: University of Washington Press, 1972.

Cairns, David and Shaun Richards. *Writing Ireland.* Manchester: Manchester University Press, 1988.

Clarke, Brenna Katz. *The Emergence of the Irish Peasant Play at the Abbey Theatre.* Ann Arbor, Mich.: UMI Research Press, 1982.

Dantanus, Ulf. *Brian Friel: A Study.* London: Faber and Faber, 1988.

Foster, R. F. *Modern Ireland 1600–1972.* London: Penguin, 1988.

Friel, Brian. *Translations.* In *Selected Plays of Brian Friel,* Irish Drama Selections 6. Gerrards Cross, Bucks: Colin Smythe; Washington: The Catholic University of American Press, 1986.

Gregory, Lady Augusta. *Our Irish Theatre.* London and New York: G. P. Putnam's Sons, 1913.

Hogan, Robert and James Kilroy. *The Abbey Theatre: The Years of Synge 1905–1909.* Dublin: The Dolman Press, 1970.

———. *The Modern Irish Drama, a documentary history II: Laying the Foundations 1902–1904.* Dublin: The Dolmen Press, 1976.

Kilroy, James. *The Playboy Riots.* Dublin: The Dolmen Press, 1971.

Mikhail, E. H. *The Abbey Theatre: Interviews and Recollections.* Totowa: Barnes and Noble, 1988.

O'Leary, Philip. "Poor Relations: Gaelic Drama and the Abbey Theatre, 1899–1913." *Journal of Irish Literature* 18 (1989) 3–24.

Pine, Richard. *Brian Friel and Ireland's Drama.* London: Routledge, 1990.

Saddlemyer, Ann, and Colin Smythe, eds. *Lady Gregory, Fifty Years After,* Irish Literary Studies 13. Gerrards Cross, Bucks: Colin Smythe; Totowa: Barnes and Nobles, 1987.

Synge, J. M. *The Complete Plays.* New York: The Modern Library, 1935.

———. *The Aran Islands and Other Writings.* New York: Vintage, 1962.

Walkley, Arthur Bingham. "The Irish National Theatre." *Times Literary Supplement* 8 May 1903.

Yeats, W. B. *Essays and Introductions.* London: Macmillan, 1961.

———. *Synge and the Ireland of his Time.* Dublin: Cuala Press, 1911.

11

DECOLONIZING THE THEATRE

Césaire, Serreau and the Drama of Negritude

Robert Eric Livingston

Poet, politician and anti-colonial theorist, Aimé Césaire is best known as one of the founders of the negritude movement. Launched as a literary movement in the hothouse of 1930s Paris, negritude rejected the French colonial policy of cultural assimilation, and espoused a renewal of African culture as a vehicle for black consciousness. The movement achieved postwar prominence with the publication of Leopold Sedar Senghor's *Anthology of New Negro and Malagasy Poetry* in 1948, which featured extended excerpts from Césaire's great autobiographical poem *Return to My Native Land* as well as an influential introduction by Jean-Paul Sartre (Mudimbe: 83–7). Preoccupied during the 1950s with the intellectual foundations of the black independence movement, Césaire turned, in the 1960s, to the theatre as a medium for advancing the political project of negritude. Working in close collaboration with the French director Jean-Marie Serreau, Césaire produced a set of dramas that together comprise a triptych of decolonization in the African world. Given the combative and dialectical energies of negritude itself, the turn towards dramatic form is hardly surprising: as early as 1946, a collection of Césaire's poetry, *Les Armes Miraculeuses*, culminated with a "lyrical oratorio," "And the dogs fell silent" (in Césaire 1990: 3–74). Where the plays of the 1960s do mark a departure, however, is in their efforts to make the visionary poetics of negritude more widely accessible. Developed explicitly for theatrical realization, Césaire's plays – *The Tragedy of King Christophe* (1964); *A Season in the Congo* (1966); and the adaptation of Shakespeare entitled *A Tempest* (1969) – seek to integrate the fierce lyric energies of negritude poetry with forms of popular festivity and cultural expression.

Given Césaire's status as a spokesman for negritude, his plays have received a fair amount of critical attention, including translation into English. Most critics, however, have seen the plays as direct extensions of Césaire's poetic vision, and have tended to ignore both the significance of dramatic form and the context of performance. Such an approach, while sensitive to the verbal density of the plays, risks homogenizing their political texture and fails to grasp the extent to which the plays reflect on the historicity of negritude. By exposing the gap between lyric vision and popular consciousness, that is, Césaire's plays register the limits of canonizing conceptions of African culture and maintain a critical awareness of the complexities of black consciousness.

Explaining his decision to explore the possibilities of theatrical performance, Césaire evoked historical, political and technical imperatives. "Politics," he declared to an audience of French students in 1967, "is the modern form of destiny; today, history is lived politics. Theatre should evoke the invention of the future. It is, especially in Africa, an essential means of communication. It must, accordingly, be directly comprehensible by the people." Inscribing his work in what he termed "an optic of development," Césaire envisioned theatrical performance as a means of combating cultural underdevelopment and facilitating the political mobilization of the newly enfranchised black nations. Drawing on previously suppressed indigenous forms and cultural traditions, articulating popular needs and aspirations, Césairean theatre was imagined as both critical and constructive, a contribution to the emergence of the culture of decolonization (Laville: 239–40).

Césaire's efforts to rearticulate the significance of negritude in the wake of decolonization owed a great deal to the theatrical vision of Jean-Marie Serreau. A follower of Jacques Copeau and Charles Dullin, Serreau was trained as an architect, and brought to his work an abiding concern for the construction – literal and figurative – of dramatic space. Early work with a provincial touring company, Jeune-France, left him fascinated with the potential of a mobile repertory company, minimally encumbered with fixed sets and capable of making theatrical activity more widely available. These two principles – construction and mobility – became hallmarks of Serreau's approach. After World War II, he emerged as one of the few directors capable of bridging the growing divide between the absurdist and existentialist "New Theatre" and the politically committed advocates of a Brecht-inspired "popular" theatre; collaborating with Roger Blin on *En Attendant Godot*, as well as works by Ionesco, Adamov and Genet, he also helped spearhead the Brecht revival with signature productions of *The Exception and the Rule* (1947) and *A Man's a Man* (1954) (Bradby: 144) Restaged at regular intervals throughout Serreau's career, the latter play, with its reconstruction of the worker Galy Gay, served as a touchstone for Serreau's treatment of dramatic character (Auclaire-Tamaroff: 87).

A resistance to both Brechtian and absurdist orthodoxies, however, coupled with the outbreak of the Algerian War, led Serreau away from the institutional centers of French theatre and towards its decolonizing margins. Starting in 1958, he began a collaboration with the Algerian poet Kateb Yacine. Their work on *Le Cadavre encerclé* proved provocative enough to force the production to move to Brussels (returning to Paris only in 1964); *La Femme sauvage* (1963) and *Les Ancêtres redoublent de ferocité* (1967) completed an epic trilogy about the Algerian Revolution. His encounter with Césaire, following a reading of *King Christophe*, developed into a parallel trilogy on the subject of negritude. Maintaining his focus on decolonization throughout the 1960s, Serreau staged major works by the Haitian René Depestre (*Arc-en-ciel pour un occident chretien*, 1967), Adrienne Kennedy's *Funnyhouse of a Negro* (1968), and, from the Ivory Coast, Bernard Dadié's *Beatrice du Congo* (1971), as well as Edward Albee's *Death of Bessie Smith* (1970). To produce these works, Serreau assembled a multinational company, working extensively with actors from throughout North Africa and black Africa.[1]

For Serreau, the turn towards an emergent Third World was neither a simple political decision nor a quest for exotic themes and colorful performance styles. Rather, it was prompted by a developing conception of the theatre as a space for collective self-definition and transformation. Seeing decolonization as a historical challenge to Western culture, Serreau looked to the poets and playwrights of the Third World for the sense of "creative contestation" necessary to a culturally vital theatre. "Until now," he argued,

> humanism has been confused with an image of the West. The period we live in renders this assimilation obsolete, and suddenly confronts our civilization and its commonplaces with other civilizations hitherto confined to the ghettos of history. It is the great strength of these poets, and our good fortune, that, while remaining other, they inhabit and enrich our language and our culture, compelling our habits of thought to transform themselves and to recover forgotten sources.
>
> (Laville: 240–1)

In practice, Serreau's notions of challenge, contestation and renewal translated into extending the expressive range of French theatre and opening dramatic space to the process of political transformation. Moving out of the little theatres of the Parisian Left Bank, Serreau sought an open or "exploded" scenic space, overtly constructed rather than self-enclosed, an environment for registering rhythmic movement rather than capturing a static scene. For Serreau, the theatrical experience was more movable feast than bounded representation, an occasion for spectacle more than a dutiful institution of culture. Incorporating music, song, dance, choral movement, political satire and audiovisual technology, Serreau crossed Brecht with McLuhan to envision a mobile theatre for the global village. "The social festival which is the theatre," he wrote, "should assemble all the various modes of expression: music, cries, dancing, each one expressing what the others can't express. This continual alternation is what constitutes the spectacle" (Laville: 261).[2]

The idea of "continual alternation" is key here. Putting Brecht's concept of interrupted action into overdrive, the Serreauvian spectacle is best grasped through its rhythmic architecture, as a set of verbal and visual movements that outline a space of transformation.[3] Building on the premises of *A Man's a Man*, character becomes construction; development takes place through the recurrent disintegration and rearticulation of the dramatic scene. Underlining the process of construction, mobile scenery facilitates the rapid multiplication of viewpoints. Alternating between fixed and fluid moments, between individual and crowd scenes, between dialogue and monologue, spoken and sung, Serreau staged the drama of decolonization as a dialectic of cultural challenge and response. Most importantly, by imagining a portable rather than permanent theatre, Serreau sought to confront the emergence of new social locations, and to build the need for rearticulation into the process of dramatic construction itself. In what Césaire termed the "theatre of development," mounting the spectacle would itself become a moment of cultural negotiation. This ideal of decolonizing cultural exchange, however, despite important interventions in Senegal, Quebec and Tunisia, remained largely unrealized.

THE TRAGEDY OF KING CHRISTOPHE

First produced at the Salzburg Festival in 1964, later reprised in Dakar and Montreal after its Parisian run, *The Tragedy of King Christophe* constitutes Césaire and Serreau's response to the first wave of decolonization. A sequel to Césaire's lengthy biography of Toussaint L'Ouverture, the play draws on the history of post-revolutionary Haiti to dramatize the challenges facing newly independent states. The urgency of cultural renewal, the dangers of rivalry and factionalism, the tensions between elites and masses, the meddling of foreign powers: these are presented, in *King Christophe*, as challenges to the visionary aspirations of independence and as pitfalls for political leadership. Casting its drama explicitly in tragic – that is, canonical – terms, the play frames decolonization as a question of social construction, the difficult elaboration of a new social order. As tragic hero, its chief protagonist functions at once as exemplary subject and political object-lesson.

At the center of the drama is Henri Christophe: slave, cook, general, king, and tyrant, as the production's publicity poster put it (Auclaire-Tamaroff: 111). Situating its drama in the conflict between Haiti's urban mulattos and the black peasantry, the play describes Christophe's efforts to realize an emancipatory vision by founding a genuinely independent black state. Driven by a desire to overcome the legacy of slavery, he transforms himself from popular tribune into autocratic ruler, increasingly isolated from the people whose hopes he embodies. Accompanied by a Fool-figure, Hugonin, who finally reveals himself as the voodoo spirit-master, Baron Samedi, Christophe remains throughout an uncompromising spokesman for negritude, justifying his actions by an appeal to the historic destiny of the black race.

According to Césaire, *The Tragedy of King Christophe* is meant to function on three distinct levels: political, existential and metaphysical (Auclaire-Tamaroff: 124).[4] The first involves the conflict between different personalities, groups and political ideals: Christophe vs. the mulatto leader Petion, blacks vs. mulattos, democracy vs. tyranny. These conflicts are essentially the subject of the play's individual scenes. At a second level, the play is unified by the overarching destiny of Christophe himself, and his transformation from visionary populist leader into isolated existential hero. Finally, at a third level, the tragic action is conceptualized in the terms of an African metaphysics, in which the play provides a meditation on the nature of power. Christophe, Césaire explains, represents Shango, the god of force and violent authority. But force

> is not the sole aspect of reality. Power tends to reify the world into immobility. That is why life, which is change, needs the intervention of humor, [which] functions by taking its distance from things, thus assuring passage, the mobility which is indispensable to life and which gives things their fluidity. That is what the character of Hugonin aims at in the play. Just as Christophe is Shango, Hugonin is Eshu, the cunning god of the Yoruba.
>
> (Auclaire-Tamaroff: 124)

From this perspective, the play's protagonist is not Christophe, towards whom the audience must necessarily be ambivalent, but the couple Shango-Eshu, the tyrant and the trickster together.[5] It is their uneasy conjunction and ultimate dissociation that provides the materials both for the tragedy and its transcendence.

To dramatize this complex cultural script, the play sets up a number of simultaneous theatrical rhythms. In a trajectory that goes from an opening scene of cock-fighting to Christophe's funeral service, there is a constant alternation between comic and tragic moments, a dialectic of parody and poetry. Thus, in an early scene, Christophe's first act as king is to assemble a court, and to receive, from the "International Technical Aid Organization," a master of ceremonies who will provide lessons in proper deportment. The satirical dig at Western aid programs is taken up in a larger carnivalesque movement, as the master of ceremonies proceeds to call out the names of Christophe's indigenous aristocracy: "His Grace the Duke of Marmalade/His Grace the Duke of Candytown/His Lordship the Count of Stinkhole" (Césaire 1964: 23). The broad comedy (compounded by translation) here conceals a political barb, for most of the names are real. The moment of humiliating laughter is then transformed into an occasion of creative defiance and self-assertion. In the first of a series of great lyrical interventions, Christophe situates his founding act in the history of slavery and decolonization: "With names of glory I will cover your slave names/ With names of pride our names of infamy/With names of redemption our orphans' names/Names of rebirth, gentlemen/ Playthings, rattles, no doubt/But thunder, too" (25–6). Fiery and inspiring, this poetic vision goes, as it were, over the heads of Christophe's compatriots and attests to his overweening power.

First played by the Senegalese actor Douta Sek, the towering figure of King Christophe dominates most of the action, and realizing Christophe's ambitions supplies the play with its central and most powerful theatrical image, the construction of an immense citadel on the cliffs of Cap Haitien, as a monumental symbol of defiant liberty. "This people has to want," Christophe proclaims as he formulates this titanic goal,

> to gain, to achieve something. Against fate, against history, against nature. That's it. Extravagant venture of our bare hands! Insane challenge of our wounded hands! On this mountain a solid corner-stone, a firm foundation. Assault on heaven or sun's resting place, I do not know – fresh troops charging in the morning . . . . No, not a palace. Not a fortress to guard my property. No, the citadel, the freedom of a whole people. Built by the whole people, men and women, young and old, and for the whole people . . . . This people, forced to its knees, needed a monument to make it stand up. There it is. Risen! A watchtower! (15).

Conjuring his vision out of sheer determination and rhetorical power, Christophe is at once a prophet of negritude and a nascent tyrant; the citadel both bodies forth the desire for liberation and becomes the site of its petrification. Built by conscripting the entire population – "labors suggesting the building of the Pyramids"(67) – the construction project presides over the second half of the play, and becomes the site of Christophe's ultimate isolation and death.[6]

If the citadel supplies a scenic emblem for the demands of nation-building, its performative equivalent is the organization of popular, festive elements into more hierarchical forms. Interludes of song and dance that, in early scenes, interrupt the action to signify popular spontaneity, gradually give way to choral and ceremonial movements: forced labor, a mass wedding, a climactic celebration of the Feast of the Assumption. An obsession with etiquette marks the stages of Christophe's growing tyranny, and his rage for order leads him to ever-harsher measures of social organization and political retribution. But as Christophe's isolation grows, so does his visionary exaltation. Lyric power thus becomes a sign of distance and estrangement, its grandeur founded on repression and the will to power. This movement culminates in the great hymn that precedes Christophe's death, in which he identifies his body with the beating heart of Africa: "Congo, I've often watched/the impetuous hummingbird in the datura blossom/and wondered how so frail a body can hold/that hammering heart without bursting/Africa, rouse my blood with your big horn/ Make it open like a giant bird" (89).

Despite the complexities of its theatrical rhythms, however, the play ultimately seeks to harmonize the conflicts it dramatizes into a moment of tragic reconciliation. Thus, the final scene makes Christophe's funeral the occasion of a choral song, in which the strands of the hero's life are woven together. According to Césaire, "Madame Christophe buries Christophe, Vastey [Christophe's secretary] buries the King, and the voodoo priestess, the 'mambo' who has accompanied Christophe all along, buries Christophe [as] the God Shango who will return to haunt the world mounted on battering rams of thunder" (Auclaire-Tamaroff: 124). Each of these attendant characters is given an extended song elaborating the dead hero's significant virtues. The funeral literally figures a moment of harmony: Christophe's death becomes the sacrifice necessary to the founding of a new social order. The closure of the play thus envisions the transcendence of social conflict, and the anticipation of independence as a collective aspiration. Christophe's destiny is to become the tragic victim of his own uncompromising social vision.

A SEASON IN THE CONGO

The Tragedy of King Christophe inscribes decolonization within the horizon of political independence. The hero embodies the aspiration towards an unconditioned freedom, and his death transforms his project into a collective social ideal. In Césaire and Serreau's next collaboration, *A Season in the Congo*, the relation between political independence and decolonization is far more problematic. Where *King Christophe* aspires to the canonical closure of tragedy, with politics subsumed by history, *A Season in the Congo* takes its subject from the immediate and still controversial past, events given renewed currency by the Congolese civil war of 1964–5.[7] Initially written in 1966, staged in Venice the following year, revised with a substantially new ending in 1973, *A Season* constitutes itself as a political intervention, an effort to resist dominant representations of decolonization.[8] As a result, the status of political independence itself is treated far more ironically, becoming the site of uncontainable conflict and the occasion of manipulation and intrigue. If *King Christophe* could plot the end of colonialism in a narrative of liberation, that is, *A Season in the Congo* finds decolonization enmeshed with the emergent structures of neo-colonialism.

The dramatic elements of *A Season* are, in significant ways, recognizable extensions of the earlier play. Once again, the center is occupied by a dynamic incarnation of negritude, whose lyric vision comes into conflict with political realities. Its protagonist is Patrice Lumumba, whose meteoric rise propelled the push for Congolese independence from Belgium in

1959–60, and whose six-month tenure as Prime Minister witnessed the outbreak of civil war, the declaration of martial law, intervention by the United Nations, and a coup d'état by Joseph Mobutu who, more than thirty years later, remains at the head of the Zairean state. Murdered by his political opponents, aided if not instigated by the United States, Lumumba became a conspicuous victim of Cold War politics and a martyr in the cause of pan-African unity; subsequent efforts by the Mobutu regime to re-habilitate Lumumba, in a cynically transparent bid for legitimacy, testify to his abiding popularity and prestige.[9]

A Season in the Congo follows the broad outlines of Lumumba's career, incorporating historical documents, political songs, and adaptations of Lumumba's own speeches and poetry in order to render the complexity of the struggle for Congolese independence. Despite this attention to the individual leader, however, the object is not "The Tragedy of Patrice Lumumba," but, as Césaire insisted, "epic theatre, more concerned with collective than individual destiny" (Harris: 126–7). The skeptical, caution-ary role that *King Christophe* had assigned to Hugonin is here held by a "joueur de sanza," an epic narrator who moves freely in and out of the action and provides a bridging commentary, often in hermetic, proverbial form. The increased importance of this figure is underscored by its being created for the powerful Senegalese actor, Douta Sek, who had previously played the role of Christophe.

If the earlier play maintained an admiring, albeit ambivalent, stance towards its heroic protagonist, *A Season in the Congo* is markedly more resistant to the visionary style of Lumumba, and guards itself against overtly hagiographic tendencies. From the first scene, in which Lumumba appears as a "bonimenteur," a fast-talking salesman for "Polar Beer," he is associated with various forms of intoxication – rhetorical, political and sexual, and his very fluency foreshadows both his popular charisma and his mercurial leadership.[10] Rather than celebrating Lumumba's politics, Césaire plays off his uncompromising defiance of colonial authority against the more plebian and oblique comments of the sanza player. Lyric exaltation, most intensely rendered at the moment of the formal transfer of power, in which Lumumba interrupts the ceremony to deliver a blistering denuncia-tion of Belgian rule and a soaring evocation of the Congolese spirit (Césaire 1966: 19–20), is pitted against both "epic" irony and popular song. The scene of decolonization is thus dialectically complicated, with discursive styles indicating differing, if related, political positions.

Indeed, both formally and politically, *A Season* is a far more complex drama than *King Christophe*, and registers a more elaborate rupture with the conventions of realist theatre. Freely intermingling historical, satirical and allegorical characters, shifting rapidly between levels of theatrical action, *A Season in the Congo* is at times closer to mass spectacle than to *King Christophe*'s self-contained tragedy. Although punctuated – and arguably flawed – by a number of expository and oratorical scenes (Laville: 258; Bradby: 149), the accelerated and intensified action aims at the fragmentation rather than the consolidation of theatrical space. With its revisionary allusion to Rimbaud's *A Season in Hell*, the play's governing trope reads the politics of Congolese independence as surrealist prose-poem, a historical literalization of what, in Rimbaud, remains an imaginary scene. The Congo becomes the site of a "systematic derangement of the senses," to cite Rimbaud's slogan. "We'll have everything," Lumumba declares upon taking power,

> and right away: mutiny, sabotage, threats, slander, blackmail, and treason. You look surprised. That's what power means: betrayal, maybe death. Death, no question. That's the Congo. See: the Congo is a place where things go fast. A seed in the ground today, tomorrow a bush, no, tomorrow a forest.
>
> (Césaire 1966: 28, translation modified)

Accordingly, interruption becomes the very motor of dramatic construction, with Lumumba increasingly at the mercy of the very forces he sets in motion.

Fragmented by the hallucinatory pacing of the drama, theatrical space in *A Season* acquires its dense texture through the accumulation of political interventions. "Above" the action, a chorus of Belgian bankers and the "Ambassador of the Great West" exert interpretive pressure and surreptitious influence; representatives of the United Nations, informed by the fervent religiosity of Dag Hammarskjöld, claim a position of strict political neutrality; from "below," masses of soldiers, religious devotees and diverse ethnic groups are repeatedly mobilized and maintain a persistent presence. Lumumba himself is surrounded by a shifting cast of allies and antagonists, whose political loyalties remain disturbingly unstable. Meanwhile, music, radio broadcasts and a variety of projected images establish a disconcerting audiovisual environment, in which the vulnerability of the unamplified voice is increasingly exposed.[11] Rather than moving, as *King Christophe* does, towards a tragic mastery of fate, *A Season in the Congo* constructs an open-ended historical texture, a rhetorical space recurrently subjected to deconstruction.

Within this texture, Lumumba's death, although heavily foreshadowed and dramatically unavoidable, cannot carry the weight of full closure. With its polemical indictment of existing political figures, the political force of Césaire's play requires that the death remain a contingent scandal rather than a tragic necessity. Consequently, the figure of Lumumba becomes increasingly problematic towards the end of the play. Although the logic of mass spectacle would tend to deny the significance of individuals – saying, with Césaire, that "after Lumumba, the season is over, history continues, another season begins" (Laville: 249) – Lumumba's status as political icon and repository of pan-African utopian hope cannot be so easily surrendered. As the moment of his death approaches, therefore, the play attempts to outline the elements of a secular martyrdom; lines like "My magic is an invulnerable idea. As invincible as a people's hope" (99) and "I'm dying my life, and that's good enough for me" (99) endow the mercurial politician with a perhaps overly schematic ethical significance.[12] In these moments, the thematic integrity of the drama is insistently reasserted against its headlong and destructive pacing.

The scenes following the death of Lumumba are more successful at preserving the open texture of the drama. Indeed, the ending itself was subjected to a number of revisions to take account of changes in the politics of the Congo. In the earliest version, in an ironic turn on the choral scene that closed *King Christophe*, speeches by Hammarskjöld, a Belgian banker, Lumumba's widow Pauline, and the sanza player offered contrasting interpretations of the leader's life and death, with the sanza player's invocation of the god Nzambi ("Hey you, the great god Nzambi/ What a big fool you are/You eat our ribs, you eat our asses" (100)) left as the last word. Rather than sublimating conflict in harmony, the ending underscored diverging, even conflicting, perspectives on resolution (Laville: 293–4).

In the play's first production, the interpretive conflict was enhanced by including addresses by characters identified as Lumumba's murderers: the Ambassador of the Great West, and the politicians Tzumbi, Kala and Mokutu. More important, however, was the addition of an epilogue dated July 1966, dramatizing an Independence Day celebration in Kinshasa in which Mokutu proclaims Lumumba's martyrdom ("Patrice, martyr, athlete, hero – I turn to you for strength to carry on my task") and dedicates a public statue to the man he had killed ("a statue erected at the gate of what was formerly Leopoldville/[will] signify to the world/that the piety of a nation will never cease/to make reparation for our crime/the crime of which we are all guilty/Congolese, let this day be the beginning/Of a new season for the Congo (103)).[13] Lest this perspective on the vicissitudes of decolonization appear too cynical, the play again concludes with a song by the sanza player, "The ballad of ambiguous times," not so much endorsing as contextualizing, with properly Brechtian irony, the inevitable revisions of the political line ("Sorghum grows/Bird rises from the ground/Why refuse man/The right to change?/A man is hungry/Do you deny him food?/Why say no to a country/Thirsting for hope?" (104; translation modified)).

A version published in 1973, however, eliminates the vestiges of historical ambiguity. With the crowd in a frenzy over Mokutu's speech ("Glory to Lumumba/Immortal glory/Down with neo-colonialism"), the president turns to one of his ministers: "Let's go. Clean it up. And quick. Let the nitwits know our powder's dry, and the show's over!" Machine-gun fire sweeps the square, and the stage is left littered with corpses, among them the sanza player (Houyoux: 345–6). Bleak, even despairing in its reading of the end of Lumumba's moment, this ending has the merit of political clarity, and perhaps the dramatic advantage of representing – rather than enacting – an arbitrary authority. Closure then becomes an event to be witnessed rather than a stance of demanding ambivalence.

A TEMPEST

Thanks to its canonical source, *A Tempest* remains Césaire's best-known play, and the one most amenable to a literary pedagogy (McNee; Smith). Indeed, recent New Historicist scholarship has stressed the colonial thematics of the Shakespearean text itself to the point of muting the audacity of Césaire and Serreau's 1969 "adaptation for a black theatre": thus is iconoclasm incorporated into a revisionary orthodoxy.[14] The anti-canonical move signalled by the title of *A Tempest*, however – interpretive modesty or sly subaltern irony? – seems already to inscribe an awareness of its own contingency. Although containing moments of radical appropriation, in which the canonical authority of Shakespeare is emphatically disrupted, the thrust of *A Tempest* is to complicate assertions of cultural autonomy by subjecting self-determination to the dialectic of master and slave.

Conceived initially for performance in Tunisia in 1969, *A Tempest* was given contemporary relevance by being cast as an allegory of American politics. According to Césaire,

> Demystified, the play [is] essentially about the master–slave relation, a relation that is still alive and which, in my opinion, explains a good deal of contemporary history: in particular, colonial history, the history of the United States. Wherever there are multiracial societies, the same drama can be found, I think.
>
> The dominated can adopt several attitudes. One is Caliban's revolt. Another is Ariel's, whose path is more complicated – but is not necessarily one of submission, that would be too simple . . . . If you want me to specify . . . I'd say that there is Malcolm X's attitude, and then there is Martin Luther King's.
>
> (Auclaire-Tamaroff: 132)

Such topical political reference-points ("Uhuru!" chants Caliban, and "Freedom Now!") were then integrated into a mythically stylized American landscape. As Serreau put it,

> We thought that the best visual climate to underscore [Césaire's reading] would be the western. *The Tempest* as a story of gangsters who are ready to kill instantly, and who finally agree to marry their son and daughter because Caliban is starting to stir. . . . So the costumes are western, symbolizing an epoch when America was peopled by pioneers

come from the old world and obliged to co-exist with slaves and Indians.

(Auclaire-Tamaroff: 128–32)

In addition, Serreau used the sails of the first scene's foundering ship as screens on which to project a range of historical and contemporary images. Rather than an integrated, naturalized representation of Shakespeare's *Tempest*, that is, Césaire and Serreau opted for a condensed – three acts in place of five – and evocative presentation, in which successive layers of colonial history are forced to the surface.

As a result, a cursory reading of the text risks overstating the formal coherence of *A Tempest* and underestimating its deconstructive force. Nevertheless, a number of textual revisions seem especially noteworthy.[15] First, in the list of characters, Prospero's two servants are identified by their race: Ariel is "ethnically a mulatto," while Caliban is specified as "a black slave." Their different relations to Prospero, as well as their visions of liberation, are thus referred to racial distinction. At the beginning of the second Act, Césaire interpolates a scene in which the two lay out their differences, with Ariel advocating non-violence and an appeal to conscience while Caliban proclaims the need for uncompromising resistance and "Freedom Now." Meanwhile, *A Tempest* also adds to the list of spirits by introducing an apparition of Eshu alongside Ceres, Iris and Juno.

Secondly, the entire drama is itself re-imagined as a mask play. In what the text calls "an atmosphere of psychodrama," the actors enter and, accompanied by the commentary of a master of ceremonies, each takes up one of the pre-existing roles. Significantly, however, the commentary emphasizes the contingency of the distribution of roles: "Let's go, gentlemen, help yourselves. To each his character, and for each a mask. You, Prospero? Why not? There are wills to power that are unsuspected" (Césaire 1969: 9). The effect of the mask-play is to de-essentialize the construction of race, to set up a tension between the racial script and its performance. The actors come to occupy allegorical roles rather than to create unified characters. Literalizing the diagnostic trope of Fanon's *Black Skin, White Masks*, the Césairean *Tempest* becomes a drama of cultural alienation and rebellion, an obsessive psychic script rather than a humanist utopia.[16]

In keeping with the dialectics of spectacle developed in the earlier plays, *A Tempest* also enhanced the importance of song and dance, from subordinate, incidental embellishments to fully active expressions of cultural mobilization. Caliban's defiance of Prospero is grounded in African culture: his work-song at the opening of Act II is a hymn to Shango, as is the marching-song of his rebellion. Most emblematic, however, is the way Césaire reworks the pastoral masque that accompanies the betrothal of Ferdinand and Miranda: into the classical order of spirits he injects the tumultuous, disruptive presence of Eshu. Drinking, dancing, demanding that twenty dogs be sacrificed to him, Eshu dispells the solemnities with shamelessly phallic vitality, singing: "Eshu has no head for carrying burdens/he's a gay one with a pointy head. When he dances/he doesn't move his shoulders/Ah, Eshu is a jolly fellow/ Eshu is a jolly fellow/With his penis, he will beat, beat, beat/With his penis" (70). What is remarkable about the apparition of the trickster-god is his ambivalent relation to the official ceremonies. Although obviously disruptive, his appearance is mischievous rather than malicious, a sign of spontaneity and vitality rather than rebellion *per se*. In the hierarchical assembly of spirits, that is, Eshu refuses to be forgotten. It is not so much the betrothal as the bloodless Western classical ceremony that he resists. Breaking up the forms of Prospero's alienating canon, Eshu's song and dance signifies the recovery of African cultural and psychic authenticity.

Despite the vigor of this counter-utopian moment, however, the central antagonism between Prospero and Caliban remains intact. In a final revision, Césaire rejects the Shakespearean vision of reconciliation and foregrounds a continuing conflict between colonizer and colonized. At the end of the play, master and slave remain locked in a specular relation of domination and defiance. With a consciousness heightened by the very failure of his rebellion, Caliban denounces Prospero's illusions and proclaims the imminent end of his own alienation:

> You lied to me so much
> about the world, about myself
> in the end you imposed an image of myself
> underdeveloped, you say
> incapable
> – that's how you made me see myself
> and that image: I hate it. It's false
> But now I know you, you old cancer
> and I know myself
> And I know that one day
> my bare fist, my one bare fist
> will be enough to smash your world. (88)

Faced with this challenge, Prospero, rather than returning to Milan, remains on the island to provoke a showdown with his old enemy. In Césaire's epilogue, Prospero appears aged and worn out, his language impoverished and stereotyped. Complaining about an invasion of oppossums and peccaries, the return of the jungle, he announces his resolve to defend civilization and to go head to head, as it were, with the former slave. In the end, Prospero is left calling out Caliban's name, while in the distance, over the sound of the surf and the cries of birds, scraps of Caliban's song can be heard: "Freedom Ohé Freedom."

Politically, the contrast between the ending of *A Tempest* and the choral conclusions of the earlier plays is striking. Caliban's animistic merging with the forces of nature suggests that freedom is elsewhere, ever-present but always elusive. As a voice in the wind, the spirit of liberation lacks visible agency: it persists as an idea rather than as a project for collective realization. The scene closes with Prospero frustrated and pathetic, but continuing to occupy center stage. The atmosphere of psychodrama is thus not entirely dispelled, even if what must be called the Arielization of Caliban points towards the final lifting of masks. The spectacle remains the scene of alienation and false consciousness, with the end of the drama symbolically raising the curtain on a different world. Whether re-enacting and ratifying the fact of decolonization, or gesturing towards a liberation yet to come, the performance of *A Tempest* thus inscribes a political relation to the site of its own production. Created for the first international cultural festival held at Hammamet, Tunisia, the play anticipates the imminent extension of decolonized territories.

CONCLUSION

In the wake of *A Tempest*, Serreau placed plans for future work under the sign of his collaboration with Césaire. Founding a "Théâtre de la Tempête," he went on to direct *A Man's a Man* in Martinique in 1972 and Paul Keinig's drama of the French Revolution, *Le Printemps des bonnets rouges* the following year. But the institutional existence of a decolonized theatre fell victim to Serreau's own untimely death in 1973, and sporadic efforts to carry on failed to integrate the disparate elements of the initial vision. A *Festschrift* assembled in 1986 attests to the range of Serreau's influence, and contains vivid testimony from his numerous collaborators. The fact that Césaire himself attributed his withdrawal from dramatic writing to Serreau's death is evidence of the intensity of their collaboration; apart from a brief collection of poems, *moi, laminaire*, issued in 1982, Césaire produced little new work in the susbsequent two decades (Auclaire-Tamaroff: 124).

It is, of course, problematic to construct a evolutionary narrative out of Césaire and Serreau's three dramas. There are, among the plays, clear lines of thematic and stylistic continuity as well as important differences in political and cultural emphasis. Historical tragedy, quasi-documentary history, revisionary adaptation: these are best grasped as three approaches to the problem of dramatizing negritude rather than definitive comments on the process of decolonization. Nevertheless, it is difficult not to remark upon the passage from a predominantly constructive figuration of decolonization in *The Tragedy of King Christophe* to the primarily deconstructive rendering of *A Tempest*. Whether this shift is best taken as an advance or a retreat, an optimistic celebration of uncompromising defiance (Nixon: 200) or a pessimistic allegory of post-colonial impasse (Mbom: 99), depends both on an assessment of the cultural politics of negritude and a reading of the history of decolonization.

Short of such a full-scale recontextualization, a few summary comments may be in order. In retrospect, what is most striking about Césaire and Serreau's collaboration is their sense of decolonization as a moment of accelerated cultural development. Theatrical performance could, in their view, both assist and reflect this development. By working with a multi-cultural troupe on pieces intended for rapid adaptation to different venues, the process of production itself became an occasion for the creative exploration of diverse performance styles and expressive traditions. The spectacle became a site for the active transformation of culture. At the same time, the plays developed were informed by the history of anti-colonial resistance, and contributed to the construction of a new global culture of decolonization. With the deceleration of Third World development in the 1970s and 1980s, the chill of a resurgent neo-colonialism left much of this vision unrealized, and exposed the utopian underpinnings of the project perhaps too clearly. Equally visible were the limits of its conception of the politics of liberation, notably an almost exclusive focus on the role of a male leadership (Mbom: 97–9; Nixon: 205). The Brechtian texture of Césaire and Serreau's epic dramaturgy, however, proved sufficiently open to allow for corrective revision; thus, a revival of *A Season in the Congo* in 1989 restaged the drama as a commemoration of the anniversary of Lumumba's death, with the role of the sanza player re-assigned to a woman (Houyoux: 508–16). Conceived as flexible constructions rather than formal products, vehicles for a decolonizing consciousness rather than canonical definitions, the plays retain their vital orientation towards a historical future.

NOTES

1 A complete listing of Serreau's collaborators is supplied by Auclaire-Tamaroff and Barthélémy (209–20).
2 Compare Césaire's comment:

> For me, song and dance are not opposed, and I don't choose between them. I don't believe there is one kind of art especially apt for conveying political conflict. For me, theatre is a complete, total art. Theatre can integrate poetry, dance, song, folklore, storytelling; it's an art of synthesis and integration.
>
> (Laville: 261)

3 Such acceleration would seem to eliminate the time for reflection necessary to the Brechtian conception. Serreau justified his pacing with an appeal to the development of modern media:

> If the spectator's eye gets bored, it's because we no longer offer an image that's alive enough, rapid enough. The modern spectator is a man who lives

in a world of perpetual movement and his powers of absorption have become breathtaking. The spectacle shouldn't be put on in a theater, the theater should be built up around each spectacle.

(Auclaire-Tamaroff: 58)

4 Cesaire's comments actually refer to the political, the *human*, and the metaphysical; I have rendered "human" as "existential" in order to preserve a sense of ascending hierarchy.

5 For a suggestive consideration of Eshu as a figure of black signification, see Henry Louis Gates, Jr. (1988), pp. 3–43.

6 For an interpretation of these events that differ in illuminating ways from Cesaire's drama, see Alejo Carpentier's 1949 novel, *El reino de este mundo* (*The Kingdom of This World*).

7 Indeed, the events surrounding the death of Patrice Lumumba continue to be a source of political controversy in Zaire, raising fundamental questions about the legitimacy of the post-colonial state. See "Zaire Reopens Old Wound: Lumumba's Death" (*New York Times* 14 June 1992).

8 With its historical background and extensive revisions, the textual history of *A Season in the Congo* is extremely vexed. An indispensable point of reference is the annotated edition, including historical documentation, prepared by Suzanne Birchaux Houyoux (unpublished Ph.D. dissertation, University of Virginia 1990).

9 An interesting perspective on these events, by one of the participants in the UN Mission, can be found in Conor Cruise O'Brien's play *Murderous Angels: a political tragedy and comedy in black and white* (1968).

10 Hoyoux reprints the advertisement for Polar Beer on which the scene is based.

11 Laville (264) remarks that "The vocal and gestural techniques of the black [African] actors differ from those of European actors to the point that it is sometimes difficult to distinguish between song, dance and spoken diction."

12 It should be noted, however, that a number of Lumumba's lines (e.g. the statement "If I have to die, I want to die like Gandhi" (89)) are virtually historical quotation (Houyoux: 298).

13 According to a letter reprinted by Houyoux (472) the scene was modeled on the canonization of Shaw's St Joan.

14 See, most notably, Paul Brown (1985), Francis Barker and Peter Hulme (1985), and Stephen Greenblatt (1990). Nixon (1987) provides a useful overview of post-colonial readings of *The Tempest*.

15 Given the problems of rendering Shakespeare into French, the differences between translation, revision and adaptation – including the status of the English version of Cesaire's text – might merit considerable reflection; a full consideration would necessarily touch on the historical uses of Shakespeare as a counter-weight to the canons of French classicism.

16 As Rob Nixon points out, the subtext for Cesaire's interpretation includes both Fanon and Césaire's own critique of Octave Mannoni's 1949 text, translated as *Prospero and Caliban: The Psychology of Colonization* (Nixon: 190–91).

WORKS CITED

Auclaire-Tamaroff, Elisabeth, and Barthélémy. *Jean-Marie Serreau: Découvreur de Théâtres*. Paris: L'Arbre Verdoyant, 1986.

Barker, Francis and Peter Hulme. "Nymphs and reapers heavily vanish: the discursive con-texts of *The Tempest*" in John Drakakis, ed. *Alternative Shakespeares*. New York: Methuen, 1985.

Bradby, David. *Modern French Drama*, 2nd edition. Cambridge: Cambridge University Press, 1991.

Brown, Paul. "'This thing of darkness I acknowledge mine': *The Tempest* and the discourse of colonialism" in Jonathan Dollimore and Alan Sinfield, eds. *Political Shakespeare: New Essays in Cultural Materialism*. Ithaca: Cornell University Press, 1985.

Césaire, Aimé. *Lyric and Dramatic Poetry 1946–82*. Trans. Clayton Eshleman and Annette Smith. Charlottesville: University Press of Virginia, 1990.

———. (1964), *La Tragédie du Roi Christophe*. Trans. Ralph Manheim, *The Tragedy of King Christophe*. New York: Grove Press, 1969.

———. (1966) *Une Saison au Congo*. Trans. Ralph Manheim, *A Season in the Congo*. New York: Grove Press, 1968]

———. (1969) *Une tempête*. Trans. Emile Snyder and Sanford Upson, *A Tempest*. New York: Third World Press, 1975.

Gates, Henry Louis, Jr. *The Signifying Monkey: A Theory of African-American Literary Criticism*. New York: Oxford University Press, 1988.

Greenblatt, Stephen. "Learning to Curse: Aspects of Linguistic Colonialism in the Sixteenth Century" in *Learning to Curse: Essays in Early Modern Culture*. New York: Routledge, 1990.

Harris, Rodney. *L'Humanisme dans le theatre d'Aimé Césaire*. Ottawa: Naaman, 1973.

Houyoux, Suzanne Brichaux. *Aimé Césaire: A Season in the Congo*. Annotated Edition. Ph.D. dissertation, Department of French, University of Virginia, 1990.

Laville, Pierre. "Aimé Césaire et Jean-Marie Serreau: Un acte politique et poétique" in *Les Voies de la création théâtrale II*, 1970.

Mbom, Clement. *Le Théâtre d'Aimé Césaire*. Paris: Fernand Nathan, 1979.

McNee, Lisa. "Teaching in the multicultural tempest." *College Literature* 19/20 (1993): 195–201.

Mudimbe, V. Y. *The Invention of Africa*. Bloomington and Indianapolis: Indiana University Press, 1988.

Nixon, Rob. "Caribbean and African Appropriations of *The Tempest*, in Robert von Hallberg, ed. *Politics and Poetic Value*. Chicago: University of Chicago Press, 1987.

Smith, Robert P. "Evoking Caliban: Césaire's response to Shakespeare." *CLA Journal* 35 (1992): 387–99

FURTHER READING

Arnold, A. James. *Modernism and Negritude*. Cambridge: Harvard University Press, 1981.

Clifford, James. "A Politics of Neologism" in *The Predicament of Culture*. Cambridge: Harvard University Press, 1988.

Hulme, Peter. *Colonial Encounters: Europe and the Native Caribbean 1492–1797*. New York: Methuen, 1986.

Pallister, Janis. *Aimé Césaire*. New York: Twayne, 1991.

12

INTERCULTURAL PERFORMANCE, THEATRE ANTHROPOLOGY, AND THE IMPERIALIST CRITIQUE

Identities, Inheritances, and Neo-Orthodoxies

Julie Stone Peters

In the first decades of the century, after Sadanji Ichikawa II's 1909 production of Ibsen's *John Gabriel Borkman*, Japanese theatre practitioners like Hōgetsu Shimamura and Shōyō Tsubouchi celebrate the importation of the Italian proscenium stage and of English, French, and Scandinavian naturalist drama (in the *Shingeki* movement) as a revolutionary liberation from the stifling Japanese traditional theatre.

In the 1920s, after having seen two American vaudeville and ragtime performers who were touring West Africa, the Ghanaian actors Ishmael "Bob" Johnson, C. B. Hutton, and J. B. Ansah, form a comedy group and develop a new theatrical genre – the "concert party" – which combines vaudeville, Ghanaian *Anansesem* narrative performance, and Liberian sea-shanties.

In 1984, a Hungarian scholar named Robert Sarlós begins the reconstruction of the 1583 Catholic Easter play, the *Luzerner Osterspiel*, attempting to train actors, dancers, and musicians in sixteenth-century style, and to dress the Swiss audience in sixteenth-century costume.

In 1985 in Zambia, a group of Ndembu led by a midwife named Seriya engage in a reconstruction of the *Kankanga* dances (the girl's initiation ceremony), using the script in Victor Turner's *The Drums of Affliction* (1968), and combining *Kaonde* performance forms with invented segments as a substitution for the naked "breast dance" the Turners had seen in the 1950s.[1]

In 1985 (following the lead of a spate of Indian theatrical, film, and television versions), Peter Brook and Jean-Claude Carrière collaborate with an international cast of actors on a grandiose theatrical adaptation of the

199

3,000-year-old Sanskrit epic, *The Mahabharata*, a production viewed by many (not just by them) as a monument of intercultural performance.

Each of these performances, it goes without saying, has a loaded political subtext. None is neutral. No two are equivalent. While *Shingeki*, the concert party, and Brook and Carrière's *Mahabharata* all involve cultural borrowing, they involve different kinds of cultural borrowing with different political implications. While both Seriya's *Kankanga* and Sarlós's *Osterspiel* involve the reconstruction of a lost piece of ritual – at once sacred and entertaining – their participants relate to these reconstructions in very different ways. While all are attempts to uncover an alien ideology and aesthetics, something either historically or geographically foreign, each has its own history. That seemingly parallel forms of cultural exchange, which a simplistic egalitarianism might deem precisely analogous, are not in fact equal – that history makes differences – now seems obvious in the face of the numerous studies of cultural imperialism produced over the last decades: studies of the superimposition of European high culture on local cultures (and hence the suppression of the local); studies of the "orientalist" (inevitably falsifying) representation of the "non-Western"; studies of the ethnographic voyeurist spectatorship that serves such representation.[2]

Few who have a recognition of the historical inequity of global cultural power (money, resources, educational institutions, prestige induced by centuries of such imbalance) would suggest that this is purely past history. The various forms of dominance – economic, military, cultural – are structurally integrated, self-bolstering, sometimes indistinguishable. When, for instance, Portuguese adventurers in sixteenth-century Brazil performed a spectacular version of the Nativity for local inhabitants that concluded with the "signing over" of land, or when in 1710 a group of Iroquois kings (allies against the French in the struggle over the riches of the colony of New York) paraded through London on their way to a performance of *Macbeth* where the mob in the upper gallery insisted that they be placed on the stage as part of the spectacle (Bond 4), or when at the 1993 presidential inauguration strains of "We Shall Overcome" rose as military planes flew over enormous screens that superimposed the images of JFK, Martin Luther King, and Bill Clinton while US forces bombed Iraq – at these moments the political, economic, and cultural become part of a unified system.

Theatre has a special place in this history because it offers an aestheticized brand of performance, of the ways things happen on the political stage or the stage of war, in the courts and on the streets. It offers a particular version (crucial to cultural self-perception in the modern period) of what Nguge Wa 'Thiongo calls "orature" (quoted Roach 1): those performances of the voice and body that serve as cultural inscriptions without the need of writing. It provides occasions for reflection on the ways texts and performances relate to each other: the ways texts may document or prescribe performances; the ways memory recorded in writing competes with the repetition of people's histories, repetitions which are at once, themselves, forms of memory and new performances. More concretely, it has been a powerful tool in the history of subordination and resistance, of cultural appropriation and reappropriation, of the constitution, breakup, and refurbishing of the modern empires. Theatre (broadly construed) and its modern mechanical offshoots have been instruments of power, whether in the invasion of the "New World," when Jesuit performances taught language and religion to the "savage," in the importation of the exotic in the nineteenth and twentieth centuries (in world fairs, in museums, in the imitation of "primitive rituals" and "oriental" dance forms), or in the twentieth-century spread of capital-intensive mechanical media (film, television, computer technologies), which have given the affluent countries a capacity to monopolize the media market, and so to reinforce the cultural hegemonies already in place – to shape global taste, and hence global consumption of culture.

The performance forms the late twentieth century has inherited, then, are deeply invested in the histories of the modern empires. And yet each performance has its own valences: each engages its own terms, its own representations, its own version of power relations. For many Japanese intellectuals, for instance, imitations of Ibsen in the 1910s and 1920s could convey a subtle resistance to the politics of Japanese imperialism, even while the Japanese imperial presence in China was spreading European (more than Japanese) theatrical forms in the Chinese theatre. For those reconstructing the *Kankanga*, the fusion of Ndembu and Kaonde forms meant an acceptance of a Zambian national (as opposed to tribal) basis for the initiation rite; it meant embracing the promises of African nationalism (the promises of liberation from the Anglo empire) through a "return" to "traditional origins" whose terms were dictated by a US anthropologist. Those who would suggest that Ishmael "Bob" Johnson's imitation of vaudeville in Ghana is the same as Peter Brook's imitation of Indian epic in London would be ignoring the history of power. But those who imply that the history of theatre in the empires is the history of two sides at war are equally mistaken.

It is tempting for cultural historians to explain cultural products as the outcome of radical polarities because they may, in so doing, place themselves on one side in a clear-cut moral universe. But such explanations are primarily the result of ideological slippage, in which arguments about particular historical situations are generalized into formal principles, and reapplied to situations different in significant ways. Those engaged in the debate *within* studies of power and global cultural exchange (for instance, that over terms like "post-colonial," "the Other," "North/South") recognize that the politics of such exchange are too multifarious to conform to a simplistic picture. Theorists who have engaged in the most careful self-scrutiny acknowledge that the "post-colonial" studies industry has often unconsciously perpetuated the unnuanced bifurcation of West and East, First and Third Worlds, developed and undeveloped, primitive and civilized.

As the debate within such studies recognizes, positionality is complex. "Heterogeneous and heteronomous representations" (to quote Teresa de Lauretis by way of Sue-Ellen Case (Case 111)) are just that, and cannot be understood by being identified with one of two polarized positions, whose scripts are seen as unchanging. If we are to understand the cultural history of the empires of the past three centuries, and if cultural exchange is to provide a basis for moving beyond that history, we must not indulge in the crude picture of "Western" cultural imposition (imperialism), appropriation (orientalism), and objectification (ethnographic voyeurism), but allow history all its complexity. If we – writers, readers, talkers, thinkers (a "we" that is complex, variegated, hardly unified, but that must nonetheless sometimes function as if unified) – if we cannot do so, then we demean the important work on imperialism of the last decades.[3]

An instance of slippage: the institution of Sanskrit poetics in Britain (as Case argues) was as much part of the imperialist project of "converting the heathen" in India as the teaching of Shakespeare there,[4] but in the hands of the Romantics, Sanskrit poetics became absorbed by Greek poetics, and lost its "indigenous" character; Brook's *Mahabharata* is the descendent of British Sanskrit poetics; therefore, Brook's *Mahabharata* is a continuation of the imperialist project.

A (broader) version of that argument: the ostensible struggle against imperialism on the part of European performance-ethnographers (Artaud and others) in the early part of the century takes the form of the suppression of local values and the imposition of European aesthetics and values on the "primitive," in combination with an ethnographic voyeurism and fetishizing orientalism;[5] much of contemporary European and North American theatre anthropology and intercultural performance is a direct descendent of just such modernist performance ethnography; therefore, these have inherited the voyeurism and orientalism – the unconscious imperialism – that marked the European attempt to assimilate non-European forms.

The logic, then, swells: theatre anthropology and the ostensibly intercultural performances that are its inheritors – from Artaud's hallucinatory ethnography, through "ritual" theatre like Genet's, through the studies of anthropologists like Victor Turner and theatre theorists and practitioners like Richard Schechner and Eugenio Barba, through performance experimentation from the 1960s on, like that of Jerzy Grotowski, Lee Breuer, or Brook – are part of the pattern of Western imperialist appropriation. Such studies and performances perpetuate the dualisms that the discipline of anthropology helped to construct, dualisms which have been complicit in post-1950s neo-imperialism: anthropologist/primitive, writing/ritual, subject/object, observer/observed. At the same time, by representing others, intercultural practitioners and anthropologists continue to refuse those "others" self-representation. The "Western" use of "non-Western" performance forms has inevitably (as Daryl Chin writes) a "hidden agenda of imperialism" (Chin 87).

In an eloquent and carefully reasoned essay, Una Chaudhuri outlines the troubled historical background to late twentieth-century "theatre anthropology" and intercultural performance. Chaudhuri merits quoting at length not only because her critique is so convincing (and hence worth challenging), but also because she adumbrates most of the central charges that critics bring against theatre anthropology and intercultural performance:

> Interculturalism has developed as both a problematic practice and an ideological – and idealistic – project. In the former guise, it has sometimes seemed to collude in another version of cultural imperialism, in which the West helps itself to the forms and images of others without taking the full measure of the cultural fabric from which these are torn. This practice (of which the prime recent example, some have argued, was Peter Brook's *Mahabharata*) claims the interculturalist label for itself and often seeks to elaborate a moral-political model of theatre as a *vital . . .* cultural *exchange*. Its critics, however, discern a less-than-equal dimension to its foundational trope: is the barter truly egalitarian, do both sides gain equally, or is there something of the "glass-beads-for-land" model of exchange at work here? Is this kind of interculturalism a sophisticated disguise for another installment of Orientalism, or worse, of cultural rape?
>
> (Chaudhuri 193)

Inegalitarian exchange pretends to be egalitarian, according to Chaudhuri and others, but becomes merely another form of cultural violation. The inauthenticity of the representation of the non-Western is evidence of the failure of the pretense of equality.

Brook and Carrière's *Mahabharata* focussed the discussion of these issues in the late 1980s and early 1990s, generating such controversy because the production was created at a moment in which it could become the axis for a collection of contested claims, of larger cultural desires and fears: the desire to represent the foreign on the part of regions that had dominated global culture since at least the eighteenth century, and the recognition that any such representation must come to terms with the history of colonialism; the desire of culturally marginalized regions to represent their own cultural histories and the fear that their histories are, by now, whatever colonialism (or its later history, "imperialism without colonies," as Harry Magdoff calls it) has made them. The discussion surrounding Brook's *Mahabharata* raised one of the crucial questions of the late twentieth century: to whom do "cultures" – and the products that configure them – belong? Not (as at mid-century), who has the right to possess cultural objects, but: Who has the right to represent them?

When Case complains that, in the *Mahabharata*, "the politics of cultural translation and historical *accuracy* gave way to the eternal values of art" (122; my italics), she is echoing Gautam Dasgupta, whose essay on "Peter Brook's Orientalism" exemplifies the attack on the *Mahabharata*'s "authenticity":

> *The Mahabharata* is nothing, an empty shell, if it is read merely as a compendium of martial legends, of revenge, valor, and bravura. . . . How else can one explain the shockingly truncated *Bhagavad-Gita* sequence, the epicenter of the poem, the fulcrum on which rests the entire thrust of this monumental drama of humanity, here rendered into whispered words never revealed to the audience?
>
> (Dasgupta 78)

Daryl Chin, in his essay on "Interculturalism, Postmodernism, and Pluralism," makes an even broader claim for authenticity. Chin argues against the decontextualization of *any* cultural material, and what he conceives as the indiscriminate admixture of elements from diverse cultures. For him, Lee Breuer's *Warrior Ant* is "one of the most egregious examples of the excesses of the intercultural approach" (Chin 87), because it becomes

> a statement about the disintegration of national boundaries implied by the collision of disparate elements from many different cultures. Thus, a Bunraku master, a Turkish belly dancer, and rap singers are all equated, rendered not so much equal as equally distracting. The distinctions between high art, folk art, and popular art which the different elements represented were blurred, without the implications being carefully considered. Instead of an attempt at synthesis, there was the formal placement of disjunction. This disjunction ultimately devalued all elements, as no element was allowed to exist within an appropriate context; appropriate, that is, in terms of the cultural context from which that element derived.
>
> (Chin 88)

For Chin, Brook's version of *The Cherry Orchard* is as troubling as his *Mahabharata*, insofar as it

> displaces the meaning of the work by denying its specificity. The equivalence of meaning, which finds formal correlatives in the international cast, the lack of dramatic emphases leveling the momentum of the play, and the bare staging, denies the structure of the play. . . . *The Cherry Orchard* is displaced. (88)

204

Inauthenticity is ostensibly one of the marks of orientalism, which establishes a pseudo-dualism in which the alien-exotic (with attendant qualities: primitive, innocent, natural, rich) is set up in opposition to the central culture (civilized, sophisticated, artful, familiar), but both are really products of the dominant aesthetic. Constructing difference by means of stereotypes, in a binarism that helps to perpetuate a politics of "them" and "us," becomes a defense against incursion from anything that might be genuinely foreign. Johannes Birringer implies as much when he asks:

> How does [Brook's] assimilation of alien ethnic styles or his "Orientalist" projection of images more accessible to Western audiences onto a sacred Indian epic differ from other commercial theatre, dance, or opera productions that have done the same?
>
> (Birringer 117)

Western description of non-Western performance as "universal" is merely a disguised form of orientalism, for in the identification of the likeness of other and self (the likeness of deep structural patterns, the likeness of emotion, the likeness of spiritual force), those ostensible "others" are simply assimilated. Difference is denied to them. Birringer, for instance, writes that "the history of colonialism and imperialism has produced different meanings of 'global culture' for countries in Latin America, Asia, Africa, and Australia" (Birringer 123). Claims to universal rules of performance tend to classify disparate global forms under categories that the "West" has identified as universal. Eurocentric categories have coerced individual "non-Western" cultures into acquiescing to them. Such classification is merely an extension of the earlier imperialist claim that Western forms represent the high point of culture because they have "universal value," and is finally a form of essentialism (seen as the basis for reifying gender, race, and ethnicity).

There is no question that it is the task of readers and spectators, as interpreters, to judge a representation better or worse (sometimes implicitly, sometimes explicitly). There is no question that it is often their task to show how that estimation of merit is part of a mesh of aesthetic and cultural meaning. Rustom Bharucha, for instance, does just that in analyzing what he refers to as "Brook's inadequate confrontation of Indian tradition . . . characterized by short cuts" (Bharucha 236), pointing out many of the weaknesses and some of the strengths of Brook's *Mahabharata*. So, differently, does Vijay Mishra's analysis of the "basic conflict between the text as performed and the humanistic interpretations advanced [by Brook] in its favor" (Mishra 202), in which he argues that in "Brook's version we return to a *Mahabharata* as spectacle, as performance, which remains deeply ambivalent about its political implications and about the possibility of order" (Mishra 204). Close interpretation of the "performance text" may have powerful political implications, as does Maria Shevtsova's reading of the Brook production, in which she replaces "argument in terms of cultural 'property'" ("simply inadequate," as she writes) with "argument in terms of interaction-interpretation" (Shevtsova 209). In each of these cases, interpretation – interpretation that teaches us something about the work – is predicated on a fundamental acceptance of the terms of cultural translation.

Complaints like those of Birringer that Brook has created an "'Orientalist' projection of images more accessible to Western audiences onto a sacred Indian epic," on the other hand, fail to acknowledge the fundamental principle of such exchange: that translation *is* indeed necessary in order for communication to take place – communication between cultures and between individual expressions within cultures; that translation is the precondition for human political life, whatever direction that politics may lead. Case decries the "displacement of the indigenous context" in scholars' attempts to "fit" Sanskrit texts to "eurocentric meanings and practices" (118). But it is hard to see how one can avoid such "displacement" in any act of translation. In describing *The Natyasastra* as "a treatise on performance, reception, and texts" (116), Case, after all, uses not only the Latin alphabet, but also terms which have (in her own words, though applied to others) "little to do with the cosmology within which the language historically operated" (113). If we don't feel altogether comfortable with Brook's description of the *Mahabharata* as "Shakespearean in the true sense of the word" (quoted Case 123), we may nonetheless acknowledge the uses of translation. What is lost in translation may be gained in communication. That is the necessary hermeneutic exchange, whatever boundaries interpretation must cross.

As J. Ndukaku Amankulor recognizes, a quasi-structuralist acknowledgement of cross-cultural similarities may be necessary if we are to resist the conventional distinction between "non-Western ritual" and "Western theatre":

> Unable to see the relationship between theatre performances in Europe and America and theatre performances in the largely non-literate cultures of the world, the anthropologists coined the phrase "ritual theatre" or "ritual drama" as a convenient label for distinguishing the "otherness" of non-Western performance traditions. . . . The narrow adoption of the sacred ceremonial interpretation . . . pushes certain types of theatre permanently into the religious domain and creates an unnecessary intercultural dichotomy. (228, 235)

Brook's attempts, in his *Mahabharata*, to avoid such an "unnecessary intercultural dichotomy" – his universalism – is anything but a disguised claim for ownership of the Indian epic:

We are not attempting a reconstruction of Dravidian and Aryan India of three thousand years ago. We are not presuming to present the symbolism of Hindu philosophy. . . . On the contrary, the many nationalities who have gathered together are trying to reflect *The Mahabharata* by bringing to it something of their own. In this way, we are trying to celebrate a work which only India could have created but which carries echoes for all mankind.

(Carrière xvi)

Again, whatever discomfort we may feel about the exclusions sublimated in the phrase "all mankind," Brook's basic sentiment is precisely what many "hands-on" practitioners (theatrical and political) recognize: that the invocation of a global humanism is not necessarily complicit with an overwhelming hegemonic order. The acknowledgement of cross-cultural similarities may produce a coercive flattening of that which is "foreign." But it may also, if rightly used, produce conversations that grow into a multi-vocal political agenda; it may produce the strategic universalism (not, I might add, necessarily a philosophic universalism) necessary to linking those who are committed to change, allowing them to move beyond the boundaries of a single insular neighborhood.[6]

One of those "hands-on" practitioners, the Yaqui activist and teacher Anselmo Valencia, describes the reception of the Yaqui deer dance quite differently than Brook describes the reception of his *Mahabharata*, but he too invokes cross-cultural sameness as a foundation for the meaning of his work, and honors those non-Yaquis who interpret the deer dance by identifying it with their own cultural experiences:

I'd always said that this belongs to the Yaquis, nobody else. But as the years go by I'm realizing that all the benefits – the spiritual benefits, obviously – do not only belong to the Yaquis but to whomever comes near it. . . . That's why I have begun to invite people in there during, for instance, the Sabado de Gloria. . . . In talking about the Gloria . . . many people unite spiritually, whether their god is Jehovah, Muhamed, Buddha, or Jesus – whatever name you call your god, it's the same.
(96–7)

The critique of productions with universalist overtones fails to acknowledge that communication across distances relies on a recognition not only of differences, but also of samenesses. Indeed, what is marked as the same is inevitably also different, or the marking of sameness would have no meaning. When the critique of "universalism" extends itself to the critique of all identification of samenesses across distance, the notion of difference itself becomes meaningless.

Those who insist on the radicality of difference feel uncomfortable with the mixing of cultures and forms. But such an insistence on authenticity (an insistence on orthodoxy) shows little recognition of the conditions of theatre, or, for that matter, of cultural pluralism (indeed culture's only condition) as a whole. When Dasgupta claims, for instance, that the "*Bhagavad-Gita* sequence, the epicenter of the poem" is, in Brook's *Mahabharata*, "shockingly truncated," he calls on theatre to reproduce cultural forms with "accuracy," rather than recognizing theatre's position as explorer in cultural forms. Similarly, when Chin complains that Brook fails to preserve cultural "specificity" in the *Mahabharata* and *The Cherry Orchard*, or that, in the *Warrior Ant*, a Bunraku master, a Turkish belly dancer, and rap singers are all equated, and that "the distinctions between high art, folk art, and popular art which the different elements represented were blurred," he refuses to recognize that the "blurring of distinctions" is a choice that rather resists "orientalizing" than confirms it. To insist that theatre represent things in their "appropriate context" (as Chin does) is to insist on the purity of cultural property, and is finally another version of the puritanical insistence that cultural identities have their unyielding boundaries. The insistence on respect for tradition implicit here and explicit in Bharucha's essay ("If we have to 'kill' our tradition today, we must be in a position to do so *respectfully*" (Bharucha 236)) – the subtle cultural conservatism in such positions – is not one I would share.

If orientalism (representation of the foreign as a fixed and uniform set of cultural features) means dangerous stereotyping, so does the claim for "authenticity." Indeed, that claim is closely akin to the kind of purist cultural self-identity (representation of one's "own" group as fixed and uniform) that is bound up with nationalist ideologies, with an us-versus-them mentality, and with the kind of protective attitude toward cultural property that even Bharucha reveals when he writes that Brook "should focus his attention on *his own* cultural artefacts, the epics of western civilization like the *Iliad* or the *Odyssey*" (Bharucha 231; my italics). Such a prescription is the equivalent of pronouncing a separate-but-equal global cultural politics: you do "yours," and we'll do "ours." Theorists like Case are uncomfortable with such binaries (us/them, West/East, First World/Third World, European/indigenous, self/Other). But they often rely on them – or slightly narrower but nonetheless oversimplifying cultural distinctions – in order to proscribe the trespassing by (most often) the "Eurocentric" on the territory of the "Other." Case acknowledges, for instance, that she has "operated here in somewhat 'monolithic figures' of colonialism," and that "by foregrounding the absence of any method of knowing the Sanskrit tradition," she has "maintained its category as Other and left it as a monolith" (124). She concedes with disarming directness that shortcomings in her training are responsible for her "singular focus on the colonial effect [which] also lends all power to the colonizer, displacing once more any strategies of resistance on the part of the colonized" (124). But she feels that this relegation of a singular "Other" to the dark spaces in the history of cultures is necessary if she is to "untie seemingly objective descriptions from their empirical shorings and reveal, instead, their collusion with colonial, imperial practices" (124).

Case avoids "suggesting a false/real binary" by choosing "not to include any seemingly objective information about the subject" (123), just as she avoids positing fixed cultural identities by choosing to leave India and Sanskrit as parts of a monolithically uniform "Other." These hardly seem justifiable sacrifices, and they are sacrifices that Chaudhuri is not willing to make. Recognizing, like Case, that the critique of imperialist cultural "appropriation" inevitably falls into the "orthodoxy" argument, Chaudhuri tries to get around the problem. To do so, she argues that a positive interculturalism may emerge from "the drama of immigrants" (196), in which an oversimplification or essentializing of cultural identity becomes impossible – in which it becomes impossible radically to subdivide the world into the "foreign" and the "familiar," the "exotic" and the "standard," "them" and "us." Chaudhuri offers David Hare's *A Map of the World* as an example of a positive interculturalism, describing two characters who disrupt audience expectations about the congruence between ideology and national identity:

> In Hare's play, where an Englishman speaks for the Third World and an Indian defends "colonial" values, there is a flagrant lack of correspondence between the antagonists' ideological positions and their national identities. Thus the conflict that ensues is at odds with the extra-textual stereotypes of such conflicts. It is not, that is to say, a simple conflict between West and East, or imperialism and liberalism, because the spokesmen for the two positions have been "switched."
>
> The non-congruence of ideology and national identity in the protagonists makes their views, at the very least, suspect. (203)

Chaudhuri's (and Hare's) point, of course, is similar to mine: that "purist" versions of cultural identity are fabrications, sometimes dangerous ones. To be sure, clusters of marginalized individuals have often needed to use the construction of group identity to dismantle orientalism-in-the-broadest-sense: the cultural stereotyping that happens when people attempt to represent others from a distance, but have only (at best) a partial view. They have sometimes needed to rely on the idea that they (in Case's phrasing) "have direct access to pure indigenous traditions" (124).

The claim for orthodoxy (which ostensibly can be achieved only by the proprietors of the cultural artifacts) stems from a similar desire to dismantle cultural stereotypes, from the justifiable fear that representation of unfamiliar things risks oversimplification at the least, and more often ends up in the reproduction of such stereotypes. It stems from the recognition that cultural stereotypes tend to fix power relations, and that when traditional power relations are under pressure or collapsing, stereotypes tend to emerge to prop them up. Minstrel shows in the United States in the late nineteenth and early twentieth century, for instance, attempted to reify images that provided a rationale for the cultural subordination of the black population, after much of the pre-Civil War legal subordination had been abolished.

Yet it is difficult not to feel that we ought to have transcended the need for officially declared congruence between ideology and identity – that we ought finally to have learned that aesthetic and intellectual positions cannot be matched to a series of categories which the world has framed as a way of simplifying its thinking about individuals. We ought to have discovered, finally, that to conceptualize culture around the individual (though that once looked like a way of perpetuating an economy of competitive isolationism) may be a way of recognizing the irreducible, multiple, changing being of the self – a self that may nonetheless feel deeply committed to other human beings, even those who are far away, even those who are radically different, even those one has never seen.

To do so may be a way of recognizing that identity politics, whatever power they can give, can sometimes be more crippling than enabling. Those who have not learned, in a world of migration, a world in which there are tens of millions of refugees, a world in which most nations are artificial constructs of the nineteenth century – those who have not learned that cultural identities (like racial ones) are fluid composites with multiple genealogies, will perpetuate for us all the sad history of racism and intercultural animosity that has been part of the human inheritance in the twentieth century.

To suggest that cultural identities are fixed is to suggest that the cultural inheritances that make up those identities are equally fixed: that we cannot change the material we have inherited. So my argument is finally about the nature of inheritances. Even if theorists and practitioners like Brook, Breuer, Schechner, and Barba have inherited practices that modernist theatre practitioners themselves inherited from colonial missionaries, these may be transformed in a (partially) post-colonial world. The inheritances of intercultural performance and theatre anthropology are as mixed, as ethically malleable, as the kaleidoscope of inheritances of which any given individual in any group might partake. We are – or at least ought to think of ourselves as – a world of immigrants, granted no fixed culture, but nonetheless granted a great deal of it continually to remake.

Who owns a culture? Who inherits it, from the moments of celebration to the documents of barbarism? Nobody, of course. For when one inherits, one inherits a global collective web, a web not concentric or symmetrical, but connected in all its parts (even if no one is privileged with seeing all parts of it at once), a web which one is meant, indeed bound, to reweave. The point is to recognize the ways in which the documents of history may be documents of barbarism, and to repossess them differently. That perplexing "right to culture" (promised in the international human rights covenants) is the right to as much of it as we can participate in, without any of it being taken away from anyone else. When Chaudhuri questions whether theatrical "barter" is "truly egalitarian," asking whether there is "something of the 'glass-beads-for-land' model of exchange at work here," her analogy is a false one, for the question is not about objects, but about representations. And cultural representations, unlike either beads or land, can be borrowed without anyone missing them or attempting to retrieve them at gunpoint; they have the grace (like human beings) to be fruitful and multiply without much training, and they have the good sense (also like human beings) to transform themselves in the process.

NOTES

1 On Japanese *Shingeki*, see Horie-Webber, and Rimer (with thanks to Richard Schechner for drawing my attention to it). On the "concert party," see Bame. On the *Luzerner Osterspiel*, see Sarlós. On the *Kankanga*, see Turner. On the *Mahabharata*, see Carrière, and Williams, ed.

2 It is, of course, only for convenience that I describe as separate these three kinds of cultural imperialism, each overlapping and dependent on the others, but each with its own point of view. Historians since Fanon have substantiated in overwhelming detail his claims about the imposition of European cultures on non-Europeans. Studies of "orientalist" (appropriating and distorting) representations of "exotic" cultural forms, drawing primarily on Said, have elaborated on cultural borrowing from the other direction. The anthropological self-critique, drawing primarily on Clifford and Marcus (with methodologies borrowed from Clifford Geertz) has made it impossible to ignore the ethnocentrism and voyeurism in the ethnographic tradition, in which the "primitive" is treated as both an object of curious scrutiny and a sign of the universal.

3 It goes without saying that work on performance has learned a great deal from the imperialist critique, which has permitted the kind of nuanced history that Roach calls "genealogy of performance": interpretations that resist the erasures of history "by taking into account the give and take of transmissions, posted in the past, arriving in the present, delivered by living messengers, speaking in tongues not entirely their own" (Roach 24). Most of it has moved far beyond the imperialist–oppressor–native–victim dichotomy. There is, for instance, general recognition of the power of colonial reappropriation of colonizers' works (though critics and spectators seem considerably less comfortable accepting that a parody of oppressive traditions of representation might be subversion . . . many found the actor Ted Danson's recent blackface parody of the minstrel show, for example, unpalatable in the face of racist history in the US).

4 Case quotes Colonel Boden of the East India Company, who endows a Chair of Sanskrit as "a means of enabling my countrymen to proceed in the conversion of the native of India to the Christian religion" (quoted Case 115).

5 For Artaud, for instance, his "Mission" to "revive" the "anachronistic" and "Primeval Race" of the "pure red Indians called the Tarahumara," ends up showing to him, in the "Rites which I know not what paganism has overlaid," the story of "the Great Celestial Healer . . . of Jesus Christ" (Artaud, *Selected Writings* 374; *Peyote Dance* 3, 72–3).

6 The necessity of using a strategic universalism becomes clear in the critical instance of the international human rights discussion (the instance that has indeed, provided me with a good deal of motivation for writing this essay). Perhaps it is needless to recall that, just as an idea of the inalterably "other" was the foundation for apartheid, an idea of what it is to be human in some (yes, even) essential way is the foundation for its official political end. Perhaps it is harder for some to acknowledge that claims for exemption from international (in effect, universal) human rights norms on the grounds of cultural differences – claims that such norms are a product of the West – are, in practice, almost always offered as a shield for human rights violations against cultural sub-groups.

WORKS CITED

Amankulor, J. Ndukaku. "The Condition of Ritual in Theatre." In Bonnie Marranca and Gautam Dasgupta, eds. *Interculturalism and Performance: Writings from PAJ.* New York: PAJ, 1991: 227–40.

Artaud, Antonin. *The Peyote Dance.* Trans. Helen Weaver. New York: Farrar, Straus and Giroux, 1976.

Artaud, Antonin. *Selected Writings.* Ed. Susan Sontag. Berkeley: University of California Press, 1976.

Bame, Kwabena N. *Come to Laugh: African Traditional Theatre in Ghana.* New York: Lilian Barber Press, 1985.

Bharucha, Rustom. "A View from India." In David Williams, ed. *Peter Brook and the Mahabharata: Critical Perspectives.* London: Routledge, 1991: 228–52.

Birringer, Johannes. "Invisible Cities/Transcultural Images." In Bonnie Marranca and Gautam Dasgupta, eds. *Interculturalism and Performance: Writings from PAJ.* New York: PAJ, 1991: 113–31.

Bond, Richmond Pugh. *Queen Anne's American Kings.* New York: Oxford University Press, 1952.

Carrière, Jean-Claude. *The Mahabharata: A Play Based Upon the Indian Classic Epic.* Trans. Peter Brook. New York: Harper & Row, 1987.

Case, Sue-Ellen. "The Eurocolonial Reception of Sanskrit Poetics." In Sue-Ellen Case and Janelle Reinelt, eds. *The Performance of Power: Theatrical Discourse and Politics.* Iowa City: University of Iowa Press, 1991: 111–27.

Chaudhuri, Una. "The Future of the Hyphen: Interculturalism, Textuality, and the Difference Within." In Bonnie Marranca and Gautam Dasgupta, eds. *Interculturalism and Performance: Writings from PAJ.* New York: PAJ, 1991: 192–207.

Chin, Daryl. "Interculturalism, Postmodernism, Pluralism." In Bonnie Marranca and Gautam Dasgupta, eds. *Interculturalism and Performance: Writings from PAJ.* New York: PAJ, 1991: 83–95.

Clifford, James, and George Marcus, eds. *Writing Culture: The Poetics and Politics of Ethnography.* Berkeley: University of California Press, 1986.

Dasgupta, Gautam. "The Mahabharata: Peter Brook's Orientalism." In Bonnie Marranca and Gautam Dasgupta, eds. *Interculturalism and Performance: Writings from PAJ.* New York: PAJ, 1991: 75–82.

Fanon, Frantz. *The Wretched of the Earth.* New York: Grove Press, 1963.

Horie-Webber, A. "Modernisation of the Japanese Theatre: The Shingeki Movement." In W. B. Beasley, ed. *Modern Japan: Aspects of History, Literature, and Society.* Berkeley: University of California Press, 1975: 147–65.

Magdoff, Harry. "Imperialism without Colonies." In Roger Owen and Bob Sutcliffe, eds. *Studies in the Theory of Imperialism,* London: Longman 1972: 144–70.

Mishra, Vijay. "The Great Indian Epic and Peter Brook." In David Williams, ed. *Peter Brook and the Mahabharata: Critical Perspectives*. London: Routledge, 1991: 195–205.

Rimer, J. Thomas. *Toward a Modern Japanese Theatre: Kishida Kunio*. Princeton: Princeton University Press, 1974.

Roach, Joseph. "Culture and Performance in the Circum-Atlantic World." Typescript, fall 1993.

Said, Edward W. *Orientalism*. New York: Vintage Books, 1978.

Sarlós, Robert K. "Performance Reconstruction: The Vital Link Between Past and Future." In Thomas Postlewait and Bruce A. McConachie, eds. *Interpreting the Theatrical Past*. Iowa City: University of Iowa Press, 1989: 198–229.

Schechner, Richard, and Willa Appel, eds. *By Means of Performance: Intercultural Studies of Theatre and Ritual*. Cambridge: Cambridge University Press, 1990.

Shevtsova, Maria. "Interaction–Interpretation: The *Mahabharata* from a Socio-Cultural Perspective." In David Williams, ed. *Peter Brook and the Mahabharata: Critical Perspectives*. London: Routledge, 1991: 206–27.

Turner, Edith. "Zambia's Kankanga Dances: The Changing Life of Ritual." In Bonnie Marranca and Gautam Dasgupta, eds. *Interculturalism and Performance: Writings from PAJ*. New York: PAJ, 1991: 168–83.

Valencia, Anselmo, Heather Valencia, and Rosamond B. Spicer. "A Yaqui Point of View: On Yaqui Ceremonies and Anthropologists." In Richard Schechner and Willa Appel, eds. *By Means of Performance: Intercultural Studies of Theatre and Ritual*. Cambridge: Cambridge University Press, 1990: 96–108.

Williams, David, ed. *Peter Brook and the Mahabharata: Critical Perspectives*. London: Routledge, 1991.

13

SATELLITE DRAMA

Imperialism, Slovakia and the Case of Peter Karvas

Michael Quinn

One of the landmarks of Czechoslovak literary scholarship during the Cold War was Milada Souckova's *A Literary Satellite: Czechoslovak–Russian Literary Relations*, in which she describes the dynamics of Soviet cultural imperialism by using Czechoslovakia as an East-European paradigm. The current widespread relief, both in Russia and elsewhere, over the dissolution of Soviet-style Communist rule in Europe has not, however, eliminated the problem of "satellite" cultures. Tito's Yugoslavia was for years the model of a multi-national state that could provide a Communist alternative to Stalinism, yet the recent terror in Bosnia has made it only too clear how power in the service of political ambition was merely repressed and contained in Yugoslavia, not eliminated from provincial ideology. Another potentially "multi-national" satellite was modern Czechoslovakia, which was greatly simplified under the Warsaw Pact specifically to avoid such comparisons and tensions. Unlike the former Yugoslav states, which were provinces in a relatively independent country, Slovakia was to some extent a satellite of a satellite. Whether it is preferable for such a small country to declare its independence, which the Slovaks have finally done for themselves, of course remains to be seen. But there is a sense in which the Slovaks, despite what are often the best intentions of their stronger partners, have for a long time been doubly obscured, doubly dominated and also doubly determined to assert their autonomy. As the focus of political resistance writing and its scholarly appreciation moves, in work like Barbara Harlow's, into the third world, it may be well to keep in mind that the history of reform writing is still not done in Eastern Europe, especially when the rebirth of nations often includes, as it may in Slovakia, the rebirth of a repressed, insufficiently examined fascism.

If it seems odd to some proponents of contemporary cultural studies, with its Marxist basis, to think of a Marxist imperialism, such was nevertheless the case in the history of Stalinist expansion. The different but sensible theories of imperialism that Marx and Lenin proposed become just

another ideological contradiction in the record of forceful political strate-
gizing compiled by the Soviets. And though the West grew used to the idea
of a united Soviet empire, as well as a world-wide sphere of Communist
influence, France, Cambodia and North Korea serve in part to remind us of
how vastly different Marxisms can become in practice. If one simply keeps
in mind Said's working definition of imperialism as "the practice, the theory
and the attitudes of a dominating metropolitan center ruling a distant
territory," then the situation in Slovakia is perfectly clear (Said, 9); and if
the Soviets colonized only with armies, not with Russian settlements, that
only provides a distinction between satellite countries like Czechoslovakia
and annexed Soviet "republics" like Latvia and Estonia. Meanwhile the
rapid dissolution of the former Soviet Union and the re-emergence of
Russian ambitions to national power impress us with how the legacy of
imperial politics continues, like nationalism, despite the lessons of history
and the changing forms of government. In this regard Slovakia is only one
small spot on the world map, not so recently heroic as some of the former
Soviet republics, nor so tormented by conflict and deprivation as many of
the southern Communist states. Nor were the Soviets the first empire to
dominate Slovakia.

The history of Slovakia is not well known, and tends to be confused with
that of many other small nationalities in the eastern half of Europe. The
Slovaks' relationship with the Czechs is especially complex, because the
cultures have overlapped and joined many times, and as a result most
commentary on Slovakia has tended either to underplay or exaggerate
the regions' differences depending upon the political strategies of the
moment. These strategies have, in the modern era, often involved the
relations of the Slovaks with imperial powers. Such changing imperial
situations, especially in times of war and occupation, have created many
large shifts in the political way of life of all Slovaks, but especially in the
lives of intellectuals. After explaining something of the general historical
situation of Slovakia with reference to the history of its drama, I will then
concentrate on a description of the career of Peter Karvas, a Slovak writer
who, while exceptional, is nevertheless a representative figure when
considering the effects of imperial Soviet policy on artists and critics.

IMPERIAL HISTORY AND DRAMATIC CONTEXT

Slovakia's historical problem of identity traces back to the ninth century,
during the period of the Great Moravian Empire, a trading center that
flourished for three hundred years despite repeated efforts by the Franks
and the Roman Catholics to conquer or colonize its territory (which included
Bohemia and Slovakia). The Magyar invasion around 900 effectively sepa-
rated the Slovaks and the Czechs, and the Slovaks became a subject people in
the Hungarian kingdom for an entire millennium. In the meantime the

Czechs founded their own royal house, which was once the seat of the Holy Roman Empire, but then endured the suppression of the Hussite reformation in 1415, the defeat of the Czech estates in 1620, and were themselves eventually occupied by Austria for three centuries. The Slovaks collaborated with Vienna in attempting to put down the Hungarian revolution of 1848, but profitted very little by betraying their neighbors; such episodes are chronicled in nationalist dramas like Jozef Gregor-Tajovsky's modern play *The Execution of George Langsfeld*. Needless to say, these different Czech/ Slovak national fortunes created vast cultural differences: of religion, language, historical understanding, political vision and artistic culture.

The Hungarian influence in Slovakia and the German influence in the Czech lands began to wane with the slow decline of joint Austro-Hungarian fortunes in the nineteenth century and the emergence of Romantic nationalism – especially Pan-Slavism, which encouraged Czechs and Slovaks to emphasize their similarities (Herder might say their innate "goodness") and make common cause against the empire. Czech served both groups as the literary language until after 1843, so that Slovak literature is still only 150 years old; nevertheless many important Czech works before that time, such as the best early stage comedies, were written by Slovaks like Jan Chalupka (who also introduced Slovak-speaking characters on stage). In theatrical terms the gradual movement of political power toward Prague was obvious; the construction of the National Theatre on the banks of the Vltava in 1881 created a visible institution that was clearly a rival to the German-language Estates Theatre, but this effort was not paralleled in Bratislava (or Pressburg as it was then known). In fact, a national theatre was next established in Brno, the center of old Moravia, during the First Czechoslovak Republic, while what would eventually become the National Theatre in Bratislava was still being run as a private enterprise, with only half its repertory performed in Slovak. The only other comparable Slovak theatre was in Kosice; meanwhile Slovakia was presented on the stage in Prague in peasant pastorals like Jiri Mahen's *Janosik*, one of several dramatic versions treating a Slovak nationalist hero who is something like Robin Hood.

The emergence of independent Czechoslovakia in 1918 provided the Slovaks with a much larger role in the affairs of the country's government, and much greater access to education and self-advancement, but the American-sponsored Republic was not a complete remedy to national ambitions. Pleased to be free of the Hungarians, the Slovaks nevertheless had to contend with a situation in which their capital city – twenty-odd miles from Vienna – was half German-speaking, and in which there were not only substantial Hungarian and Romany minorities, but also a large Ukrainian-speaking minority in Sub-Carpathian Ruthenia; consequently, the Czech language became more important for political life. The Slovaks were represented proportionately in the Prague legislature (especially after a reorganization of Slovak administration in 1927), and certainly the territory made gains under the new government, which provided incentives for investment in Slovakia. But the growth of the Slovak middle class, especially in the allocation of government positions along party lines, was still rather slow, and many Slovaks continued to choose emigration. Though the work of ethnographers like the Russian emigré Petr Bogatyrev on literary and folk culture – especially traditional costumes and folk drama – was not intended as nationalism, the writings that he and members of the faculty at the new post-1918 Comenius University (Igor Hrusovsky, Andreja Melichercik, etc.) carried out also had the effect of constructing, sometimes for the first time, anthropological and historical cases for separate Slovak and Ruthenian identities. Most Slovak political parties during the presidencies of Masaryk and Benes were configured as opposition groups, though few took such extreme stances as the autonomist Hlinka party or the russophile Communists, both of whom argued that the bourgeois Czechs had taken advantage of a cheap Slovak work force. Their implication was that wherever the Habsburgs had left off, the Czech and German capitalists had taken over. These and other absurdities were very effectively satirized by the best Slovak dramatist of the inter-war years, Ivan Stodola; in *Jozko Pucik and His Career*, for example, Stodola told the story of a poor, naive Slovak clerk whose low standard of living actually improved when he was declared a criminal and made the beneficiary of several charitable organizations.

After the Munich accords in 1938 effectively conceded the autonomy of Czechoslovakia to Hitler, the ambitions of Slovak nationalists took on a decidedly ugly character. President Benes, facing invasion with the knowledge that no help was coming, moved the Republic's government abroad; meanwhile a second Republic was declared, then superseded as Hitler occupied the Czech speaking "protectorate" territories. Slovakia's minority of "clerico-fascist" nationalist politicians, led by Monsignor Jozef Tiso, reorganized through political collaboration to form a separate, supposedly autonomous Slovak Republic with Nazi sponsorship. This arrangement led to such regrettable results as the deployment of Slovak troops against the Poles and the Red Army, Slovak implication in the extermination of Jews, and the conversion of Slovak industry to military production. By 1944 the German army occupied Slovakia anyway, with the Czech and Slovak resistance working together despite major setbacks like the failure of the anti-fascist Slovak National Uprising at Banska Bystrica. The Communists in Moscow were much more willing to express their support of Slovakia near the war's end than were the Western powers, and Moscow maintained contact with the Slovak Communist party even though it had been forced underground. Among the other results of post-war political maneuvering were the annexation of Ruthenia by the Soviets (who refused to withdraw their army), the expulsion of the German population (over two million, especially the Sudeten Germans who provoked the Munich agreement) and the attempt to repatriate the Hungarian minority (eventually 160,000 were exchanged for Slovaks from Hungary). The Slovak perspective on the horrors of war, and the subsequent terrors of Stalinism, would wait for dramatic expression until about 1960, when Karvas took up the burden.

During the war the Slovak National Theatre, strategically placed in a commanding position on Hviezdoslavovo namestie, was nationalized and converted to an all-Slovak repertory, and in 1946 it added a second stage. A predictable mix of directors were working on Slovak productions: the older Stanislavsky school was represented by Jan Borodac, while the inter-war expressionist influence came through Jan Jamnicky (with a playwriting equivalent in works like Julius Barc-Ivan's 1934 strike drama, *The 3000 Men*). A younger generation came into its own after the war – especially Jozef Budsky and K. L. Zachar. Though the period between the war's end and the Communist takeover in 1948 was confused, and relatively short, it was a time in which the arts were granted an unusual importance in the reorganization of Czechoslovakia. In "On the Artistic Situation of the Contemporary Czech Theatre (1945)," Jan Mukarovsky theorized the "re-composition" of reality by a theatre that had been "decomposed" by modernist fragmentation and fascist force: "How to arrive at such a reality in the theatre can be decided only by the artists, and then not through some theoretical cogitation but rather through the praxis of their creating." Unfortunately this open moment quickly disappeared with the Communist takeover, and the institution of the standard self-sacrificing themes of Socialist Realism, as in Stefan Kralik's *Play without Love* (1946). At this point it became clear to many Slovaks that earlier expressions of Moscow's support for Slovak nationhood were mere leverage, and that political concerns centered on Slovakia would now be considered symptoms of "bourgeois nationalism," punishable by official actions like the 1952 Slansky trials. Even those party officials like Vladimir Clementis, the poet Laco Novomesky or Gustav Husak, who had orchestrated the Communist takeover through the manipulation of the Slovak cabinet, were tried and shot, or in Husak's case sentenced to life in prison (he was pardoned in 1960).

The Communist takeover did have the impact of strengthening several cultural institutions in Slovakia, like Matica Slovenska, the Slovak center for folk culture in Martin. Though political power was centralized under Gottwald and then Novotny in Prague (the latter was both party chief and President), investment in Slovak schools, heavy industry and artistic institutions continued. The Comintern had been disbanded, and also eventually its replacement, Cominform, so the primary pressures from the Soviet Union on the Warsaw pact countries were economic, with Comecon struggling to outpace Tito's alternative model. It was soon clear that the new Czechoslovak economy was collapsing in concert with

Kruschev's revelations about Stalinism, for though Czechoslovakia had more people working than ever before (in gradually shorter work weeks), enjoyed a higher rate of capital development, and compared favorably to other Soviet economies, the average wages of workers actually declined, as did industrial productivity. Five-year plans were scrapped as efforts to convert a complex economy to primitive heavy industry failed, and pressure for internal economic initiatives was especially strong from Slovakia, where by 1963 a fairly open press developed under the apparently negligent gaze of local party chief Alexander Dubcek. And Husak resurfaced as a political columnist and historian, gaining great credibility with his heroic account of the Slovak National Uprising. Theatrically this period allowed the emergence of a short-lived satirical theatre of real vigor, the Divadlo na Korze of Milan Lasica and Julius Satinsky, and eventually the socially conscious plays of Ivan Bukovcan (*Until the Cock Ceases to Sing*, 1969). Though there was only a limited upsurge of talent in Slovakia in the 1960s, not comparable to that in Czech drama, there was nevertheless an atmosphere of great creative freedom, one which did not take much note of the replacement of Kruschev in 1964 by Brezhnev and Kosygin. Yet surprisingly, when the Czech writers made their crucial play at the 1967 Czechoslovak Writers Congress, the Slovaks complacently refused to support the challenge to Novotny; even so, when Novotny was replaced as Party Chief in January 1968, it was by Dubcek, a Slovak who had initiated a later Party debate that forced the change.

One of the first important changes for Slovaks in the "Prague Spring" was the re-acknowledgement of Bratislava as the Slovak capital, and the promise to reorganize Czechoslovakia along federal rather than central lines. Yet this long-sought recognition came at a high price. Husak and other conservative Slovak party members constructed a false opposition between federation and democratization, in an attempt to slow the process of change in Slovakia and save their own positions. In fact this strategy resulted in Husak's eventual appointment as head of the Slovak Communist Party, and finally as chief executive of the "normalization" of Czechoslovakia after the August 1968 Soviet invasion. Husak, still in Bratislava, oversaw the realization of the new federal structure in January 1969, but there was no cause for Slovak celebration. The leading reform magazine, *Kulturny zivot*, was closed in Slovakia (even though it had been Husak's journalistic base all through the previous decade); similar retrenchments and betrayals characterized every aspect of the reorganization of daily life. By the time Husak was appointed head of the whole Czechoslovak party in April he was supported by only 23 percent of all Slovaks; the rank and file citizens were much more concerned with his role as negotiator with imperial Russia than with their small gains of autonomy. Protests to the invasion were widespread, but repression was effective and relatively swift, so that even post-invasion acts by lame-duck Czechoslovak officials had been overturned by pro-Soviet politicians by the end of 1970. For twenty years the pall of repression hovered over all Czechs and Slovaks. Churches and theatres were closed for decades, supposedly awaiting improvement. Even finished improvements took on a sinister character; the National Gallery in Bratislava, for example, underwent a horrific remodelling in which its lovely, arched stucco courtyard was fronted by a massive, elevated trapezoidal addition of corrugated iron – it stands today as a monument to willful ugliness. In the Slovak theatre the only possible dissident political expressions were in the tradition of Svejk, a kind of dumb compliance with authority that revealed the idiocy of those in control by simply co-operating with their stupidity; the Radosin Naive Theater was probably the most successful with this tactic, and its earthy humor was popularized in several recordings. But the best authors and directors, like their Czech colleagues, were simply not allowed performances; the only theatre artists who seemed to be exempt were designers, which allowed the emergence of Ladislav Vychodil as a scenographer roughly equivalent in Slovakia to the Czech National Theatre's Josef Svoboda.

The impossible, exhausting project of panoptic party surveillance and repressive police work, together with the successful communicative strategies of the Czechoslovak resistance movements, gradually led to government lapses that allowed grass-roots democratic reforms to gain some momentum. The faltering leadership succession of the Soviet Union provided an opening for these developments, as did the emergence of Gorbachev as a leader with almost no interest in empire. If Czech companies like Theater on a String were able to gain solid reputations in Brno (and even, by 1988, to produce a play by Havel in Prague), artists working in the margins of Slovak institutions were similarly successful; the most prominent case is probably the director Blaho Uhlar, who by 1990 had completed a long project that dramatized, with designer Jan Zavarsky, the decay of repressive power through a "non-conformist" style of *mise-en-scène*. Probably the most significant protest movement intitiated in Slovakia was the 1987 "Bratislava Aloud" program, in which official data on the state of the environment were used by a citizens' group to convince the public of the extent of the ecological damage in the country.

Once the political dam broke in 1989, Slovaks worked in concert with Czechs for reform, only to have their common interests once again derailed by the old nationalism. Though veterans of Slovak political reform like Miroslav Kusy, the rector of Comenius University, saw such nationalism as a basic failure of the political imagination, he understood that many Slovak "patriots" were "in the realm of nationalist totalitarian mythology," and – like most Czechs – he and other Slovak intellectuals were more or less resigned to the way a vocal, organized minority, in the context of a post-revolutionary scene in which no single party could claim majority privileges, might force the issue for the whole country without ever calling a vote. For many Slovaks the *idea* of a Czech majority was much worse than its *practice*, particularly after the assurances of disproportionate Slovak power that the federal reforms of 1969 had guaranteed, yet the same process of aggressive minority party leverage that had effected the Fascist and Communist takeovers eventually produced the obnoxious Vladimir Meciar's Nationalist seccession of 1993. Small wonder, then, that humanists like Havel and the Slovak revolutionary leader Jan Carnogursky refused to encourage Slovak independence. Unfortunately the misplaced political confidence of Slovaks who supported seccession is further isolating Slovakia, retarding its progress toward such stated nationalist goals as membership in the European Economic Community.

In theatrical terms the effects of separation are more immediately apparent. The planned new stage of the National Theatre, in a prime building site on the bank of the Danube, has been suspended until funds can be raised to complete its construction. The theatrical community is, at least for the moment, well supplied with good dramatic materials from the time when so many plays were forbidden, but as in the Czech Republic it is a difficult period for new writers. A few unconventional initiatives, like Uhlar's new company, are gaining some notoriety. But in the meantime the minority Hungarian theatres outside the capital, like the Thalia Theatre in Kosice, have become important community centers for a minority that feels threatened by Slovak policies like the Soviet-style diversion of the Danube, the removal of alternative Hungarian place-names from roadsigns, and similar nationalist maneuvers. At the very least it is clear that any new Slovak government will have a difficult time managing the transition from minoritarian dissent to leadership in what remains a multi-ethnic state.

PETER KARVAS

One figure whose career spans most of these modern difficulties is Peter Karvas, the leading dramatist of modern Slovakia, one of its most influential novelists, a belle-lettrist and travel writer of some ideological weight, and also the country's leading theatre theorist. Karvas is virtually unknown in the West – none of his plays or novels have been fully translated into English – but his exclusion only confirms that not one of Slovakia's writers has ever achieved real international exposure or recognition, beyond an occasional mention within the containing umbrella of a hybridized "Czech-o-slovak" culture (typically appended to a survey in which Slovak matters are covered after the major account – of Czech literature – is complete). Certainly it would be difficult for any small country to match the productivity and interest of the post-war generation of Czech novelists and playwrights, with major figures in world literature like Kundera, Havel, Klima and Skvorecky. Yet in Karvas's case the exclusion of such a witty, inventive, disputatious master of intellectual dialogue is surely not due to the lower quality of the work, but is more nearly a matter of the difficulty of the language, the marginality of his cultural context, and the vexing contradictions of a long writing career carried out in an unpredictable political climate.

Karvas, born in 1920, grew up in the liberal atmosphere of the First Republic. His college education began in the year of the German invasion, 1938, and his studies continued sporadically while he began a career in drama by writing anti-fascist, satirical resistance plays for the radio, often under a pseudonym, with self-consciously literary themes. Nevertheless he was able to study for a time in Prague, and through the close ties of Czech and Slovak universities Karvas was able to count as his major intellectual guides both Jan Mukarovsky, the philosophical master of Prague School structuralism, and Jiri Veltrusky, the Prague School's most incisive theatre theorist and critic (in Veltrusky's case, the two men have still never met). Like the young Chekhov, Karvas began with satirical sketches, and wrote quickly under sometimes extraordinary pressures; in one year alone, 1941, Karvas's output included seven short plays, with titles like "Scandal in the Editor's Desk," "Contribution to the University Library," and "The Manuscript of Archibald, the Pirate." By 1944 Karvas was contributing this kind of writing, as well as more serious commentary, to what was called in Slovakia the "whispering resistance," conducted through channels like the Free Slovak Radio (his first book was on radio, in 1948).

Karvas felt the power of wartime oppression in very personal terms, despite his high-spirited writing style. Though he was raised in a home that observed no religious ceremony, Karvas's family had a Jewish background, and both of his parents perished in the Nazi camps. He continued to support himself during the war by doing work in fields like advertising graphics and building design, meanwhile also editing a journal for student writers which, because of its marginal status during the war, was able to publish writings by some major figures whose works might otherwise have been proscribed.

Karvas was also working on longer dramatic works, and shortly after the war ended, in 1945, his play *Meteor* was chosen to reopen the Slovak National Theatre. Karvas himself was appointed as the dramaturg for its new experimental stage. *Meteor,* the story of five astronomers who discover a large, ominous meteor and seek to interpret its significance in a series of philosophical discussions, was one of the most important plays in post-war Czechoslovakia, since its dialogue was generally interpreted as an informed, balanced argument about the country's future, as well as its ambivalent response to Hitler (anticipating the use of a similar metaphor by Friedrich Durrenmatt twenty years later). Karvas finished his doctorate in 1946 at Comenius University in Bratislava; his dissertation, *Introduction to the Fundamental Elements of the Theater,* is the most complete Czechoslovak synthesis of Prague School theatre theory (the book has been in constant use since that time as the basis of courses at the state drama academy, though for many years Karvas's name was removed; he has recently finished an updated edition). He also wrote an analysis of the post-war situation in drama, *Toward the Fundamental Question of the Contemporary Slovak Theater* (1948). In the brief window between Nazi and Soviet domination, Karvas established himself as the most innovative, accomplished young writer on Slovakia's theatrical and theoretical scene. His other allegorical plays from this period included *Coming Back to Life* (1946) and *The Fort* (1948), as well as the satirical comedy *Hannibal Before the Gates* (1947). Karvas was also assigned, for a short time, to the cultural office of the Czechoslovak embassy in Bucharest (where his plays were also very successful).

Karvas's fortunes changed after 1948, when the new Communist government offered him a post in dramatic criticism and playwriting at the national theatre academy. Like the other remaining Prague School writers (e.g. Jan Mukarovsky) he renounced his earlier structuralist writings; in Karvas's case an official statement was printed in *Slovenske Pohl'ady*, the region's leading literary journal. But like many of the Prague School theatre writers, such as Jindrich Honzl and Miroslav Kouril, Karvas saw no great contradiction between the sociologically-informed structuralism of the pre-war years and the socialism that seemed to be emerging at the time. Karvas was asked to renounce his theatre theory, but not his artistic works. In some respects Karvas was trying to continue the philosophical humanism of Karel Capek, the great Czech observer of the charms of daily life that he met once in his youth, and so even in the midst of political upheaval Karvas could confirm the steady politics of neighborhood values in his satirical comedy *The People Living in Our Street* (1950). For a few years Karvas, a hopeful young Communist, devoted his work to the official aesthetic, i.e. serious socialist realism, as in his 1953 work, *A Heart Full of Love* and the hospital drama *Patient 113* (1955). Like many of the young writers tempted in the beginning to believe in the Soviet project, Karvas was given a travel grant for a guided tour of Soviet capitals, and when he returned he praised Russian revolutionary culture in his *Leningrad Letters*. His works entered the repertories of state theatres throughout eastern Europe, in Russian, German, Hungarian – even in Romanian, into which nine of his plays were translated. Karvas freely admits today that this period seemed to him to be a success, that the international exposure and personal benefits of party writing created the illusion that he was having an important, successful career. In retrospect, Karvas's attitude today is somewhat apologetic, but fairly simple: "I was mistaken," he explains in an interview. "I can see now that the work is not as good as I thought, and that the ideas in my other plays are much more complex and interesting."

During the post-1956 thaw, when the dark side of Soviet history was beginning to emerge, Karvas began once again to write politically prescient dramas, especially *Midnight Mass* (1959), an examination of the Slovak moral situation at the end of the war that pitted the heroes of the National Uprising against the petty bourgeois, and *The Scar* (1963), which dramatized the political errors and harmful effects of Stalin's personality cult; the former was performed throughout the country, and abroad. In one of his most often-produced plays, *Antigone and the Others* (1962), Karvas used the metaphor of the immured heroine to dramatize the horror of the Nazi concentration camps. In 1968 Karvas, who is a lucid self-critic in the structuralist style of alternative possibilities, explained his role in dramatizing such crucial events as the National Uprising this way:

I have often read that I belong to the generation of the National Uprising. That is a definition that leads to all sorts of interesting possibilities. You can narrow it down to include only the actual participants of the Uprising, and then you lose many writers of works thematically anchored in the Uprising. Or, to take the other extreme, you broaden the definition to include the entire literature concerned with the Uprising, and suddenly, you find that you have room for several generations of writers. It appears that this confusion has nothing to do with the chronological nature of literary development, but rather with the changing evaluation of the Uprising as a historical event and a literary subject.

If we limit our discussion to the literary aspect, the matter is in essence rather simple. The Uprising as subject matter and inspiration has undoubtedly played a tremendous role in Slovak literature. Its thematic contributions are such that modern Slovak literature is unthinkable without it. The Uprising has provided a fund of material which has served to fortify Slovak literature during periods of waning vitality. It can even be said that attempts at discovering the truth of the Uprising compensated Slovak literature for its inability to penetrate to the reality of subsequent periods. It is significant that during a certain period it was as dangerous to publish truths about the Uprising as it was to objectively discuss current conflicts of contemporary society.

When it became necessary to impute guilt to the key figure of the Uprising, the entire movement had to be condemned as well. This period, during which interest in other people was limited to speculations about their guilt or innocence, was also marked by systematic distortion of the real nature of the Slovak National Uprising. Through a coincidence of circumstances literature was thus destined to stimulate the awareness of a historic phenomenon, which historiography itself – due to "objective reasons" – had to disregard until much later. I don't want to go into historical details nor to gloss over the obvious fact that even literature was not entirely free from errors and distortions insofar as the true face of the Uprising was concerned. But if I were to define the generation of the Uprising in literary terms, I believe that the decisive criterion would be based on the extent to which a writer regarded the Uprising as a historical event rather than as a complex human problem. Many have gotten rid of the Uprising by relegating it to the area of history, glory, and, above all, official celebration. Others appropriate it as personal property on which it is possible to collect interest. When I speak of the generation of the Uprising, I am thinking of artists for whom the Uprising is not a literary crutch but a decisive life-experience, with all its complexities, errors and guilt. I don't believe that my fellow citizens could ever perform anything purer, better or more sincere than the Uprising. Pure art derived from the experience will live, whereas official Uprising literature will be solemnly and ceremoniously buried in monuments.

(Liehm, 346–47)

Like the late efforts of resistance in Prague, narrated in such crucial post-war works as Skvorecky's *The Cowards*, the matter of the Slovak war experience helped to make Karvas an important writer, but it also left him vulnerable to criticism from other historians of the uprising, like Gustav Husak (particularly when it is linked, as it is in Liehm's interview, with structuralist theories of art and culture).

But in addition to this serious writing, so important to a country that needed to take some account of its fascist past, Karvas continued to write satirical comedies. *The Great Wig* is a fable about the political scapegoating of a bald-headed minority. The wig becomes a theatrical metaphor for the intellectual litmus test, and the state minister who goes bald in the play goes to absurd lengths to conceal what has happened to – and in – his head, as he discovers the implications of a transportation from dominant to marginal status. This play, along with another Slovak satire by Zdenek Mahler, was described in Marketa Goetz-Stankiewicz's *The Silenced Theatre* (the only English-language survey to deal with any recent Slovak plays). Yet this was only the most successful of a string of popular works in Slovakia's strongest genre, satire; others include plays with whimsical British characters, like *Diplomats*, which chronicles the misadventures of ambassador Oliver Cox in an unnamed South American embassay.

Karvas, who like Capek often included a strong technological element in his futuristic plays, went too far with his apocalyptic indictment of official science in *Experiment Damocles* (1967). He produced one more play at the National Theatre in 1968, ironically titled *Absolutely Forbidden*, and after the Warsaw Pact invasion in 1968 he was not produced again until the Gorbachev thaw had begun. Even today Karvas has not forgotten that during the years of the crackdown he felt absolutely alone. Karvas had worked for the reforms of the Prague Spring, and was one of a few prominent Slovak signatories of Charter 77. Consequently he was expelled from the writers' union (in 1950 he had been its secretary), and his plays and novels were refused publication. His foreign audience was not in the West, as with many Czech writers, but in the other Eastern Bloc countries, where he was similarly censored. In 1974, in the later stages of the purge and the Soviet "normalization" of post-counter-revolutionary Czechoslovakia, Karvas was dismissed from the drama academy. Husak's government would have denied him any official position, but Karvas was saved through the loyalty of Slovak Minister of Culture Miroslav Volek, and given a non-teaching position, at minimal rank, in the Institute for Cultural Research. These frequent reassignments were extremely common as a coercive, materialistic state practice in which political loyalty was rewarded with better work – a better standard of living – and dissent meant the sacrifice of comforts, and the withdrawal of access to communication. Personal tragedy again accompanied political reversal, as Karvas endured the suicides of two family members. Karvas nevertheless revived his theoretical work, miraculously publishing four new theoretical books that acknowledged Soviet scholarship (and hence seemed acceptable to the authorities) but in effect continued the project of liberal Prague School theoretical writing (with a socialist twist) that he had began forty years earlier. The most important of these books is probably *Space in the Theater and the Theater in Space*, the most comprehensive semiotic study of theatrical space yet undertaken in a country known for the excellence of its designers. Karvas also produced major studies on the comic, on theatre and modern media, and on dialogue.

Karvas was not suddenly and dramatically swept back into favor after the 1989 revolution, but instead gradually regained some access to publishing. He brought out a few novels and stories in the 1980s, and in 1986 his substantial one-act play, *A Private Celebration*, was produced by the National Theatre. In 1987 Karvas was able to publish seven plays that had, except for the one-act, not been produced, dating back to his 1966 drama *The Twentieth Night*, which considers the conscience of a man who killed a romantic rival during the war and then worked for the next twenty years as a devoted physician to try to redeem his crime. Since then Karvas has been staged twice more, and is a featured playwright on the dramatic stage of the National Theatre. Both of the plays currently in the repertory are Karvas-style British satires, but as Karvas says, "I have written about England because it was impossible to write about Bratislava." In *The Back Door, or Pleasure on Tuesday after Midnight*, Karvas uses a confrontation between prostitutes and the politicians who are their clients to dramatize the collapse of a revolution. The sophisticated prostitutes first threaten to unionize, but when the men simply abstain they threaten to go public. This, too, generates no surprise, but at the end of the play the womens' leader has fallen in love with Lord Henderson's butler, and the two begin new lives together.

Even more absurd, and consequently more easily related to the Slovak political situation, is *Patriots of the Town of Yo, or A Kingdom for a Murderer.* Like Milos Forman's *Fireman's Ball*, Karvas's play uses a small town to satirize larger political issues. Deciding that the tricentennial of their town jail needs an execution in order to attract the proper official attention, the Yo town council searches high and low for a murderer, but can't find one. Undeterred, they invent one (who will enter a posh "witness protection program" after a faked death), only to have dozens of townspeople then volunteer as substitutes. But the death penalty is abolished in London, and the celebration begins to unravel, until a solution is finally discovered; the burghers announce that the building's origin was actually three years later, which buys them three more years of planning time. This sort of satire is adaptable not only from England to Soviet Czechoslovakia, but also to the transition from Communist satellite to independent capitalist state. Karvas notes that he writes primarily for an educated audience – criticism for scholars, novels for playful, literate readers, and dramatic art for relatively intimate production in traditional, sophisticated settings.

Karvas's beliefs, though apparently changeable from the standpoint of official politics, are based in a consistent conviction that discussion and understanding should be the basis for the decisions that guide a just socialist society – that a corrupt situation or a buried anxiety must be recognized by audiences, whose common perceptions of political problems can provide the basis for critical judgments, whether those produce a new interpretation of the past, a ridiculous comic critique of the present or a visionary consideration of the future. From this standpoint Karvas's politics, like those of Habermas or the Prague School, resist imperialism through communicative ethics, through a belief in the importance of complete, accessible arguments and negotiable social contracts to the cultural life of a democratic society. Such a view, as it is dramatized by Karvas and received by his contemporary audience, conceives of margins and centers as divisive political control strategies, which can be remedied by a collaborative, coherent, inclusive government that escapes the dogmatic excesses of Soviet culture. This is not the kind of government the Meciar seccession appears to have encouraged, so in Karvas's view the contemporary situation is unique, and will require new critical efforts. Unfortunately Karvas himself is writing very little at the moment; his eyesight is diminishing, and he is recovering from surgery on a facial nerve. If there is a dramatist of similar caliber on the horizon in Slovakia, who might take up the task, it's not clear yet who that might be.

Karvas does not qualify as a political hero; like most resistance writers, he was sometimes courageous, he sometimes lacked the knowledge to see things clearly, and he was sometimes tempted to compromise. Yet through all these changes he also became a great writer, capable of expression not only in drama, but in an acclaimed series of novels, in collections of comic sketches (like those collected in 1989 in *Niet pristavov* and *Posledne homoresky a ine kratochvile*), and in major critical works. A resistance writer and semiotic structuralist who turned Communist and social realist, and then turned back, Karvas continued to compose this diverse outpouring of books despite frequent, unpredictable changes of political fortune. A victim of several historical turns, he also contributed to the energies of positive reform. Certainly his work deserves, like Slovak culture in general, to come out of the compromising orbit of an imperial Soviet culture and into a more general, international context of recognition that respects his so-called "provincial" environment. Now that Slovakia has emerged as an independent country, he will certainly be promoted at home as one of its most distinctive, accomplished writers.

WORKS CITED

Bakosova-Hlavenkova. *Cas Cinohry.* Bratislava: Ustav umeleckej kritiky a divadelnej documentacie, 1990.

Cincura, Andrew. *An Anthology of Slovak Literature.* Riverside, CA: University Hardcovers, 1976.

Dickinson, Thomas. *The Theatre in a Changing Europe.* New York: Henry Holt, 1937.

Goetz-Stankiewicz, Marketa. *The Silenced Theatre: Czech Playwrights Without a Stage.* Toronto University Press, 1979.

Harlow, Barbara. *Resistance Literature.* New York: Methuen, 1987.

Heneka, A. *et al. A Besieged Culture: Czechoslovakia Ten Years after Helsinki.* Stockholm and Vienna: Charta 77 Foundation, 1985.

Hruby, P. *Fools and Heroes: The Changing Role of Communist Intellectuals in Czechoslovakia.* Oxford University Press, 1980.

Karvas, Peter. *Fascikel S.* Bratislava: Slovensky spisovatel, 1988.

———. *Humoresky a ine kratochvile.* Bratislava: Slovenske spisovatel, 1984.

———. Interview with Michael Quinn, Bratislava, 20 October 1993.

———. *Kapitolky o rozhlase.* Bratislava, 1948.

———. *Kniha ul'avy: Humoresky, apokryfy, podobenstva.* Bratislava: Slovenske spisovatel, 1970.

———. *Meteor a ine hry.* Bratislava: Lita, 1990.

———. *My/Co nechceme byt menovani.* Bratislava: Praca, 1992.

———. *Niet pristavov (tri novely).* 2 Vols. (six novels). Bratislava: Tatran, 1989 and 1990.

———. *Nove humoresky a ine kratochvile.* Bratislava: Slovensky spisovatel, 1986.

———. *Pol'ahcujuca okolnost'.* Bratislava: Slovensky spisovatel, 1991.

———. *Posledne humoresky a ine kratochvile.* Bratislava: Slovensky spisovatel, 1989.

———. *Priestory v divadle a divadlo v priestore.* Bratislava: Tatran, 1984.

———. *Restructuracia umelecyche potrieb a premeny dramatickych umeni.* Bratislava, 1982.

———. *Rozhlasove umenie vo veku televizie.* Bratislava: Slovensky rozhlas, 1992.

———. *Sedem hier.* Bratislava: Slovensky spisovatel, 1987.

———. *Toto pokolenie.* Bratislava: Smena, 1985.

———. *Umenie dramy a fenomen televizie.* Bratislava: Vyskumny ustav kultury, 1985.

———. *V Hniezde.* Bratislava: Slovensky spisovatel, 1981.

———. *Velikan, cize Zivot a dielo profesora Bagovica.* Bratislava: Slovensky spisovatel, 1993.

————. *Velka parochna a ine hry.* Bratislava: Lita, 1990.

————. *Zamysleni nad dramaturgii.* Prague: Czeskoslovensky spisovatel, 1969.

————. *Zastaveny cas: Humoresky, satiry, poviedky, causerie, 1941–1966.* Bratislava: Slovensky spisovatel, 1990.

Kieran, V. G. *Marxism and Imperialism.* New York: St Martins, 1974.

Kusin, Vladimir. *The Intellectual Origins of the Prague Spring: The Development of Reformist Ideas in Czechoslovakia.* Cambridge: Cambridge University Press, 1971.

Liehm, Antonin. *The Politics of Culture.* trans. Peter Kussi. New York: Grove, 1970.

Mistrik, Milos. *Sto slovenskych hier.* Bratislava: Lita, 1992.

Mrlian, Rudolf. *Sucasna Slovenska drama.* Bratislava: Slovenske spisovatel, 1981.

Quinn, Michael. "Uncertain Slovakia: Blaho Uhlar, Stoka and Vres," *Slavic and East European Performance*, 1994.

Rampak, Zoltan. *Cesty dramy.* Bratislava: Tatran, 1984.

Renner, Hans. *A History of Czechoslovakia Since 1945.* London: Routledge, 1989.

Said, Edward W. *Culture and Imperialism.* New York: Knopf, 1993.

Shepard, Gordon. *Russia's Danubian Empire.* London: Heinemann, 1954.

Souckova, Milada. A Literary Satellite: Czechoslovak–Russian Literary Relations. Chicago University Press, 1970.

Steiner, Eugen. *The Slovak Dilemma.* Cambridge: Cambridge University Press, 1973.

Wheaton, Bernard and Zdenek Kavan, *The Velvet Revolution: Czechoslovakia 1988–91.* Boulder, CO: Westview, 1992.

Whipple, Tim D., ed. *After the Velvet Revolution: Vaclav Havel and the New Leaders of Czechoslovakia Speak Out.* Focus on Issues, No. 14. New York: Freedom House, 1991.

14

ON JEAN GENET'S LATE WORKS

Edward W. Said

for Ben Sonnenberg

The first time I saw Jean Genet was in the spring of 1970, a theatrically turbulent and inchoate season when energies and ambitions were released from the social imagination of America into its social body. There was always some excitement to celebrate, some occasion to get up for, some new moment in the Indochinese war either to lament or demonstrate against. Just a couple of weeks before the American invasion of Cambodia, at what seemed the very height of the spring events at Columbia University – which, it should be recalled, had still not recovered from the upheavals of 1968: its administration feeling uncertain, its faculty badly divided, its students perpetually exercised both in and out of the classroom – a noon rally was announced in support of the Black Panthers. It was to take place on the steps of Low Library, Columbia's imposing administration building, and I was especially eager to attend because the rumour was that Jean Genet was going to speak. As I left Hamilton Hall for the rally, I met a student of mine who had been particularly active on campus and who assured me that Genet was indeed going to speak and that he, the student, would be Genet's simultaneous interpreter.

It was an unforgettable scene for two reasons. One was the deeply moving sight of Genet himself, who stood at the center of a large crowd of Panthers and students – he was planted in the middle of the steps with his audience all around him rather than in front of him – dressed in his black leather jacket, blue shirt, and, I think, scruffy jeans. He seemed absolutely at rest, rather like the portrait of him by Giacometti, who catches the man's astounding combination of storminess, relentless control, and almost religious stillness. What I have never forgotten was the gaze of Genet's piercing blue eyes; they seemed to reach out across the distance and fix you with an enigmatic and curiously neutral look.

The other memorable aspect of that rally was the stark contrast between the declarative simplicity of Genet's French remarks in support of the Panthers, and the immensely baroque embellishment of them by my erstwhile student. Genet would say, for example, "The blacks are the most oppressed class in the United States." This would emerge in the translator's colorful ornamentation as something like "In this mother-fucking son-of-a-bitch country, in which reactionary capitalism oppresses and fucks over all the people, not just some of them, etc. etc." Genet stood through this appalling tirade unruffled, and even though the tables were sufficiently turned that translator and not speaker dominated the proceedings, the great writer never so much as blinked. This added to my respect and interest in the man, who was swept away without a flourish at the end of his all-too-brief comments. Having known Genet's literary achievements through teaching *Notre-Dame des fleurs* and *The Thief's Journal*, I was surprised at what appeared from a distance to be his immaculate modesty, quite different from the violent and eccentric sentiments attributed to him by his translator, who allowed himself to ignore what Genet said during the rally in preference for the bordello and prison scatology of some of the plays and prose writings.

When I next saw Genet, it was in the late fall of 1972 in Beirut, where I was spending a sabbatical year. An old school friend of mine, Hanna (John) Mikhail, had called me some time before and said that he would like to bring Genet around to meet me, but I hadn't taken the offer very seriously at first, partly because I couldn't imagine Hanna and Genet as friends, and partly because I still knew nothing about Genet's already considerable involvement with the Palestinian resistance movement.

In any event, Hanna Mikhail deserves to be remembered seventeen years after the fact a little more substantially than I've just presented him. Hanna and I were exact contemporaries, he as a Palestinian undergraduate at Haverford in the mid-1950s, I at Princeton. We went to graduate school at Harvard at the same time, although he was in political science and Middle Eastern studies and I was in comparative literature and English. He was always an exceptionally decent, quiet, and intellectually brilliant man, who expressed to me a quite unique Palestinian Christian background, firmly rooted in the Quaker community of Ramallah. He was committed to Arab nationalism and, very much more than I, at home in both the Arab world and the West. I was flabbergasted when in 1969, after what I gathered was a difficult divorce from his American wife, he quit a good teaching position at the University of Washington and enlisted in the revolution, as we called it, which was headquartered in Amman. I met him there in 1969 and again in 1970 when, both before Black September and in its early days, he played a leading role as the head of information for Fateh.

Hanna's movement name was Abu Omar, and it is in that capacity and by that name that he appears in Genet's posthumous autobiographical work *Un Captif amoureux* (the English title, *Prisoner of Love*, misses much that is subtly interesting in the French original), which I think Genet considered to be a continuation of *The Thief's Journal*. Published in 1986, *Un Captif* is an astonishingly rich and rambling account of Genet's experiences with, feelings about, and reflections on the Palestinians, with whom he

231

associated for about fifteen years. As I said, at the time of his visit I had no idea of Genet's already quite long involvement with the Palestinians, nor, in fact, did I know anything at all about his North African engagements, personal or political. Hanna had called at about eight that evening to say that they would both be dropping by a little later, and so after putting our infant son to bed, Mariam and I sat down to wait in the attractively warm and quiet Beirut evening.

I feel hesitant about reading too much into Genet's presence in that part of the world at that time, but in retrospect there is a correspondence between this unsettlingly brilliant *poéte maudit* and much that has been bewildering and disturbing about recent events in Jordan, Palestine, and Lebanon. Genet was no ordinary visitor, no simple observer or Western traveler in search of exotic peoples and places to write up in some future book. Now, in recollection, his movements through Jordan and Lebanon had something like the effect of a seismographic reading, drawing and exposing the fault lines that a largely normal surface had hidden. I say this mainly because at the time I met him, 1972, although I had not read or seen *Les Paravents (The Screens)*, his gigantic and iconoclastic drama about French colonialism and the Algerian resistance, and although *Un Captif amoureux* had not been written and would not appear for fourteen years, I sensed that this titanic personality had fully intuited the scope and drama of what we were living through, in Lebanon, Palestine, and elsewhere. The Lebanese Civil War would break out almost exactly three years later; Hanna would be killed four years later; the Israeli invasion of Lebanon would occur ten years later; and, very important indeed from my point of view, the *intifada* that would lead to the declaration of a Palestinian state was to explode into actuality fifteen years after. I could not have felt what I feel now, that the dislocating and yet rigorous energies and visions that informed *The Screens* would not, could not, be stilled after Algerian independence in 1962, but would, like the nomadic figures spoken of by Gilles Deleuze and Felix Guattari in *Mille plateaux*, wander elsewhere in search of acknowledgment and fulfillment.

In manner and appearance, Genet was as quiet and as modest as he had seemed at the Columbia rally. He and Hanna arrived a little after ten and stayed till almost three in the morning. I don't think I could narrate the meandering discussions of that evening, but I do want to register a few impressions and anecdotes. Hanna remained fairly quiet throughout; he later told me that he had wanted to let me feel the full force of Genet's vision of things without distraction. Later I was able to read back into that gesture some of the forgiving permission that Hanna had extended to everyone around him, and how that permission, that allowance for people to be themselves, was the true focus of Hanna's search for liberation. Certainly it was clear that Genet appreciated this aspect of his companion's political mission; it was the deep bond between them, that both men in effect had united passion with an almost self-abnegating tolerance.

At the outset it seemed appropriate to tell Genet my spectator's side of the Panther rally and get his reaction to his interpreter's embellishments. He seemed unfazed: "I may not have said all those things," he said, "but," he added solemnly, "je les pensais." We talked about Sartre, whose enormous tome on Genet, I suggested, must have made its subject slightly uneasy. Not at all, Genet replied unaffectedly, "If the guy wanted to make a saint of me, that's fine." In any case, he went on to say, about Sartre's strong pro-Israeli position, "He's a bit of a coward for fear that his friends in Paris might accuse him of anti-Semitism if he ever said anything in support of Palestinian rights." Seven years later, when I was invited to a seminar in Paris about the Middle East organized by Simone de Beauvoir and Sartre, I remembered Genet's comment. I was struck by how this great Western intellectual, whose work I had long admired, was held so in thrall to Zionism (and to Pierre Victor, his manipulative young associate of the time) that he was prevented from saying a single word about what the Palestinians had endured at the hands of Israel for so many decades. (This is easily verified in the Spring 1980 issue of *Les Temps modernes*, which appeared with the full transcript of our seminar's desultory discussions.)

And so the conversation went for many hours, punctuated by Genet's long, puzzling, and yet compellingly impressive silences. We spoke about his experiences in Jordan and Lebanon, his life and friends in France (toward most of whom he expressed either deep hatred or total indifference). He smoked constantly, and he also drank, but he never seemed to change much with drink, emotion, or thought. I recall that once during the evening he said something very positive and surprisingly warm about Jacques Derrida – "un copain," remarked Genet – whom I had thought of as a quietist Heideggerian type at the time; *Glas* had not yet been published, and it was only six months later, when Mariam, our little son, and I spent a few weeks in Paris in April 1973, that I learned from Derrida himself that his friendship with Genet had been sealed as the two of them watched soccer matches together, which I though was a nice touch. There is a brief allusion in *Glas* to our encounter at Reid Hall in Paris, although I've always been slightly miffed that Derrida should refer to me only anonymously, as "un ami" who brought him news of Genet.

But to return to Genet in Beirut: my overwhelming impression was that he seemed totally unlike anything of his that I had read. And I then understood what he had said on a number of occasions (most notably in a letter about *The Screens* to its first director, Roger Blin), that in fact everything he wrote was "contre moi-même," a motif that turns up again in his 1977 interview with Hubert Fichte in the *New Review*, where he says that only when he is alone does he tell the truth. This notion is elaborated somewhat in his interview with *La Revue d'études palestiniennes*, in 1983: "The moment I begin to speak, I am betrayed by the situation. I am betrayed by whoever listens to me, simply because of communication itself. I am betrayed by my choice of words." These comments helped me to interpret his disconcertingly long silences, particularly at a time when, in his visits with the Palestinians, he was quite consciously acting in support of people for whom he cared, and for whom, he says in the Fichte interview, he felt an erotic attraction.

Still, it is the case with Genet's work that, unlike that of any other major writer, you feel that his words, the situations he describes, the characters he depicts – no matter how intensely, no matter how forcefully – are provisional. It is always the propulsive force within himself and his characters that Genet delivers most accurately, and not the correctness of what is said, or its content, or how people think or feel. His later, more overtly political works, most notably *The Screens* and *Un Captif amoureux*, are quite as explicit, indeed scandalous, in this regard as his earlier, more personal works. Much more important than commitment to a cause, much more beautiful and true, he says, is betraying it, which I read as another version of his unceasing search for the freedom of the negative identity that reduces all language to empty posturing, all action to the theatrics of a society he abhors. And yet Genet's essentially antithetical mode oughtn't to be denied either. He was in fact in love with the Arabs he draws in *The Screens* and in *Un Captif amoureux*, a truth that does shine through the denials and negations.

The Thief's Journal (1949) is full of this contradiction. A picaresque account of his early life of "betrayal, theft, and homosexuality," the *Journal* lauds the beauty of a betrayal "that cannot be justified by any heroic excuse. The sneaky, cringing kind, elicited by the least noble of sentiments: envy, hatred . . . greed." Betrayal for Genet is better if it is meaner, not that of Lucifer, but the kind we associate with a police informer or a collaborator. "It is enough," Genet continues, "if the betrayer be aware of his betrayal, that he will it, that he be able to break the bonds of love uniting him with mankind. Indispensable for achieving beauty, love. And cruelty shattering that love." For Genet, to betray is to assert that "exceptional" identity foisted unjustly on him by a society that has found him to be a guilty criminal, but it is also to assert his power to elude any attempts to rehabilitate or reclaim him. Better the destabilizing effects of a permanent will to betray, always keeping him one step out of everyone's reach, than a permanent identity as a crook who can be punished or forgiven by others.

The irony here, and in his later work, is that notwithstanding his repeated betrayals and his claims to dispassionate meanness, Genet's writing also records the emergence of a recognizable and indeed strongly marked social being with real, albeit threatened, bonds connecting him to people and ideas. In part this is because Genet, the character whose adventures are being told, wants his readers to get a pretty firm grip on who and what he is, for all his wandering delinquency and surprising vagabondage. He stands for, and in fact becomes, the outcast unconfined by ordinary social formality or "human" norms. But it is also true that Genet's work is undeniably influenced by the history and the politics of his time; in that setting and throughout that world Genet's addiction to betrayal is a clearly perceptible element. Far from occurring in the abstract, however, it is interpretable as part of his radical politics, which have allied him with Black Panthers, Algerians, and Palestinians. To betray them is not to abandon them exactly, but to retain for himself the right not to belong, not to be accountable, not to be tied down.

Does his love for the Palestinians nevertheless amount to a kind of overturned or exploded Orientalism? Or is it a sort of reformulated colonialist love of handsomely dark young men? Genet did allow his love for Arabs to be his approach to them, but there is no indication that he aspired to a special position, like some benevolent White Father, when he was with them or wrote about them. On the other hand, he never tried to go native, be someone other than he was. There is no evidence at all that he relied on colonial knowledge or lore to guide him, and he did not resort in what he wrote or said to clichés about Arab customs, or mentality, or a tribal past, which he might have used to interpret what he saw or felt. However he might have made his initial contacts with the Arabs (*Un Captif* suggests that he first fell in love with an Arab while an 18 year-old soldier in Damascus half a century ago), he entered the Arab space and lived in it not as an investigator of exoticism but as someone for whom the Arabs had actuality and a presence that he enjoyed, felt comfortable with, even though he was, and remained, different. In the context of a dominant Orientalism that commanded, codified, articulated virtually all Western knowledge and experience of the Arab/Islamic world, there is something quietly but heroically subversive about Genet's extraordinary relationship with the Arabs.

These matters lay a special kind of obligation on Arab readers and critics of Genet, which compels us to read him with unusual attention. Yes, he was a lover of Arabs – something not many of us are accustomed to from Western writers and thinkers, who have found an adversarial relationship with us more congenial – and it is this particular emotion that stamps his last major works. Both were written in a frankly partisan mode – *The Screens* in support of Algerian resistance during the height of the colonial struggle, *Un Captif* in support of Palestinian resistance from the late 1960s until his death in 1986– so that one is left in no doubt where Genet stood. His anger and enmity against France had autobiographical roots; on one level, therefore, to attack France in *The Screens* was to transgress against the government that had judged him and imprisoned him in places like La Mettray. But on another level, France represents the authority into which all social movements normally harden once they have achieved success. Genet celebrates the betrayal by Saïd, the protagonist of *The Screens*, not only because it guarantees the prerogatives of freedom and beauty for an individual in perpetual revolt, but also because its preemptive violence is a way of forestalling what revolutions in course never admit, that their first great enemies – and victims – after they triumph are likely to be the artists and intellectuals who supported the revolution out of love, not out of the accidents of nationality, or the likelihood of success, or the dictates of theory.

Genet's attachment to Palestine was intermittent. After some years in reserve, it was revived in the fall of 1982, when he returned to Beirut and wrote his memorable piece on the Sabra and Shatila massacres. He makes clear, however (in the concluding pages of *Un Captif*), that what ties him to Palestine is that revolution continued there *after* it was forgotten in Algeria. Precisely what is obdurate, defiant, radically transgressive in Saïd's gestures, and in the life-after-death speeches of the Mother, Leila, and Khadija in *The Screens*, is alive in the Palestinian resistance. Yet in that last great prose work of his, one can see Genet's self-absorption struggling with his self-forgetfulness while his Western, French, Christian identity grapples with an entirely different culture. And it is in this encounter that Genet's exemplary greatness comes forward and, in an almost Proustian way, retrospectively illuminates *The Screens*.

For the greatness of the play, in all its lurid and unremitting, often comic theatricality, is its deliberate and logical dismantling not just of French identity – France as empire, as power, as history – but of the very notion of identity itself. Both the nationalism in whose name France has subjugated Algeria and the nationalism in whose name the Algerians have resisted France since 1830 rely to a very great extent upon a politics of identity. As Genet said to Roger Blin, for the French it was all one big event without beginning or end: the connection between the Dey's *coup d'éventail* in 1830 and the invention by 800,000 *pieds noirs* of Tixier-Vignancour, the extreme right-wing French lawyer who defended General Raoul Salan in the trials of 1962. France, France, France, as in the slogan *Algérie française*. But the opposite and equal reaction of the Algerians is also an affirmation of identity, by which the affiliation between combatants, the suffusing presence of patriotism, even the justified violence of the oppressed to which Genet always gave his unequivocal support, are all mobilized in the single-minded cause of *Algérie pour les Algériens*. The gestures that contain the extreme radicality of Genet's anti-identitarian logic are of course Saïd's betrayal of his comrades, and the various incantations to evil pronounced by the women. It is also to be found in the intended decor, costumes, and verbal as well as gestural impropriety that gives the play its terrible force. "Pas de joliesse," said Genet to Blin, for if there was one thing the force of the play could not tolerate, it was prettification, or palliation, or any sort of inconstancy to its rigor.

We are closer to Genet's solitary truth – as opposed to his sense of compromise whenever language is used – when we take seriously his description of the play as a *poetic deflagration*, an artifically started and hastened chemical fire whose purpose is to light up the landscape as it turns all identities into combustible things, like Mr Blankensee's rosebushes, which are set aflame by the Algerians in *The Screens* even as he prates on unheedingly. This notion also explains Genet's various, often very tentatively expressed requests that the play not be performed too many times. Genet was too serious a mind to assume that audiences, or actors and directors for that matter, can live through the apocalyptic purifications of the loss of identity on a daily basis. *The Screens* has to be experienced as something altogether rare.

No less uncompromising is *Un Captif amoureux*. There is no narrative in it, no sequential or thematically organized reflection on politics, love, or history. Indeed, one of the book's most remarkable accomplishments is that it somehow pulls one along uncomplainingly in its meandering, often startlingly abrupt shifts of mood and logic. To read Genet is in the end to accept the utterly undomesticated peculiarity of his sensibility, which returns constantly to the area where revolt, passion, death, and regeneration are linked:

> What was to become of you after the storms of fire and steel? What were you to do?
>
> Burn, shriek, turn into a brand, blacken, turn to ashes, let yourself be slowly covered first with dust and then with earth, seeds, moss, leaving behind nothing but your jawbone and teeth, and finally becoming a little funeral mound with flowers growing on it and nothing inside.

In their movement of regenerative rebellion, the Palestinians, like the Algerians and Black Panthers before them, show Genet a new language, not of orderly communication but of astonishing lyricism, of an instinctive and yet highly wrought intensity that delivers "moments of wonder and . . . flashes of comprehension." Many of the most memorable fragments in the mysteriously digressive structure of *Un Captif amoureux* meditate on language, which Genet always wants to transform from a force for identity and statement into a transgressive, disruptive, and perhaps even consciously evil mode of betrayal. "Once we see in the need to 'translate' the obvious need to 'betray', we shall see the temptation to betray as something desirable, comparable perhaps to erotic exaltation. Anyone who hasn't experienced the ecstasy of betrayal knows nothing about ecstasy at all." There is in this admission – dubious, even repellent, on moral and political grounds, tolerable, if at all, only as an aesthetic or rhetorical credo – the very same dark force that motivates the Mother, Khadija, Leila, and Saïd in *The Screens*, partisans of Algerian liberation who nevertheless exultantly betray their comrades.

237

The challenge of Genet's writing, therefore, is its fierce antinomianism. Here is a man in love with "the other," an outcast and stranger himself, feeling the deepest sympathy for the Palestinian revolution as the "metaphysical" uprising of outcasts and strangers – "my heart was in it, my body was in it, my spirit was in it" – yet neither his "total belief" nor "the whole of myself" could be in it. The consciousness of being a sham, an unstable personality perpetually at the border ("where human personality expresses itself most fully, whether in harmony or in contradiction with itself"), is the central experience of the book. "My whole life was made up of unimportant trifles cleverly blown up into acts of daring." One is immediately reminded here of T. E. Lawrence, an imperial agent amongst the Arabs (though pretending to be otherwise) half a century earlier, but Lawrence's assertiveness and instinct for detached domination is superseded in Genet (who was no agent) by eroticism and an authentic submission to the political sweep of a passionate commitment.

Identity is what we impose on ourselves through our lives as social, historical, political, and even spiritual beings. The logic of culture and of families doubles the strength of identity, which for someone like Genet, who was a victim of the identity forced on him by his delinquency, his isolation, his transgressive talents and delights, is something to be resolutely opposed. Above all, given Genet's choice of sites like Algeria and Palestine, identity is the process by which the stronger culture, and the more developed society, imposes itself violently upon those who, by the same identity process, are decreed to be a lesser people. Imperialism is the export of identity.

Genet, therefore, is the traveler across identities, the tourist whose purpose is marriage with a foreign cause, so long as that cause is both revolutionary and in constant agitation. Despite their prohibitions, he says in *Un Captif*, frontiers are fascinating because a Jacobin who crosses frontiers must change into a Machiavellian. The revolutionary, in other words, will occasionally accommodate himself to the customs post, haggling, brandishing a passport, applying for visas, humbling himself before the State. Genet tried artfully to avoid this: in Beirut, he spoke to us with rare joviality of how he once entered the United States from Canada surreptitiously and illegally. But crossing to Algeria and Palestine was not an occasion for such adventurism, but rather the expression of a dangerous and subversive politics involving borders to be negotiated, expectations to be fulfilled, dangers to be confronted. And, to speak here as a Palestinian, I believe that Genet's choice of Palestine in the 1970s and 1980s was the most dangerous political choice, the scariest journey of all. Only Palestine has not been co-opted in the West by either the dominant liberal or the dominant establishment political culture. Ask any Palestinian and he or she will tell you how our identity is still the only criminalized and delinquent selfhood – whose code word is terrorism – in a historical period in the West that has liberated or variously dignified most other races and nationalities. So the choice first of Algeria in the 1950s, then of Palestine in the period thereafter, is and ought to be understood as a vital act of Genet's solidarity, his willingly enraptured identification with other identities whose existence involves a strenuously contested struggle.

So identity grates against identity. Genet's is thus the most antithetical of imaginations. Ruling all his endeavors, housing all his nomadic energy, are precision and grace, embodied in one of the greatest formal French styles since Chateaubriand (here I quote Richard Howard). One never feels any sort of sloppiness or diversion in what he does, any more than one would expect Genet to have worn a three-piece suit and worked in an office. Genius ("le génie"), he once said, "c'est la rigeur dans le désespoir." How perfectly that sense is caught in Khadija's great ode to "le mal" in scene 12 of *The Screens*, with its combination of hieratic severity and its surprising self-deflation, all contained in a rhythm of high formality that suggests an unlikely combination of Racine and Zazie.

Genet is like that other great modern dissolver of identity, Adorno, for whom no thought is translatable into any other equivalent, yet whose relentless urge to communicate his precision and desperation — with the fineness and counter-narratival energy that makes *Minima Moralia* his masterpiece — furnishes a perfect metaphysical accompaniment to Genet's funereal pomp and scabrous raucousness. What we miss in Adorno is Genet's scurrilous humor, so evident in his booming send-ups of Sir Harold and his son, the vamps and missionaries, whores and French soldiers of *The Screens*. In both, however, a fantastic decision is enacted to be eccentric, and to be so with unbendable, unmodifiable rigor, to write of triviality or degradation with an almost metaphysically driven grandeur that is compelling, melancholy, heartrending. Such solitude as theirs is resistance and hopelessness together, to be neither emulated nor routinized, no matter how much the reader may appreciate (or appropriate) some of what they say.

Adorno, however, is a minimalist whose distrust and hatred of the totality cause him to work entirely in fragments, aphorisms, essays and digressions. As opposed to Adorno's micrologics, Genet is a poet of large Dionysiac forms, of ceremonies and carnivalesque display: his work is related to the Ibsen of *Peer Gynt*, to Artaud, Peter Weiss, and Aimé Césaire. His characters do not interest us because of their psychology but because in their own obsessive ways they are the paradoxically casual and yet formalistic bearers of a very finely imagined and understood history. Genet made the step, crossed the legal borders, that very few white men or women even attempted. He traversed the space from the metropolitan center to the colony; his unquestioned solidarity was with the very same oppressed identified and so passionately analyzed by Fanon.

I don't think it is wrong to say that in the twentieth century, with very few exceptions, great art in a colonial situation appears only in support of what Genet in *Un Captif* calls the metaphysical uprising of the natives. Lesser art fudges or trims, but ends up being for the status quo. The cause of Algeria produced *The Screens*, Pontecorvo's *Battle of Algiers*, Fanon's books, and the works of the great Algerian novelist Kateb Yacine, who died in 1989. Compared with these, Camus pales, his novels, essays, and stories the desperate gestures of a frightened, finally ungenerous mind. In Palestine the same is true, since the radical, the transformative, difficult, and visionary work comes from and on behalf of the Palestinians – Habibi, Darwish, Jabra, Kanafani, Kassem, Genet – not from the Israelis who oppose them. Genet's works are, to borrow a phrase from Raymond Williams, resources of hope. In 1961 he could complete an overwhelmingly theatrical work like *The Screens* because, I believe, victory for the FLN was very near at hand: the play catches the moral exhaustion of France and the moral triumph of the FLN. When it came to Palestine, however, Genet found the revolution in an apparently uncertain phase, with the disasters of Jordan and Lebanon recently behind the Palestinians and the dangers of more dispossession, exile, and dispersion all around them. Hence, the ruminative, exploratory, and intimate quality of *Un Captif amoureux* – antitheatrical, radically contradictory, rich in memory and speculation:

> This is *my* Palestinian revolution, told in my own chosen order. As well as mine there is the other, probably many others. Trying to think the revolution is like waking up and trying to see the logic in a dream. There's no point, in the middle of a drought, in imagining how to cross the river when the bridge has been swept away. When, half awake, I think about the revolution, I see it as the tail of a caged tiger, starting to lash out in a vast sweep, then falling back wearily on the prisoner's flank.

One wishes Genet were alive today for many reasons, not least because of the *intifada*, which has been continuing since late 1987. It is not farfetched to say that *The Screens* is Genet's version of an Algerian *intifada*, given flesh and blood in the beauty and exuberance of the Palestinian *intifada*. Life imitates art, but so also does art imitate life and, insofar as it can be imitated, death.

Genet's last works are saturated with images of death, especially *Un Captif*, part of whose melancholy for the reader is the knowledge that Genet was dying as he wrote it and that so many of the Palestinians he saw, knew, and wrote about were also to die. It is curious, however, that both *Un Captif* and *The Screens* end with affirmative recollections of a mother and her son who, although dead or about to die, are reunited by Genet in his own mind: the act of reconciliation and recollection that occurs at the end of *The Screens*, as Saïd and the unnamed Mother are seen together, prefigures Genet's last prose work by twenty-five years.

These are firmly unsentimental scenes, partly because Genet seems determined to present death as a weightless and largely unchallenging thing, partly, too, because he wants to retain for his own purposes the priority and affective comfort of the relationship between an almost savagely archetypal mother and a loyal but somewhat aloof, often harsh son.

In *Un Captif*, the primordial relationship – fierce, loving, enduring – of the maternally defined pair (Hamza and his mother) is imagined as persisting beyond death. Yet so meticulous is Genet's refusal to concede that any good can come from permanence or bourgeois, and heterosexual, stability that he dissolves even these positive images of death in the ceaseless social turbulence and revolutionary disruption that are central to his interest. Yet it is the mother in both works who is strangely unyielding, uncompromising, difficult. "Tu ne vas pas flancher," his mother reminds Saïd, you are not to be co-opted, and you are not to become a domesticated symbol or a martyr for the revolution. When Saïd finally disappears at the end of the play, undoubtedly killed, it is once again the Mother who with considerable anxiety and, I think, disgust suggests that Saïd *might* be forced by his comrades to come back in a commemorative revolutionary song.

Genet does not want the death that awaits and will surely claim him and his characters to invade, arrest, or seriously modify any aspect of the rushing turmoil that his work represents as deflagration, which he imagines to be centrally, even mystically important. It is startling to find this irreducibly religious conviction so close to his heart at the end. For whether demon or divinity, the Absolute for Genet is perceptible neither in the form of human identity nor as a personified deity, but precisely in what, after everything is said and done, will not settle down, will not be incorporated or domesticated. That such a force must somehow be represented and cared for by people who are absorbed in it and, at the same time, must risk its own disclosure or personification is Genet's final, most intransigent paradox. Even when we close the book or leave the theater once the performance is over, his work instructs us also to block the song, doubt the narrative and memory, disregard the aesthetic experience that brought us those images for which we now have a genuinely strong affection. That so impersonal and true a philosophical dignity should also be allied with so poignantly human a sensibility is what gives Genet's work the unreconciled and tense note it communicates. In no other late-twentieth-century writer are the dangers of catastrophe and the lyrical delicacy of affective response to them sustained together as grandly and fearlessly.

EDITOR'S NOTE

JoAnne Akalaitis's production of Jean Genet's *The Screens* ran at the Guthrie Theatre in Minneapolis, Minnesota (USA) from October 24 to November 19,

1989. The play received much critical attention and outstanding reviews in both the local and national press.[1] Genet's 1961 play had not been staged in America since the 1971 production at the Chelsea Theater Center, and reviewers of the Guthrie production made particular note of the new currency of the play, given the clear resonances between the Algerian revolution of its setting and the Palestinian *intifada* then in full force.[2]

The University of Minnesota, in conjunction with the Guthrie Theatre, sponsored a symposium on the play in November 1989, and invited Edward Said to participate.[3] His remarks on that occasion, which I heard as a member of the audience, were later published in essay form in *Grand Street* (36).[4] That essay is reprinted here with the permission of the author. I am most grateful to Professor Said for allowing me to include this piece in the collection.

NOTES

1 See, for example, Jack Kroll, "Major Doings in Minneapolis," *Newsweek* 20 November 1989: 76.
2 See, for example, Jennifer Wicke, "The Screens," *Nation* 2 April 1990: 464–66.
3 For details on the symposium, see Marc Robinson, "The Conversion of Saint Genet," *American Theatre* (March 1990), 15–19, 57–58. I am grateful to the Guthrie Theatre for providing me with this and other articles on their production, and to my assistant, Kornelia Tancheva, for her research on its reviews.
4 Edward Said, *Grand Street* (36) vol 9, no. 4 (1990), 26–42.

15

STRATEGIES FOR SURVIVAL
Anti-Imperialist Theatrical Forms in the Anglophone Caribbean

Elaine Savory

[The] association of wealth with whites and poverty with blacks is not accidental. It is the nature of the imperialist relationship that enriches the metropolis at the expense of the colony i.e. it makes the whites richer and the blacks poorer.

> Walter Rodney, *The Groundings With My Brothers,* 1969: 19

That imperialism which today is fighting against a true liberation of mankind leaves in its wake here and there tinctures of decay which we must search out and mercilessly expel from our land and our spirits.

> Frantz Fanon, *The Wretched of the Earth,* 1967: 200

The neo-colonialism of today represents imperialism in its final and perhaps its most dangerous stage.

> Kwame Nkrumah, *Neo-Colonialism: The Last Stage of Imperialism,* 1965: ix

The birth of a people (their emergent consciousness) is a fascinating spectacle. The theater that accompanies it is a moving experience.

> Edouard Glissant, *Caribbean Discourse,* 1992: 196

"Who with the Devil tries to play fair,
  Weaves the net of his own despair."

> Derek Walcott, *Tijean and His Brothers,* 1972: 156–157

"Len, Len, son, listen to me, son. Your soul is in bondage! A have to release you! A have to set you free!"

> Trevor Rhone, *Old Story Time,* 1981: 60–61

In the Caribbean,[1] imperialism and strategies for defeating its ever mutating forms are not abstract, theoretical concepts, but lived, experienced realities which have gone on since the first settlements of Europeans and their arrangements for the provision of cheap plentiful labour. I have no space here[2] for an extensive discussion of the conflicted issues surrounding the term imperialism, especially in the forms which are most relevant to this discussion, namely cultural imperialism (Tomlinson 1991) and neo-imperialism (Nkrumah 1965) and so must settle for a working definition compatible with Caribbean discourses on the subject. Imperialism, then, as Walter Rodney remarks, and Frantz Fanon explored (1968) has been about racial domination as much as about who has economic and political power.

Anti-imperialisms[3] in the Caribbean have generally been the significant history of resistance in a multitude of successive forms, from the suicides and infanticides of Africans captured as slaves, to slave rebellions,[4] to the nurturing of alternative world views to the colonial, to the development of Creole languages (Roberts 1988; Devonish 1986). Furthermore, with a few exceptions, the most intense signs of rebellion were, and often still are, concentrated in the poorest members of society, who were (and still often are) darkest in skin colour and closest to African identity both physically and culturally.

The plantocracy attempted in many ways to eradicate African cultural continuity, from which the most sustained resistance has come, and the colonial government often tried to silence particularly African modes of expression,[5] but the African presence stubbornly went on, sometimes protected within a hard-won space inside imperial society (such as the Maroon community living in the hills of rural Jamaica[6]), sometimes remaining an unspoken subtext of everyday life in colonial society.[7] African forms of expression, love of the word and the inventive use of music, masking, dance, possession and ritual survived in the Caribbean despite attempts on the part of colonial authorities to eradicate them. They are most developed in postcolonial society in neo-African, creolized cults such as pocomania, Rastafarianism, vodoun, Shango worship and the African-centred Baptist church, and these, and to a lesser extent Indo-Caribbean festivals,[8] provide important vocabularies for theatrical performance of all kinds. It is important to recognize that such vocabularies are both inherently theatrical and inherently political, moving towards liberating a community from the fear which would assure their acquiescence to a brutal and hostile governing power.

The past struggle against overt imperialisms and the present one against neo-imperialisms have informed the whole of Caribbean social life, and given a strongly political identity to Caribbean art forms of all kinds.[9] This essay focuses, necessarily very briefly, on some central performance elements which four contemporary Caribbean playwrights utilize and which are developed from folk forms. These forms give a sense of identity to a people struggling to resist co-option into a dominant culture as second-class members. I have therefore termed them "strategies for survival."

Performance forms, such as the crucially central culture of cricket[10] and Carnival, have contributed greatly to anti-imperialism in the Caribbean, but commercial interests increasingly threaten the older elements of public ritual and performance because of the extent of the tourist industry.[11]

The playwright's resources include the most informal of encounters on the street, so often theatrical in the Caribbean, story-telling and the enactment of ritual within the context of religions like Shango worship,[12] African-centred Baptist Christianity or Hinduism. The Caribbean play has been increasingly interrelated with popular culture, especially as the middle-class theatre-going public has realized the importance of pride in ethnic identity and culture.[13] It draws on a range of theatrical possibilities, such as rituals, festivals, creole usages, topical allusions or concerns, local custom, and performance strategies utilized by calypsonians, speech-makers[14] or folk singers/dancers. Thus though formal theatre in the Caribbean, i.e. the making of plays to be seen in theatres, traces its ancestry directly to the expatriate and Creole[15] entertainments which drew their inspiration from European models, it has become successful in recent times as an openly anti-imperialist force because of inventive revisioning.[16]

The European play as genre has a history of upper- and middle-class audiences, and European dramatists such as Brecht have sought ways to fracture their complacency. The African-Caribbean middle-class have, as the twentieth century comes to a close, acknowledged their origins in slavery and an impoverished working class and therefore have been willing in recent times to re-enter their traditions in the theatre. This means that Caribbean playwrights have an audience when they seek to rehabilitate ritual and festival elements from African or Indian culture on the stage.

Whereas within Euro-American theatre performance styles are often clearly demarcated by genre (the predominantly verbal play, the musical, the cabaret act etc.), in Caribbean theatre the boundaries between genres are continually being explored and tested. Dramatists struggle to unite with the idea of the play the oral and performance traditions which have long constituted their people's identity and defence against colonial intrusion as well as local hegemonies. What I am speaking about here is a movement towards rehabilitating popular traditions as anti-imperialist forms, a movement which can serve many anti-imperialist agendas, including that of feminism,[17] though that is not our concern here. A "strategy for survival," then, in the context of the Caribbean, draws on the "little tradition"[18] or suppressed inheritance and is expressed in a mode which both releases the self-defining energy of reconnection with a past ancestry denied by colonialism and carves out space in a given context of repression. The emphasis here is on community identity and the search for what heals and strengthens communally.

Such strategies have tended to develop first in one territory. Calypso, for example, first turned into a highly organized art form in Trinidad. It originated as a song of resistance[19] on the plantation among the slaves, and behind this is probably an ancestry in satirical African orature. Survival strategies which I propose to discuss here are theatrical in themselves and have both been prevalent anti-imperialist reinforcers within the culture and useful devices in theatrical performance with an anti-imperialist intent. They are masking, possession, speech-making, the use of music and/or dance and story-telling. Each of these is an important element in both contemporary Caribbean folk culture and in African cultures,[20] where the secular and spiritual are closely interwoven. In the Caribbean, spirituality in the poorest communities is often a site of anti-imperialist resistance. Thus what is particularly interesting is that in the Caribbean logocentrism, the power of the word, and especially the performed word, has a long history of being a powerful, inventive and successful site of resistance to oppression.

Possession, the entry of a god into the living body of a celebrant, which is witnessed by many in the Caribbean at religious rituals, is a complex issue for the dramatist. Even if the actor has no fear of undergoing the experience of pretending to possession (with the risk of actually becoming possessed), the audience is going to be watching with the possibility in mind that this could be real or become real.[21] Even middle-class actors can retain a sense of caution about the portrayal of the dead on stage or in certain rituals. But precisely because there is through the idea of possession the meaningful notion of multiple selves[22] and connection to an ancestral past (reinforced also by the convention of masking), it is a particularly useful theatrical mode. It gives a deeper meaning to the actor switching roles during performance, for example. There may or may not be a residual belief in reincarnation in African-Caribbean culture.[23] If so, this reflects the belief systems of Africa, where a conception of the eternal cycle of life from the unborn through the living and the dead and back to the unborn is a cornerstone of many cultures. An acceptance of the possibility of reincarnation and of possession gives a profound sense of the inter-relationship of generations, strengthens community and communal reading of history, and undermines excessive pursuit of individual self-centredness. This is what makes the idea of possession a possibility as a theatrical strategy of survival, a means of siting resistance to colonial, i.e. imperial, influences.

Dennis Scott's *Echo in the Bone* (1985) is set in rural Jamaica at a "nine nights" ceremony to honour a death. The anti-imperialist movement of the play is in the direction of freeing a family and village community from the burden of a past full of the pain and destructiveness of racism and economic oppression. By extension, the family becomes Jamaica as a whole. Scott utilizes the idea of possession to bring the dead man back to tell his own version of the story of his last days. Indeed, the only way Crew is portrayed throughout the play is by his enactment by other characters, which reinforces the idea that he lives in them as an embodiment of their connection to their collective history. Early in the play, Rattler begins to dance, and there is real concern for his welfare because Crew's spirit is abroad:

RATTLER: (*In a high voice*) Ah ah ah ah ah . . .

STONE: (*At the door, pointing, a paper in his hand*)
Crew, show yourself!

246

P: Crew? Where?

MADAM: Hold him, Stone, him going to kill himself!

STONE: Jesus! Dream, what happen?

P: The spirit take him, just so, and him start to dance.

STONE: Then is him I see!

P: Who?

STONE: Is the dead man walking the air. Is Crew! . . .

MADAM: Hold him Stone! He inside the boy trying to get out and the
heart will break open if the oil is not put on his head and his mouth
soon. (81)

Scott uses a number of historical moments to convey a sense of
unbroken history through the fragmented collective memory of his characters. The device of possession, or multiple identity, assists in weaving their
role-playing together as a coherent explanation of how Crew came to
murder Mr Charles and what this means: instead of seeing the act as a
single criminal brutality, we see black and white locked into a violent
history, one killing the other in different ways. Charles' death and Crew's
disappearance bring them together as joint victims of communal refusal to
defeat human negativity and essentialism. Their joint ends may, in the ritual
of the nine nights and their dissolution of the boundaries of self, begin a
kind of communal healing.

As in African festival, the use of masks in Caribbean ritual conveys a
sense of identity which is at times fluid. The mask enables the human
personality to be presented as connected to a cycle of change, from the
metaphysical to the physical and again, after death, to the metaphysical.
Thus ancestors and gods may enter the human world through masking,
whether or not possession occurs. This has been a particularly important
strategy for Caribbean peoples of African descent whose sense of freedom
was often confined to religious imagery, from slavery times, when an
African believed that to die was to return home to Africa and be reunited
with the ancestors, to the notion that a poor black person could become
filled with power and dignity through the transformative experience of
wearing a mask either in religious rite or in Carnival. Once again the
notion of masking is particularly interesting when utilized in theatrical
contexts where it permits the idea of character and identity to be complex
and shifting. Use of a mask of course in performance can be simply a
matter of dramatic costume (in the way masks function in Carnival, for
example), or it can suggest a complex perception of the relation of
individual personality to communally understood symbol, as well as the
possibility of the possession of the individual by spiritual powers.

Derek Walcott's *Dream on Monkey Mountain* (1972) and *Tijean and His
Brothers* (1972) both utilize masking extensively. The white apparition
who haunts Makak in *Dream* and whom he finally beheads to free himself

of self-delusion and self-hate, is female, an image of "La Diablesse", a Creole image of the Devil. This has to be both Carnival mask and intensely powerful spirit, whereas when Makak appears in a dream as African king with his followers the effect is only that of a gorgeous Carnival band. This emphasizes the distance between Africa the idea and Africa the reality, for Makak must work his way through to honouring his identity as an African-Caribbean peasant, not evading it into romantic notions of Africa. Basil, the carpenter and coffin-maker, is the other highly "masked" character, with dramatic facepaint and sinister clothing at the beginning of the play, when he looks somewhat like Baron Samedi, the guardian of the graveyard in Haitian vodoun ritual. This appearance suggests his communications with an unseen world of spirits, both creative and destructive, and indeed, Makak's rehabilitation depends upon his working through false or misleading apparitions to a solid vision of spiritual health.

In *Tijean*, the Devil and the Bolom are similarly manifestations of the spirit world. The Devil must mask himself in order to be able to move among humans with maximum devastation. The Bolom is masked in the sense of not yet being liberated from the prebirth state of uninterpreted human form. Thus their masking is of two quite different moral orders: the one a deliberate, intelligent and amoral pursuit of predatory supremacy, the other a frustration of possibility. The play utilizes these two poles of masking as active theatrical metaphors: to cause the Devil to drop his mask and to feel produces the chance that the Bolom can be freed from a state of suspended development.

There are also more subtle conventions of masking at work in many Caribbean plays, for racism and class divisions give rise to a good deal of masking or role-playing, and, in their function as anti-imperialist performance, plays can expose and reverse dangerous self-disguising. In Trevor Rhone's *Old Story Time* (1981), class and skin shade are intertwined, so that a form of masking which has to be shed is the preference for middle-class and light-skinned persons and cultural traits. Mama, who has schemed for a light bride for her son Len, is possessed by what are described as "evil spirits" in the last scene of the play, and delivered by the whole family holding her and singing a chant, "Omnia n Twi. Mia Kuru. Omnia n ani," and the twenty-third Psalm. Mama is delivered not just from evil spirits but from her wish to part her son and his wife. Thus we see the combined force of belief in Christian and African images of good and evil: the complex question of how to balance them occupies the community's energies to a serious degree. The objective of unmasking is to restore honest feeling, even if the community will continue to live across divides of shade, class and gender.

Story-telling was until recently a popular way for Caribbean families to gather, often around the grandmother as designated teller of tales, under the full moon. The purpose of such stories was often not just entertainment but moral teaching as well. The story-teller, then, is the guardian of the community's inheritance and protects that inheritance from being destroyed by imperialism or neo-imperialism. Also, story-tellers understand the power of the word, and the punning and verbal play which characterizes the African tradition.

As in African story-telling, Caribbean story-telling often has a set of ritual addresses and responses which mark the boundaries of the story. "Crick Crack"[24] is one such popular frame, and this is played upon by Derek Walcott at the opening of his play *Tijean and His Brothers*, where the frog says "Greek-croak", and at the end, where he says " . . . creek Crack," thus bringing together both the notion of the Greek chorus and the Caribbean (African) story-teller.[25] Theatrical use of this kind of folk tradition immediately brings together contemporary issues with a sense of African-Caribbean history and community.

Trevor Rhone's *Old Story Time* portrays story-telling as a major avenue of reconnection for the audience with their past and also of political reworking of their present. The story-teller, Papa Ben, has a dialogue with the audience and the actors play an extension of that audience in the opening scene, as yet undifferentiated into the parts they will play. Pa Ben explains the tradition of story-telling and its function for a village as he passes through the auditorium, carrying a lantern:

> You don't have voice to answer me?
> Everybody hearty? . . . (*To the audience*) Make
> yourselves comfortable on them nice
> chairs. You people lucky, years ago when A
> was a boy and A use to go to listen to
> story, it was never in no fancy place like
> this, with all them fandangles, pretty
> lights and whatnot[. . . .] On an evening in the
> district we would gather at the village
> square, everybody gather round the shop
> piazza, some sit 'pon old drum, others
> 'pon the old crocus bags filled with salt,
> everybody chatting, some meddling in
> people's business [. . .] my father was the
> chief Storyteller when him feel in the
> mood[. . . .] But A tell you, give him a bottle
> of whites, an' two twos him was slap bang
> in the mood. (8–9).

He opens up a bottle of white rum, wets his throat, and after a little more byplay with one of the actors, goes into his house chanting "Ol' Story Time." The by-play between Pa Ben as story-teller (who controls the fiction) and Pa Ben the community memory (who sometimes does not know what happened) is a central strategy of the play–audience relation.

Whereas folk dancing may, in an industrial culture, become simply an entertaining illustration of a lost past, in the Caribbean, folk dances performed as a serious part of culture (as opposed to hotel entertainments for tourists) convey a powerful sense of a repressed culture reawakening, and of the pleasure of rehabilitating a sense of identity as publicly and centrally important after generations suffered the imposition of colonial alienation from the underground culture which in fact sustained most of the people. Similarly, music and singing, rather than turning a play into a "musical," almost synonymous with trivializing it or associating it with sophisticated escapism in Western industrial culture,[26] takes the Caribbean play closer to festival and ritual in which both have a symbolic significance, as they do in African culture.

As might be expected in a play named after a style of song, Earl Lovelace's *Jestina's Calypso* (1984) exploits the calypso form. Calypso is more than a form of popular song, it is a tradition of subversive response to all kinds of authority. It is also a system of moral comment on behaviour. Above all, and this is explained well by Gordon Rohlehr, the calypsonian is a wordsmith who conveys the spiritual power of language as a decolonizing or liberating force: Rohlehr speaks here of the early development of song as part of the African-centred culture of the poor masses in Trinidad:

> the man who was recognised as a possessor of the word and as a spokesman for the group, occupied a position of supreme importance. Such a man would have been the chantwel of the Calinda bands[. . . .] One of the roles of the chantwel was to reinforce obeah with verbal magic. He has to support the boasting speech of his own champion or "chief king" by impressing the rival that dire injuries would be dealt him if he did not desist. (52)

Thus it is appropriate that Jestina's speech-making and the songs which the actors sing about her should be clever, amusing and provocative. They also contribute a serious comment on the superficiality of basing human worth on outside appearances. The whole play is Jestina's calypso, her satirical and highly political essay on female images and their relation to the nation of Trinidad and Tobago itself. Lovelace created this play at a time when female calypsonians were beginning to emerge in Trinidad and Tobago and the rest of the Caribbean, and gave a feminist reading to a tradition which has mostly been quite explicitly sexist (Boyce Davies 1990).

The role of music and dance in Walcott's plays, and even sometimes in the more verbally orientated dramas of Rhone, reflects the centrality of music as a series of interconnected languages within Caribbean culture. For example, Walcott's *Dream on Monkey Mountain* opens with music and dance, which together with the lighting of the scene give a strong sense of the strands of important symbolism which the play will explore: African identity in the Caribbean, the meaning of life and death, imprisonment, the moon as one symbol of whiteness and therefore potential death to the black community, the possibility of all things being able to be themselves and their opposites:

> A spotlight warms the white disc of an African drum until it glows like the round moon above it. Below the moon is the stark silhouette of a volcanic mountain. Reversed, the moon becomes the sun. A dancer enters and sits astride the drum. From the opposite side of the stage a top-hatted, frock-coated figure with white gloves, his face halved by white make-up like the figure of Baron Samedi, enters and crouches behind the dancer. As the lament begins, dancer and figure wave their arms slowly, sinuously, with a spidery motion. The figure rises during the lament and touches the disc of the moon. The drummer rises, dancing as if in slow motion, indicating, as their areas grow distinct, two prison cages on either side of the stage. In one cell, TIGRE and SOURIS, two half-naked felons, are squabbling. The figure strides off slowly, the CONTEUR and CHORUS, off-stage, increase the volume of their lament. (212).

One of the most important aspects of recent Caribbean performance arts is the flood of orature that draws upon "nation language," Edward Kamau Brathwaite's term for the language(s)[27] which Caribbean peoples speak. This is a creative development unique to each territory and born of the enforced containment of African and Asian languages within a colonial language but informed by a spirit of subversion in response to this oppression. Therefore language is a particularly heightened political space in Caribbean writing, and theatrical writing can draw on a huge variety of linguistic possibilities, all of them understood by local audiences within the context of politics. Language plays an important role in defining anti-imperial and colonial elements in most Caribbean plays, and is frequently, as in African cultural contexts, inseparable from musical forms, as in the case of calypso.

In *Tijean*, the Devil/Planter/Papa Bois character has immense and dangerous linguistic skills but they tend to the self-defeatingly comic – "To hell with dependence and the second-lieutenancy!" (152) – so that although he suitably enough speaks in international English, he lacks the poetic resonance of Tiijean or his mother. Tijean, for example, says as he looks on the Devil's face, "this is like looking/At the blinding gaze of God" (143). The Devil's greatest deficiency is his inability to have any communal experience, and his language correspondingly has become the empty rhetoric of one who has no faith and no integrity and for whom language carries so much irony that it almost ceases to carry meaning: "Oh Christ, how weary it is to be immortal" (151). Creole speech denotes connection to the Caribbean in *Tijean*, as when Mijean talks to the Bird: "Bird, you disturbing me! Too much whistling without sense,/Is animal you are, so please know your place" (115). This is a Creole made accessible to outsiders but it serves to indicate a world in which the poor have their own language, whereas the Devil speaks in a more cosmopolitan register. Tijean, like Makak, speaks both in Creole and in international English, often with a highly poetic resonance.

Makak in *Dream* is given to speeches of great melancholic poetry which characterize this abjectly poor and self-doubting man as a gifted maker of words. The decolonizing movement of *Dream* gives Makak the greatest gift of language, which in a culture admiring of words is significant. We can see how important an emphasis this is when we think of Shakespearian plays in which the most important characters often have the highest rank as well the most poetic and striking facility with words, and the low-born are often only comically witty, and sometimes downright farcical. In Caribbean plays, the least articulate folk are likely to be the most elite and often white, whereas the most verbally dextrous are most likely those who come from the poorest and most African-centred masses. This is not only a political perception, but a reflection of the way in which Caribbean people have seen language utilized by folk culture on the one hand and a restrictive colonial bureaucracy on the other.

My point has been that Caribbean plays draw on the strongly anti-imperialist character of popular culture and utilize it to carry their own themes of challenge to invasive, elitist or foreign influence. As the song from *Tijean* rightly points out, playing fair with the Devil is not likely to work, and it has always been known in the Caribbean that resistance to imperialisms requires creative and innovative strategies which both protect the oppressed and aggressively engage with the oppressor. In utilizing the folk traditions which in the Caribbean have been so long subversive and anti-imperialist in themselves, dramatists give themselves a vocabulary which connects them to the contemporary struggle against neo-imperialisms which threaten the survival of folk culture and thereby the identity of the people who created it as their protection in a hostile world.

NOTES

1 I have restricted my discussion, in terms of examples of theatrical usage, to anglophone plays. Of course the Caribbean is multi-lingual in very complex ways, reflecting its immense cultural pluralism. See, for example, Lewis (1968) for an introduction.

2 This essay has been cut to a quarter of its original length, thereby sacrificing much of the illustration of the argument, because of space available in the volume. If I knew I was writing for a community of scholars conversant with Caribbean issues, producing this argument in a small number of pages would be very much easier. As it is, I have been unable to approach the level of discussion

which can assume considerable knowledge in the reader. This is, in itself, a side effect of most publishing originating in industrialized countries which pay little attention to Caribbean culture. I hope this essay may help spark a demand for more information on it.

3 I have used the plural form because the after-effects of European rule are now compounded by new intrusions through the electronic media, especially from the United States, and because intellectual debate rages as to the meaning of the term imperialism in different contexts.

4 There are many good accounts of slave resistance in the Caribbean, but I would recommend Beckles (1987); James (1963); Millette (1985); and Thompson (1987). All of these studies are written by established Caribbean scholars and all deal with resistance to imperialism.

5 For example, the kalinda drums which were silenced in Trinidad in the late nineteenth century, with resulting civil disorder and also the subsequent invention of steel pan. See: Brereton (1981); Rohlehr (1990); and Savory Fido (1990).

6 See Price (1979).

7 See, for excellent discussions of the rediscovery of this subtext, Brathwaite (1974); Cobley and Thompson (1990); and Simpson (1980).

8 See John La Guerre (1985) for a discussion of Indo-Caribbean culture in Trinidad.

9 By this I mean those forms which have gradually developed in the Caribbean from a creolization process working on various cultural influences possessed by each generation of people who arrived in whatever circumstances. Obvious examples are calypso, steel band, reggae.

10 See James (1963).

11 Carnival in Trinidad has many of the characteristics of African festival, not least in its amalgam of secular and non-secular elements. In recent times Carnival has been becoming more of a tourist entertainment and has lost some of the popular aspects of its character, including some of the old dance steps and band formations which were prevalent in earlier times.

12 See particularly the discussion of religious cults by Simpson (1980). See also Warner-Lewis (1991) for an excellent linguistic introduction to Yoruba survivals in Trinidad. The worship of Yoruba *orisha* or gods in Trinidad is known as Shango worship after one of the *orisha*.

13 See Gibbons (1979) for a very interesting survey of the theatrical character of various Trinidadian cultural elements including Indo-Trinidadian festivals.

14 By this I mean those who would speak at tea-meetings, for example, or the clergy who made good sermons, for there were and still are many occasions in Caribbean society where "speechifying" is important and sustains the high level of popular respect for those gifted with words.

15 Creole here means Caribbean people of European or predominantly European descent, but when used for the way in which Caribbean culture and language has grown up from many different ethnic origins, it signifies the whole society. See Brathwaite (1974) for an important discussion of the meaning of the term.

16 See Kole Omotoso (1982) for a historical overview.

17 See Savory Fido (1984; 1990; 1993).

18 Edward Kamau Brathwaite has explained the "great tradition" as the one which was imposed as so-called mainstream by colonial culture, and the "little tradition" as that which was marginalized or suppressed, i.e. African-centred culture in the Caribbean.

19 See Rohlehr (1990). It should also be said that dub and rap are strongly

present in Jamaican culture now, and again celebrate the wordsmith in an anti-imperialist spirit.

20 African theatre and drama theorists have stressed the relation between English-language drama in Africa and aspects of traditional cultures. See Etherton (1982); Traore (1972); Ogunba and Irele (1978) and Ogunbiyi (1981).

21 At a recent talk given at the Studio Museum in Harlem, Julie Dash, director of *Daughters in the Dust*, spoke of one of her actors becoming possessed during the walking on water scene in the film. Someone else mentioned that Spike Lee had said the same thing of Denzel Washington in parts of the filming of Malcolm X. In both cases, the actor remembered nothing of the experience afterwards, and the director was unable to make the actor hear her/his decision to cut the scene. This account shows how much the idea of possession is still associated with the portrayal of a dead person in African cultures.

22 A multiple self is a self incorporated into community both synchronically and diachronically, and thus more deeply bonded to the past, present and future of a given society. Some version of this belief is often present in African-Caribbean culture without necessarily being linked to African belief systems. But such belief can obviously strongly inform an actor's response to a certain part or play.

23 Reincarnation represents a belief in the circular process of life, death and rebirth in many African cultures. In this cycle the role of ancestors is particularly important, a role which the Middle Passage weakened without destroying. That is why funeral rites are still so important in Africa and indeed in the Caribbean where Christianity has displaced beliefs in reincarnation very widely.

24 An important Caribbean literary text which incorporates the idea of story-telling is Merle Hodge's *Crick Crack Monkey* (1970).

25 Lawrence A. Breiner makes the point in his essay "Walcott's Early Drama" that the sneeze made by the frog at the opening of *Tijean* is a European tradition which confirms the truth of the coming tale, rather than a Caribbean one (1991: 75). The frog's "Greek croak" and "Aeschylus me" therefore set a parallel course of cultural echo from "Crick Crack".

26 It is important to make clear here that whilst musicals contain at their best remarkably original lyrical and musical work, their ultimate aim is most often to avoid really disturbing reality. The Caribbean could of course decide to challenge that statement, as Derek Walcott seemed to do when he collaborated with Galt MacDermot (who wrote the music for *Hair*) for *The Joker of Seville* and *O Babylon* (both published 1978), the first, a reworking of the Don Juan myth in a Caribbean context, much more successful than the second, which brought real social issues about Rastafarianism and government policy in Jamaica to the stage.

27 See Edward Kamau Brathwaite's *History of the Voice* (1984). The term "nation language" is inspired because it captures the unique development of Creole language in each Caribbean territory, and the fact that linguists recognize that these are entire language systems made up of a number of linguistic elements (like English, African languages, Indian languages) which have become translated into their new context systematically. At the moment all kinds of oral poetry, some combined with music, flourish as the Caribbean expresses a new respect for the creative resources of Creoles.

WORKS CITED

Beckles, Hilary *Black Rebellion in Barbados: The Struggle Against Slavery 1627–1838* Bridgetown, Barbados: Carib Research and Publications Inc., 1987.

Boyce-Davies, Carole " 'Woman is a Nation . . . ': woman in Caribbean Oral Literature," in *Out of the Kumbla: Caribbean Women and Literature* eds Carole Boyce-Davies and Elaine Savory Fido, Trenton, NJ: Africa World Press, 1990, 165–194.

Brathwaite, Edward Kamau *Contradictory Omens: Cultural Diversity and Integration in the Caribbean* Mona, Jamaica: Savacou Publications, 1974.

——— *History of the Voice* London and Port of Spain: New Beacon Books, 1984.

Breiner, Lawrence A. "Walcott's Early Drama," in *The Art of Derek Walcott* ed. Stewart Brown, Bridgend, Wales, UK: Seren Books 1991, 69–84.

Brereton, Bridget *A History of Modern Trinidad* Kingston and London: Heinemann, 1981.

Cobley, Alan Gregor and Alvin Thompson *The African-Caribbean Connection: Historical and Cultural Perspectives* Bridgetown, Barbados: Department of History and National Cultural Foundation, 1990.

Devonish, Herbert *Language and Liberation: Creole Language Politics in the Caribbean* London: Karia Press, 1986.

Etherton, Michael *The Development of African Drama* New York: Africana Publishing Company, 1982.

Fanon, Frantz *The Wretched of the Earth* Harmondsworth, UK: Penguin, 1967.

——— *Black Skin, White Masks* London: Paladin, 1968.

Gibbons, Rawle "Traditional Enactments of Trinidad: Towards a Third Theatre" M.Phil. thesis, St Augustine, Trinidad: University of the West Indies, 1979.

Glissant, Edouard *Caribbean Discourse*, trans. Michael Dash, Charlottesville: University Press of Virginia, 1992.

Hodge, Merle *Crick Crack Monkey* London: Andre Deutsch, 1970.

James, C. L. R. *The Black Jacobins: Toussaint L'Ouverture and the San Domingo Revolution* New York: Vintage Books, 1963.

——— *Beyond the Boundary* (1963) New York: Pantheon, 1983.

La Guerre, John *Calcutta to Caroni: The East Indians of Trinidad* St Augustine, Trinidad: University of the West Indies Extramural Unit, 1985.

Lewis, Gordon *The Growth of the Modern West Indies* New York and London: Modern Reader Paperbacks, 1968.

Lovelace, Earl *Jestina's Calypso* London: Heinemann, 1984.

Millette, James *Society and Politics in Colonial Trinidad* Trinidad: Omega Bookshops, and London: Zed Books, 1985.

Nkrumah, Kwame *Neo-Colonialism: The Last Stage of Imperialism* London: Heinemann, 1965.

Ogunba, Oyin and Abiola Irele (eds) *Theatre in Africa* Ibadan: Ibadan University Press, 1978.

Ogunbiyi, Yemi (ed.) *Drama and Theatre in Nigeria: A Critical Source Book* Ibadan: Nigeria Magazine, 1981.

Omotoso, Kole *The Theatrical into Theatre: A Study of the Drama and Theatre of the English Speaking Caribbean* London: New Beacon Books, 1982.

Price, Richard *Maroon Societies: Rebel Slave Communities in the Americas* Baltimore and London: Johns Hopkins University Press, 1979.

Rhone, Trevor *Old Story Time and Other Plays* Harlow, UK: Longman, 1981.

Roberts, Peter *West Indians and their Language* Cambridge: Cambridge University Press, 1988.

Rodney, Walter *The Groundings With My Brothers* (1969) London: Bogle-L'Ouverture Publications, 1975.

Rohlehr, Gordon *Calypso and Society in Pre-Independence Trinidad* Gordon Rohlehr: Tunapuna (self-published) Trinidad, 1990

Savory Fido, Elaine "Radical Woman: Woman and Theatre in the Anglophone Caribbean" *Critical Issues in West Indian Literature* Parkersburg, Va.: Caribbean Books, 1984, 33–45.

———— "Finding a Truer Form: Rawle Gibbons's Carnival Play *I Lawah*" *Theatre Research International* Vol. 15 no. 3, 1990, 249–259.

———— "Finding a Way to Tell It: Methodology and Commitment in Theatre About Women in Jamaica and Barbados," in *Out of the Kumbla: Caribbean Women and Literature* eds Carole Boyce Davies and Elaine Savory Fido, Trenton, NJ: Africa World Press, 1990, 331–334.

———— "Freeing Up: Politics, Gender and Theatrical Form in the Anglophone Caribbean" in *Gender and Performance* ed. Lawrence Senelick, University of New England Press, 1992, 281–298.

Scott, Dennis *An Echo in the Bone* in *Plays for Today* Harlow, UK: Longman, 1985, 73–137.

Simpson, George Eaton *Religious Cults of the Caribbean: Trinidad, Jamaica, Haiti* Puerto Rico: Institute of Caribbean Studies, University of Puerto Rico, 1980.

Thompson, Alvin *Colonialism and Underdevelopment in Guyana 1580–1803* Bridgetown, Barbados: Carib Research and Publications Inc., 1987.

Tomlinson, John *Cultural Imperialism* Baltimore: Johns Hopkins University Press, 1991.

Traore, Bakary *The Black African Theatre and its Social Functions* Ibadan: Ibadan University Press, 1972.

Walcott, Derek *Dream on Monkey Mountain* and *Tijean and his Brothers* in *Dream on Monkey Mountain and Other Plays* London: Jonathan Cape, 1972.

———— *The Joker of Seville and O Babylon!* New York: Farrar, Straus and Giroux, 1978.

Warner-Lewis, Maureen *Guinea's Other Suns* Dover, Mass.: The Majority Press, 1991.

INDEX

Page numbers in bold denote a chapter/major section devoted to subject. Page numbers in italic denote an illustration. n denotes a footnote.

257

INDEX

Case, Sue-Ellen 204, 207, 208–9
Caste Wars 73
Césaire, Aimé: collaboration with
  Serreau 182, 183, 195, 196; and
  founding of negritude movement
  182–3; poetry 182
  PLAYS: *A Season in the Congo* 182,
  188–92, 196; *A Tempest* 182, **192–5**;
  The Tragedy of King Christophe 182, 183,
  185–8, 189, 190, 195
Chalupka, Jan 216
Chaudhuri, Una 203, 209, 211
Cheo tradition 6–7, 8, 9–10
Cherry Orchard, The (Brook) 204–5, 208
Chi, Jimmy: *Bran Nue Dae* 126–9
Chiapanecs 79–80, 82
Chiapas 72, 73
Chiaroscuro (Kay) 46–9
Chin, Daryl 203, 204, 208
class: unifying of through melodrama
  133, 135, 136–8, 139–44
Clifford, James 79
Clive, Robert 21, 34
clothing *see* costume
colonized women 94; depiction of in
  French entertainment 92–3, *95*, 96,
  99; and wearing of veils 94
Congo: independence of depicted in *A
  Season in the Congo* 188–9, 190
Conrad, Joseph 135, 136; *Heart of
  Darkness* 133
costume **104–29**; and Aboriginal
  protest against white imperialism
  123–7; of 'Aussie digger' 108–9, 111;
  body's ritualized markings in Davis'
  plays 124, 126; as colonizing tools in
  Visions 116; and contemporary
  theatre practice 104; cross-gender
  and cross-race dressing in *Shimada*
  109, 111–12, 113; focus on politics
  106–7; functions of in process of
  imperialism 104–5; and gender
  difference 106–7, **118–23**; instigation
  of hierarchies of power 105–6, 113;
  in *The Man From Mukinupin* 121–3; in
  Men Without Wives 118–19; soldiers
  attire in *Inside the Island* 113, 115–16;
  in *The Tempest* 105; in *Touch of Silk* 120
cross-gender dressing 106; in *Shimada*
  109, 111–12
cross-race dressing 106 in *Shimada*
  111–12, 113

Culture and Imperialism (Said) 132–3,
  134, 135, 141
Culture and Working Life Project
  (CWLP) 158
Czechoslovakia 214, 215, 216, 217,
  218–19, 220, 221; *see also* Slovakia

Dance of the Seven Veils 85;
  performed by Loie Fuller 86, 88, 90
Dasgupta, Gautam 204, 208
David Copperfield (Dickens) 139
Davis, Jack: *The Dreamers* 124, *125*, 126;
  The First Born 126; *Kullark* 124, 126;
  No Sugar 124, 126
De Brunhoff, Jean: *Babar the Elephant*
  99–100
De Groen, Alma: *The Rivers of China*
  120–1
De Vos, Jan 78, 79
Derrida, Jacques 233
Dickens, Charles 139
Disney, Walt 99, 100
Dorfman, Ariel 99–101
Drake-Brockman, Henrietta: *Men
  Without Wives* 118–19
Dream on Monkey Mountain (Walcott)
  247–8, 250–1, 252
Dreamers, The (Davis) 124, *125*, 126
Dubcek, Alexander 219
Durban Workers Cultural Local
  (DWCL) 157, 158, 159
Dutta, Michael Madhūsudan 19, 27, 31;
  Kṛṣṇākumārī 28–9, 33; *Śarmiṣṭhā* 27–8,
  29
Dynasty of Jaguars (Sna Jtz'ibajom) 71,
  78–82
Dzul Ek, Carlos Armando 82; *The
  Inquisition, or the Colliding of Two
  Cultures* 71, **74–8**, 81; and Sac Nicté
  71, 72, *74*, 82, 83n

Echo in the Bone (Scott) 246–7
Egoli (Manaka) 152
England *see* Britain
English (language): and Irish language
  in Abbey Theatre 164–5, 168, 170;
  and *Translations* 172–8
Erlmann, Veit 154
Experiment Damocles (Karvas) 225
Exposition Universelle *see* World Fair
Eyre, E.J. 140, 141

259

263